PLAGUE OF JUSTICE

a true crime story

PLAGUE OF JUSTICE

a true crime story

BY STAN TUREL

PLAGUE OF JUSTICE: A TRUE CRIME STORY

© 2009 BY STAN TUREL
all rights reserved
stan@plagueofjustice.com
www.plagueofjustice.com

Special quantity discounts for bulk purchases for sales promotion, premiums, fundraising, book clubs, and educational or institutional uses are available through the distributor, or contact the author at stan@plagueofjustice.com.

The *60 Minutes* episode, 'Plague of Justice,' is available on YouTube.com (type in "Stan Turel" or "Plague of Justice" in the SEARCH blank) or go to: http://www.plagueofjustice.com.

This book is a work of nonfiction although some of the names have been changed to protect the privacy of individuals.

The author has based this book on facts as they occurred, actual notes made by the homicide detectives, transcripts of witnesses' tape recordings, sworn testimony, and the contents of frivolous lawsuits filed by the convicted murderers. There are additional crimes alleged to have been committed by the guilty parties and their co-conspirators for which authorities did not follow through with charges. The District Attorneys' offices felt that spending taxpayer's money on further charges would have been a waste because the guilty parties had already been sentenced to life imprisonment. The validity of these additional crimes has not been proven since there were no follow up investigations.

Turel, Stan
Plague of Justice: a true crime story/
ISBN-13: 978-1-892076-56-4
Library of Congress Control Number: 2008910290
1. Title; 2. True Crime - Murder; 3. Frivolous Lawsuits; 4. Victim's Rights; 5. Prisoner's Rights; 6. Crime Victim Legislation; 7. Abuse of Oregon Legal System.

Cover art by Stan Turel.
Cover design and production by Mandish Design, Inc.
Editing and book design by Carla Perry.

Manufactured in the United States of America

FIRST EDITION

Dedication

This book is dedicated to murder victims and to the families of murder victims whose crimes have not yet been solved. Nothing is more painful than continuing to live without knowing who killed a loved one and why. Hopefully, with modern methods of forensic discovery and new DNA technology, many cold cases will be solved.

A further dedication must be given to all the detectives, police officers, judges, and district attorneys' offices throughout the world who are trying to bring criminals to justice.

While I was painting the art used on this book cover, I wrote the following poem:

WHILE WE SLEEP

The city is busy at night I know
Many will work until we awake
To protect us from those who take
Others help the sick and keep the lights aglow.

Twinkle of stars and lights it shows
Only nature's God truly knows
Every light has a purpose
In the distance stars a hope still glows.

To lovers, last night was a daze
From whose life begins with a rose
For others, it's a rest from all their woes
Only to awaken by sunlight's morning toll.

—Stanley Turel

Acknowledgments

I would not have written this book if it were not for the suggestion made by reporter and CBS correspondent Morley Safer. His *60 Minutes* segment, "Plague of Justice," broadcast on December 12, 1982, was about this murder case. My book presents the true story of the 14-year battle in pursuit of justice regarding the man who killed my father. Shortly after the trials ended I collected over 10,000 pages of court transcripts, documents, letters, articles, and notes in anticipation of writing this book someday. This story involves murder, arsons, securities fraud, romance and the legal battles that ensued.

This true crime story has been over 30 years in the making. Most all the details of the crime, arrest, conviction, and what happened afterwards are based on facts as they occurred, actual notes made by the homicide detectives, sworn testimony, and the contents of frivolous lawsuits filed by the convicted murderers. The names of the detectives, prosecutors, judges, co-conspirators and criminals involved are true names. However, the names of some witnesses, girlfriends, and minor characters not directly involved with the murder have been changed to protect their identity.

I thank everyone who cooperated in the research and editing of this book including, but not limited to Carla Perry, Debbie Laufman, Joel Clements, Chris and Pam Cheney, Joanne Santos Eastman, and Robert Skimin.

Also I wish to profoundly thank: detectives Orlando "Blackie" Yazzolino, Stewart Wells, Rod Englert, and Joe Woods; Multnomah County District Attorneys Michael Schrunk and Norm Frink; Multnomah County Senior Deputy District Attorney Forrest "Joe" Rieke; Deputy Sheriff "Mac" McRedmond; Norm Frank; attorney Jim, and his wife Pat Auxier; Dr. Ronald Turco; Dr. Stan Abrams; my friends John Winters, Chris Cheney, Simone Paddock, Lynn Dobson, and Ernesto Santos and his family. Also the Winningstad family, and my uncle Ray and Aunt Lorraine, and other relatives who helped contribute to my positive attitude about the future. Thanks also to my brother, Gary Turel, and to my sisters, who showed great patience over the years during this saga.

Additionally, I cannot thank enough the number of Columbia Bookkeeping staff members who stuck with me during those challenging years while helping me build a successful business enterprise. They include—but are not limited to: Julie Syler, Sherri Cronin, Wanda Fuller, Judy Krussow, Dorothy Hyde, Bob Rounds, and Trudi and Al Kempin. In the end, we persevered in most of our endeavors.

Most of this story happened just as I've relayed with some poetic license regarding the dates and places of my romantic relationships. I have deliberately not used the real name of the lady I dated. Regarding my personal life with my wife, all references to her and my children have been intentionally omitted in an attempt to retain their privacy, considering the nature of this book.

I hope you, your family, and friends are never the victim of a serious crime. But if you are, I wrote this book hoping it will encourage you to pursue justice by exercising your rights. Your rights may include compensation from the criminal, the right to assist in solving the crime, the right to be heard at sentencing, the right to speak at parole hearings, and financial assistance at no cost from government agencies. The Appendix at the end of this book contains a list of organizations and agencies that can help. Or better yet, call your local district attorney's office for assistance.

Contents

Contents (continued)

Chapter 1: Murder Scene Discovered

On the clear summer morning of August 29, 1974, Julie Syler was driving to work. As head bookkeeper at the Columbia Bookkeeping Service, it was Julie's job to arrive promptly at 8 o'clock in the morning to open the office. August 29 was a Thursday and she was looking forward to the upcoming Labor Day weekend. As she entered the parking lot of the two-story office building, she noticed the new golden Cadillac belonging to her boss, Jim Turel, was already parked in his place in front of the building. She thought that was odd, since Jim rarely arrived at work that early.

As Julie entered the building, she was hit with a strange odor. She walked down the dark hallway on the plush red carpet, and then turned on the master light switches. She turned the corner leading to her office but stopped abruptly, startled by a gruesome sight. Her boss, Jim Turel, was lying on the carpet, motionless, in a pool of drying blood. She screamed, "Oh my God!" as she noticed his broken crutches lying beside him. She saw blood splattered on the door and hallway walls. Julie reached down gently to touch Mr. Turel's hand. It was cold. Carefully, she backed up, turned, then rushed to the front lobby to call the police.

When the operator answered, Julie, with a trembling voice, said, "I think my boss is dead!" After answering a few brief questions, she hung up and called her husband, a corrections officer at Rocky Butte Jail. Crying and near hysterics, Julie stuttered that Mr. Turel appeared dead and that it was a horrible sight. While still on the phone, Julie heard the approaching sirens.

The first to arrive was an EMT unit, the Medical Fireman, who, within moments, determined that Mr. Turel was dead.

Next, Officer Scott, from the Multnomah Sheriff's office, pulled to a quick stop in front of the building and rushed through the front door Julie had left open. Julie was sitting quietly, but still trembling from shock. Officer Scott, in his crisp green uniform, unlatched his holster as he walked past Julie. All she could do was point—in that direction. After quickly assessing the situation, he advised Julie Syler to sit in the front lobby until more officers arrived. "Don't touch anything," Officer Scott said. "Just sit there for now and try to calm down."

Soon, a number of detectives, police cars, and a van from the Multnomah County Scientific Investigation Department arrived, led by Detective Lewis Rice who reviewed the scene. Rice noted that Mr. Turel was lying face down in a pool of his own blood. Turel's wallet lay at a right angle to the body, open, with no cash. He also noticed the cash register was open. Detective Rice asked Julie Syler why the damaged crutches were there.

"Jim Turel is crippled from polio and walks ... walked ... with crutches," she said in a subdued voice, tears rolling down her face. Julie Syler had been working for Mr. Turel for four years. Her boss was 49 years old and he depended on her to keep things organized.

At first, Detective Rice considered it possible that the crippled man had fallen down the stairs since his body lay near the foot of the stairway. The metal crutches lay bent next to Jim Turel's body. He also noticed smudges of blood splattered on the walls and ceiling. The congealed blood pooled near the victim's head had been disturbed, was in fact smeared across the rug. The deceased man's metal crutch handles were bent. There were no marks on the stairway walls to indicate a fall had taken place, but Detective Rice did find hair on a crutch handle.

Upon further examination of the body, he noticed swollen tissue that ringed the man's neck, so it seemed more likely the victim had been strangled and beaten with his own crutches. "This does not look like an accident," he wrote on his notepad. "Appears as though Mr. Turel has been strangled." Detective Rice immediately instructed the officers to secure the building and parking lot as a crime scene. The death was likely a homicide.

By 8:50 a.m., the lead homicide detectives, Blackie Yazzolino and Stewart Wells, arrived. As Detective Yazzolino entered the parking lot of the office building he noticed the police cars, plus a brand new gold colored Cadillac Seville parked at an odd angle by the front door. Inside, he met Detective Rice who had already instructed the other officers not to touch anything and to stay in the front of the lobby.

At first, Detective Yazzolino suspected a robbery and instructed that all door handles, doorways, file cabinets and desks be dusted for fingerprints. "When was the last time you saw Mr. Turel alive?" Yazzolino asked Julie Syler.

"Last night, about 5 o'clock, when the office closed," Julie said, wiping her eyes. Then she verified Mr. Turel would have had about $100 on him as she had cashed a check for him the day before.

"All the money in his wallet is gone," Yazzolino said.

At 9:00 a.m., Rod Addicks, Columbia Bookkeeping's CPA, entered the building. He seemed dazed when he saw the swarm of policemen. Mr. Addicks was in his mid-thirties, well dressed in a tailored two-piece dark suit. He was of average build, had a professional demeanor, and at first handled himself with a strong air of self-confidence. When told that Mr. Turel had probably been murdered, Mr. Addicks first looked stunned, then sat down and quietly said, "I cannot believe it." Then he asked, "Is there anything I can do?"

Detective Wells stepped into a separate office to interview Rod Addicks while Yazzolino continued his interview with the petite, red-haired, 33-year-old bookkeeper, Julie Syler.

"Has Bernie Turel been called yet?" Yazzolino asked Julie. Bernie was Jim Turel's wife.

"No," Julie said.

"I want to be the one to tell her," Yazzolino said. "Julie, while I call her, would you walk around the office to see if anything else is missing? But, Julie, don't touch anything."

Julie quickly discovered that someone had entered the locked vault and left its door open. Julie Syler was one hundred percent sure she had locked the vault the previous night, since it was part of her regular routine. The desk drawer where she normally hid the vault key was left partway open and the key was still inside it, but not in its normal place.

It seemed obvious that a robbery had taken place. However, there was no sign of forced entry, suggesting that Jim Turel must have known his assailant and let the robber in. None of the other 10 desks or 15 file cabinets appeared to have been disturbed. Each desk was still tidy. The giant, newly purchased room-size Burroughs bookkeeping computer was undisturbed, and still in good working order.

While Blackie Yazzolino walked through the various offices with Julie Syler, Detective Wells continued talking with Rod Addicks. "When did you last see Mr. Turel?"

"I went out to dinner last night with Jim," said Addicks. "We had drinks at the Kitchen Kettle restaurant between 6 and about 8 o'clock. We returned to the office just after 8 p.m."

Addicks then told the detective that upon returning to the office parking lot he and Jim Turel had a short conversation and, as he left the parking lot, he saw Jim at the front door of the office building, about to go in. But when Rod Addicks was questioned again, he changed his story. "No, Jim was standing out at the curb talking with a tall, long-haired fellow who had a car that was parked in the parking lot."

Rod Addicks appeared nervous, which was a normal reaction to the situation. He sat quietly, but his thumbs obsessively twitched against each other. Addicks explained that he and Mr. Turel were good friends as well as business partners. He said that he owned 38 percent of the tax business.

Detectives Yazzolino and Wells left the crime scene at 9:45 a.m. and went directly to the Turel home to break the bad news. The Turels lived on the outskirts of East Portland in a modest 900-square-foot home. The detectives explored the property. They found an indoor swimming pool in the backyard. The pool house was detached from, but much larger than the small house. The acre-size yard was well kept with plants, fruit trees, and dozens of large rhododendrons.

When the detectives rang the doorbell, a thin 55-year-old lady answered the door. Showing their badges, the detectives asked if they could talk to her, and she invited them in. The house was neat and tidy.

When Detective Yazzolino said her husband had been found dead at his office, Mrs. Turel showed little emotion. She sat down slowly in a rocking chair. "How can that be? He is supposed to be in Bend, at a tax seminar. He left yesterday. How did Jim die?"

"He appears to have been murdered, Mrs. Turel," Yazzolino said.

"What!"

"I'm sorry to have to give you that news, Mrs. Turel. I have to ask you some personal questions now. Would that be alright?" Yazzolino said. When she agreed, he said, "How many credit cards did Mr. Turel have?"

"Two," said Bernie. "An American Express and one other credit card. Why?"

"It may have been a robbery, since his cash and credit cards were missing from his wallet."

Blackie Yazzolino chose not to show his hand. He wanted to remain open-minded as to all possible motives. Was it truly a robbery? Yazzolino did not think so; the office was too neat and orderly. There was no evidence of robbery, except for the money missing from the victim's wallet and the cash register. Whoever murdered Mr. Turel knew the office layout. The vault door had been opened with a key hidden inside Julie Syler's desk. Sure, it could have been a robbery, but if so, there should have been more of a mess. Robbers can really wreck a place as they search for money. Or, it might have been an inside job. Maybe Jim Turel knew the murderer and let him in. If so, it could have been any of the two thousand accounting clients who had their taxes prepared by Columbia Bookkeeping.

"Do you have any idea who might want to kill your husband?" Yazzolino asked Bernie Turel.

"I don't know anyone who could do something like that! Can't you tell me what happened?"

"No, I'm sorry, but we can't, ma'am," Yazzolino said. Then, delicately, he asked if she knew about any other women in her husband's life.

"I was aware he was having an affair with someone, if that's what you mean," Bernie said. "But I don't know who." She admitted she and Jim had broken up several times in the recent past and were seriously discussing divorce plans. "My husband met with our attorney to arrange an offer for a divorce, but I turned that one down."

"When was the last time you saw your husband, Mrs. Turel?"

"Yesterday afternoon, when I went to the office to wash the Cadillac. I usually pack his overnight bag for all his trips and yesterday I put the packed bag in the trunk of the Cadillac."

"And what does that bag look like," asked Yazzolino.

"White handles, so that Jim could place the bag on his crutches and carry it while he walks. I can't believe what you're telling me. Jim is supposed to be in Bend."

A jealous wife, one who is aware her husband was seeing another woman, could be a possible suspect. "What were you doing last night?" Yazzolino asked Bernie Turel.

"Home. Alone. Watching TV," she answered. Bernie was calm. She answered all the detective's questions without hesitation. She sat quietly.

Based on the viciousness of the wounds, Yazzolino surmised the attack of the crippled husband would likely have been done by someone angry. Other family members may have had motives as well. "Do you know what is in your husband's will?" Yazzolino asked.

"In 1969 I saw a will Jim prepared," Bernie Turel said. "That will leave most of the tax company to Jim's son, Stan. The rest of the assets are to be distributed equally among his children, and to my daughter from a prior marriage."

"Do you know the name of your husband's attorney?"

"Jim Auxier. From downtown. I can give you his phone number."

"Thank you, ma'am."

"According to my husband's will, I get our home free and clear of any debt plus some money from a life insurance policy. I have a copy of the will," said Bernie. "Would you like to see it?"

"First tell me about your husband's children."

"Jim has two sons and two daughters," she replied. "The youngest daughter just got married. Two weeks ago."

"Do you have someone you can call to come over and sit with you?"

"Well, Stan could come. Or Jim's older daughter. I could call Stan; Jim told me to call Stan if he ever died."

"Where does the daughter live?" Detective Yazzolino asked.

"Milwaukie, a suburb in southeast Portland. She works at a company called ADP. Both sons live here in Portland."

"Can we call her now? I'd like to speak with her."

When Detective Yazzolino spoke to Jim's daughter, she began crying. She said she didn't believe the news. But she agreed to come over to her stepmother's house right away. First, she would try to reach her brother, Gary, Jim's youngest son. Detective Yazzolino placed a call to the phone number for Stan Turel, Jim's oldest son, but reached Stan's answering service. He left an urgent message to call Detective Yazzolino immediately.

"Mrs. Turel," Detective Yazzolino continued, "Did all of Jim's children get along with their father? Were there any problems? Any discord?"

"They all got along fine with their father," Bernie said.

"Does Gary work with his dad at Columbia Bookkeeping?"

"No."

"Tell me about your husband's business."

"I don't know much. Only that Jim told me if he became sick or unable to sign checks, that his son, Stan, could sign checks for the business. But Stan has refused to work in the business with his dad. Except for one thing. Stan helped his father build the swimming pool building behind our house, and something else—he bought and remodeled an office building for his dad in Beaverton a year ago."

Detective Blackie Yazzolino tried again to reach Stan Turel, but again the lady at the answering service said, "Stan Turel isn't available. He flew to Seattle this morning, on business. Can I give him a message?"

Yazzolino was troubled that the oldest son could not be reached by phone. "Yes, please ask him to call Detective Blackie Yazzolino as soon as possible."

Bernie Turel hadn't moved. She was still sitting absolutely still, as if in a trance. Either the woman was going into shock, or she was putting on a very good act.

"Mrs. Turel, do you know if any of Jim Turel's children had a drug or drinking problem?"

"No. They're all straight arrows. My daughter is too."

"Can you tell me what each of them does for a living?"

"Well, my daughter's husband has been a problem but she is divorced and lives in Salem. And Gary, Jim's youngest son, has a small tax office called College Crest Tax Services on the other side of town in North Portland, on Lombard Street. Stan, Jim's oldest son, owns a corporation called Air Auto Waxing, which does business in Oregon and Washington. Oh, and Stan owns some rental properties and an apartment building in Washington State."

"What about Jim's daughters?" said Yazzolino.

"Jim's youngest daughter lives in Los Angeles, but she's on her honeymoon now, I think. The older daughter works for ADP processing as their specialist for Louisiana Pacific's computer input.

"You said your husband's son Stan had check-signing authority if something happened to Mr. Turel. Did Rod Addicks, your husband's CPA and partner at Columbia Bookkeeping, have check-signing authority?" Yazzolino asked.

"No he didn't, Jim didn't trust Rod Addicks with money. He didn't want to give Rod that kind of authority. Jim said that Rod Addicks is always short on money and on the edge of going broke."

"And why did Jim not give you check-signing authority?"

Bernie lowered her head and said quietly, "I don't know enough about business and I'm afraid Jim didn't trust me either." Then she looked up. "However, I am secretary of the company and have to sign some papers from time to time. When we first got married, I helped him open his first bookkeeping office. Oh, I just remembered something about Jim's will."

"What would that be?"

"Well, about a year ago Stan asked his dad to make him and Gary equals in the company as Stan didn't want jealousy to develop. But I don't know if the will was changed or not."

"Mrs. Turel, Jim's older daughter is on her way here now, so we'll be leaving."

"Do I need to get an attorney?" Bernie asked. "Am I a suspect?"

"I have no suspects yet, Mrs. Turel. But I'll let you know if we think you should have legal representation. Perhaps it would be wise to call your attorney to discuss your husband's will and make funeral arrangements."

Columbia Bookkeeping parking lot with golden Cadillac on left, August 29, 1974.

Chapter 2: Detectives Investigate Crime Scene

By 11:30 a.m., the detectives returned to the Columbia Bookkeeping office. The Scientific Investigation Department was gone, but they had done a good job securing the crime scene. There were still police officers in the parking lot and in the lobby. Rod Addicks and Julie Syler, who were confined to the lobby, were talking on the phone and explaining to clients that the office was closed today. The police were still there making sure no unauthorized person entered the hallway. Detectives Blackie Yazzolino and Stewart Wells nodded as they passed the policemen and walked down the hallway to assess the crime scene once more.

The detectives had begun assembling a list of possible suspects: the murder victim's wife, his two sons, Rod Addicks—the last person to see Mr. Turel alive, another Columbia Bookkeeping employee, a robber, a girlfriend, or a business client.

About that time, Jim's youngest son arrived. Gary Turel was unaware his father was dead. He said he was in the area and decided to just drop in and ask his dad out for lunch. Gary saw the police cars and the barricade tape, but ducked under it and entered the building. Gary entered the lobby and saw Julie Syler, Rod Addicks, and the detectives sitting at the front desk.

"What's going on here!" Gary demanded.

Blackie Yazzolino had seen that determined expression of anger and shock before. After Julie explained to Gary that his father appeared to have been robbed and murdered, Gary insisted on seeing exactly where his dad had died. Yazzolino let Gary view the murder scene because his father's body had already been transferred downtown to the coroner's office.

"Gary, my assistant Detective Wells would like to ask you some questions," Yazzolino said. "It would help us to understand a few things. Detective Wells, I'll take over the interview with Rod Addicks." With that, Yazzolino left the room.

Scientific Investigator Lewis Rice dusting Jim Turel's crutch for fingerprints.

"Gary, you are the youngest son of Jim Turel, is that correct?" Detective Wells began.

"Yes."

"Can you tell me where you were last night?"

"I was out with friends last night until almost midnight."

"Where do you live? And can we have your phone and home address so we can talk to you later?"

"I live in a bedroom in my Lombard tax office," Gary said as he handed the detective a business card."

Detective Wells noted that Gary was a handsome young man who appeared to be in shock. He was a clean-cut kid, visibly upset, but wanting to help. "When was the last time you saw your father?" Wells asked.

"A few days ago. I had dinner with him last Sunday."

"Do you have a key to your father's office?"

"No," Gary said.

"That's all the questions I have for now. Gary, I'd suggest you go to your stepmother's house and join your sister who's already there."

Wells wrote in his notebook that Gary seemed sincere and quite upset when he left.

Meanwhile, Detective Yazzolino had introduced himself to Rod Addicks and began questioning him about the last time he saw Jim Turel alive, and his activities that day.

According to the Detective Yazzolino's testimony, Mr. Addicks explained again what transpired that evening. "Mr. Addicks stated that he and Mr. Turel went down to the Kitchen Kettle and had some drinks and they came back to the office sometime around 8 or 8:30 p.m. and that some cars were illegally parked in the office parking lot. Addicks said that Mr. Turel was upset about these cars, and that he had written some notes and placed them on the windshields of a couple of the cars. As he placed the notes under the windshield wipers a very tall, thin man approached and Mr. Turel and the man began talking about the automobiles. Mr. Addicks said he stayed inside his car while this was going on. Mr. Addicks said Jim Turel then returned to the car and made the remark, "I think I have taken care of the parking problem" Mr. Addicks stated that he then left for home. Mr. Turel was standing outside on the sidewalk in front of the Columbia Bookkeeping office building as he drove away and that was the last time he saw Mr. Turel.

Addicks then told Detective Yazzolino that Mr. Turel was supposed to leave that night and drive to Bend for a conference. He said this was one of their ploys to cover up their nighttime activities. He said Mr. Turel was in a hurry to leave the Kitchen Kettle and return to the Columbia Bookkeeping office, possibly because Mr. Turel had planned to meet a woman there. However, once they returned to the office parking lot, Mr. Turel did not seem to be in a hurry about anything. Mr. Turel said he needed a shave and the canvas bag in the back of his car had a Norelco shaver in it.

Mr. Addicks told Detective Yazzolino that Mr. Turel was having problems with his wife in that she was unresponsive to him and once he had offered her $10,000 for a divorce. Mrs. Turel had refused and they continued to live together, although periodically they each moved out, then would return.

"Do you need the name of Jim's attorney?" Rod Addicks asked.

"Yes," said Detective Yazzolino.

"Jim Auxier. He's got an office downtown and I already talked to him to see if there is anything I can do to help."

"Thank you, Mr. Addicks, I appreciate your help. I don't have any further questions right now, but let me know if you think of anything you want to add. I'd like to speak with you again after I talk with the others."

"I'll help you in any way I can, Detective. I want to see this case solved and Jim's murderer brought to justice. I'm going to head over to Bernie Turel's home to offer my condolences and see if there's anything I can do for her. Poor woman. This must be a horrible nightmare for her."

Blackie Yazzolino had his suspicions about everyone he'd spoken to so far, but his main person of interest was Stan Turel, the victim's eldest son. Stan had not yet called him back, so Yazzolino placed another call to Stan's number.

The answering service lady said, "Stan usually checks in at the end of each day. Can I tell him what this is about?"

"No. Just ask him to call Detective Blackie Yazzolino."

The detectives decided an officer and a police car should remain at the tax office overnight. He told the policeman standing guard that the building should remain locked and sealed, and that no employees or clients were allowed to enter.

"Take notes about anyone who calls or shows up," Yazzolino said. Then he and Detective Wells left Columbia Bookkeeping to return to their office downtown to review their notes. After comparing their notes, they realized they had conflicting versions from Rod Addicks, which raised concerns. Was Mr. Turel standing on the sidewalk outside the office? Or was he talking to the tall, blond man in the parking lot?

Later that afternoon, around 4 o'clock, the detectives returned to the crime scene. They had retrieved the keys to the Cadillac from the dead man's pocket and opened the trunk to examine its contents. The flight bag Bernie Turel had said she'd packed the previous afternoon and placed in the trunk was not there. It also appeared as though Jim Turel had not moved his car between the time his wife arrived and the time he died.

Yazzolino knew that the first 48 hours after a body is discovered is the most crucial time to determine the course of an investigation. He was hoping to hear from Stan Turel in order to move forward. He again called Stan's answering service, and was again told they had not heard from Stan Turel yet. "We have, however, received a couple of urgent messages for

Stan to call his sister, his stepmother, his mother, and his brother. We're hoping he'll call in soon," the answering service lady said. Detective Yazzolino then called Mrs. Turel again, just to make sure she was okay.

"Yes, I'm okay," Bernie said. "Rod Addicks was here visiting just a bit ago. He offered to help. He also brought $200 for me that I asked the attorney to get, since I have no emergency cash. Both Gary and his older sister are here with me. Oh, Stan just called. I told him what happened. He's on his way home."

Just then a call came in to the detectives from Stan Turel.

"Is it true? That my dad is dead? What's going on?" Stan asked the detective.

"I'd like to meet with you today," said Yazzolino. "I'm at your father's office now. How soon can you be here?"

Chapter 3: I Cannot Believe My Dad Is Dead!

I am Stan Turel and I have just been told that my dad is dead. I can't even imagine what these words mean. They make no sense to me.

That call to Detective Blackie Yazzolino was my first step into the real nightmare of what was to come.

"I'll be back in Portland as soon as possible," I told the detective. "I'm with my girlfriend in Seattle. We flew up here this morning in my private plane on business."

I started taking big, deep breaths while trying to hold back the tears. Then I said, "But I'm in no condition to fly. I can't think straight. I'm going to rent a car. I'll be there by 7:30 tonight. Please don't let anyone in the office, especially my dad's CPA, Rod Addicks, or any of the people from the massage parlors accounts!"

"Okay," said Yazzolino. We'll meet you back here at 7:30 tonight."

"I can't believe what I just heard," I said to my girlfriend Janet in a trembling voice. Last night I asked Janet if maybe we could live together to learn more about each other and how compatible we would be, and she had agreed. This morning, she and I flew up to Gavin's Flight Office at Boeing Field in Seattle, Washington. We were going to take care of a bit of business, and when that was done, our plan was to fly to Vancouver, British Columbia. I had planned a nice Labor Day weekend with Janet to celebrate our commitment. But before leaving Seattle, I placed a call to my answering service in Portland just to check in.

That call changed my life.

This is how my day had begun...

Janet and I woke early this morning, packed our bags, placed them in my little single-engine plane, and flew north from Troutdale, Oregon, towards Boeing Field in Seattle. I was happy and relaxed as I flew above the light morning mist that coated the land below. I could see the line of trees and green valleys. My attention was drawn to a large pasture and I remember thinking, if I could land down there, I would make love with Janet, right in the middle of that meadow. Such thoughts are not uncommon for a man excited about sitting next to such a beautiful lady who I was in love with and becoming totally attached to in more ways than one. However, I kept my thoughts to myself because I figured a classy lady like her would want to wait for a romantic setting, something more like a bedroom with candles in an upscale hotel in Vancouver, B.C.

Just before we entered the Seattle airspace, around 8:30 a.m., a heavy, sick feeling sent chills down my neck. It was as if my dad was transmitting words into my head. I distinctly heard, "It's your problem now. You are on your own and good luck in the future," as if he was dying. The thought left me feeling lonely. No, no, no, I thought, I don't want that. I shook off the nauseous feeling and focused on the instructions coming through my earphones from Seattle Approach Control regarding air traffic.

I've had premonitions in the past, and dreams, where my visions turned out to be true, so I didn't dismiss the feeling entirely, yet I had to push it aside and deal with landing the plane and paying attention to the beautiful lady sitting beside me.

Yet the nagging sensation stayed with me. Just the week before, on my return from Mexico City on a commercial flight from Los Angeles to Portland, I sat next to a former Air Force psychiatrist. This man mentioned that his specialty had been to interview and debrief Air Force pilots after a crash or any strange encounter. Dr. Ron Turco was a well-dressed man in his thirties. He and I spent the three-hour commute talking about the possibility of a fourth dimension—something like extra sensory perception. That conversation was the first time I'd had the opportunity to speak with a professional about my premonitions and dreams. I explained that sometimes my dreams included crashes or bizarre events that came true within a week or so.

"That phenomenon is called "precognitory premonition," Dr. Turco told me. "It's as if there is a connection to the future or past."

I assumed Dr. Turco and my paths would never cross again and I was grateful for all I learned during that brief flight. But 15 years later I found out we had a more earth-bound connection. Maurice Lucas, the famous basketball player with the Portland Trail Blazers, became a partner in one of my family-owned office buildings. It turned out Maurice had rented space to that very same psychiatrist.

Plus, coincidentally, 30 years later, on a return from Mexico, I caught a connecting flight from Los Angeles to Portland and sat next to Dr. Turco again. At first we did not recognize each other. His hair had turned gray and he'd grown a beard. We were again sitting next to each other and deep in conversation before we realized we'd met before. It was the same airline, the same flight, in adjacent seats. Doctor Turco and I then had a long talk about destiny!

Janet broke into my thoughts and brought me back to the present by pointing out how beautiful Seattle is from the perspective of the front window of a small plane. I was glad she appreciated the splendor of it all. Another great thing about Janet was that she occasionally helped me clean and wax airplanes for clients, which made me remember an incident from last month when she and I were waxing a million-dollar airplane for Swede Ralston at Aero Air very late one night. Swede came over and said, "Stan, if this is your idea of a date, marry that woman! She attracts business."

But I pushed my memories aside as I was anxious to complete my business projects and get on to the festivities of the weekend with my sweetheart.

Anyway, with business complete at Gavin's Flight Office, we prepared to board my plane again for a short hop to Vancouver, B.C. I checked in with the FAA weather site, and then called my answering service. It was 4:30 p.m. by then. The operator said my brother, sister, and stepmother had been trying to reach me all day. And a Detective Blackie Yazzolino. She said it sounded urgent. "Your dad is the only family member who hasn't left a message for you!"

I could tell by the young lady's voice that something serious had happened and again a chill went down the back of my neck. "What happened?" I asked her.

"I don't know! Oh, Stan, call your family right away!"

I called my stepmother immediately. She was very direct. "Stan, your dad was found dead in his office today."

I thought she said someone shot him. "I can't believe he was shot!" I said.

"No, no. He wasn't shot," Bernie said.

"Bernie, I'm in Seattle, but I'm coming home. Right now."

"Wait! Stan, I have a message from a police detective. His name is

Blackie Yazzolino. You're supposed to call him right away. I have his number for you."

I dialed Detective Yazzolino's number and he answered the phone after one ring. "Is it true my dad was killed?"

Blackie Yazzolino said, "Yes."

"What happened? How did it happen? Who shot him?" I asked.

"I can't discuss that with you over the phone," he replied.

"Detective Yazzolino, please make sure no one gets into my dad's office! The answers to what happened might still be there!"

We agreed to meet at my dad's office in three hours. The detective said he would be there when I arrived.

I hung up and, still in the phone booth, began to sob. Janet was watching me. I opened the folding door, "My dad was murdered this morning!" I said. "No, I must have misunderstood Bernie. That couldn't be what she said. I just spoke with a detective, but maybe he said my father was in the hospital."

"Stan, you're in no condition to fly us back to Portland. We are going to rent a car."

I agreed.

As Janet drove, I kept going over and over the words my stepmother said. 'Stan, your dad was found dead in his office today.' Every few minutes I would start to cry, and then I'd get angry. Who would do such a thing? Why would anyone want to kill my father? Then I wondered, was he really killed in his office? If so, there had to be clues left behind. I thought about times when Dad tried to talk me into becoming an accountant with his firm and how I'd refused.

But who could hate my father enough to do this? Maybe some angry client who thought he paid too much in taxes? Maybe my dad had discovered something illegal and was killed to keep him silent! Maybe he wasn't dead at all. Maybe it was just a close call. My thoughts were spinning, round and round they went, no answers, just questions. Over and over. I don't think I said one word aloud on the entire trip home.

As Janet and I approached the Columbia Bookkeeping office at 7:30, the sun, still bright in the early evening sky, was beginning to set. I noticed three police cars and yellow crime scene tape surrounding the entire area. Janet parked on the street. As I walked past the yellow tape barricade I noticed my dad's Cadillac parked at a funny angle near the entrance. I tried to open the front door of the office, but it was locked. When I knocked, a sheriff came out and I introduced myself as Stan Turel, Jim Turel's son. "Is it true my father is dead?" I said.

"Yes, he is," the officer said. "Could you hold on a minute?"

Within 30 seconds, out came a short, stocky man in his late 50s. "I am Detective Blackie Yazzolino," he said, as he handed me his card.

"Is my father dead?" I asked, trying to hold back tears.

In a deep voice Yazzolino said, "Yes." The detective's graying crew cut and facial features resembled my father's and I immediately felt I could put my trust in him. He motioned for me to enter the front lobby. "Stan, don't go beyond the lobby, they're still investigating the rest of the crime scene. Look, Stan, I'm real sorry about all this and it's never easy to talk about what happened with a murder, but I will do everything possible to find out who committed the crime."

"How did my dad die?"

"I'll talk with you later about the details."

"Well, please just make sure no one else is allowed to enter," I said. "Everything has to be examined. If my dad was murdered here, then answers might still be in the office." I still wasn't thinking totally straight, but I knew I didn't want Rod Addicks or my stepmother prowling around the scene. "Detective Yazzolino, will you post a policeman at the door? At all times?" I asked.

"Yes, I will."

"So no one can get in?"

"Yes. It's Labor Day weekend, Stan. A holiday."

"Oh, right" I said. I'd completely forgotten about the holiday.

"Stan, I will do everything possible to determine what happened here," Yazzolino said. But first I'd like to ask you some questions to determine where you were last night, and what you know."

"I was with my girlfriend at her apartment. Oh, but I promised my stepmother I'd go see her right after this. I came straight here from Seattle to meet you. My girlfriend is in the car, would you like to meet her? My brother and sister are waiting for me at Dad's house."

Blackie Yazzolino walked with me to the car and introduced himself to Janet. "Are you willing to meet me after you visit with your family?"

"Here?" I asked.

"No, not here. Somewhere we could talk privately."

"Where is my father now? His body."

"At the Multnomah County Coroner's office," Yazzolino said.

"Did my father suffer?" I could hardly get the words out. "How did he die?"

"We'll talk about that later," Yazzolino said. "Right now, you should go and visit your stepmother."

We agreed to meet in two hours at my home, which was only a mile away. Yazzolino put his arm around my shoulder, which made me even more emotional, and he said, "Don't worry. We are going to get to the bottom of this."

I choked out, "I'm available any time, Detective Yazzolino." And I gave him my home phone number and address.

Back in my car, Janet was white as a sheet. She looked like she was upset, too. "I can drive now," I said.

"No, I don't think so," Janet said. I got in on the passenger's side and we headed for my dad's home on the outskirts of Portland. As she drove, I leaned against the window in a daze. I scanned the trees and pastures as we drove by. I was thinking—this is what my dad saw every day when he drove home from work. Then the tears would run down my trembling face. I looked at her, and she put her hand on my knee.

When we turned down the driveway of Dad's home, I felt a sense of absolute loneliness knowing my father would not be coming home that night. My father was only 49 years old. I thought about the coincidence of Granddad Turel, my father's dad, who died in an accident when he was only 48 years old. I wondered if I'd live to be 49. My granddad had owned a cedar mill and thousands of acres of timber rights at the time of his death. My father was only 16 when his father died. I again held the tears back, thinking of the loneliness my father must have felt when he was so young.

There was no room to park in front of the house, so Janet parked the car on the grass between the rhododendrons and fruit trees my brother and I had planted years ago. I remembered helping to frame and build the indoor pool building for Dad's swimming therapy. He used that pool every day of his life to ease the discomforts of the polio. The pool building was larger than my dad's house.

As we entered the living room we were greeted with somber hugs from my older sister and my brother, Gary. My stepmother, Bernie, did not get out of her chair. She sat there stern and erect, her face devoid of emotion. Maybe she's in shock, I thought, or perhaps she is just bottling up her feelings. My sister and her husband were there as well. No one in the room, except Bernie and I, knew that two weeks ago I had seen her arguing with my father about a divorce. Sometimes I felt sorry for Bernie, knowing my dad's temper and how hard my dad was to live with. But Bernie had always seemed so cold to us children. We had never felt comfortable in her home because we'd never been made to feel welcome. However, at Dad's insistence, Bernie would occasionally cook wonderful dinners for my girlfriend and me when we came to visit.

No one was eager to talk. We couldn't believe Dad was dead. Finally, I began asking questions, not of my family, but just in general. "Who could have done such a thing? Do any of you know any details?"

No, no one knew anything other than Dad had been murdered. Yazzolino had talked to them all, separately, but never divulged what he knew or suspected.

"How was he killed?" I asked. "Was he shot?"

"The police aren't talking," Gary said.

"His secretary and bookkeeper, Julie Syler, found him dead this morning when she opened the office at 8 o'clock in the morning," my sister said. "Other than that, all they know for sure is Dad was murdered, and that at first it appeared to be a robbery."

"How was he murdered?" I asked again.

"The police won't say," Gary repeated. "But Yazzolino said Dad must have put up a fight."

"Dad would have given a robber a lecture," I said. "Maybe he got so mad, he refused to give the robber any money, and they got into a fight." Janet put her hand on my thigh and the five of us sank back into our own silences. A bunch of other possibilities rolled around in my head, but I dared not say them in front of my stepmother, Bernie.

"You'd better call your dad's attorney, Stan," said Bernie. "You're in charge of his estate."

I groaned. The thought made me sick. "This isn't the time to think about that," I said.

"I don't want a large funeral for him," Bernie continued. "There's no money to hold a large funeral."

"I don't think this is a good time to talk about his funeral, Bernie. We can talk about that later." I was sure we were all caught in some bad dream. "Look," I said. "Janet and I need to meet with Detective Yazzolino now and we agreed to meet him back at my home, so I have to leave."

"Perhaps you need to get some rest, Bernie," Janet suggested.

"Yes, Bernie needs to rest," I agreed. Maybe we all should go."

"I will stay here overnight," my older sister said. "So she won't be alone. And a distant cousin of Dad's is driving up and will stay with Bernie a few days." I was glad to hear that she would be there soon because she was somebody I could count on.

"Oh, by the way, Stan," my sister said, "Rod Addicks came by here this afternoon."

"What was he doing here?"

"He came by to give Bernie some emergency money. He offered his condolences."

"Rod was the last person to see your dad last night," Bernie said.

"What time was that?"

"It must have been after dark," my sister said. "Because Rod mentioned he had to turn on his car lights when he left the office. But I got into a little discussion with Rod about that. I pointed out it couldn't have been that early since darkness came later. I said he wouldn't have needed to turn on his car lights yet if he left at 8 o'clock. Rod kept rubbing his left shoulder the whole time he was here."

Janet and I drove back to my house, 15 minutes away. We arrived at 9:30 p.m. and saw Detective Blackie Yazzolino already parked on the street in an unmarked tan police car. I noticed an antenna on the back of the car.

We met the detectives in the driveway and Janet and I led them downstairs to the living room of my basement apartment. Blackie Yazzolino introduced the younger man, Detective Stewart Wells. The four of us sat down and just looked at each other for what seemed like a very long time. It was probably less than a minute. I shook my head in disbelief that this was happening. Janet sat next to me with her hand on my lap, which comforted me.

Yazzolino explained that he and Detective Wells had talked to many people already, and apologized for getting together with me so late. "But, Stan, I wanted to talk to you specifically, since I've been told you got along with your father the best of all his children. Excuse my directness, but what do you know about your father's personal life and his business affairs."

"Where should I begin?" I asked. "Wait, before that, what have you found out?"

"Stan, the S-I Department is doing everything possible to find leads in the office building."

"What's the S-I Department?"

"The department that houses the scientific investigators. They've been taking hundreds of fingerprints. They've been examining the crime scene, looking for clues."

I couldn't sit still. While Yazzolino explained in detail how the S-I Department operated, I began pacing. Yazzolino paused. "Do you rent the upstairs apartment to someone else?"

"Yes," I answered, and explained who they were. The detective was checking out my place, I thought to myself. But I didn't care.

"Detective Yazzolino," I said, "When exactly did my father die?"

"It appears as though he died sometime last night, August 28."

"I need to know," I said. "Did he suffer?" The tears came rolling down my cheeks.

"They can't tell at this point."

"Was it a robbery?"

"Maybe," said Yazzolino. "Maybe. But there are many possibilities. Let's go over a few points that could help us get a better idea of where this investigation should go. Stan, can you deal with this now?"

"Yes," I said, pulling myself together.

"These questions are the standard questions we ask relatives and friends when something tragic like this happens," Yazzolino explained. "First, we consider if the crime was a robbery, but then we make a list of everyone who might benefit from the victim's death. Next we make a list of the people who had the opportunity and might have been crazy enough to kill your father."

"First, Mr. Turel," said Detective Wells. "We want to review each person who could benefit from your father's death. Let's start with relatives, then talk about his employees, customers, and anyone you can think of who might help us in this investigation. Who would your father have confided in, besides yourself? Someone else we could talk to."

"I don't work in my father's business," I said. "So, I don't know much about his customers. But I want to help you any way I can. Dad's number one employee and CPA is Rod Addicks. Then there's his secretary and bookkeepers, Julie Syler, and Peg. And of course Dad's wife, Bernie. But I can't imagine anyone mad or crazy enough to want to kill him. It must have been robbery since sometimes there's lots of money in the office."

Yazzolino asked me a series of questions: Why did you two go to Seattle this morning? What were you doing in Mexico two weeks ago? When was the last time you saw your father? What do you know about the workings of your father's business? I was calm as I answered the detective's questions but I had some questions of my own. Detective Yazzolino repeated that we'd get to my questions later.

"We've been told by your stepmother that you were the child closest to your father. Why don't you go back a few weeks and tell me more about your Mexico trip," Yazzolino said. "Maybe explaining what you did will help you relax, which will help you remember some more details of your last meetings or discussions with your father."

Chapter 4: Victim, Two Weeks Prior to the Murder

**Jim Turel and his ex-wife at their daughter's wedding,
two weeks before his murder in 1974.**

It is a bright August summer morning in Portland, Oregon, but all I can hear is a horrendously loud argument above me. I've remodeled my split-level house into a duplex and I live downstairs. The deluxe, expensive part of the house is rented to a couple whose favorite recreation is verbal fighting. Their noise usually doesn't bother me, since the rent they pay covers my mortgage.

Last weekend was my younger sister's wedding. It was a beautiful church ceremony with lots of relatives and friends present. For the first time in years, we got a picture of my dad and mother together, even though they are divorced, with my sister standing between them. Dad and Mom both looked so proud. I love to see them like that. My stepmother, Bernie, stood stern-faced in the background. I wondered if Mom being there bothered her.

Today I'm packing for Mexico City. I'm off on vacation to get out of Portland for the hot month of August 1974. I'm 26 years old and single. I've been dating a girl named Janet on and off for the last three years.

Let me say this bluntly. I have a commitment problem and more than one woman has told me she was tired of waiting for me to pop the question. Eventually they start dating someone else and it breaks my heart. When I was 22, I fell in love with a woman named Susan, the first woman with whom I had an intimate relationship. Susan eventually left me because I was not mature in that relationship, meaning I was afraid to make a commitment to her. Losing her was my own fault. Since then I've dated a few women, which was educational, unpredictable, entertaining, and romantic.

My little sister's wedding made me think about my relationship with Janet. What better way of sorting out my doubts than to get away from everyone and everything by taking the time to visit my best friend and old college roommate, Ernesto Santos, who lives in Mexico City. I decided to take Ernesto up on his invitation to spend a week as a guest in his parents' home, where Ernesto and his sisters also live. Their home is a stately affair with maids and large family dinners.

So, off to Mexico City I went.

Since Ernesto worked during the day, his little sister, Laura, aged 18, was assigned as my guide and interpreter. Laura drove me around Mexico City every day and our close proximity and constant companionship caused feelings of affection to awaken inside me. I became very fond of Laura, yet I kept that information to myself and refrained from asking her out on a real date. Laura is engaged to a good man named Eduardo. Laura's hair is silky brown and she has beautiful brown eyes. I dared not tell her how I felt and couldn't ask if she felt the same way about me. Neither of us did or said anything to impinge her engagement. To do so would have been a dishonor to my friend and their family.

After my week in Mexico, I returned to Oregon and decided to visit Janet that very night to see her in person and from there, determine how I felt about her. We went out for dinner on August 27 and when we returned to her apartment we spent the whole night talking about our relationship. I still loved Janet, I decided. That night I decided to think seriously about asking if we could live together.

The next day I headed for the Troutdale airport. I spent a few minutes talking with Ken Smith, the aircraft painter, about his proposal to paint my single-engine aircraft, the first plane I ever bought, my dream machine. Then I took off for a scenic flight over the hills around Portland. I used the time to strategize my plan for a live-in proposal to my beautiful roommate to-be. Flying the plane makes me feel connected to nature and the true grace of life. It's a freedom that only pilots and birds can understand.

As I meandered, as graceful as an eagle over the green foothills east of Portland city limits, I wondered if Janet would be receptive to the idea of moving in together. She had kind of hinted about it before, but I was wasn't ready to commit. I knew she was attracted to another man, but how serious was it for her? This would be the first time I was willing to make a serious commitment. I kept wondering, would Janet say yes?

I thought, there's no time to lose and decided to pop the big question before I lost my nerve. I envisioned myself getting down on one knee like they do in movies. Yes, I decided, that's exactly what I'll do, and with my plan set, I flew back to the Troutdale airport and made a perfect landing.

But as I secured the plane, an old doubt leapt to the forefront. Well, I reasoned, if Janet turns me down, at least I will have told her how I feel.

It was 5 o'clock in the evening by the time I arrived at Janet's apartment. Janet wasn't home from work yet, so I quietly rehearsed what I was going to say. I listened intently for the distinctive sound of her Pinto rounding the corner. A year ago, that car had become an issue between us. For spite, since I refused to make a commitment, Janet threatened to buy a sports car, specifically to attract other men.

But when Janet drove up in her little green Pinto, I made a prayer of thanks. I would have lost her for sure if she traded up for a sports car. Men are definitely attracted to such things, especially if a sexy lady like Janet was sitting in the driver's seat.

Janet was surprised to see me sitting there in front of her apartment, waiting. I hadn't called in advance. I probably should have. As she walked toward me I couldn't help but admire how good she looked with her short skirt hugging her perfect curves.

"I've got something important to say to you," I said.

"Then I suppose I should invite you in."

After a few minutes working up my nerve, I bent down on one knee and blurted it out. "Janet," I said, "what do you think of the idea of us moving in together? But before you give me an answer, I want to explain why I am asking you this question. Since I have not seen you much lately, I realize how much I miss you. Also, it is time to either move forward with this relationship or not. In the past we have discussed this topic but I was afraid of making any kind of commitment. We've been dating for several years and I think it's time to find out if we are compatible enough to move on to the next step."

Janet got up out of her chair and kneeled down to be with me on the floor. She gave me a big hug and wet kiss.

"You're crying," I said.

"Because I'm so happy," said Janet. "The answer is, yes."

I started crying a little, too.

"Yes? Yes! Oh, Janet! To celebrate, let's make some special plans for this weekend," I said.

"Sure," she said.

We agreed that in the morning we would fly to Seattle in my plane. I had business appointments I'd have to handle, but I suggested that from there, we could fly to Vancouver, British Columbia, for the Labor Day weekend. That was fine with Janet. My heart filled with love and excitement as we cuddled throughout the night.

It took over ten minutes to explain my story to Detective Blackie Yazzolino. The detectives let me ramble, probably to help me relax. It felt good to talk about something other than the murder for a few minutes. But once detectives Yazzolino and Wells got back to the discussion about the upcoming investigation, they began asking direct questions.

"Okay, Stan, that brings us up through your activities of this morning. Now I'd like to talk about your stepmother's relationship with your father."

"Well, my last few visits to my dad's home weren't terribly pleasant. Bernie and my dad argued about getting a divorce. When I ribbed my dad about it later, he told me to stop giving him a bad time. I told him he was being rude to Bernie when he joked about his recent fun time at the computer seminar in San Diego and the Tijuana entertainment. The last time I had lunch with Dad he said he'd offered to buy Bernie out of the marriage for $20,000 cash."

"What about your personal relationship with Bernie?" Yazzolino asked.

"Bernie's relationship with all us kids is strained. She's stingy. For Christmas for the past seven years, Dad and Bernie gave my brother and me one pair of black socks each. Nothing else. It was the same every year, just one pair of black socks."

"How old is Gary? Did he work with your father?"

"Gary is 24. My dad sold some tax clients to my brother to get him started in business on the other side of town. Also he sold a few pieces of furniture to Gary for his office."

"Rod Addicks, your father's CPA, mentioned that your father and brother had a disagreement in the office at Columbia Bookkeeping a few months ago. What can you tell me about that incident?"

"I think Rod is jealous of my brother because Gary worked for H&R Block for two tax seasons, and then he opened his own tax business. Rod is probably exaggerating. Maybe the disagreement was something minor."

"Tell me about your sisters," Detective Wells said.

"One lives in Los Angeles, and the other sister lives in Milwaukie, Oregon. Neither of them have problems," I said. "Detective, are they under investigation? None of my siblings could have done such a ghastly thing!"

"Everyone in your family is being very cooperative," Yazzolino said. "But your sisters and brother had no idea that Jim and Bernie had been talking about getting divorced."

"My little sister just got married. She's still on her honeymoon!"

"I know, we located them and they're on their way here, now," Yazzolino said.

"How did you find them?"

"Police located them on a state highway in California. They're okay. They'll be arriving in Portland tomorrow."

I thought, what a honeymoon! I was remembering that my dad seemed so happy at their wedding.

"Let's move on to your mother. She and your father divorced ten years ago. Is that correct?"

"Yes," I said.

"And your mother took your father to court several times over a property dispute?"

"How did you know that?" I asked.

"Your stepmother, Bernie, mentioned it," Yazzolino said.

"It wasn't property. Six years ago, my dad was way behind on his child support so my mother had to take him to court, several times, to make him pay up. My mother is a very kind and gentle lady. Is she a suspect? She'd never even step on a bug. Another thing is, she remarried. She doesn't even have a driver's license. She couldn't have murdered my father!"

"I'm not suggesting she did, Stan. Did your father have any girlfriends?"

"No, of course not! Oh, wait a minute. He and I had an odd conversation in my driveway about a month ago. Dad told me he was selling a rundown cabin at the beach to a woman on a contract, with nothing down. He had a smirk on his face when he told me this. I said to him, as a joke, 'There must be more here than meets the eye! How old is she?' He then had the biggest smile and said, 'Too old for you. You'll never know.'"

"Explain to me why you are so intent on having the police keep the bookkeeping office locked," Yazzolino said.

"My father had many customers, so who knows who did this. The company has over 2,000 tax and accounting clients including a large account that operates 12 massage parlors in Portland. When Dad told me about that client, I wondered if the massage parlors were a front for prostitution."

"Can I break in here?" said Detective Wells, leaning forward. "Two young ladies who worked for massage parlors in Portland were found badly beaten this year. We strongly believe the parlors are, in fact, fronts for prostitution."

His comment made me a bit paranoid and no one said anything for a moment. Then Detective Wells leaned back and got ready to take more notes.

Wells appeared to be about 35, too young to be a senior detective. I found out that Stewart Wells use to be a schoolteacher. What a strange transition, I thought to myself.

Then Blackie Yazzolino said, "Let's talk about his employees and their relationships with your father."

"My dad was suspicious about one of his employees, Rod Addicks, the CPA. Rod bought a rental house that burned down 60 days after it was purchased. Dad told me the fire looked suspicious to him. That was about a year ago. He said he felt uneasy because Addicks wasn't upset about the fire. In fact, he told me that Addicks seemed gleeful about having enough insurance to cover the loss, plus make a little profit. Dad said he planned to investigate further into Addicks' background because the fire incident troubled him. He said it was just a feeling he had, nothing concrete. Dad also mentioned that Rod had no credit card. Addicks is the employee who bought out part of my dad's business."

"Rod Addicks worked as a CPA for your father, but he owned part of the business?" Yazzolino asked.

"Yes," I said.

"Did you father mention any other suspicions?"

"Dad mentioned Sam Moll's junky car was stolen and it sounded fishy to him. Sam Moll is a accountant and Rod's friend."

"That's okay. Who had keys to the office?"

"I don't know."

"Do you have a key?" Yazzolino asked.

"No."

"Do you know Jim Auxier?"

"Who's he?"

"Your father's attorney."

"No. I've never met him."

"Do you have a copy of your father's will?"

"No," I said. "But I guess his attorney would."

"Had your father mentioned what was in his will?"

"Only that about four years ago he told me he planned to leave the majority of his tax business to me, and a minor interest to my brother and sisters. I told my dad it wouldn't be fair to them, so I suggested that we get equal benefits, of whatever it would be. Then, about a year ago, Dad said he made things more equal between my brother and me. I don't know what he did in the end. That was the last discussion I had with my father about his will."

"Stan, I don't want to alarm you," Yazzolino said, alarming me, "but I'd suggest you keep a notebook where you jot down any suspicions or other things that come to you which might have some bearing on his murder. Conversations, observations, anything that might shed light on what brought on his murder."

"Okay," I said.

"Rod Addicks has been talking to us," Yazzolino said. "Addicks' theory was that the murder was either due to a botched robbery, a girlfriend killed him, or his wife, Bernie Turel."

"What do you think?" I asked.

"I'm still gathering information."

"How did my father die?"

"Your father must have put up a good fight. There was a struggle. Maybe he let someone in the office. There was no sign of forced entry. Rod Addicks was aware of a possible divorce between your father and stepmother."

We talked for over an hour and then Yazzolino said, "I'm surprised you know so much about your father's personal and business life. Do you know a lady named Nora?"

"No," I answered. "Who is she?"

"Are you aware he went to Hawaii with a lady that bought a house from your father?"

"No. You're kidding," I said. "Well then, I guess my suspicions were correct."

"Can you meet with me again tomorrow?" Yazzolino said. "I think we've covered enough ground for one night. You'd better get some sleep. I'd like to caution you not to speak to anyone else about your suspicions regarding the murder or arson. It appears as though your father didn't talk to anyone about his concerns regarding Addicks and Bernie, except you."

"Yes, I can meet again tomorrow. I'll do anything to help. What time?"

"Sometime in the morning, I'll call you later with a specific time. Where are you staying tonight?" Yazzolino asked.

"Janet and I decided to stay overnight at her apartment." I gave Detective Yazzolino Janet's phone number and address. Detective Wells wrote it down in his four-by-six note pad. He didn't talk much. Both detectives were very polite, gentle and professionally dressed.

We said goodbye to detectives Yazzolino and Wells, and Janet drove us to her apartment in Beaverton, Oregon. When we arrived there, we immediately went to bed. I couldn't sleep. My head was spinning. How did my dad die? Did he suffer? What brought this on? Who did it? Why would anyone do such a thing? Who murdered my father? Who murdered my father? Who murdered my father?

Janet was asleep next to me and I tried not to disturb her.

—————

Around midnight, the phone rang and I reached over to pick it up. It was Detective Blackie Yazzolino. "Can you meet me at my office downtown at 9 o'clock tomorrow morning?" he asked.

"Of course," I said.

"And here's the number of your father's attorney, Jim Auxier. I suggest you call him and get a copy of the will."

"Now?" I asked

"No, not now," Yazzolino said. "Sorry to have called so late."

"Is the office building locked and off limits?" I asked.

"No one will be allowed into the office. The police are guarding the building now. They'll be stationed there for the next five days, through Labor Day weekend.

Chapter 5: The Victim and His Family

The next day, August 30, 1974, Janet and I awoke about 7 o'clock. We took a nice hot shower together, got dressed, and after a big hug and kiss, she left for work at State Farm Insurance. We agreed to meet at her apartment that evening for dinner. I called my answering service and informed them of what had happened and asked them to take careful notes whenever any message came in. I dressed in my only nice suit so I could be taken more seriously. I like to dress in sport slacks and a suit jacket as it makes me feel more professional. In high school and college I was skinny as a rail. My nickname was Beanpole. Actually, I was a school nerd, which became an inferiority complex that stuck with me for years.

I drove to the sheriff's office in downtown Portland, which at that time was located at 222 SW Pine Street. I walked up the white marble stairway to a large office on the fourth floor where three detectives greeted me. One was Fire Inspector Millard of the Portland Fire Bureau who, unbeknownst to me, Yazzolino had called at 7:30 that morning to find out if they had information on Rod Addicks, which they did. Also present was a man from the FBI who was interested in the massage parlor connection. A few large whiteboards hung on the walls. The detectives' desks were disheveled, with stacks of paper piled high. Detective Yazzolino pointed to a whiteboard that contained a list of possible suspects, many of whom we'd already discussed, plus a separate list of people who would benefit from Dad's death. That list included my sisters, my brother, me, my stepmother, and several names I didn't recognize. Yazzolino confirmed that the City Fire Department was aware of the suspicious nature of the fire that gutted the rental house Rod Addicks owned. A list under "Motives" included robbery, jealousy, extra-marital affairs.

One of the detectives said I was lucky to get Blackie Yazzolino working on this murder case, as it would be one of his last cases before he retired. Detective Blackie Yazzolino was 60 years old.

I sat down and breathed deep a couple of times. The detectives asked me if I was ready to go over the lists and answer some questions.

"Yes," I said.

We went over some of the same territory I'd explained last night to detectives Yazzolino and Wells. They wanted me to talk about what I knew regarding my dad's impending divorce and business dealings with his CPA, Rod Addicks. They asked me to describe how my dad started out in the tax business. Then they wanted to get an understanding about the family's past. Where did we live while growing up? Who were my dad's friends? They wanted to know about my travels and how I acquired my business investments. Did my dad tell me anything about the massage parlor businesses? I spent an hour explaining everything I could think of. They just let me talk and every once in a while, one of them asked a direct question. Detective Yazzolino asked me to start as far back as I could remember regarding my dad's past.

"I have fond memories of my life as a child. Should I start my story there?" I asked.

"Yes, that's good," Yazzolino said.

"Okay," I said. "When I was three or four years old, I remember waiting anxiously for the sight of my father's large logging truck to return home each evening. He would sometimes bring home candy as a surprise.

When I was four, our family moved from the mountains of Sweethome, Oregon, to Gold Beach, on the Oregon coast. In Gold Beach, I recall windy walks along the sandy ocean beaches with my mother. Other memories include riding with my father on the coastal highway in his logging truck. I was so proud of my dad.

"I remember when our dog, Blackie, was run over by a car and died. In 1955, I watched my mother cry as my father became bedridden, and eventually crippled from what turned out to be polio. An emergency Life Flight plane flew low over our home on a cloudy day, heading north to a Eugene hospital with my dad aboard. My younger brother and I waved goodbye as the plane flew overhead. I wondered if he would ever return. My dad was only 26 years old at the time.

"Since polio was a contagious disease, my older sister and I were quarantined and taken out of school. I had just begun the first grade. The polio vaccine came out just a few months after he contracted the disease.

Jim Turel with his log truck, Sweethome, Oregon 1949.

"By the time Dad was out of the hospital, many months later, he was crippled for life and our family was broke. The logging trucks were sold, and then our dream home overlooking the ocean was sold. I had watched my dad build that house.

"Our family was surrounded by relatives who believed a person could become whatever they want to, as long as they maintain their principles, think positive, and work hard. Our aunts and uncles all gathered around us and encouraged us by their actions. Also the March of Dimes and our neighbors helped in many ways. We ended up on Welfare.

"We watched our dad struggle after returning from the hospital. At first he was restricted to a wheelchair, but later he began walking with crutches. During the four years following my dad's return home from the hospital, he was fortunate to borrow money from the State of Oregon to attend Lewis & Clark College in Portland and soon he received a degree in

Jim Turel stands proudly with his young wife and family, 1950.

accounting and business. Being restricted physically, my dad was angry a lot of the time, yet determined to remove himself from the restraints of welfare.

"In 1957, my mother's father, Grandpa George, engineered and installed one of the first handicapped auto devices in Oregon, which enabled my father to drive himself in his own automobile, a 1953 Hudson. There were four of us children. We spent summers at Grandpa George's farm in Grandview, Washington. Our grandparents were positive thinkers with good Christian values, which they instilled in all of us. From the age of nine through 15, while living in Portland and Lebanon, all of us kids, except my little sister, picked beans, raspberries, and strawberries to pay for most of our school clothes. Both our mother and father were into strict discipline and kept us busy with chores. By the time I was in the sixth grade, I had been enrolled in four different grade schools due to our various moves during those years.

Jim Turel with Stan and older sister, Gold Beach, Oregon, 1952.

"My father, Jim Turel, was successful at whatever he did before the polio crippled him from the waist down. He was a proud man and determined to make something of himself even after becoming crippled.

"When he received his accounting degree from Lewis & Clark College, he took a job as office manager at Barton & Abby Logging Company back in Sweethome. In the evenings, however, he started a small accounting and tax business in our living room in nearby Lebanon.

**Turel Family when Jim Turel returned from the hospital after contracting polio.
From *Curry County News* article, 1956.**

**Jim Turel in 1961
following his Lewis and Clark College graduation.**

"Not to sugarcoat it, being restricted by polio made Dad a difficult man to live with. When people are crippled, they sometimes become irrationally angry with the ones closest to them. Dad's behavior ruined the marriage between my mother and father. After 17 years together, my dad filed for a divorce, even though my mother objected. I watched my loving mother's life and self-esteem shatter.

I paused and asked the detectives, "Are you sure you want me to continue with this kind of background?"

"Yes. It will give us a better idea of all the personalities and family background. Please continue," Yazzolino said as the detectives made more notes on their small pads.

"After the divorce, we children stayed with my mother while my father went off. We moved to Portland and adjusted to a tight standard of living once again. Two years after their divorce, my older sister and I went to a Parents Without Partners picnic with our dad. A man who was then 30 years old began making eyes at my 17-year-old sister. He was following her around like a puppy dog and continually drinking from a bottle of booze, which he kept in a paper sack. The man was unshaven and his clothes were wrinkled. My sister, a Good Samaritan, felt sorry for him and told him she had a 25-year-old cousin she would introduce him to. She figured this would get rid of him. But one week later, the man showed up at our house for dinner to meet our cousin. My sister's plan backfired as he immediately made a play for our 36-year-old mother, who was still a beautiful lady."

"Tell us more about your stepfather. Was he a violent man?" Yazzolino asked.

"My brother, Gary, and my sisters and I watched with horror as our mother married that man who, to us, represented the exact opposite in character, hygiene, and ambition from that of our father. I know my mother slept with only two men in her lifetime. Our stepfather, Tom, was from a poor family from Arkansas. He had no table manners and no stable employment. He was physically threatening, and even roughed up our mom at times. His negative attitude about everything and everyone was contrary to the way we were being raised.

"By then my mother had a stable job at *The Oregonian* newspaper in Portland, and she used her income to support Tom until she retired at 72 years of age. *The Oregonian* was her social life and her escape from a stressful life with her husband. My mom would play classical music from memory, which was something she and all of us enjoyed. Tom worked at various jobs for minimum wage between long periods of unemployment. His attitude was 'society always keeps the poor man down.' He would turn on us whenever we'd intervene as he and our mother had physically abusive arguments. My brother and I tried to keep Tom away from our mom during violent episodes, but Mom usually sided with Tom and would chastise us for making trouble. My older sister escaped our home by moving into a Christian college in another part of town. It sickened me when I'd see him sit close to my sister and drool over her when my mother wasn't around.

"To me, it felt like we were living in a nut house. My mom could not admit to herself that she had married the wrong man, and I was worried that she would have a nervous breakdown. Some of their fights led to cracked and broken sheetrock in the hallways. None of her sisters or brothers had ever been divorced and to divorce again would have been the ultimate shame in her family. She couldn't do it."

"Tell us more about how you and your brother became interested in airplanes," Detective Wells said. "How could you afford your own airplane at such a young age?"

"When I was 16, Gary and I began to hang around local airports, partly just to get out of the house. But we were also crazy about airplanes, so we joined the Civil Air Patrol and a teenage flying club that had its own two-seat aircraft. The airplane was donated from Western Skyways of Troutdale, Oregon. The founder, Ernie Helms, saw to it that the airplane was taken care of by his mechanics free of charge for this young group of 15 teenagers.

"The club, SkyTeens, was lead by Chris Cheney, an 18-year-old commercial pilot. That group of young student pilots turned out to be a great inspiration to my brother and me. During our high school vacation breaks, three friends and I would rent a single engine plane, load up our sleeping bags, and fly anywhere we chose to go. Some flights took us to Canada, and some even as far south as Los Angeles. Yes, we were daring and adventurous, but not one person in that group went astray. We all turned out to be winners in one way or another, with most of us becoming licensed pilots. Of course there were a few mischievous situations. For instance, the time two small planes buzzed a football field during halftime, flying low between the grandstands, causing the school's marching band to drop to the ground in a wet mess. Chris Cheney and Don Riegelhuth lost their license for six months."

Detective Wells stood up and crossed the room. "I'm curious," he said. "Tell us how you got started in business."

"At first, Gary and I cleaned the bottom of a couple of airplanes in exchange for free rides with aircraft owners. Gary landed a job at the local airport as a line boy, gassing private airplanes in exchange for flying lessons. In addition to my 4 a.m. paper route, I started waxing airplanes for money and formed a business called Turel Enterprises. I also started waxing airplanes at Seattle's Boeing field. I hitched rides with a man named Don Riddel, who flew his plane back and forth to Seattle weekly on business. In one day, I could generally bum a free flight in a private plane to Seattle and back or end up in California. Some of these pilots took us under their wings, so to speak. While washing and waxing airplanes for money, I also received free airplanes rides from most of my clients. Flying allowed Gary and me to imagine that we could make something of ourselves.

"My stepfather told us often that the people around the airport were giving us false encouragement. 'Rich people don't care about poor people,' he would say. He lectured us regularly that we were going to earn minimum wage, just like him. 'You'll never get ahead,' he told us, over and over.

"During the summers before I had a car, I would spend a week at a time in Seattle with my Uncle Ray and Aunt Lorraine. Uncle Ray would give me rides to Boeing Field. During the rest of the year I'd just hitch a plane ride up to Seattle whenever I could. One weekend when my Uncle and Aunt weren't home, I slept under the wing of an airplane on a bed of newspapers, then hitched a ride back to Oregon the next day. Mr. Galvin, of Galvin's Flight Service, sometimes gave me planes to wax and let me hang around his flight office until I could hitch a ride with a pilot flying back to Portland. It was a tough beginning.

"My brother and I both found ways to avoid conflicts with our stepfather by hitchhiking or arranging rides from home to reach the Hillsboro airport after school and on weekends. Then I bought an old Volkswagen van.

"At home one night, I accidentally took the first helping of food from a large bowl of stew that had just been removed from the oven. My stepfather's rule was that no one was allowed to place any food on his plate until after he served himself a helping of everything first. I assumed it was an Arkansas family tradition. But that one evening I forgot to wait for my stepfather to fill his plate. He was sitting at the opposite end of the table. When he saw me spoon the stew into my bowl, he stood up and lifted his end of the table three feet in the air. The pot of hot boiling stew slid right into my lap. I was severely scalded on my stomach but fortunately, my family jewels were not damaged.

"My Uncle Ray and Aunt Lorraine recognized the difficult situation at home and they invited me to move to Seattle to live with them for nine months during my junior year of high school. Living with them gave me a concept of what a normal loving home life could be. When I returned home for my senior year of high school, the problem with my stepfather and mother was even worse. My mother lived in fear of my stepdad's temper, but refused to do anything about it. She was a gentle and kind lady from the old school that sticks by their man, no matter what.

"One of the local pilot families, Norm and Dolores Winningstad, realized our situation and agreed that my brother and I could move in with them. We were friends with Norm's sons and jumped at the chance to participate in an incredible healthy situation that removed us from an abusive home life. Gary and I could not have moved in with our dad since he had remarried and our new stepmom was cold and uninviting. Also, my mom and dad were repeatedly in court, fighting over child support. The Winningstad family instilled the type of positive energy that my brother and I needed at that time in our lives. They even paid for our room and board during our first year of college, and helped us in many other ways. Living with the Winningstads, plus my Uncle Ray and Aunt Lorraine, gave me hope that someday I would raise a family in a healthy environment. A few years later my younger sister found the situation at home intolerable and moved in with my dad across town.

"Throughout high school and college, I expanded my aircraft waxing business and ended up servicing 25 airports throughout Washington and Oregon. My brother, Gary, maintained a strong focus on aviation, and received his Private Pilot license before me, at the age of 17. I focused on saving money and running my business with the help and encouragement of local pilots and businessmen. Also, for two years, I spent three nights each week in the Emergency Room at Good Samaritan Hospital in Portland as an Explorer Scout volunteer. I wanted to become a doctor but found out that most doctors had very little time for a personal life. Those pilots and the staff at Good Sam were positive influences and I cannot thank them enough. I had become a workaholic before the age of 20. I did not drink, smoke, or take drugs."

I hesitated, looked at the detectives, and decided it was time to ask them some questions. But before I could, Detective Yazzolino looked directly at me and said, "Stan, can you tell me how you got into real estate deals at such a young age?"

"My friend, Chris Cheney, the man who started the SkyTeens flying club, got together with me to talk about how we could make some money together. We were both attending Portland State University when we decided to pool our money and start buying rental properties and playing the stock market. We were bored with the college curriculum and needed projects to occupy our ambitions. During my second year of college I talked the Dean of the Business School at Portland State into letting me skip the basics and go directly to graduate classes in business law, marketing, real estate, finance, and taxes. I learned to use some of that knowledge in business right away. From outside seminars, Chris and I learned a lot about limited partnerships and the stock market. We limited our potential purchase of properties to those that would pay their own way. That meant the rent collected must cover the mortgage, taxes and insurance. We predicted, and counted on, an average inflation factor of five percent per year to make us rich.

"The first property we selected to purchase was a 100-year-old converted triplex. When we approached Pete Wilson Reality about buying the property, we met the most fantastic looking lady who worked in their office. Chris asked her out on a date and found that she was 30 years old. She laughed at his boldness, but encouraged our efforts in buying rental property. Chris Cheney and I talked with Pete Wilson, and with that lady's assistance, Mr. Wilson agreed to carry his commission. Even so, we needed to put down $1,200 to secure the property. Chris and I together could come up with only $800, so I talked my brother into investing $400. However, that deal went bad when the City of Portland condemned the house four months after we filed for a permit to improve the electrical wiring. Chris and I talked to the realtor again and convinced him to take the property back. He agreed to return our money.

"One month later we found a six-unit apartment building in Camas, Washington, which Pete Wilson had listed. Chris and I invested $800 down on that property and Pete Wilson agreed to carry a note for his $4,500 commission. Later we bought several more properties in a similar fashion. Chris and I bought a house in Corvallis, a college town 100 miles south of Portland, and rented it to some of our buddies who attended Oregon State University.

"When I told my dad what Chris Cheney and I were up to, he was shocked that we could tie up so many properties at such a young age. In fact, the realtors never told the sellers how young we were and he arranged to have them carry private contracts on the properties. Two years later I bought my own plane.

"In the meantime, my brother and Chris Cheney joined the Oregon Air National Guard. I stayed in college because I didn't qualify for military service. I was classified as 4F since I was legally blinded in one eye from a childhood accident. Shortly afterwards, Chris Cheney got married and became an Air Force fighter pilot. Gary got a job with a construction company in Lewiston Idaho.

"In 1970, my dad began inviting me to lunches to talk about his business. He encouraged me to obtain an accounting degree then join him in the tax business. I rejected the idea because of all those troubled years we had after Mom and Dad's divorce. I felt my father had treated my mother unfairly. I despised the idea of becoming a bookkeeper, but found tax and law classes intriguing, like a chess game. I told Dad several times I wasn't interested in joining his business.

"When I was 22, Dad and I agreed to move forward and put the past behind us. He apologized for his behavior regarding Mom and admitted it was a huge mistake to have divorced her. At one lunch he said he wanted me to assist him in purchasing an office building or house in Beaverton so he could convert it into a tax office. With his $10,000 down payment, I went looking for a building. While driving along with my large white Samoyed dog in my red Ford Econoline aircraft waxing van, I approached the owner of a duplex and made a deal without a realtor. Three weeks later, I bought the duplex in my dad's name and converted it into an office building. The owner even agreed to a private contract. By the beginning of 1974, Columbia Bookkeeping had three accounting and tax offices located in the Portland area.

"After that," I said to Detective Blackie Yazzolino, "my dad began to talk to me about some of his physical, marital, and business problems. He asked again if I would come to work with him. But I said I wanted to go in my own direction. My dad told me he knew that no matter what direction I choose, I would succeed."

Yazzolino suggested we all get up to stretch, but brought the topic of the murder back into focus. "Have you had a chance to contact Jim Auxier, your father's attorney?" he asked.

"Yes," I said. "I made an appointment with him this afternoon in fact. To go over Dad's will."

Blackie Yazzolino explained that he and his detectives were checking with some of their informants into the massage parlors. They wondered if my father was doing any accounting for several other businesses about which they had questions. I said I did not know much about his accounts, only that I had my suspicions about the massage parlors. Julie, the bookkeeper, had told me that Rod Addicks oversaw most of those accounts.

"I'd like to go there with you, to Auxier's office," Yazzolino said. "To find out about the will, and a few other items."

I was surprised, but said, "Yes, of course."

Blackie Yazzolino was not going to leave any stone unturned.

I could tell by the detectives' questions about the family's history that my brother, stepmother, stepdad, and I were all considered suspects. However, at that point I could only guess who might be a murderer. Was it Dad's girlfriend, someone connected to the massage parlors? Was the murder just part of a robbery? Did Dad stumble into an arson ring? No, that couldn't be it, I thought as I slowly walked down the cold stairway from the detectives' office. The murderer couldn't be anyone I know.

Before going to the attorney's office, which was also downtown, I stopped by McDonalds for a bite to eat. I was so uptight that I couldn't drink my glass of ice water, or bite into the 49-cent cheeseburger. Added to that, I had a massive headache.

Chapter 6: Dad's Will and Funeral Arrangements

When I arrived at Jim Auxier's fourth floor law office in downtown Portland, near the corner of Southwest Morrison Street and 12th Avenue, I was surprised to find the two detectives, Blackie Yazzolino and Stewart Wells, already there waiting for me. Auxier's office suite was old and comfortable, with marble floors and rich wood trim. When we were ushered into Jim Auxier's private office, I smelled tobacco residue from a pipe or cigar. Auxier looked like an ex-football player: healthy, stocky, in his late 30s, and with a firm handshake which I liked. His deep voice sounded commanding and confident.

When we sat down, Auxier introduced himself to all three of us as "Jim." First, he offered his condolences to me. "I really liked your father, Stan, and I respect how hard he worked to get where he had gotten."

I thanked him and made an effort to keep my emotions in check.

"I'm glad you called, Stan," Auxier continued. "There's quite a number of items to go over with you because, according to your father's will, you are the executor of his estate. Here's a copy of his will. Excuse me a moment." He buzzed his secretary and asked her to make another copy of the will for the detectives. I had never seen my dad's will before.

As I sat there staring at the document, my head spun in disbelief. This wasn't happening. I had to take a big deep breath.

The four of us went over details in the will and found that my dad had placed Columbia Bookkeeping, his two office buildings, plus two contract receivables into the Turel Family Trust. His wife, Bernie Turel, was to receive her home, the cars, plus monthly income from the Turel Trust to support her as long as the assets in the trust lasted. None of us kids would receive any money from his death or from the Trust, unless there was money left over after Bernie died.

Auxier also showed us a will my dad had prepared in 1969, which would have left the majority of the business to me. I was glad that the new will reflected equal disbursements for Gary and me. I wanted to avoid bad feelings with my brother.

"Was Bernie present when this will was drafted?" asked Detective Yazzolino.

"No," Auxier answered, "but Rod Addicks was. This will was signed several years ago."

My dad's file also contained a buy-sell/stock purchase agreement for Columbia Bookkeeping stock between Addicks and my dad. Rod Addicks had exercised an option to buy up to 38 percent of the tax business. That agreement had been signed two years earlier. "You're lucky a professional CPA like Rod Addicks is available to run the business now that your dad is dead," Auxier said. I wondered, did the agreement contain a statement that gave Addicks the first right of refusal to buy the whole company from the Trust if the family wanted to sell?

"Stan, your dad and Rod Addicks also formed a business called Quality Financial Planning."

"Can you give me more details about the company?" I asked.

"Rod Addicks had talked clients into investing in three different apartment complexes, and he took a monthly fee for managing them. Also Addicks owns a minor interest in two other business deals, one of which is a small mobile home park in Florence, Oregon."

All this was news to me.

"I'd suggest we meet with your stepmother, Bernie, after Labor Day," Auxier said, "so we can go over funeral arrangements. Bernie already called me and said she needed emergency money, so yesterday I asked Rod Addicks to take a few hundred dollars over to her. From now on, however, as the executor of your father's will, you have the right to okay such requests until things get settled."

"Would it help to have my brother and sisters available for the meeting, too?"

"We can talk to them together or individually," Auxier said. "If necessary."

"Who will be running the company?" asked Detective Yazzolino.

"Rod Addicks called me and said he'd be available to run the company," Auxier said, "until the family decides what it wants to do with it. In case the decision is to sell. Addicks said to tell you he'd help in any way possible."

"Mr. Auxier, do you mind if I ask you a few questions that pertain to this case?" said Blackie Yazzolino.

"Not at all, detective. It's your job. Do you mind if I smoke?" he said, lighting his pipe while leaning back in his dark leather chair.

"Do you know of anyone having trouble with Jim Turel? Anyone that might profit from Mr. Turel's death?"

"Jim Turel came to my office a number of times in the last few months and asked what it would cost to prepare divorce papers. He said he and his wife were having serious troubles."

"Have you done any legal work for the massage parlors that Addicks brought to the business?"

"No," Auxier said. "Why?"

"It's possible that something involving the massage parlors may have contributed to Jim Turel's death," Yazzolino answered. "Have you done any of the legal work on Addicks' insurance claim for a house that burned down?"

"Yes," said Auxier. "But neither I, nor the insurance company, thought Addicks was involved in arson since Addicks had an ironclad alibi, which is why the insurance company paid Addicks on the claim."

"Who prepared the legal documents for the apartment deals?"

"I did," said Jim Auxier. "Based on instructions from Rod Addicks. They all appeared to be normal transactions. Jim Turel called me a number of times for clarifications regarding the deals that Addicks was forming. Mr. Turel wanted to ensure that Addicks would not drag him into any trouble from a liability standpoint. Mr. Turel seemed overly concerned in the last few months about his pending divorce."

"What can you tell me about Rod Addicks?"

"Well, Mr. Turel placed a lot of trust and faith in Rod Addicks. At Addicks' request, for instance, Mr. Turel agreed to give Addicks an option for buying part of the tax business. He didn't want to lose Addicks because he was the top producer for the company."

"Explain what you mean by 'producer,'" said Yazzolino.

"Columbia Bookkeeping hires four temporary tax preparers and three bookkeepers during each tax season. Rod Addicks and Mr. Turel were the only tax accountants after April 15 of each year."

Just then, a call came in and the attorney excused himself. He returned in a minute.

"That was Rod Addicks," said Auxier. "He mentioned a $50,000 life insurance policy in effect payable to the tax company. Also Stan, Addicks wants you to know that he would work for a reasonable fee per month to help run the company."

"Mr. Auxier, can I have a copy of all your records regarding the apartment deals, communications, and corporate minutes for Mr. Turel's various businesses?" said Detective Yazzolino.

"Well, Mr. Yazzolino, some of that information is confidential and I would need to receive a subpoena from you or authorization from the persons involved to release that information."

"Of course," Yazzolino said.

"I wouldn't want to lose my license over improper disclosure of information," Auxier said. "I'm not trying to be difficult."

"I understand," said Yazzolino.

"Gentlemen, I will cooperate with you in any way possible," said Auxier. Then he faced me. "Most of the legal responsibly will fall to you, Stan, regarding your dad's business, since you are his executor. Check with me regarding what information you can give out without a subpoena."

"Okay," I said.

"All the tax and accounting records for the company's 2,800 clients are confidential and it requires a subpoena before someone can go through any tax client's records. Let's be reasonable about this," Auxier said, "as we don't want to scare away the clients and in the process ruin the tax business."

The detectives did not seem happy with this. "Jim, I'll have to trust your judgment on this," I said, "but I don't want to do anything to slow down the investigation."

"That's all I have for now," said Yazzolino, and he and the note-taking Detective Wells shook hands with us and departed.

I stayed with Jim Auxier for another hour, talking over my dad's various business arrangements. "Jim," I said, "I want to make sure my dad's tax business doesn't fall apart. I don't want to see my dad's entire lifelong efforts wasted. If eventually we need to sell the business, then we must preserve the value of the company. This is important to me. Our family went through something like this once before and it almost destroyed my father's generation. Granddad Turel died in an accident and his timber rights and lumber business was sold. My father forever after resented the fact that he was not given the opportunity to continue with his father's lumber mill business. Dad's mother, my grandmother, sold everything at ten cents on the dollar, and today those timber rights would have been worth millions."

"You have two options," said Auxier. "The Trust agreement is very clear. You can either choose to run the business yourself for the benefit of the Trust and your stepmother, or you can turn it over to a bank trust and watch what happens. I can't think of anyone except maybe Bernie or a burglar who would be mad enough to kill your father. And since Bernie was offered several ridiculously low offers to divorce your dad, she might have hated your father, but it's highly unlikely she could have physically murdered him. "Be careful not to jump to conclusions," Jim Auxier warned me, "as the police sometimes get focused in one area, which leads down the wrong path. Many people could be considered a suspect in this case. But due to your suspicions about your stepmother, the massage parlors, and Rod Addicks' house burning down, I urge you to just wait and see what the investigation turns up before you make any accusations or decisions. Maybe someone robbed your father since it happened sometime between the hours of 8 and 10 p.m."

"You know for sure that was the time of the murder?"

"I thought that's what the detectives said," Auxier replied.

Auxier then went through the process of how I could retain control of the business and ensure that Rod Addicks understood he was an important part of the future of Columbia Bookkeeping. "Rod told me he'd like to get the office re-opened as soon as possible," Auxier said. "The business will fall apart without him there, I assure you. Rod is concerned about you and Gary. He doesn't want either of you to worry or to get too involved, because he can handle it. The clients will be very nervous if too many changes take place under these circumstances."

"Jim, not to disagree, but I have a lot more business experience than perhaps you and Rod realize. I've taken graduate classes in corporate, income tax and business law at Portland State University. Most importantly, Jim, I want to make sure that no one, including my stepmother Bernie and Rod Addicks, will have access to my dad's checking and savings accounts. I have a personal banker. His name is Jack Miller. He worked with my father as well. I trust Jack Miller. But before I go any further on this, I want to get into the tax office and go through my dad's personal books and find out what his financial situation is. I don't want Addicks or my stepmother going through Dad's office until after the detectives and I look at everything."

"Then I guess you and I are done for now, Stan," Auxier said. "Again, let me express my condolences for your father's untimely death."

"Do you mind if use your phone, Jim?" I asked.

"Be my guest," he said, striking a match to relight his pipe.

I called Blackie Yazzolino's number and asked if he could have someone haul Dad's private two-drawer file cabinet to the detective's downtown office. "I'd like to bring my banker down there so we could both go through it."

"Yes, good idea," agreed Yazzolino. "But Stan, please do not tell anyone what you hear or see during our conversations. And please be careful what you say to Jim Auxier. He was the attorney representing the estates of both Addicks and your father. Remember, according to the Fire Marshall's arson investigation, Jim Auxier handled the insurance claim for Addicks' fire."

When I got off the phone I asked Jim Auxier to set up a corporate meeting for both Columbia Bookkeeping and Quality Financial. "Until I know more about the murder," I said, "what do you recommend we do until we figure out what happened?"

"I would recommend that you, Stan, be named president of the company and remove any check-signing authority from Rod Addicks and Bernie Turel. According to the Turel Family Trust Agreement, this is spelled out in the will. That's what should be done anyway to maintain control of the business."

"When should we do that?" I asked.

"It should be done right away, Stan," Auxier said. "I'll arrange meetings with Rod and Bernie for tomorrow or early next week, after Labor Day. Also, I will advise Addicks that he must get a different lawyer if he needs one in his business affairs since I represent your father's estate and Columbia Bookkeeping."

A few days after my dad died, I hired a young ex-marine named Jimmy Frances to drive my van to the various airports each day to handle my scheduled aircraft waxing appointments. For two days I trained him on how to detail aircraft. Our arrangement was to meet each morning at the tax office and I would provide the worksheets that identified his assignments. I had airplanes lined up for Jimmy to wax and/or detail since I could not complete the work myself. I reduced my appointments in the Seattle area so I could remain in town all the time. Jimmy would pick up my Ford van each morning and return it by 5 o'clock in the evening.

I had met Rod Addicks only a few times before my dad's death so I called him to talk about the investigation and to discuss when we should re-open the tax office. I decided to let him know that the police would not be allowing anyone into the office for at least a week. Addicks sounded shocked and upset over the phone.

"The police won't find anything there!" Addicks said. "It was most likely a robbery, or maybe your father's wife committed the murder."

I pretended I was just following Jim Auxier's instructions, not wanting to sound like I was going to run things. Jim and Detective Yazzolino had instructed me not to mention my suspicions to anyone yet. "The attorney, Jim Auxier, will be calling you to arrange a meeting," I said, "so you can re-open the office soon."

"Okay. That's a good plan," Addicks said. "I'll be waiting for Auxier's call. Stan, I want you to know I will do anything to help you guys, just let me know if you need anything."

Then I called my stepmother, Bernie, and told her that Jim Auxier, Dad's attorney, wanted to meet her downtown tomorrow or early next week.

"I'll be there," she said.

On the books, Bernie was Columbia Bookkeeping's secretary, my dad was president, and Rod Addicks was vice president. Addicks was also listed as president of Quality Financial Planning, the business that set up the apartment building purchases and operations for investors.

Then I called Jim Auxier and asked him to make it appear as if it was his idea to turn over temporary control to me, even though it was set up in the will that way. "Jim," I said, "I do not want Rod Addicks or my stepmother to become offended by the sudden change in corporate structure." Auxier agreed to my suggestion. In the back of my mind I was being careful. I didn't want to upset either of them with my suspicions. I wanted to act as if I knew nothing regarding the police.

The next day Bernie and all of us kids met at Bernie's house to discuss funeral plans. Dad's body could not be released by the Homicide

Department until the following week. We arranged for his funeral to be held in Gresham, Oregon.

I explained to the family that I'd gone with Dad to a graveyard recently. I'd been out to the Springwater Pioneer Cemetery, southeast of Estacada, with Dad just a few months before, when my dad's favorite uncle, Jack Marrs, was laid to rest. The original Turel homestead was built in 1903 and the area was special to his family. Dad and I remained at Uncle Jack's grave after most of the other mourners had left because Dad wanted to spend some time there. He said the quiet Pioneer Cemetery was where he wanted to be buried, too, when it was his time.

"Stan, I want you to remember this place," Dad told me.

"Oh, Dad," I said. "Don't think like that."

But with him standing with his crutches at the foot of Uncle Jack's grave, Dad reminded me that several times in his life he had faced death. "No one knows when the end will come."

Dad reminisced about his tour of duty in the Navy during World War II on the aircraft carrier Yorktown. The "Jap Kamikazes," as he called them, attacked his ship many times. During an air attack, Dad was standing next to one of his best friends when the young man was literally shot in half. Dad said he watched the life in the eyes of his friend go slowly out.

Another time he was driving a full logging truck down a narrow logging road. On a steep hillside, when he came around a corner, he saw a pickup crossways in the middle of the road. Three drunken teenagers had stopped their truck right there. Dad could not stop so he ran the truck, logs and all, right down the steep embankment. He careened for over 500 feet before the truck came to a stop. Dad said he felt lucky to be alive because the truck was completely destroyed. For saving those young kids' lives he received a hero's thanks in the local newspaper and the State Industrial Accident Agency Award.

A few years later, he said, in 1955, a log had snapped on a hill above his truck and rolled right over him, which broke one of his legs six months prior to his contracting polio.

And Dad reminded me that even I had a close call with death. I was a passenger in a twin-engine plane crash when I was 18. I escaped with minor scratches but had several hernia surgeries in the following years due to the impact. Dad took out a life insurance policy on Gary and me after that. "Anyway," I said to everyone at Bernie's house as we discussed funeral plans, "Dad asked to be buried at Springwater, and I recommend we grant him that request."

So, the group decision was to bury Dad there.

My sisters began crying. Our gathering turned into an impromptu memorial as each of us described memories of Dad. This nightmare, that he was murdered, was finally sinking in. We agreed that Dad had led a lucky but unlucky life.

"It would be cheaper to cremate Jim," my stepmother Bernie said. "I don't want to waste a lot of money on a funeral. I vote for keeping it simple."

The rest of us looked at each other and shook our heads. No, we didn't like that idea.

"Then we should spend at the most $300 on a simple gravestone," Bernie suggested. "The Veteran's Administration will cover that amount."

While arranging pallbearers for the funeral, I called Rod Addicks to ask him if he would be one since he was my dad's best friend. Addicks paused, then sighed, then said, "You know Stan, I do not feel up to it since I am so upset." As he said those words, I felt a chill, as if something was wrong. Perhaps he was going through a bit of remorse, or having feelings of guilt, I thought. Or perhaps Rod Addicks had an aversion to carrying Dad's coffin. It was just one of those strange sensations.

We went along with Bernie's budget, since we wanted to avoid upsetting her with our personal opinions. However the family insisted on a nice coffin for Dad to be buried in.

After that meeting, in the early afternoon, I drove Bernie downtown to Jim Auxier's law office. Rod Addicks and the lawyer were already deep in discussion when we got there. The three of us sat quietly while Jim Auxier went over a number of items: banking, corporate resolutions, and the $50,000 life insurance policy.

"Just to make it clear," Rod Addicks said, "the life insurance money is company money, not mine personally. Your family will need to decide if you want to sell the business, or keep it. Either way, I assure you, I'm here to help in any way I can." Addicks was compassionate, sincere, and supportive of whatever Jim Auxier recommended.

The lawyer handled the details perfectly. All parties agreed to move control of the business from my dad to myself as trustee of the Turel Family Trust and Estate. Jim Auxier made it sound as though this meeting was being carried out per the terms of the Will and Trust Agreement, which in fact, it was. The Trust Agreement made it very clear that I was "given full control to operate and continue the tax business as if I were the owner." Frankly, I was surprised Dad had made such a clear directive in his will.

Over Labor Day weekend Bernie burned all of my dad's clothes in the backyard. We found out about it later and I can tell you both Gary and I were quite upset about that. We wondered: is she destroying evidence? We made a call to Detective Blackie Yazzolino voicing our individual suspicions and concerns. To their credit, the police and detectives were patient and respectful to all of us. I was reminded by my brother and sister that perhaps Bernie was pissed off at Dad since she had found out about Dad's girlfriend from the police.

Chapter 7: Investigating Suspects and the Tax Business

Late on Tuesday, the day after Labor Day, I met again with Detective Blackie Yazzolino, but this time at my dad's office. A marked police car was still posted in the parking lot. I noticed all the dark dusted finger print smudges that stood out against the gold paint on the back of the Cadillac. I paused to get my grief under control, and took a big deep breath as I walked past the car. It was only a year ago that Dad flew to the Cadillac factory back east to pick it up. He was so proud of his car. The yellow crime scene tape had been removed from the front door earlier that day.

As I entered the building I noticed hundreds of dark fingerprint smudges all over the inside of the main offices, hallways, doors, and file cabinets. I was stunned, and shocked, to find the hallway, walls and ceiling leading to my dad's office splattered with blood. The rug in the hallway where he died was saturated with a large dark area that I had to assume was dried blood. It made me queasy to see where my dad had died. I thought the police would have cleaned up the mess before they allowed the family in, but they said usually the owners of the property do the cleaning. I asked them again if they would take my dad's locked personal two-drawer filing cabinet downtown for us to review.

The hot and stuffy office held the sickening odor of death. I had to go outside to get some fresh air before I crumbled with nausea. I could not believe I was going to be the one arranging the clean up.

I called a carpet company to replace the carpet, and painters to apply a fresh coat in the hallways. Once that was done, I had the regular office cleaning lady, Betty Smith, clean the whole building. It was as difficult for her as it was for me to see the mess. She had a key; did that make her a suspect too? The police interviewed her but she had an airtight alibi. She was a kind woman, and terribly upset, as she had liked my dad a lot. Later that day, Detective Yazzolino, my stepmother Bernie Turel, Jim Auxier, a representative from the State of Oregon, and I met at the First Interstate Bank to open Dad's safe deposit box. An original of Dad's will and his agreements with Addicks was inside.

Detective Yazzolino agreed to meet the next morning with me, and Jack Miller from First Interstate Bank, at the Sheriff's office downtown. There, we went through all of my dad's personal books and checking account records. We found that Dad owed his bank $16,000 on a 90-day loan, due the day he died. All his personal accounting records were in excellent shape, with good details. However the books and records of Quality Financial Planning were entirely missing.

From the Sheriff's office, I went to Columbia Bookkeeping's banks with a copy of the new corporate resolutions. I checked with each bank account's signature card and removed the names of Bernie Turel and Rod Addicks from any check-signing authority for all business accounts except Quality Financial Planning, which had very little cash in it. I verified that Addicks did not have check-signing authority on Columbia Bookkeeping's main account. I originally agreed with Addicks' idea to set up a small payroll account with limited funds for him to use if I was not in the office. But I decided not to put that into effect just yet.

A quick total of Dad's business assets and properties put his gross estate value at just over half a million dollars. Once I subtracted the company debts, that half-million dollar estate value dwindled to less than a $140,000 net worth in the Turel Family Trust, if the tax business was sold and liquidated right then. My dilemma was, should I try to save the tax business while it attempted to support my stepmother, or should I sell it? In order to make a decision, I consulted with my banker, Jack Miller, and Rod Addicks, several times over several days. We found that Dad and Bernie's personal account had only a few hundred dollars in it. Bernie could keep that account separate from the estate. According to Dad's will, Bernie would receive their home and cars free and clear of any debt, plus a small life insurance policy.

The First Interstate Bank's Trust Department, from which I sought advice next, told me that based on the value of the company and net assets, the Turel Family Trust money would last at most seven years while it supported my stepmother. They showed me an actuarial table that predicted Bernie could live 25 more years. That meant there would be no residual money left for Dad's children, including myself, since the Trust would be out of money within seven years. Also, they suggested that I sell the tax company right away and they could help handle that sale, since trust departments of banks do not normally run small companies in their trust portfolios.

I didn't like First Interstate's advice. Considering how hard my dad had worked his whole life, and considering how angry I was that someone stole the remaining years of his life, I decided not to sell. I refused to let whoever murdered my father also destroy his life's efforts. I remembered again how much my dad regretted not having the chance to save Grandpa Turel's business in 1939. Since my stepmother and Rod Addicks were suspects, why sell it now? Addicks may have been the only logical person to buy the tax business, and I didn't want to go there. No, I wouldn't do it. I decided to set myself up in my dad's office, at least until we found out who killed him and why. My brother and I agreed, without telling Addicks, that when the office reopened, we would both stay on the premises for the first week or so.

After I made my decision not to sell, doubts continued to haunt me. Should I sell the business or turn it over to the bank? Could I make enough profit running the business while supporting Bernie for years, and keep it up long enough for my brother and sisters to inherit something? Due to my dad's suspicions about Addicks, could I even work with him? At one point I didn't think so. But I kept my doubts to myself.

Again I went to our lawyer, Jim Auxier, and asked for his advice about turning over the Turel Trust to a bank. During our two-hour discussion Auxier said, "Let me use my own past experience concerning my mother's Trust which a bank ran for years. The bank never made any money for my mother's Trust. All they did was charge high fees to run it. You and your family would be better off in the long run if you keep the company and work with Rod Addicks as long as you can. Addicks seems very cooperative. I'm sure he knows nothing about the murder and the only reason the police are interested in him is because he was the last person to see your dad alive. Stan, if you turn the Trust over to a bank, the bank will sell the company to Addicks or someone else and Bernie will use up all the Turel Trust money in about seven years. There will be no inheritance for any of you or your siblings unless you make a go of it. I think you can do a lot with the company. That is what your father told me and that is why he set up the Trust the way he did. He felt you could run the company."

At one point during that conversation with Auxier, Rod Addicks called with the news that Bernie should receive SAIF Workers Compensation, since my dad was killed in his office. That meant that Bernie would receive an additional $750 per month until she died or remarried.

With Detective Yazzolino's okay, I decided to reopen the tax office several days after Labor Day weekend. Also, I asked for and received a subpoena, which allowed Multnomah County to have their own CPA, the IRS, and the FBI review the books, records, checkbooks and the partnerships documents that Rod Addicks had formed. On the day after Labor Day, my dad's two-drawer filing cabinet was given to me for safekeeping, which I transferred to Janet's apartment. I spread papers and files all over her neat apartment, familiarizing myself with my dad's books and documents in every detail. I think the long hours obsessing about the investigation and funeral plans was getting to her. It wasn't exactly the romantic getaway we had planned.

Several days before the funeral, I was back in Blackie Yazzolino's downtown office scanning their long list of potential suspects when an idea hit me. The building that housed Columbia Bookkeeping rented out extra suites to other firms. One of the tenants was Scientific Investigations, a business that conducted polygraph tests. I wrote myself a note to meet with the owner to ask him how reliable lie detector tests were. When we spoke in person, I learned the owner was a retired specialist from the Multnomah County Sheriff's office. He said the tests were very reliable. Based on that conversation, I called up Detective Yazzolino to ask if he thought it made sense for all potential suspects, including myself, to take lie detector tests. "Wouldn't that help speed up the investigation?" I asked Yazzolino.

"Yes, it's a really good idea. In fact, I'm already working on it."

I described my meeting with the tenant next door and asked if he wanted his contact information.

"No," Yazzolino said. "No need. We'll provide the best specialist in the State of Oregon at no charge. It's part of our normal investigation process."

I found out later that Yazzolino had already talked to a state examiner about initiating polygraph tests. We decided to use the Columbia

Bookkeeping office as the location of the tests, and they were set to begin in five days. I called my brother, sisters, and stepmother. Everyone I talked to agreed to take the test. I also asked the detectives if we should offer a $5,000 reward for information leading to the arrest and conviction of the murderer. Yazzolino said, "Not yet, maybe later. First we'll administer the tests, and then we'll follow up on the suspicions we talked about before."

When I called Rod Addicks, asking him to take the polygraph test, he said he would have to talk to his attorney first since he didn't trust lie detector tests. "You'd better not take the test either, Stan," he advised me. "You should definitely talk to Jim Auxier, your dad's attorney, first."

"I think the tests are a good idea, Rod," I said.

"I'm not trying to be difficult, Stan," Addicks said, using his short, nervous laughing voice. "I'm just being cautious since I've heard bad things about those tests."

"Rod, if you refuse, this will only draw attention to you since everyone else is cooperating. I want to get the investigation going and eliminate as many suspects as possible."

"It was probably just a robbery, Stan," Addicks said. "Most likely a stranger did it."

"Yes, I agree with you," I said. "It could have been a stranger and a bungled robbery, but I still think it's a good idea to eliminate all the potential suspects up front." I called Addicks several times about the test but I could tell the calls were irritating him, so I backed off.

In the back of my mind I felt there was a really strong possibility that the murder had something to do with the massage parlors. Did my dad stumble onto something illegal with the massage parlor business? Was that business involved in arson and connected with organized crime?

"Look, Stan," Addicks said, "I assure you I can keep the business going. But if you really want to sell, I know a few people who might want to buy it."

I thanked Addicks for his consideration then asked him again, "Rod, are you interested in being a pallbearer, since you were such a close friend of my dad?"

"I'm going to pass on that one, Stan. I feel too bad about what happened." He hesitated for a moment and then, in low voice, said, "Sincerely, Stan, you will never know how bad I feel about this."

Chills raced down my back again when Rod Addicks said those

words. But I dismissed the thought again because it just wasn't possible he was connected with the murder. After all, Addicks was a professional and I could sense how seriously this had affected him. His voice over the phone sounded calm, friendly and logical. During that discussion, I asked Addicks if he had contacted the seasonal tax preparers about the funeral arrangements. And I specifically asked him if he had gotten in touch with John Bell and Sam Moll, our seasonal tax preparers. Addicks told me he didn't know how to reach Sam Moll because Moll didn't have a phone.

Since Bernie and all my siblings had agreed to take a polygraph test, I reasoned that Dad might have been murdered by someone Addicks knew. Someone from the massage parlors. Was Addicks afraid to talk?

I wrote down a note for Detective Yazzolino. Something in the conversation with Rod Addicks had made me uneasy.

Due to the fact that Dad was murdered and an investigation underway, my dad's body and his autopsy report could not be released by the Sherriff's Special Investigations Department for over a week. The day before the funeral I decided to take some action on my own since I had assembled my own list of possible suspects. I decided that in the next few weeks I would make a point of talking with as many people as I could that had even a minor connection to the investigation.

I wondered if the murderer would show up at the funeral. My dad had many clients and I needed a way to identify all the people who attended. So, I hired a photographer to hide in the bushes of the cemetery near the funeral home to take pictures of license plates and everyone who came to show their respects. I thought that maybe the murderer might come to the funeral because he or she had a guilty conscience. Yazzolino said I was wasting my money, but later the police asked for the pictures anyway. The only strange picture taken during the funeral was an elderly man drinking from a Clorox bottle, which I think must have contained whisky. He drank from it only after his wife went inside the funeral home.

The evening prior to the funeral, I called my friend John Wayland who owned a radio and guitar shop, and asked if he could build a compact transmitter for me, capable of transmitting a few blocks away. John is a young, inventive guy and a Citizen's Band nut who had outfitted the cars of many of my friend's with various CB's, shortwave, and stereo systems.

I gave John a brief rundown about what was going on—that my dad had been murdered and I had suspicions I wanted to follow up on. I told him I wanted to record my conversations with possible suspects.

"Sure, no problem," John said, and set about designing a compact transmitter that used a remote AM channel. I paid him $400 and when I picked up the little unit, I was surprised that it was small enough to be hidden in a cigarette pack. It had a three-foot wire that ran across my chest and was taped two feet down my back. The only problem was that I didn't smoke and everyone knew it. So, I decided to hide the pack by taping it to my skinny stomach under my shirt.

I did not tell the police, nor ask for permission to use it because my attorney told me it was illegal.

Many of my father's relatives, employees, and friends came to the funeral in Gresham and most followed us for the 30-mile drive to the cemetery. Detectives Yazzolino and Wells arrived early. I had a hard time stopping myself from breaking down emotionally, but I kept my focus by staying alert for anything that could be construed as suspicious. Talking with relatives and friends helped me control my tears, but watching my 73-year-old Uncle Ted cry nonstop undid me. Uncle Ted Turel, my grandfather's brother, had treated my dad like a son since he never had children of his own.

Then there was my, oh so very sad, Aunt Sally Fox. When my dad was a teenager he left home and lived with Sally for a year. When Dad married Mom after World War II, Sally gave him a whole beef for the freezer as a wedding present. When my dad divorced my mom 17 years later, Aunt Sally sent my dad a bill for the cow. Strange, the things you remember when you see people at a funeral.

Everyone was polite but grief-stricken. Few asked any questions about the investigation. The detectives stood in the background and observed. Occasionally they meandered up to me to ask who this person or that person was.

I was exhausted by the end of the day, so Janet and I went back to the apartment before dark. By then I had started taking different routes home every day, checking my rear view mirror, staying alert to anyone who might be following us. Yes, I had become more than a little paranoid ever since Blackie Yazzolino told me to keep my eyes open for anything suspicious. By then everything seemed suspicious to me. When Janet and I arrived back at her apartment, I hid my bright red van on a back street. I went inside, then crashed on the sofa and fell into a deep sleep.

The day after the funeral, on September 6, my brother, Gary, and I made sure we met the detectives at the tax office before Julie Syler's arrival at 8 o'clock. As usual, I was dressed in my only good suit and Gary was dressed casually. A policeman was already there, removing the remaining crime scene tape from around the building and parking lot.

Detectives Yazzolino and Wells arrived in their tan, unmarked police car a few minutes later. Dad's golden Cadillac still sat in the number one parking spot near the front door, looking abandoned. I again noticed the black smudge marks on the car from the fingerprinting. It felt strange, and sad, to realize that his parking spot was the last place my dad drove to on the night he died. The Cadillac remained where it was until later that day when the detectives said it was okay for Bernie to take it home with her.

Detective Yazzolino, Gary, and I entered the large lobby together. The policeman stayed outside in his patrol car. I could smell the new carpet, which overwhelmed the deathly odor present the last time I was there. And I could still see groove marks under the freshly painted sheetrock. The light brown pine molding around the bathroom doorway was still damaged and served as a reminder of the struggle that had taken place. I felt profound loss as I walked down the hallway where Dad inhaled his last breath.

Yazzolino said, "The police will leave after everyone arrives for work."

We all greeted Julie Syler in the front lobby. The first thing everyone notices about Julie is her bright red hair. She gave Gary and me a hug. "Oh Stan, I still can't believe what happened. When I saw your father in the hallway, it was like a bad dream. I'm just so sorry. I wish there was something I could do."

"Julie, either Gary or I, or even both of us will be here in the office every day until they catch the person who committed the murder."

"Oh, Stan! I'm so relieved to hear that. I'm just so glad to see you both. I feel better knowing the two of you will be around."

Next to arrive was Peg, a tall and slender woman in her 30s. With her dark black hair and tailored clothing, she looked like a well-dressed executive. Peg was the only other bookkeeper who worked in the office between tax seasons. She had just returned from her Hawaiian vacation.

Detective Yazzolino, Gary, Julie and I went into Dad's office. We closed the door behind us. At first, Gary and I sat in the two chairs in front of Dad's large oak desk. Looking across the table at Dad's empty chair made the room feel empty. His large oak desk was three feet by six feet, with a spotless clear glass top.

Yazzolino stood at the window, looking through the glass at the parking lot. "Does anyone know what time Rod Addicks comes to work?" he asked.

"Rod generally arrives between 9 and 10 a.m. each morning," said Julie. "He lives in Kelso, Washington, at least a forty-five minute drive."

I got up and I walked over to Dad's side of the desk and hesitantly sat down in his comfortable leather swivel chair. I decided to go through Dad's desk one more time, looking for anything that could possibly be a clue. Gary walked over and watched me intensely as I examined papers, pens and notes Dad had left behind.

While waiting for Addicks, Julie left the room and detectives Yazzolino and Wells took the opportunity to update Gary and me on the lie detector specialist scheduled for September 19, 1974. We decided to hold the polygraph tests in the accounting office upstairs, a large 30-foot by 15-foot space, with white walls. This room is used heavily during tax season by the copying and checking staff, but otherwise remains empty the rest of the year. The door at the top of the stairs could be shut giving the polygraph examiner maximum privacy.

"Stan, I'm surprised you've been able to talk everyone into taking the lie detector test, Yazzolino said. "Except, of course, Rod Addicks." The people who the detectives were most interested in were my stepmother Bernie, Gary, myself, one of the bookkeepers, and my dad's newly-discovered girlfriend whose name, we found out, was Nora Banks. My sister agreed to take a test, but the detectives said that was not necessary.

"Will the man who owns the massage parlors be asked to take the test?" I asked.

"I don't want what we're doing here to interfere with that part of the investigation," Yazzolino said. "At least not at this time. This test will eliminate a number of persons, such as you and four others."

"Now can you give me details on how Dad was murdered?" I asked.

"Your dad must have put up a good fight as he apparently fell to the ground while struggling with his attacker," Yazzolino said. "It appears the murderer tried to beat your father to death with his metal crutches, but the cause of death was strangulation. Look, Stan, this is still in the early stages of our investigation and I can't discuss the details. If a crackpot confesses to the crime, but the details of a confession do not match the crime scene, then we'll know he's not our man."

"So, it was a man who murdered Dad?"

"No, I'm not saying that. Your father may have been waiting for a date, according to Rod Addicks. And Bernie said there was an overnight bag packed for your father in the trunk of his car. He was headed for a one-day business trip to Bend. The bag was blue with white handles. But your father's bag is missing from the trunk of his Cadillac and it wasn't found in the office." Yazzolino paused and then said, "Maybe your father was getting ready for a date, and maybe he shaved in the bathroom and had his overnight bag in the office. It appears your father was attacked when he came out of the bathroom, near the hallway, where he died."

"You think his date hit him, then strangled him?"

Blackie Yazzolino said, "We don't know. Let's ask Julie, the bookkeeper, to come join us. Maybe she can help fill in a few blanks."

I walked out to Julie's office and brought her back in with me.

"Julie, did you notice anything unusual around the tax office in the last few months?" Yazzolino said. "Anything out of the ordinary that you observed about Mr. Turel?"

"Well," said Julie. "About a year ago, Jim insisted that every piece of mail arriving in the office had to first be placed on his desk. Jim would review all the mail prior to distributing it to others."

"Who pays the bills for Quality Financial Planning and the four partnership complexes that Rod Addicks manages?"

"Rod handles most of those customers."

Detective Yazzolino then asked about the working relationship between Rod Addicks and Dad.

"Rod is a really a nice man who gets along with everyone. There was never any sign of problems between Jim and Rod Addicks," Julie answered, with a puzzled look on her face.

"Did Jim Turel have any shady clients?"

"Well, there's the massage parlors," Julie replied, "But Mr. Turel didn't handle those. In fact, Jim Turel is a very honest businessman, I mean was. In fact, if a client ever asked him to dummy up the books or their tax returns, he told them to find another accountant."

"How are you doing with all this, Julie?" Yazzolino asked in a gentler voice.

"I had a nightmare about Jim after finding his body, but I'm okay." Julie clearly didn't want to talk about herself. "Rod Addicks handled about seventy percent of all the new client work since he joined our company. Jim seemed to be taking it easier than he used to, but he always reviewed whatever was going on all the time. Most clients would be introduced to Jim Turel first, then Jim would pass on the work to Rod."

Between the high-intensity tax season, which took place from January 1 through April 30 each year, Columbia Bookkeeping would normally drop its employees to only three bookkeepers, plus Rod Addicks and Dad. But during the tax season, the company would hire at least three additional licensed tax preparers, plus three receptionists, one for each of the three offices. The three most recent tax accountants added last year included a beautiful 27-year-old lady named Jan Hildreth, plus Sam Moll, and John Bell. Yazzolino requested contact information for all three.

"I don't have a phone number for Sam Moll," Julie Syler said. "He lives near Tacoma, Washington, on the Puyallup Indian Reservation."

"Who owns the two new Cadillacs that your father and Rod Addicks were driving?" Yazzolino asked.

Julie didn't know, so I said, "While reviewing the books with Jack Miller, my banker, we found that Columbia Bookkeeping bought and owned the new, bright red Cadillac Rod Addicks was driving, as well as Dad's golden Cadillac. It appears the red Caddy was part of Addicks' fringe benefits, in addition to the commission on work he performed in the name of the company."

"Thank you, Stan. Thank you, Julie. We'll get to the bottom of this," Detective Yazzolino said. "Stan, I'd like you and Gary to make a point of talking to Rod Addicks about what he knows and how he feels about what went on. If he retains a lawyer, from now on, we won't be able to interview him unless we read him his Miranda rights, which means we won't be able to interview him any further after that."

"Make sure to take notes and call us about anything unusual," Detective Wells added.

At 10:45 a.m. the same day, September 16, Rod Addicks drove up in the tax company's red Cadillac, entered the building and said, "Hi," as he passed the reception area. He went to his office and sat down at his desk.

His office was next door to my dad's private office. The detectives walked over to Addicks' office and, still standing in the hallway, asked to talk to him for a few minutes.

I heard Addicks' nervous cackle and when the detectives asked if they could talk to him. Addicks replied, "I hope you find the guy that did this as Jim Turel was a close friend of mine." Then the detectives entered Addicks' office and closed the door behind them. They were in there for several hours. When at last they emerged, they thanked Addicks for his time, said goodbye to Gary and me, and left.

I called a meeting with the two bookkeepers and Rod Addicks. "I just want to say this has been a tough time and we appreciate you coming back to work. Rod is going to be in charge, but if you notice anything fishy or if you remember something that strikes you as suspicious, please let the police or me know."

Julie brought out a handkerchief.

"The crime looks like it was a robbery or the act of someone who hated my dad. If you think of anyone who might have wanted my dad dead, please let me know." I'd been told not to speak of my suspicions about Rod Addicks and the massage parlors to the staff.

Addicks said, "Stan, I am available to help your family in any way that I can. I'm confident I can take care of all our customers. So you don't have to worry about that part."

"Thank you, Rod," I said. "We need your help and are grateful you're here."

"I can prepare taxes," Gary offered, "if Rod needs any help."

"Thanks, but no," said Addicks. "That won't be necessary since most of the returns we prepare are a lot more complicated than what you're experienced with."

"Rod," I said, "my brother, Gary, and I are not here to run the place. We'll be around just temporarily, to help things along." Addicks' comment to Gary sounded to me like a deliberate putdown, but Gary and I had agreed that as long as Addicks was cooperating, we wouldn't threaten him or oppose his opinions in any way. Maybe we could discover some leads. I had begun to think Addicks was hiding something, but I kept that to myself.

As the day progressed I opened the mail that had accumulated. There was a stack of normal business correspondence plus numerous condolence letters from clients. I felt the time was right to try and get to know a little more about Rod Addicks.

"Gary, will you stay here in Dad's office and listen through the wall?" I asked. "I'm going next door to have a conversation with Rod Addicks."

Gary was ready. He even had a glass in his hand that he placed against the adjoining office wall. As I walked out of the room, Gary put his ear up against the glass.

I walked next door and into Addicks' office, which was neat as a pin. On the wall hung his diploma from Linfield College and his Washington State CPA certification. I started asking questions about how the business and apartments partnerships operated. I spent an hour talking to Addicks behind closed doors. I explained why I felt he should take the polygraph test, especially since the examiner was coming here next week and it would be free. I even drew a graph on a piece of paper for Addicks. It contained a list of original potential suspects and indicated how most of us could be eliminated as suspects after taking the test. Addicks elaborated that he thought it might be a jealous husband of some woman my father may have dated, or Bernie, who killed my dad. "You know, Stan," Addicks said, "your father had a serious temper and he could have gotten into a serious argument with a customer. Who knows?"

"Why not take the test?" I asked Addicks, "Since you'll probably pass, that would clear you. And that would allow the detectives to move on to other possible suspects."

"Oh, Stan, I'm a nervous type of guy. And the test isn't legal as evidence in Oregon anymore anyway."

"I understand, Rod, but honestly, no harm could come from it, since you're sure to pass, and especially so if test results aren't admissible in court. If all of us take the test, you should feel more comfortable about it. It's just that I would sure hate for the police to waste their time wondering about you."

Addicks laughed, but it was a strained laugh. "I'm truly sorry, Stan," he said. "But my lawyer says I shouldn't since these test results are always so inaccurate."

Oh great, I thought. Now he's talking to a lawyer!

I left Rod Addicks' office feeling disgusted and trusted him even less than before. If he were truly Dad's friend, he would take the test.

I talked to Rod Addicks, privately, a few more times as the day moved along, and each time I asked him to try to imagine someone Dad knew who could have carried out the murder.

"Only an angry woman could have deliberately done such a thing," Addicks said. "Have you considered that maybe the murder was accidental? Perhaps it was just a robbery."

"Rod, do you think maybe we should offer a reward for information leading to the arrest of the murderer?" For some reason, when I said those words, a $5,000 amount popped into my head. "Do you think $5,000 would attract someone?" I asked him.

Rod leaned back in his swivel chair, looked up at the ceiling, then leaned forward with a sincere but peculiar look on his face and said, "I don't think it would be a good idea to offer any reward because whoever did it probably won't talk anyway. Maybe later, I don't know. Maybe you should wait and ask the detectives. You shouldn't do anything that would interfere with their investigation."

Addicks and I talked at length about possibilities. I let him know I was relying on his judgment regarding which direction we should go. I continued to reassure Addicks, in deliberate, pretentious ways, that I wanted him to stay and run the business. I wanted him to believe I was there only to make the ladies feel more comfortable. I explained that I had to hire someone to run my aircraft waxing company so that I could stay here. I hoped we could continue to work together and I would let him run the company just as my dad and he had planned. All this coddling seemed to ease his mind. I also let him know that the police would be issuing a subpoena for the books of Columbia Bookkeeping and Quality Financial Planning to search for information to help the investigation.

"I have nothing to hide," Addicks kept saying. "You're always welcome to look over the books any time, they're always up-to-date. The police will find nothing and you'll soon learn that. The sooner they get out of here the sooner they will focus somewhere else and find the murderer."

Rod Addicks, if involved with the murder, was a master of self-control who used his innocent, baby-face looks most effectively. He seemed so sincere and concerned, so confident and reassuring in his professional demeanor while sitting there. The longer we talked, the more convinced I became that he could not have committed such a gruesome crime. Yet, at the same time I kept getting the feeling that he was hiding something. Why would he refuse to take the lie detector test?

As I was leaving his room, I turned towards Addicks and said, "Oh, by the way, Detective Yazzolino called and said if you don't take the test, it will make you look suspicious. Do you want to change your mind and take the test?"

His answer was, "No, I still do not trust those tests."

At the end of each conversation, Addicks would reassure me of his willingness to help and his capabilities, and then cackle that nervous laugh, which always made me think he was hiding something. Then, when we finished talking, Addicks would go directly to the bathroom. I noticed he went there every time our conversation steered towards the murder.

Later that day, Detective Yazzolino called me on the phone and said, "Stan, were you able to convince Rod Addicks to take the test?" I had to tell him no.

Someone murdered my dad and I had a strong desire to find out who and why. And, I'm not afraid to admit, I had a strong desire to get even. If Rod Addicks had anything to do with this horrendous situation, then he was going to jail for life to pay for his deed. I began going through the business ledgers with the Multnomah County CPA.

Later, I started doing a quick scan through the check register accounts Addicks handled for the apartments. When I spoke with the investors, I had to reassure a few that I was just learning the business, and asked them to have patience with me. I talked frankly to a few of the investors like Mary and Al Foglio, and Dr. Joe Rand, who I trusted. I kept the rest in the dark about the murder investigation details. They were surprised I knew so much about their personal apartment deals.

However, I never mentioned to anyone that Addicks, my stepmother, and the massage parlor managers were my prime suspects. I felt there was a strong possibility the massage parlors were involved with organized crime, which had been implied by Detective Yazzolino. I figured, maybe Addicks feared the mafia would harm him if he divulged information implicating his involvement in organized crime. Would this explain his refusal to take the lie detector test?

Later that same day, September 6, Rod Addicks became quite upset during his two-hour interview with the detectives. He told them he had nothing to hide but repeated what he said to me: that he'd heard bad things about lie detector tests. Finally he said that since he and my dad had gone out for dinner the night my dad was murdered, he should be careful, so he didn't want to say much of anything. Yazzolino then received a call from a Mr. Hanson, Addicks' attorney. I was later informed by Yazzolino that Addicks had retained a new attorney because Jim Auxier was representing the Turel Estate and Columbia Bookkeeping. Wow, I thought, Addicks has a new attorney now. I wonder what that means.

During one of my subsequent discussions with Addicks, he mentioned that a lot of cash was collected in this type of business. He also implied that if no one was keeping track of that cash, it would be very difficult for the IRS to determine what was collected. An uncomfortable thought went through the back of my mind, wondering if Addicks was doing work for cash and not reporting it. Maybe this was another reason why my dad did not trust him.

Chapter 8: D.B. Cooper, Massage Parlors, Sniper Shooting, and Aircraft Sabotage?

At the end of the first few days, when the tax office closed for the night, my brother, Gary, and I would carefully search for clues. We examined the lobby, then went through each of the building's individual rooms and all the filing cabinets. On top of one of the filing cabinets we found a stapled stack of papers that had "D.B. Cooper" written on it. We skimmed through the papers only to realize that Rod Addicks was attempting to summarize the D.B. Cooper hijacking escapade. I turned this 50-page typed summary over to Detective Blackie Yazzolino. It looked to me like Addicks might have been planning to write a book. Or, was it possible he was involved in the D.B. Cooper hijacking? After all, he lived in the Kelso, Washington, area where D.B. Cooper was alleged to have bailed out. Detective Yazzolino copied the original and returned it the next day.

To give you a bit of history: D.B. Cooper was the hijacker of a Boeing 727 en route from Portland to Seattle in 1971. He demanded one million dollars in ransom and a parachute, before releasing his passengers in Seattle. Then the jet took off again, heading for Las Vegas with a crew of three plus the hijacker, who sat in the back of the plane. At 10,000 feet, over the mountains east of Kelso, Washington, the rear door opened and it was suspected that D.B. Cooper jumped out shortly thereafter. He was never seen again. The case has never been solved even though some of the money was found years later along the banks of the Columbia River. Gary and I pondered the Kelso connection. We knew Rod hunted in those woods.

Soon after, I received a call from Charles Turner from the local U.S. Attorney General's office, expressing his condolences regarding my dad's death. He also thanked me for my cooperation with everyone assigned to the case and assured me that Rod Addicks was almost certainly not involved in the D.B. Cooper hijacking. I said that we figured not, and suggested that perhaps we were getting a little paranoid.

"Detectives are checking evidence to determine if the massage parlors are involved in organized crime. Please do let us know if you find out anything suspicious," Turner said. "If you ever need our help, let me know."

I cannot tell you how much I appreciated all the law enforcement agency's efforts. Everyone was discreet and sincere in their intentions, which encouraged me to follow the law in my effort to find out who committed this crime.

As the days passed, I would step into Rod Addicks' office to speak with him alone, privately, for a half hour or so several times each day. I would close the door and start talking about the case and the detectives' suspicions about him, and the arson. I acted as if I was totally naïve and wanted his version of what happened in the fire that burned down his house. I would always agree with his version and pretend I was totally convinced he was innocent and that the police were barking up the wrong tree, all the while trying to rattle him a bit.

Gary and I continued our afterhours sleuthing. We investigated files and desks everywhere throughout the office building. Detective Blackie Yazzolino had given Gary and me a list of arson suspects so we could check their names against past client lists. We looked for Dad's flight bag, which the detectives said was still missing. We inspected the attic and crawl spaces, and searched through the ductwork looking for anything that may have been hidden. The attic was 80 feet long and 30 feet wide. I reviewed the blueprints for the office, then examined all the places my dad's flight bag might have been hidden.

During one of those evenings in September, I opened a small envelope lying on top Addicks' desk. It was addressed to Rod Addicks at Columbia Bookkeeping. The return address was William Stebbins of the Cavalier Beachfront Condominiums on the Oregon Coast. The letter inside, dated September 2, 1974, extended his sympathy to Rod and the staff at Columbia Bookkeeping. One paragraph caught my eye since I recently learned William Stebbins was the insurance agent who placed the $50,000 life insurance policy on my dad.

Stebbins wrote, "Rod, as you know, I did not know Jim well, only through my association with you, but he felt so strongly in his determination for what he wanted to do for us."

I previously had wondered whose idea it was for Dad to get the life insurance policy and that letter gave me the answer: Rod Addicks. When I met William Stebbins a few days later, he was very professional and sincere in his condolences to my brother and me.

One morning I entered Addicks office, closed the door and sat down. I had a notepad in my hand with a list of questions.

"Rod," I said, "I don't want to interfere with your running the company but I need to figure out if this murder investigation is going to scare away clients and employees this coming tax season. What are your thoughts?"

"Well, Stan," Addicks said. "I figure it depends on whether we can continue, especially if this is not solved before tax season. I think the bookkeepers will stay but I can't say for sure about the others."

"What about the tax preparers? Have you talked to Sam Moll?"

"No," Addicks replied. "I haven't seen or talked to Sam since last tax season."

"Have you tried to call him, or can you give me his phone number so I can call him and just let him know he is welcome to come back? We need to know who plans to return. I'm afraid if we don't call these people we won't know until the last minute that we need to hire someone else."

Addicks said, "Sam is fishing at his Puyallup Indian Reservation in Tacoma and I have no phone number or way getting a hold of him since he has no phone."

"Is there any way we can leave a message for him at the tribe's office to find out his plans?" I asked.

"No Stan," Addicks said in a reassuring manner. "We have to wait for him to contact us, just before tax time."

I left that meeting saying that the family was counting on him to make the arrangements, we didn't want to interfere. Just before I stepped out of his office, Addicks said, "Stan, we received this in the mail today."

The envelope was from Rob Letherman, a broker, and it contained an offer from E. W. Arnold stating he had someone interested in buying the bookkeeping business, if we were interested in selling. "I'm surprised someone is already interested in buying us," Addicks said. "But I don't think this is the right time to sell. Besides, that broker would charge us ten percent of the sales price if we sold it through him."

The envelope was marked September 6, just a week after Dad died. "The vultures are already circulating," Addicks said, and laughed.

To relieve my own stress, I went flying that evening and headed for the graveyard where my dad is buried. I circled overhead and executed a low flyby in a quiet manner, saying a prayer for Dad, while wagging my wings goodbye as I flew away.

At 9:45 a.m. on September 19, a dark-suited gentleman whose face seemed to disappear beneath his thick glasses, showed up with polygraph equipment. I was surprised that it all fit into a regular suitcase. I guess I expected him to have bulkier equipment. And I had imagined someone younger would be handling this. Yazzolino assured us that this man was the best, and the most experienced examiner he knew. He said he had been using the man for years in other criminal cases.

Shortly after the examiner set up his equipment Bernie arrived. Gary drove up a short time later and waited in the lobby with my stepmother. Blackie Yazzolino had arranged for Nora Banks, who I had not yet met, to arrive at a different time. We didn't want any overlap between my stepmom and Dad's girlfriend. Yazzolino had mentioned to me that this lady had gone to Hawaii with my dad. That was the trip when he'd told Bernie he was headed for San Diego for a computer class.

It was decided I would be the first to take the lie detector test. I was more curious about how it worked than I was nervous. The examiner said I should try to relax, that the test would take only 15 minutes. He hooked me up to the machine by attaching a series of wires to the ends of my fingers and on my arms and other areas. He said he would ask each of us the same questions. At first, the questions would be basic and simple, obviously meant to relax me. Then would come specific questions such as: What is your name? What is your age? Then the examiner got personal: When did you last see your father? Do you know who killed your father? Did you kill your father? When did you learn that your father was dead? Were you around when your father died? Did you know your father was going to be killed?

When my test was complete, I went downstairs and told those in the lobby that it was simple. I said I really appreciated them agreeing to take the test, as it would give the detectives a chance to focus on other possibilities.

"Rod Addicks still hasn't shown up," said Detective Yazzolino.

Nora Banks arrived after most of the others had completed their tests. Miss Banks was a classy looking woman in her mid-30s. She was quite slender, with long dark hair. In fact, she looked a lot like my mother— when Mom was in her prime. She even had the same soft voice like my mom. Gary and I talked with Miss Banks for a few minutes and found her to be quite charming. I was glad my stepmom had already finished her test and left.

"I would like to talk to you later since I owe your father money on the cabin at the beach," Miss Banks softly whispered in my ear. She told me what a wonderful man my dad was and even showed me pictures of my dad in Hawaii with her. Dad was standing with his crutches, in a bathing suit, with ocean waves in the background. He had the silly smirk of a guilty man on his face. I enjoyed seeing that he had such a good time in the last few months of his life. Miss Banks was worried that I was going to call in the loan on the beach house my dad had sold to her for nothing down. I assured her that as long as she made payments, she would have no problems.

I excused myself and returned with Gary and Detective Yazzolino to Dad's office. Yazzolino closed the door. "I can see why your father liked this woman," Yazzolino said. It's obvious she's taken your father's death hard." Yazzolino lowered his voice. "Since Rod Addicks was the last person to see your father alive, Addicks is going to be someone we will focus on, especially since he refused to take a lie detector test and chose to retain an attorney," Yazzolino said. "Now that Addicks has a lawyer, we may need to read him his Miranda rights if he becomes one of our main suspects. He seemed a little too nervous when we last talked with him. And by the way, Stan, you need to remember that the fire at the house Addicks owned has been determined to be an act of arson, but we have no proof that Addicks was involved. He has an alibi. You and Gary can talk to Addicks since you are not the police. But if you notice anything fishy call and let us know."

"I've been keeping notes," I said, intentionally not mentioning the wire transmitter.

"Be careful not to become aggressive with him," Yazzolino cautioned quietly. "That could make him stop talking with you, too. Remember, Stan, Addicks is only one of several suspects we still need to investigate."

Later I learned the detectives had read Addicks his Miranda rights on

September 19, plus I was told we all passed the lie detector test with flying colors.

For the first few weeks after the tax office reopened, both Gary and I spent most of our days at the office. Gary gradually reduced his time at the office. Then he would occasionally show up to paint the outside of the office building, and would show up again after hours, especially if I was there alone with Rod Addicks. Gary and I developed a plan to keep in touch daily by phone, no matter what.

During the third week after reopening, I picked up and tested the secret transmitter I had John Wayland construct for me, and wired it to my back. To test it, Gary drove down the street and waited about a block away. Then he tuned me in while I talked behind closed doors with Addicks. It worked! From then on, I secretly taped many of my conversations with Addicks.

Rod Addicks is a short man and has the innocent face of a baby. He is so convincing when he speaks that I decided I needed to replay some of our conversations because I began to mistrust my own recollections of conflicting stories. By recording the conversations, I was able to crosscheck what Addicks told me and found I was definitely getting different versions of the same stories. The more we spoke, and the more I reviewed what he said, the more I felt as though Rod Addicks was hiding something. I still did not tell the detectives about the tape recordings.

Gary, meanwhile, in a very sincere offer, said he wanted to keep his own tax business separate from the family business, but he also wanted to share control of Dad's business as co-president. Two presidents? I had never heard of two presidents in a company. I decided to consult with Dad's attorney.

Jim Auxier's response was, "What? You're kidding! Columbia Bookkeeping cannot afford two presidents. Also, Gary would have a conflict of interest with the Turel Family Trust if he became co-president since he wants to keep his own tax business separate. You should keep your marketing and expansion plans secret from Gary. You need to treat him the same as if you're talking to a competitor, even though he is your brother. The Trust Agreement says you are to run the business as if you are the sole owner, even though the value of the business will be split with your siblings after Bernie dies. If Gary is involved, you'll have ongoing squabbles and conflicts with him."

"But I don't want to hurt Gary's feelings."

"Stan, your obligations and loyalty is to the Turel Family Trust, not your brother's personal interests."

"But he's my little brother. I have to look out for him."

"Not in this case, Stan. He may have some tax preparation experience, but you have more experience running a business," Auxier said. "You've also been dealing in real estate, which will come in handy regarding the real estate partnerships Rod Addicks has organized. Plus, having two extra bosses will confuse the staff. Besides," Auxier continued, "Addicks might quit right now if he thinks Gary is getting involved with the day-to-day business of running Columbia Bookkeeping. And furthermore, clients might think you are both too young to run the company."

After pondering the pros and cons, I decided that I felt comfortable enough handling Rod Addicks and keeping the current staff from quitting. Most of the staff now knew Rod Addicks was a suspect and they seemed nervous about it. The office did not need more confusion. So, I had a talk with Gary where I explained the reasons why there should be only one chief. Gary was upset and disappointed, but we agreed we would still cooperate on important business issues and on the murder investigation. I understood that I'd just hurt Gary's feelings, and felt bad about it. As he left Gary said, "If I were the older brother, I'd be in charge." Gary was right, it could easily have turned out that way.

In late September, Janet and I moved into our new apartment. We had decided against continuing to live in the basement of my home since the tenants upstairs fought so much and we wanted to live in a secret place. I had become totally obsessed with the notion that I had to keep on top of the investigation and business in order to learn who murdered Dad. Also, it became important that I stay razor sharp when dealing with Rod Addicks and the tax office routine. Each day I would drive my red waxing van to and from the tax office, while looking in the rearview mirror checking to see if anyone was following me. My new Air Auto Waxing employee, Jimmy Frances, the ex-marine who was handling my contracts for detailing airplanes, continued to use the van most of the day and then would return it to the Columbia Bookkeeping parking lot at night. Because I could not focus on the waxing business, I gradually reduced the number of aircraft accounts I maintained, and subsequently the detailing business declined.

My efforts at the tax office began affecting my sleep and dreams. Twice in the first three weeks after the murder, I had a vividly real dream where I saw my dad walking down the driveway of his home, on his metal crutches, after returning from the hospital. He looked healthy. He put his hand on my shoulder and said, 'Everything is okay now.' Then he said, 'Don't worry. The two men who tried to kill me are in jail now.' Dad looked so alive and relaxed. And he assured me that he would take care of things from here on because the murder was solved, which made me happy.

The dreams were so real, yet I would wake up crying. The dreams were sad, yes, but I felt great relief in the dream because the murder and investigation was over! I found that being awake was the real nightmare. My subconscious was working overtime with wishful thinking, assuring me that everything was already solved. On the other hand, I wondered if the dreams were a message from someone who knew something. I didn't put much credence in the dreams, but I couldn't shake the image of my happy dad after I woke up. Does the spirit of a deceased person hang around for a while? I could only wonder. I don't believe in ghosts. But I felt better after talking to our bookkeeper Peg about my dreams. Peg was a religious sort.

Throughout the first month of closed-door discussions with Rod Addicks, I repeatedly brought up the subject of the police investigation. Occasionally he would get angry, stand up and say something like, 'If you do not back off and stop pestering me I will leave this place! The police have nothing. It's just a bunch of bullshit. If I leave, you'll be here alone to float the boat all by yourself. They've got nothing on me, or they would have arrested me by now!' I could feel my heart begin to race as he spoke, but I tried to appear calm on the outside.

Then Addicks would calm down and say, "I am only following my attorney's advice. I don't mean to get upset." He really had this ability to calm himself down at the end and our conversation would end on a positive note, even when he was upset.

"Oh, no, I totally understand," I said. "We want you to stay, and we agree that the police are barking up the wrong tree." I'd apologize for upsetting him. I hated having to disguise my own anger.

"You know Stan," Addicks said, "I considered your father one of my best friends and I want to get to the bottom of this, too."

Every time I broached a touchy subject, I was careful to push Addicks only so far. Frankly, I was hoping he would slip up when angered and say something that would give us some better leads. I practiced learning how far I could push Addicks, and then I would back down. I did not want him to leave the business before I learned more. If he knew something, I was determined to find out. I felt like I was playing a high-stakes bluff in a poker game.

I began another approach. I told Addicks I was trying to help him and together we might discover leads to solve the crime. "Let's go over the situation with the apartments you are managing. Is it possible that Dad had an argument with one of the managers?"

Addicks would discuss this subject as long as no one implied he was involved. I asked him about the massage parlors, which tended to elicit his odd cackling laugh. "The police are wasting their time looking at me and the massage parlors," Addicks said. He kept to his theory that the murder was the work of some angry woman, or a robber on drugs. He would always end his conversation with, "I don't know, Stan. You probably know more than me since the police won't give me the time of day." Then he would laugh again.

I acted as if I didn't know anything either and I'd leave his office biting my tongue. I felt that by pretending I was naïve, a dumb kid, he would continue to think he was winning me over with his talk. Most of the time I was the one asking questions and a few times Gary joined us. Later, Gary and I would compare notes to see if Addicks changed the details in his stories.

On October 7, I received a Grand Jury Subpoena requiring me to bring all the books and accounts of Columbia Bookkeeping and Quality Financial Planning to the Multnomah County Courthouse by October 14. However, the subpoena said it could be satisfied by allowing Mr. Vince Johnson, CPA, to conduct an audit at the Columbia Bookkeeping office and report the findings to the Grand Jury.

Rod Addicks was surprised, then he turned bright red when I told him about the subpoena. Then he laughed and said, "They're not going to find anything in the account books! They don't even know what they're looking for." When I showed him the subpoena he sat down and said, "That's okay, but they're wasting taxpayer's money." Addicks went out to lunch and when he returned I could smell alcohol on his breath.

During the first week of October, Gary attended a tax class and met a man named Mr. Lawrence, who said he was a friend of Sam Moll, our seasonal tax preparer. Lawrence told Gary about a conversation he'd had with Moll about the murder of someone named Mr. Turel, and that Moll said he'd heard about it from Rod Addicks when Addicks called him in early September. Gary and I informed Detective Yazzolino about this conversation and pointed out Addicks' lie to me, when he said he had no way to contact Sam Moll.

For several weeks, my daily conversations with Rod Addicks began by talking about the business, but pretty soon I would insert statements about the detectives. Or, I'd ask him which customer or client could possibly have killed my father. At the same time I had to keep my cool to prevent Addicks from leaving the business.

One time I offered my help to Addicks—perhaps I could handle some of the day-to-day problems with the apartments, which would allow him to focus on running the accounting practice without my interference. He liked that idea. I think it made him feel better about my presence and persistent questions.

A week after Multnomah County's audit of our books, their CPA reported back that they had found nothing suspicious or out of order. This brought a smile to Addicks' face. "I told you so, Stan. There is nothing wrong here."

Six weeks after the murder, and without Addicks finding out, I was still reviewing all the previous years' monthly checks written on the four partnership accounts that Addicks managed. Most of the checks were documented with receipts. In late September and early October, several checks for $500 popped up for a Lee's Construction Company. Then the same company name popped up in a second checkbook. One check was for $600. I asked Addicks if my dad might have had a falling out with this man.

"No," said Addicks. "Look at all the records from before your father died. You will never see a check written to Lee's Construction before that date. Lee's Construction never did any work for us until afterwards. Your father never met the man. Don't worry about him."

"Who is this Lee of Lee's Construction?" I asked.

"Oh, he's just an old friend of mine who needed some work, so I can vouch for him. Hiring him is saving the partnership a lot of money,"

Addicks said in a very calm and convincing manner.

"What about using other vendors?" I asked. "The ones the firm hired before Dad's death?" But Addicks brushed off my inquiry with that nervous chuckle.

Seven weeks after the office was re-opened, Addicks announced, "I'm headed out to visit some friends in San Francisco. I'll be gone until next Tuesday. Don't worry about a thing, Stan. The girls will take care of everything," he said as he put his arm on my shoulder in a reassuring gesture. As he left, he seemed to be in a relaxed and jovial mood.

Two days later, Friday, Jimmy Frances, the man who drove my red waxing van to the airports every day to handle my airplane clients, returned my waxing van around 4:30. He walked into the tax office and his body was visibly shaking. He was obviously very agitated. "I've just been shot at! In the parking lot!" Frances said.

"Our parking lot?" I asked. "Are you sure it was a bullet?"

"Right outside, Stan! In your parking lot! I'm a Vietnam Vet! I think I know when a bullet whizzes by my head!" Frances turned in his keys and quit right then.

"Wait, Jimmy," I said. "Calm down. Tell me what just happened."

"Someone mistook me for you, Stan. We're similar enough in size and build. I had just parked your van, opened the driver's door and stepped out when it happened. They were gunning for you, Stan! I'm sorry, but this is way too dangerous. I'm sorry but I can't work for you anymore!"

My van had personalized license plates with the name TUREL on it. I called the police and they came right away, but after a quick search of the area across the street, they came back and said no bullet casing was found. My impression was that they did not take the shooting seriously.

This incident with Jimmy Frances began to make me feel even more nervous while driving back home to Janet, patiently waiting in our new apartment each night. I deliberately took even more complex routes home to verify if someone was following me. Sometimes it appeared as if I was correct.

The next day, Saturday, I decided it was time to relax by flying my plane, which I kept tied down outside at the Troutdale airport. During the preflight of my aircraft I found that one of the vital hinge pins in the rear horizontal stabilizer had been removed. That had never happened before in all the years I've been flying. Also, a quart of water was found in the bottom of my gas tank. I was so suspicious by then that I became truly paranoid. I even had the gas analyzed by Western Skyways to see if there was anything else wrong. Since Addicks and my dad had come out to see my plane the prior summer, I was thinking that maybe Addicks was the one who tampered with it. I decided not to fly at that point, and did not return to flying until months later. Was I getting closer to finding Dad's murderer? Had Dad stumbled onto an arson ring? And was he killed because of it? When Addicks returned from San Francisco, he asked me if anything happened while he was gone. I just said, 'No.'

A week after Addicks returned from San Francisco, I was with Gary in the tax office when I was introduced to Lee Cartwright of Lee's Construction. Actually, I had to specifically ask Addicks to introduce me when a thin, scraggly man in his mid-30s walked into the lobby and Addicks met with him there. Gary, who was in the lobby at the time, discreetly walked outside to get the Washington license plate number on the faded red 'Lee's Construction' pickup. He called the license number in to Detective Blackie Yazzolino. The report back was that the registered owner of the truck was a Dennis Lee Cartwright who lived in Kelso, Washington, the same town where Rod Addicks lived. It also turned out that a Dennis Lee Cartwright was on parole in Washington for assault and battery. If this was the same man, he was violating his parole by being in Oregon. Yazzolino said they wouldn't send someone to arrest him yet, as they wanted to see how he fit into the broader picture.

Rod Addicks mentioned that Cartwright was a hunting buddy. I wondered if Cartwright had also been a parachutist years ago in the army. It was the D.B. Cooper question again. Also, I wondered, could this be the man who shot at Jimmy Frances while Addicks was out of town?

That next weekend, on Sunday morning, I arranged to have a $600 bulletproof window installed in my personal office. By then I was too paranoid to sit at my dad's desk all day with my back to the window. No one knew about that window glass replacement except Gary and me.

Since I already had quite a bit of experience with my own apartment operations, I interviewed each manager of each complex operated by Rod Addicks, knowing he would find out. Then, secretly, at night, I'd return to the office to track what each apartment complex should have collected each month. One apartment complex at Southeast 52nd and Woodstock was showing more vacancies than it should have. I questioned the manager, Paula Travington, several times, "Why is there such a high vacancy factor? There should be more renters." I explained to the manager that I was just trying to figure out what we might do to help rent out the vacant units. After checking each vacant apartment myself, it turned out more units were rented than what the records showed. The manager said those units had just become occupied. I knew better, but acted as if I accepted the manager's answers. Had Dad discovered money missing in the apartment building accounts?

Needless to say, Addicks was angry because I was interfering with his management. He said the managers were uptight about all the questions I was asking. I explained I was just trying to help rent out empty units. I said, "Look at this Rod, at the Woodstock Apartments for the previous ten months, I estimate that the managers could have stolen $3,000 in rent and never reported it to you."

What I didn't say was, Or else you're in on it. The female manager of that apartment building was attractive. I wondered if perhaps Addicks was having an affair with her, or if together they were embezzling money. The reason I even wondered was because Detective Yazzolino asked me to verify if certain ladies were clients of ours. He also mentioned that detectives had visited a number of restaurants and bars in the area and found that Addicks was known to frequent them and was quite the ladies' man. In fact some of the waitresses noted that he usually was with another man or lady, not my dad, and drank quite a bit plus tipped triple the normal amount in cash. A few of the waitresses said he would often tip them each $20 in cash, a really big tip in the 1970s. One of them had actually dated him and had no idea he was married.

So Addicks is a big tipper. Interesting to know, I thought to myself. I recalled a previous discussion with Addicks when he mentioned how easy it would be to pocket a lot of cash in the tax business because clients often paid in cash. Maybe my dad suspected Addicks was doing exactly that, which would also explain why Addicks could be such a large cash tipper. Addicks could put four times as much money in his pocket if he prepared returns in the office and collected the cash without my dad ever knowing, versus the 30 percent tax-free fee he would earn from going through the proper Columbia Bookkeeping channels. This might have been another reason my dad didn't trust Addicks with money. Maybe they had a fight about this.

Detective Yazzolino stopped by the tax office in October and asked to speak to me alone. "Stan," he said, "I have a small picture I would like you to look at. Tell me if you recognize either of these two guys." The picture was a painting of two men. One looked sort of like Lee Cartwright, and the other kind of looked like Rod Addicks. "Where did you get these and what do they mean?" I asked.

"Well, sometimes we take a personal object, such as the watch your father was wearing when he died, to a well-known psychic. And sometimes the psychic can sense something connected to a murder victim's demise. Yes, I know it's strange, but this lady has helped us solve crimes before. She lives in Lake Oswego. I know it sounds weird Stan, but keep this picture for a while and let us know if it rings any bells. Please don't mention how we got these pictures to anyone else."

That is weird, I thought to myself. A few weeks later, the detectives asked for the picture back and said, "Forget you ever saw them." I laughed, as I thought this was a strange approach anyway.

Soon it was November 1974. I was still checking the billing records that contained handwritten invoices from Lee's Construction. I visited all the apartments to verify if the work being billed had been completed. I did not like all those round dollar numbers on the checks, accompanied by vague handwritten invoices. The apartments also had an account with Copeland Lumber in Oregon City. The monthly summary from Copeland was there, but individual charge slips were missing. All the missing charge slips were from purchases in August. I secretly visited Copeland Lumber and explained to them that I was investigating the murder of my dad and needed copies of all the individual charge slips. I gave them Blackie Yazzolino's phone number and said the detective would confirm who I was. Copeland Lumber was instructed by the police—and me—not to mention to Rod Addicks or anyone else what I was asking for or doing.

Surprise! I found that Lee's Construction had charged items to the account several weeks before my dad died. Lee Cartwright had even charged something to the Copeland Lumber account the day my dad was murdered. I remembered that Addicks said Lee Cartwright had never met my dad nor worked on the apartments prior to Dad's death. I forwarded the Copeland Lumber information to the detectives and they said they would check it out later.

During my next discussion at the office with Rod Addicks, when I cautiously asked a few more questions about the work Lee's Construction was doing for our company, Addicks became agitated and sarcastic. I never told Addicks what I was uncovering about Lee Cartwright, nor that the police said Cartwright was on parole in Washington State. I thought it strange that Addicks kept going to the bathroom after most of my short sessions in his office.

I discovered that Rod Addicks owed $2,000 to the same bank branch where my banker friend Jack Miller worked. I found this out when Addicks said he needed more money from the company to pay off this loan. I delayed decisions like that, blaming it on the attorney's instruction not to change the pay arrangement we made previously. I did not want Addicks to have any extra money in case he was going to be a flight risk. We had previously guaranteed Addicks a $20,000 annual salary to cover the slow months in addition to his commissions during tax season.

As the months moved along, I continued talking with a few more of the property investors and a couple of clients who had been directly involved with Addicks. All expressed disbelief that Addicks could be involved in my dad's murder, as they had all trusted him. I explained, 'We're going to get to the bottom of this soon, and I'm sure Rod Addicks is innocent, too.' But I was lying to them. I didn't want them to freak out.

Rod Addicks became increasingly upset as the detectives began following up with the short list of company clients I provided to them. Mr. Hanson, Rod Addicks' new attorney, contacted Multnomah County and the District Attorney's office and threatened a lawsuit suit against the City of Portland and the Multnomah County Commissioners for defamation of character. Apparently, the detectives were told by their superiors to ease up unless they had some better proof that Rod Addicks was involved in the murder or arson. Thereafter, the detectives still kept in touch with me, but not as often. It appeared as though nothing was panning out and the detectives had other cases to solve.

In some of my conversations with Rod Addicks, I would raise the topic of seasonal staff he would need to hire. I'd repeatedly ask him if all the same staff would return. Addicks informed me that due to the way he was being treated by the police and my continuing interference, Sam Moll, the second highest producing tax accountant in our previous tax season, would probably not return.

"Have you talked with Sam Moll recently?" I asked

"I've heard from him only once," Addicks said.

"Can I have Sam Moll's phone number?" I asked.

"Sorry, Stan. I don't have a phone number for him. Remember, he lives on an Indian Reservation in Washington and is always out fishing."

Addicks stood up from his desk, the anger evident as he raised his voice, "Look, stop pestering me about everything. I told you before, if you want me to run the company I can, but you need to stop interfering with what I am doing!" Then he calmed down and said, "Stan, don't worry. I am sure Jan Hildreth and John Bell are both returning. They are good tax preparers. But if you keep sticking your nose into everything they might not return either."

Hummm, I thought. Addicks' standing up was obviously meant to be a signal for me to leave his office, so I said in my apologetic manner, "I guess the company will suffer if Sam doesn't return. I'm sure sorry if I've been bugging you too much. I'll try to reduce my pestering, but I only want to know what's going on. I want you to stay, Rod. I agree the company would fall apart without you. We need you here, more than ever, since we don't have Sam." I was afraid Addicks was about to walk!

I did not want to lose him yet as I still had a few more issues and leads that might connect Addicks to arson, plus I did not have a replacement for him yet.

As I slowly got up and backed out of his room I told him that if he felt I was getting in his way, in a few weeks I would stop coming in because I did not want to get that involved in the tax business. Addicks responded by saying, "Stan, that might be a good idea for both of us. I like working with you but I assure you, I can really handle things from here and maybe you need to get back to your aircraft waxing business so you can make some money." By then, Addicks had returned to his normal sweet disposition and as far as he was concerned, the meeting actually ended on a good note. But I was lying through my teeth as I had no intention of backing off. I could tell we were both playing a cat and mouse game. I wondered, does he really know what I am up to?

I had secretly been interviewing a few other prospective accountants I knew who I hoped would work out as replacements for Rod Addicks and Sam Moll. Julie Syler, whose office was across from Addicks, could tell there was stress between Rod and me because she sometimes heard patches of our loud conversations. It bothered me when Julie mentioned that Rod Addicks and Sam Moll were best friends who went out drinking together most evenings during tax season. It didn't make sense that Rod would have no way of contacting Sam Moll if they were such good friends.

In a phone conversation with the arson detectives from the Fire Department it was confirmed that Sam Moll was Addicks' only alibi. Their account verified that both Addicks and Moll had been fishing in Ilwaco, Washington, that weekend. I asked the arson detective to follow up on Sam Moll, but the detectives explained they already spent money on the case over a year ago and would need permission and funding from their bosses to travel to Tacoma.

I knew Rod Addicks made most of his money working at Columbia Bookkeeping during the tax season since his salary was based on the money collected from his tax clients. Fall was Addicks' slowest time regarding earnings. After the last tense discussion with him I wanted to tempt him with the lure of the upcoming tax season money. A few days later I decided I would try to ease Addicks' irritation by pretending the detectives were looking in other directions. I thought he would be more open to discussing the case with me and we'd go over his original version of the murderer's motivation.

This time I entered his room and asked if I could talk to him for a few minutes. After he said, "Sure," I entered, closed the door and sat down.

"Rod, let's just hope the police solve the murder case soon," I said. "I know you did not have anything to do with it. The detectives told me they are now seriously looking at the possibility that it was a robbery or angry husband of someone Dad might have dated. That's why the detectives aren't coming around here so often." These statements were boldface lies. I continued, "Rod, even if you are upset with me, please don't leave, as you have a lot invested in this company and I would hate to see all of us lose out on what you have worked so hard to build." By watching his face and body movements, I could tell our interaction was going in a very positive direction.

Leading him to believe the detectives had moved on from considering him as a suspect made Addicks relax. He leaned back in his leather swivel chair and began to talk. "It certainly appears as though someone, an angry lady or man could have done it. You know, Stan, as I told you numerous times before, I suspected right from the beginning that it must have been a robbery, or someone who got into an argument with Jim, or someone who hated him. A lot of people know your father was a wealthy man. Because he was crippled he may have looked like someone who would be an easy person to rob. In fact, it could have been one of those kids from the apartments across the street who park their cars in our parking lot. Your father was always giving them a bad time. He may have had a fight with one of them and they decided to rob him, who knows? But I hope they catch the guy who did this soon. You know, I really liked your father. He was one of my best friends. I miss him more than you'll ever know."

Addicks was so convincing that I left his office doubting he could have really killed Dad. However, in the back of my mind I still had my doubts about his honesty, what he knew about the murder, and his involvement with the arson issue. Maybe Addicks had his own suspicions about who committed the murder. Why else would he refuse to take the lie detector test? Why else would he hire his own lawyer?

Addicks drove that fancy new red Cadillac, but Columbia Bookkeeping owned the car. My limited investigations showed that Addicks had very little money in savings. I knew he was always cash poor since he often asked for advances. He didn't even have a credit card, so he used a company card to buy his gas. Also, I knew from the bank loan that he was living hand-to-mouth. It was strange how everyone else, except the detectives, were totally ignorant of the show Addicks was putting on, pretending he was some rich guy in a Cadillac. He had no funds to back up his posturing.

I still wanted to keep Rod Addicks around the business a little while longer even though my ultimate goal was to get Addicks out of the company since he was, by then, my prime murder and arson suspect. I thought Addicks was involved with the massage parlors, especially because he was the one who I thought handled that account. Due to his occasional temper outbursts and lack of cooperation on the investigation, my only conclusion was I could not trust him.

I had been consulting with our lawyer, Jim Auxier, to find a way to get Rod Addicks out of the business without the estate being sued. Auxier and the detectives repeatedly warned me to be careful. If Rod Addicks was involved with my dad's murder, they said to avoid situations where I was alone with him. I was informed by my own attorney that if I was wrong, Addicks could sue me personally, as well as sue the Turel Estate for every penny it was worth. "But if you're right," they said, "watch out. He's dangerous." Apparently Mr. Hanson, Addicks' attorney, called Auxier several times, warning Auxier indirectly, complaining that I was totally out of line in my dealings with Addicks. Hanson told Auxier that Rod Addicks was not going to put up with my behavior much longer and that they'd be forced to sue the Turel Estate if I didn't stop harassing him. Hanson wanted Jim Auxier to constrain me.

The detectives updated me on more details regarding Rod Addicks alleged securities fraud violations and a lawsuit filed by clients of his accounting practice in Tacoma, Washington, from back in 1966. This was several years before Addicks applied for a job in my dad's tax business. At that time Addicks was a registered CPA in the State of Washington. The charges alleged that Rod Addicks had misappropriated money from a real estate investment in Tacoma that ended up losing money. The charges against Addicks were that he took money on the pretense that property had been bought in Oregon, when in fact Addicks used the money for his own personal business needs. Jim Auxier agreed, "It's time to get him out of the business now. I can't believe that Addicks appears to have been involved in so much trouble. No one would ever have suspected it. It's shocking."

To me it looked fishy that Addicks lived in the Kelso area, which was where D.B. Cooper had jumped from the plane. I also knew that Addicks claimed he frequently hunted in that area. When I asked the detectives to investigate Lee's Construction, they told me their superiors made them back off because of Addicks' threatened lawsuit. "If we get more solid leads, we will go into Washington State," they said. Their apparent lack of interest bothered me deep inside my gut.

Politics was getting in the way. Detective Blackie Yazzolino said, "Be patient, Stan. The truth will come out some day. Just be careful, you may be pushing Addicks too hard."

Rod Addicks was smug after the Multnomah County and IRS criminal investigators found nothing wrong with the books of Columbia Bookkeeping or its assorted partnerships. Personally, I thought the Multnomah County CPAs had not spent enough time looking through the records. Addicks appeared more relaxed after his attorney's threat of lawsuits had their desired effect. "The detectives appear to be onto another track," he told me.

Occasionally, in the evening, I would call Addicks at his home to apologize for my persistent inquiries about how everything was going at the office. I tried to assure him my intention wasn't to interfere with the business and I'd say I wanted him to know how much we appreciated him sticking with the company. I'd say that in the near future I would be reducing my time at the office, limiting my involvement to only the things he needed help with. I was still lying through my teeth. I had no intention of backing off. But the conversations seemed to ease the tensions between us.

But what Addicks didn't know was that I was still staying in touch with the detectives on every little lead I thought was important. Generally, I spoke with Detective Blackie Yazzolino two or three times a week. Detective Yazzolino said he was surprised at the intensity of my efforts in dealing with Rod Addicks, even though we both suspected he was somehow involved in Dad's murder. Gary would also occasionally call Yazzolino.

And Addicks continued to get upset with me, claiming I was still asking him too many questions. He objected when I introduced myself to customers and was annoyed that I continued to do so even after he voiced his objection. But the detectives would still drop by occasionally, without advance notice, and Addicks was forced to remain in a state of agitation.

One day I was sitting in Addicks' office with the door open when the detectives came by.

Yazzolino looked in and said, "Hi!"

"Hi," Addicks said, back to them. "And don't worry guys, I am not hiding anything. Stan here has the right to go through this office and anything in it since it is his father's business and building, not mine. I wish I could talk to you but I have to follow my attorney's advice." Then Addicks laughed that nervous cackle.

"Stan, you mind if we step into your office and go over a few things?" Yazzolino said, as Detective Wells pulled out his notepad.

I walked out of Addicks office and went into mine. The detectives and I spoke for a bit, then they left. After they were gone, Rod Addicks headed straight for the bathroom.

My brother, Gary, continued to decrease his daily involvement at Columbia Bookkeeping, eventually settling on just part of a day, once a week. In early November, in the evenings, I quietly began interviewing prospects to be Rod Addicks' replacement.

Simultaneously, Addicks interviewed—and hired—a man named

Marvin Bridge who had previously worked for an accounting and tax firm in Reno, Nevada. Marvin Bridge was intended to be the replacement for Sam Moll. At first I was suspicious of Addicks' recommendation to hire Bridge, just because the man was Addicks' choice. I wondered if he had mafia or massage parlor connections, or was involved in gambling since he was from Reno. I was thoroughly paranoid, no doubt about it. But perhaps my paranoia was justified.

Addicks mentioned that he had previously encouraged Sam Moll to start a gambling casino with him at the Puyallup Indian Reservation in Tacoma, Washington. Addicks claimed it was his idea. That set me to wondering. Had Addicks known Marvin Bridge before Dad was murdered? I quietly checked out Bridge's background and found he had a clean record. In fact, he was an IRS Enrolled Agent. Okay, I figured, maybe I can relax my concerns about this man.

Occasionally I would listen to the taped conversations I had recorded with Addicks to make sure I hadn't misinterpreted his changing stories. The inconsistencies regarding Sam Moll and Lee's Construction didn't make sense. I could tell by the changes in Addicks' voice tone that over time he was gradually becoming more stressed. Also, after listening to my voice on the recordings, I realized I needed to be smoother and more cautious, clearer and more patient. I could tell I was pushing him, perhaps too hard, perhaps hard enough to leave. I kept these tapes hidden at the apartment I shared with Janet.

During the first four months after the murder, I talked to several potential buyers of Columbia Bookkeeping. It still bothered me that Addicks presented the broker's letter with an offer to list the company the same week my dad died. A few more calls and offers came in, but when they found out my dad had been murdered and that a possible suspect was Rod Addicks, every one of them backed off.

One serious buyer, Dave Lieberman from Triple Check Tax Franchise, flew up from Los Angeles and invited me to lunch. But when he found out Rod Addicks was a murder suspect, even he stopped the negotiations. What would the 2,800 clients think if they found out Addicks was an arson and murder suspect, not to mention his security fraud involvement from 1966? It looked to me as though the company would truly fall apart.

Once, when I voiced my concerns about the potential buyers to Rod

Addicks he said, "I will buy the company if no one else wants it. We can work out some sort of down payment with the insurance proceeds and get the money to the estate that way."

It became obvious to me that I was going to have to stay involved in Dad's business fulltime, since my brother, Gary, was going to be fully occupied in his own tax business across town. Gary had about 200 clients then, and lived in his 500-square-foot tax office. I admired him for his humble beginnings. I took no salary from Columbia Bookkeeping because I still had income from my own businesses. I paid Gary $800 for painting and staining half the outside of the office building. I felt more comfortable knowing he would intermittently be nearby in case I had a problem with Rod Addicks. I didn't mention this arrangement to Addicks, who continued to be upset whenever Gary and I were both in the building.

Rod Addicks told the others that Gary and I were both losers. He called us 'ne'er do wells' who didn't know anything about business. I was glad Addicks underestimated us. He figured if the police couldn't find anything, then why worry about the Turel boys?

By the way, on September 16, 1974, I had given Detective Yazzolino the name of Tom Messler, which I had found in Addicks' phone directory. I was concerned and suspicious because there were so many scribblings around his name and several phone numbers crossed out. After I read Yazzolino's notes years later, I wondered if my dad had stumbled onto this guy, because the detectives' investigation recorded that Rod Addicks went to Beaverton, Oregon, and paid Messler $2,000 as a settlement in an old lawsuit the day before my dad was murdered.

An excerpt from Yazzolino's notes of November 28, 1974 that reference Tom Messler are as follows:

From Blackie Yazzolino's notes
Continuation Report, from page 2 of 4 pages
Case Number 74-18471   Classification: MURDER I
Reporting Officer: OY

MR. MESSLER states that he met MR. ADDICK at Linfield College and that MR. ADDICK graduated from the school a half a year before he, MR. MESSLER graduated. MR. MESSLER stated that he went into the Army and from there went to Vietnam where he stayed for approximately five years coming out as a Captain and that while in *the army he sent money home to his father, MR. CHARLES MESSLER, in the amount of $4,000.00 which in turn was sent by check to ROD ADDICK as an investment for MR. MESSLER in a corporation that had purchased some land near Fort Lewis Washington along with a tavern and a trailer court. MR. MESSLER also invested in some land in Eastern Washington and that upon his return from Vietnam which was late in 1969 he found that the suspect MR. ROD ADDICK had taken in other investors into the corporation which was known as Gold Banks Corporation... In May of 1970 ... MR. MESSLER attempted to contact MR. ADDICK and found that he had taken all the proceeds that were kept by the Gold Bank Corporation and left the area. MR. MESSLER stated he then found out that there were many suits filed against the Gold Bank Corporation along with himself and the other investors and that the amount of money that MR. ADDICK had left with was approximately $7,000.00, also MR. MESSLER was informed that the subject ADDICK had left the country entirely and was going to South America, however, investigation by writer it was revealed that he did not go to South America, but simply returned to his home town of Kelso where he stayed there under the name of ROD UNGER.*

As to MR. ADDICKS' personal life, MR. MESSLER could only state that he knew Addicks was known as a swinger, too that ADDICKS loved to gamble and also that on many occasions MR. MESSLER had been told by MR. ADDICKS that he, ADDICKS, only took out married women as he did not want to get involved with single women because of his own belief that a married woman could not cause him problems with his own wife, and they also had to keep the affair secret.

Chapter 9: Arson Ring Discovered

During October and November 1974, I continued my diligent examination of every invoice and every check that went through Quality Financial Planning. And I continued to secretly visit the people involved with every partnership Rod Addicks was managing, which continued to piss him off. I would go to them, explain my concerns about Addicks and his lawsuits in Washington State, and say I was not accusing Rod Addicks of anything. But I'd suggest they call Detective Blackie Yazzolino to verify my information. I asked them to keep the information I divulged to them confidential, to specifically refrain from mentioning it to Rod Addicks.

Addicks had a 25 percent interest in the Big Spruce Mobile Home Park in Florence, Oregon. The majority of that partnership was owned by a lifelong friend of my dad's, Al Foglio. I decided to go visit Mr. and Mrs. Foglio, to provide details about my mounting concerns and to warn them to stay alert.

The flight to the small airport on the central Oregon coast was a beautiful uplifting escape from the intense pressures at the office. I picked a day when the weather was nice, with broken clouds at 5,000 feet. The clouds cleared up just north of the Florence airport. Trees and sand dunes line the sparse area between the airport and the Pacific Ocean. As I approached the airport in my small plane, I hit 35mph crosswinds. When I made my landing, the crosswind's wind speed dropped and my landing was smooth as glass. Al Foglio met me there.

Al Foglio is a heavy-built, teddy bear of a man who is instantly liked by everyone he meets. He's known my father since the time I was born. I have always felt an extremely strong bond to Mr. Foglio's entire family because Al and my dad started out logging together after the war and they kept in touch for the rest of Dad's life. Foglio Trucking began the same time my father started his logging truck business.

When Al and I joined up with his wife Mary, I mentioned Addicks' refusal to take a polygraph test and the lawsuits filed against him for securities fraud in Washington State. I divulged that Addicks was a serious suspect regarding arson and murder. I told them I was watching every move Rod Addicks made. I let them know I would need their assistance in removing Addicks from the business. And I said I would need their help when it became time to buy out his interests from their partnerships.

The Foglios were shocked, of course. Al and Mary said they had four separate real estate deals that involved Rod Addicks but they would take the steps necessary to remove him from their business investments. They agreed to keep me informed, and to accompany me when telling the other partners in the Big Spruce Mobile Home Park about my concerns.

After I shared my suspicions about Rod Addicks with a few of the other partners, they agreed to buy out Rod Addicks' share, but not until such time that we had more proof of his guilt regarding the securities fraud and the arson investigation. They also agreed to keep my suspicions under their hats. I wanted to keep Addicks as broke as possible in the meantime. And since Addicks was friendly with the Foglios, I had to make sure he was kept in the dark about my flying to Florence to look over the Big Spruce Mobile Home Park situation.

Two of the dozen partners in the Portland-area deals slipped and told Addicks I was asking questions about the apartments, plus forwarding names and phone numbers to the detectives. Addicks became even more irritated with me when he heard this. He accused me of interfering with the operation of his partnerships. "Mr. Hanson, my attorney, is suggesting I sue you, Stan," Addicks threatened. "You personally as an individual, and Columbia Bookkeeping as well! For defamation of character!"

I said, quietly and humbly, "Rod, you know that Blackie Yazzolino may be the one telling them things. I told only a few of the partners, and only when they asked. All I said was that they should talk to Detective Blackie Yazzolino if they had questions, since I don't know that much." Of course, I was still lying to Addicks. I had been deliberately approaching these people and I definitely wanted them to know Rod Addicks had security fraud issues and was a possible arson suspect.

During my continuing review of the business and checking accounts, I noticed that one check written to Lee's Construction for $600 turned out to be an advance check. I contacted the manager of the Woodstock Apartments and found out that no work by Lee's Construction had been done for over a month. When I approached Rod Addicks about this he said it was for an advance on materials, and that he, personally, had already verified they were delivered to the Woodstock Apartments.

I decided to continue to act stupid and accept this answer, but I found no evidence at the apartment that materials had been delivered. I will check on that later, I told myself, as I added a note to my to-do list.

I forwarded the information about the suspicious checks made out to Lee's Construction to the detectives and felt sure we were on to something. Rod Addicks still came into the office at least four days a week. On the days he did not come in, I went through every single drawer in his desk, including the files in the three-drawer cabinet in his office. I was looking for information that conflicted with what he was telling me.

From Day One after the office reopened, Addicks had become more and more uncomfortable regarding my involvement with business operations. I spent hours with Addicks discussing the possible motives of others in an effort to make him feel as though I did not suspect him. Addicks knew I did not like, nor trust, the owner of the massage parlors. But I think I was doing a good job acting as if everything was okay.

It was hard to believe that I spent day after day sitting across the table from a man I suspected of having murdered my dad. If he hadn't committed the crime himself, I thought he knew who did. I was sure he was holding back vital information that could solve the case. I cannot tell you how many times, while talking with Rod Addicks, that I just pretended everything was okay, even though his stories about Sam Moll and Lee's Construction did not add up. I was raised to see the good in people and not assume the worst. However, Addicks' anger level was definitely increasing due to my continued presence around the tax office.

One evening in November, after Addicks left the office, I found his personal checking records in his desk drawer. A year and a half of his personal bank statements were neatly stacked inside bank envelopes. I had a hard time believing that he would leave all that in an unlocked desk drawer. I looked through the paperwork to see if anything might tie him to persons of interest or to the massage parlors. I reviewed all the documents carefully, including earnest money agreements on a number of houses that contained the names of Rod Addicks or Sam Moll. Were they both involved in arson? Again, the paperwork increased my suspicions since Sam Moll had decided not to return to work for Columbia Bookkeeping.

$600 check written to Lee's Construction which led to the investigation of
Dennis Lee Cartwright in murder for hire.

$2 check written by Rod Addicks transferring property from Sam Moll
to Dennis Lee Cartwright in arson scheme.

Among those banking records, I found a few checks that appeared to
be loans of large sums of money to Sam Moll. In one bank statement was a
cancelled check written by Rod Addicks to Clackamas County in the
amount of $2. As usual, I tried to figure out what that check was for
because the notation stated, "Re — Moll to Cartwright." I called Detective
Blackie Yazzolino and asked him to check it out. Yazzolino called me
back with interesting news. He was told by the County that the check was
related to a property title transfer between two persons. Aha! I thought, and
I turned a copy of the check over to the police.

I was then informed that Sam Moll's name was matched to an arson
fire on a second house with which Addicks, supposedly, had no
connection. Now the evidence showed that Addicks had transferred a third
house from Sam Moll to Lee Cartwright.

"What was Addicks doing transferring other people's names between properties?" I asked Detective Yazzolino. "These three people are now prime suspects. Let's do something about it! We've got three suspicious characters connected with this $2 check!"

Reflecting back to September, just after Dad's death, Gary and I had looked through our clients' tax files for names that matched any on the detectives' lists of possible arson suspects. Since Dad had previously told me he suspected Addicks was involved in arson, we first wondered if he might have stumbled onto an arson ring. Was that the reason our dad had been murdered?

That's it, I thought. Dad was right. Addicks is an arsonist!

Another night, Rod Addicks forgot to take his company briefcase home with him. The case was not locked, so I opened it expecting to find something related to Columbia Bookkeeping. I did find information relating to a few clients' taxes, but I also discovered Addicks' personal financial statement that showed his assets and net worth. It struck me as curious that he showed a nice net worth in Columbia Bookkeeping even though he had not paid off the contract for the purchase of stock he had the option to buy. Also, the financial statement listed a home in Kelso, Washington, as belonging to him. But I had previously learned that the house was in his mother's name and that Addicks had no phone number listed in his name anywhere. Detective Yazzolino said he already knew this information. By that time I figured the detectives were just collecting stuff, but had no time to follow through.

I felt sure something was amiss, if, as Rod Addicks claimed, he had no contact with Sam Moll anymore. There were just too many connections between Addicks and Moll and Cartwright.

On November 10, 1974, based on the information I found in Rod Addicks' desk, I summarized the man's potential net worth. I forwarded my written summary to the detectives in an effort to highlight what Addicks would have lost if my dad had kicked him out of the tax business and if Addicks lost his interest in the apartment deals. According to my calculations, Addicks would have lost over $107,000. But with Dad out of the picture, Rod Addicks was the logical person to buy the tax company from Dad's estate.

Addicks had mentioned several times that the $50,000 life insurance money could be used as a down payment to buy the business from Dad's estate. "I could pay off the balance on a contract within a few years," he said. "That is, only if the family wants to get the money out of the company without paying ordinary income tax on it. When you sell stock that has been owned for over a year, you pay only half the amount of tax since it would be considered a long-term gain."

By December 1, I had handed over so much documentation to the police that I wondered if they knew which item to follow. They probably felt many of my leads weren't important enough to investigate. Maybe the detectives had so many other murder cases to investigate they couldn't spend much time on this case. I felt my communication with Detective Blackie Yazzolino was becoming a one-way street. I finally made the assumption that a lot of the information I turned over to them was immaterial. I wondered if I had become just a paranoid pest.

On the other hand, I became frustrated with the detectives and lack of their progress. They didn't seem to be investigating my suspicions about Addicks' lies, Sam Moll, the curious checks, or the mysterious payments made to Lee's Construction. The detectives were still polite to me, but it seemed as though they were just compiling the information I forwarded to them, then not acting on that information. They did warn me several times to take it easy, as Addicks might be a dangerous man. They also reminded me that they had to be very careful about what they said to me. I knew the detectives were feeling pressure from their superiors to tread lightly with Rod Addicks due to the threatened defamation of character lawsuits. My own lawyer was also putting pressure on me to slow down. 'Stay cool,' Jim Auxier told me often enough. Maybe the detectives were just not telling me everything they knew.

The police seemed unimpressed with my summary of Rod Addicks' finances, but I felt it might show motive. If the estate sold the business to anyone besides Rod Addicks, then Addicks would be entitled to part of that insurance money, as it belonged to Columbia Bookkeeping.

During the night of December 10, I had another nightmare. In this dream I was talking to Rod Addicks about Lee's Construction. He got mad and started yelling 'Bullshit!' All of a sudden Addicks stood up, pulled a gun from his desk drawer and shot me in the stomach. I jolted awake in a heavy sweat the moment the bullet hit me. I decided right then I was pushing Addicks too hard. "Back off," I said to myself.

The next day I was surprised by a call from Detective Blackie

Yazzolino. "Stan," he said, "I don't want to alarm you, but we just found out that Rod Addicks recently obtained a permit to carry a gun. He keeps it in the glove compartment of the Cadillac." Wow, I thought, I better really back off for a few weeks. My subconscious was working overtime.

A week later, Detective Yazzolino called to say he was going to retire the next week, but he would still stay in touch with me and follow the case. "You're probably on the right track, Stan and I agree with you. I feel strongly that Rod Addicks was involved with the murder or has suspicions of who did it. I've got to say, I admire your ability to stay so intensely focused on this investigation, yet still work with the man. You're doing great keeping your cool while continually pumping Addicks for whatever information he's hiding. I want you to know, Stan, we appreciate all that information you've been providing, but I have to caution you to be more careful."

"Have you discovered any connection between my dad and the massage parlors?" I asked.

"Stan, you know I can't discuss any details, but according to my informants, your father's murder had nothing to do with them."

"Detective Yazzolino," I said, "I really appreciate what you've done so far. But who's going to be continuing the investigation?"

"Detective Wells will stay on the job until another homicide detective is assigned."

"Don't take this the wrong way, Detective Yazzolino," I said, "but I am really concerned. Detective Wells doesn't have the experience and wisdom that you do."

"You don't have to worry about that, Stan. Sooner or later the truth will come out. Usually a murderer cannot help it, he has to brag or tell someone what he did, which will get back to us somehow."

"Well, are you following up on my concerns about Sam Moll and Lee's Construction?"

"I assure you," Yazzolino said, "we have all your information, but we don't have permission or funding to go to the Seattle area at this time. The new detectives will follow up on the issue about Rod Addicks, Sam Moll, and Lee Cartwright."

"When?"

"In the near future," said Detective Blackie Yazzolino.

I was not too happy with the loss of Yazzolino's participation in the investigation. Maybe I had just worn out the detectives with too many calls and bits of information. Was I wrong to be so persistent? Maybe. They probably had other, more important murder investigations to solve.

Before we hung up, I asked Blackie Yazzolino, for the third time, if Columbia Bookkeeping should offer a reward. "I think $5,000 would attract attention," I said. "Maybe someone would come forward with information."

"Maybe in the future," Yazzolino said, "if the case doesn't move forward."

I thanked him for his efforts and wished him the best in his retirement. That afternoon, I instructed my lawyer, Jim Auxier, to type up a reward statement, just to have something ready in case the future arrived. If the investigation was going to dissipate, maybe I needed to consider offering a reward despite Detective Yazzolino's suggestion to hold off. Jim Auxier called me back the next day and dictated a one-page reward notice that I typed on Columbia Bookkeeping letterhead.

Chapter 10: CPA Resigns

In early December, I approached Rod Addicks again and asked him about the $600 advance check written to Lee's Construction.

"Lee's Construction took that advance so it could buy the appliances at Cronkite Plumbing," Addicks said. "And I have already been over to the Woodstock Apartments to verify the materials are there." Addicks' voice was calm and he had me convinced because he was so relaxed while looking directly into my eyes. "We can always get the money back if he doesn't finish the job. Or, we can return the materials to Cronkite Plumbing if necessary. Stan, we talked about this over a week ago."

"Oh, that's right," I said. "I forgot. That's great," I responded, putting my hand over my forehead, acting stupid. "That explains everything."

Addicks continued, "Plus this guy is probably getting the work done for half price, which makes it a good deal for us. Now let's move on and talk about ordering tax season supplies." I just nodded in a positive and friendly manner. I acted as though his knowledge and experience impressed me as we discussed a short to-do list for the upcoming tax season. Rod Addicks was such a smooth liar, I couldn't believe it. I had just checked out the apartments the day before and absolutely no materials had been delivered.

The next morning, without Addicks knowing, I went to Cronkite Plumbing and discreetly asked Mr. Cronkite if Lee's Construction had purchased any materials. The answer was no. Mr. Cronkite remembered that Dennis Lee Cartwright had come into the store a few weeks ago and looked over some items, but hadn't bought anything. I asked Mr. Cronkite not to mention my visit to Rod Addicks or to Dennis Cartwright. I gave him Detective Blackie Yazzolino's phone number to verify that I had the right to obtain the information. When I arrived back at the office, I did not confront Addicks, nor did I say anything about what I had learned.

On Friday of that week, I went to Jim Auxier's office to let him know

I was planning on removing Rod Addicks from the business before the next tax season began. "Jim," I said. "I fear that Addicks' possible involvement in arson and his Washington securities fraud accusations could destroy the reputation of our business. I am also convinced there is something fishy about the relationship between Rod Addicks, Sam Moll, and Dennis Lee Cartwright. And I think Addicks might know something about the murder."

But I felt my hands were tied. Even though I trusted Jim Auxier, I couldn't keep him totally informed about everything I had forwarded to the police. I felt my information was too confidential for that. But I did tell my brother, Gary, everything, on a regular basis. In order to feel like I was accomplishing something in my effort to get Addicks out of the business, I scheduled a Corporate Board of Directors meeting for Friday, December 20, 1974. I decided that at that meeting I would either fire Rod Addicks, or give him the opportunity to resign. Gary agreed, "Let's get rid of him."

I called Rod a few evenings prior to the meeting and said I would recommend that he get a year-end bonus at the upcoming stockholders meeting. I wanted to make sure he would show up.

Jim Auxier helped me strategize. He said to make sure all board members were present, which meant attendees would need to include directors Bernie Turel, Rod Addicks, our corporate attorney Jim Auxier, and me. I knew that if Addicks resigned, he would not be entitled to unemployment benefits, but if I fired him he would receive it. I planned to push him hard to get him to resign from both companies. If I fired him, he would surely sue Columbia Bookkeeping and me personally for wrongful termination and defamation of character.

Also, I had to get him out of Dad's business without enriching his cash reserves. I called my banker, Jack Miller, and suggested that he put pressure on Addicks several days in advance of the meeting, urging Addicks to pay off his 90-day loan. Miller agreed to tell Addicks that the police had been asking him for further information about Addicks, but that Miller was hesitant to say anything to the detectives about Addicks' past-due loans. I reasoned that if Addicks felt background pressure, he would be more likely to resign in an attempt to get his money quickly.

I also made a list of items I intended to present at the board meeting. The list included occasions when Addicks had failed in his fiduciary responsibilities to the clients of both Columbia Bookkeeping and Quality

Financial Planning. I asked my brother, Gary, to come to the office at the time of the board meeting. I wanted him to stand by in case there was a problem during, or after, the board of directors meeting.

On December 20, my stepmother Bernie Turel, and our attorney Jim Auxier arrived before Rod Addicks returned from a late lunch. While looking through the windows we could see Addicks drive up in his beautiful bright red Cadillac. It was a wet winter day with the wind blowing hard against the building. I wondered if Addicks noticed the darker green color of the bulletproof glass as he walked by and waved to us. No one, except my brother, knew I had installed that special glass.

I was feeling nervous so I asked Julie Syler, the bookkeeper and secretary, plus Gary, to stand in the hallway just outside the meeting room. I had prearranged that no other appointments were scheduled for that afternoon. I instructed them to call the police if things got out of hand. When Addicks entered my office, he looked shocked to see Jim Auxier there. I started the meeting at 3:30 p.m.

When Addicks entered the room and sat down I said, "Rod, I want you to know how much we all appreciate what you've done for the company." Addicks looked relaxed, even jovial, as he was expecting one of the reasons the meeting had been called was to approve payment of his year end-bonus.

"However," I continued, "we have some current and potential problems facing the corporation." I provided a quick accounting of instances where Addicks had mishandled accounts and failed to prepare timely financial reports concerning the apartment buildings he managed. I said Addicks had advanced $600 to Lee's Construction without materials or work being completed. I also referred to the investigation being conducted by the Homicide Department for the murder of my dad. "Further," I said, "we have learned from the detectives that numerous lawsuits had been filed against you in Washington State six years earlier for securities violations."

Rod Addicks sat stone-faced, with his lips pressed tightly together as I spoke.

"In summary," I said, "based on all that information, Columbia Bookkeeping is removing all check-signing authority from you regarding the apartment building management. And I am making a motion to restrict you from orchestrating any more real estate investments or putting together any deals on behalf of Columbia Bookkeeping or Quality Financial Planning."

Rod Addicks began to sweat and shift in his seat while his dark black eyes drove daggers into me. His face turned red. I could tell he was trying to control his anger, just as I had seen him do so many times during our previous talks. My heart was pounding with fear and nervousness. But I also felt in control. My agenda was that one way or another I would get him out of the business. My hope was that Addicks would not dare do anything violent, as there were too many witnesses.

After an interminable pause, I made a motion to remove Rod Addicks as president of Quality Financial Planning. But before the motion could be seconded, Addicks leaned back in his chair and laughed. "You don't have to do all that if I resign from both companies," he said.

No one else spoke.

Addicks said, "Okay. I hereby resign in the best interest of both companies." Then he laughed that edgy cackle of his again. "I'll make you this offer. In exchange for my year-end bonus of $5,500 in cash, I'll take the Cadillac."

"Rod, as you know both companies have very little money," I said, "but I'm prepared to give you some cash in the near future, as long as we can come to an agreement today." Which we did. Columbia Bookkeeping agreed to give Rod Addicks $2,000 as a down payment, with the balance of his year-end bonus payable at the end of the upcoming tax season, March 1975. "Rod," I continued, "regarding the Cadillac, we can't find the title. But we'll forward the paperwork to you later, when we find it, after we figure out which company owns it." I was straight-out lying. I had the title and knew which company owned it. "In the meantime, we'll keep up the insurance on the Cadillac until the title is clear."

Addicks agreed to all this, as he wanted to drive the Cadillac home and use it as his own personal vehicle. I didn't want Addicks to receive any money until we got to the bottom of the murder case. However, I felt I should give him something now, just to make it appear as if I was speaking in earnest. "Rod, I am sorry it had come to this, but I am following our attorney's instructions, trying to protect the reputation of the company." I was lying about that, too, as I knew a lot more than Rod Addicks or Jim Auxier realized.

Near the end of the board meeting Rod Addicks said, "Does this mean I'm being fired?" He sounded hopeful, as if he finally realized that by quitting, he would not receive unemployment benefits.

"No," I said. "You've already resigned. We can't fire you."

"That's right," said Bernie, my stepmother. "It's too late. You quit an hour ago and we accepted your resignation."

"Let's stay in contact," I suggested to Addicks. "We'll need to create the formal paperwork to reflect the agreement we just made before we can give you the rest of your money. And I think we should let you clean out your desk while you're here."

Addicks looked at me and shook his head, while making that nervous laugh of his. "I think you're making a big mistake, Stan," he said. "This company is going to fall apart without me and you'll be left here alone to float the boat by yourself."

"I am only following my attorney's advice," I replied. "I know that the police are probably on the wrong path regarding the murder and arsons, but those security fraud problems in Tacoma, Washington, really bother me. I hope you understand." The lies just flowed out of my mouth. I was trying not to react to Addicks' bait. The last thing I wanted was to cause a scene. My sole focus was on getting Addicks out of Columbia Bookkeeping before the tax season started up again.

The board meeting lasted just over one hour. As Addicks went through his desk, Gary and I reviewed every item he removed. Addicks took the brief case I thought belonged to the company, and a few pencils and papers. He tried to take customer files, but I stopped him, saying they related to our clients. He took the files of one client who he said was his own separate client. He became angry when I contested his perceived ownership of the briefcase and that one file. But then I said, "Okay, take them," because it seemed as though I was pushing him to the limit.

"I want to take my phone directory," Addicks said.

"No, that's ours," I said. The flip-up directory contained names and addresses of our clients and I knew the company had paid for it.

By then, Addicks was breathing hard. "That's bullshit," he said.

"Can I have the keys to this office, please?" I said.

He handed the keys to me and tried to shake my hand, but I couldn't take it. I wanted to tell him he was a phony, a liar, a con man and an arsonist. But I kept my mouth shut. After he left, I thanked Jim Auxier and Gary for their help in making the meeting go so well.

Immediately, I called the locksmith I had prearranged to be available, and he was able to rekey all the locks within 15 minutes. I felt so relieved that Addicks was finally gone and out of the business, but I was still shaking inside because I wondered what he would do next.

"Oh, Stan," Julie Syler said, "Peg and I are really relieved to have Addicks out of here. We've been aware of your suspicions and we know about his prior lawsuits in Washington State. He frightens us."

"Julie," I said. "Everything is going to turn out okay."

With the help of Julie and Peg, I composed a letter that would be sent to all our bookkeeping clients. We announced that Rod Addicks had resigned from the firm because he had to move back to Washington to handle personal problems. I provided the name of the CPA we'd hired to start the following Monday. I also explained that all the bookkeepers and their respective accounting records remained in our office, indirectly clarifying that Rod Addicks had no claim to them and would no longer handle their account. I invited each client in for a free year-end tax consultation. The letter was mailed out on the following Saturday.

Then, I talked to Gary and called my sisters that evening, explaining the details of Rod Addicks' resignation. I left a message for Detective Blackie Yazzolino, but Detective Wells returned my call and said he would forward my message. When I called our lawyer the next day, Jim Auxier said, "You'd better be careful when talking to the clients about Rod Addicks, as you're on the edge of being sued."

"I won't discuss the details of Addicks' problems with our clients," I told Auxier, "but I can talk to them about the lawsuits for securities fraud in Washington if I feel I need to destroy their confidence in him."

A few days later I received a $480 refund check in the mail from Lee's Construction regarding that $600 advance. It was a cashier's check. I called Rod Addicks at his home about the remaining $120 and was told it was probably for the time Lee's Construction spent checking on materials and measuring the intended project. I asked for Lee's Construction's phone number and Rod said, "He doesn't have a phone number and I don't know where to reach him."

Right, I thought, Rod Addicks is lying about everything. And I hung up the phone.

Chapter 11: Saving Dad's Business

The following Monday I set about getting organized for the upcoming tax season. I worked with the bookkeepers and compiled a detailed list of all the supplies and items needed, based on our records from prior years. The CPA I had secretly hired to replace Addicks was a 50-year-old man named Mr. Smith. I had worked with Mr. Smith in the past, when he served as manager of a local aviation company. In addition, Marvin Bridge, hired by Addicks as a replacement for Sam Moll, was ready to begin work. I leveled with Marvin Bridge and Mr. Smith about the problems I'd been having with Rod Addicks, and let everyone know that Addicks was not to be given access to the building, nor information about the company from here on into the future unless I approved it.

Within a week of Rod Addicks' departure, eight of the apartment partnership members responded to my letter. Some were upset or concerned about their investments. Who would manage the apartments? Why was Addicks gone? I reassured them that their investments were not at risk and explained my business background. I told them I had been managing my own rentals and apartment for many years. However, I could tell a few of the partners had been contacted by Addicks. I suspected he put them up to asking leading questions to backup a defamation of character lawsuit against me. In each case I referred them to the detectives. For this, I truly was following the advice of my lawyer, Jim Auxier, who said I was walking a tightrope regarding Addicks' character and my suspicions.

I requested that the apartment building partners immediately advance the necessary money to their partnerships to catch up on overdue bills. I was surprised at how convincing I was. Perhaps it was just coincidence, but shortly after Rod Addicks left Columbia Bookkeeping employment, Paula Travington, the woman who managed the Woodstock apartments, resigned and moved out of the state. I turned this information over to the police as I still suspected that $3,000 was missing from the Woodstock apartment account.

Several of the partners wanted out of the apartment business deals and refused to contribute more money to support their losses. Two in particular said that if they lost money they would sue Columbia Bookkeeping and me personally. I asked them for patience, and they all agreed. Most of them said they admired my dad and respected how I was trying to keep the company going.

With the help of Julie and Peg, we set up meetings with a number of bookkeeping clients in conjunction with their year-end tax planning. Since these clients owned rentals and businesses I was sure they would have tax questions for our new CPA. I wanted to sit in on the meetings to see how the new CPA handled the clients. When asked questions by clients, Mr. Smith kept saying, "I'll have to research that, since it's so complicated." I was surprised Mr. Smith didn't know more about tax deductions for businesses and apartments. It seemed I knew more about current tax law and rules than he did. When Smith would defer an answer to a client, I'd say I had already researched that particular aspect in relation to my own businesses and rental properties and could answer their question. At the end of a few sessions like that, most of the clients realized I was not quite the dummy Rod Addicks had implied.

After a week, when I asked Mr. Smith about his lack of knowledge, he appeared embarrassed. "I usually delegated tax research to other specialists, and then I'd get back to the client with answers. Columbia Bookkeeping can charge more, for the research, if we continue doing it this way," he suggested.

Frankly, I was disappointed in Mr. Smith's lack of knowledge and had to let him go at the end of that first week. But I learned my lesson. From that day on, I interviewed each prospective tax accountant or licensed professional using reverse strategy. When a tax accountant applicant came in for an interview, I'd tell them they were going to interview me.

"Pretend I'm a prospective tax client with questions," I would say to an applicant. I'd act ignorant, but ask tricky questions about deductible expenses, or what depreciation ranges could be used for various assets in a business or apartment building. It was a quick way to learn the extent of their knowledge. To check their integrity, I would ask questions about shady attempts at tax evasion, just to see if they would write off items that were not legitimately deductible. Over half the licensed professionals I interviewed could not come up with the right answers. I was shocked that so many replied, 'I will have to research that,' before they could give me an answer. If they didn't know tax law regarding rentals and business off the top of their head, they were not hired. I found that my personal business experience and tax knowledge regarding managing properties exceeded most of these licensed applicants. I remembered Norm Winningstad's advice: Always hire professionals who exceed or equal your knowledge base.

I interviewed Marvin Bridge in the same fashion. I decided he was as sharp as or even more knowledgeable than I in tax law, so, I promoted him to general manager. He was just the person I needed and very professional. I made sure, however, that I personally interviewed all the rest of our potential employees, including the secretaries. Most of the secretaries I ended up hiring attended the Church of Christ. My trust in humanity was not at its peak at this time, and I felt that people who feared God or believed in a higher authority would be less likely to steal money.

Pat Auxier, the wife of Jim Auxier our attorney, was a Licensed Tax Consultant with several years of experience. I hired her for the tax season and let her use my dad's office to interview clients. Pat was in her mid-30s, a classy woman with a calming professional demeanor. I needed older people on my staff to project the image of experience. She was perfect.

Just before Christmas I found myself occupied with handling client inquires and personally signing and mailing 2,800 year-end letters to tax clients. I was also worrying about Rod Addicks' next move. Meanwhile, Jim Auxier was handling Rod Addicks' attorney, Mr. Hanson, and sending me letters warning me of a forthcoming lawsuit if did not turn over the title of the Cadillac to Rod Addicks immediately. But I continued to stall. In fact, I refused to do what they asked.

"I'm not going to give another dime to Rod Addicks until my suspicions are laid to rest," I told Auxier. But I was apprehensive since neither the detectives nor the police were doing anything about the case. I was worried that they were delaying the investigation because the homicide department was short on staff due to the retirement of Blackie Yazzolino.

In late December, a break-in took place at our main Stark Street office. The intruder smashed the sliding glass door in the back of Julie Syler's office and glass lay shattered all over the place. He, or they, attempted to get into the vaulted steel door but did not gain access. There was evidence they searched through my desk as well as the eight other desks in the building. The offices were a mess. Earlier, I'd had special steel rods inserted into all the file cabinets and that prevented access, so no file cabinets were opened. My first thought was that Addicks put someone up to it.

Remember Janet, my girlfriend? I had to push aside my sleuthing obsession to find private time with her and so, a few weeks before Christmas, I took her out to buy and decorate a Christmas tree for our apartment. Yes, we were living in sin prior to a possible engagement, but I effectively rationalized it to myself. Her presence in my life had helped me immeasurably through the past four months of turmoil. Janet and I tried to keep it a secret that we were living together because we knew our relatives would not approve. But how can a man have it any better than to cuddle with a woman he loves, every night, no matter how rotten or tough the daily routine is?

One weekend Janet and I visited my Aunt Sally Fox. Aunt Sally looked at Janet and said, "Stan, why buy the cow when the milk is so cheap?" I guess the family already knew we were sharing an apartment.

My Aunt Sally is a real character. At 67, she had more energy than any twenty-year-old. When Janet and I took Aunt Sally to her favorite store in Molalla, she chewed out the manager because the drip and spray system in the vegetable department was not working properly, and then she showed the manager how to fix it. I found it amusing how she had to make every dime count using coupons, even though she was a wealthy woman. Sadly, Aunt Sally was murdered six years later by a young man who worked for her. He had recently been released on parole, but high on drugs when he decided to commit a robbery. The man beat Aunt Sally to death with the butt end of her own rifle when she caught him stealing. The murderer was apprehended in Texas a week later, after cashing some of the checks he stole from Aunt Sally's home. It turned out the young man was the son of a local sheriff who had worked for Aunt Sally twenty-five years earlier on her farm. The sheriff had asked Aunt Sally to hire his son as a favor, so she could instill good morals and a work ethic.

In the previous month I had made a few commitments to wax aircraft for Aero Air, Flightcraft, and Western Skyways on weekends. I thought if Janet and I spent some time working together on these jobs, and then had a nice dinner afterwards, it would provide valuable time together. But that was not her idea of a romantic weekend and Janet put her foot down.

These long hours at the office were taking its toll on our relationship. She told me straight out that we were not spending enough quality time with each other, and she was right. So, we made plans to get away for a few days. We decided to spend the first night of our trip at the Inn at Spanish Head in Lincoln City on the Oregon coast, then fly to Las Vegas, Nevada, for two days. Neither of us had ever gambled nor been to Las Vegas. We agreed to take $200 cash for gambling.

The day of our departure was warm and sunny, rare for Oregon, so we decided to first fly my plane to a nice picnic spot on a small grass runway north of Battleground, Washington. The place I had in mind was a romantic location with private meadows and no homes or roads nearby.

The airplane gently skimmed the soft grass as we landed. I could see the river next to the runway was still flowing within its banks. The yellow and white paint job of the plane was a beautiful contrast to the green park-like setting.

As soon as we landed Janet asked, "Where's the bathroom?"

"Oops," I said. "There aren't any out here." Embarrassed, she disappeared among ferns and trees and quickly returned. But just as we set out the blanket on the warm grass, clouds started to roll in. We were determined to persevere and were enjoying a very romantic picnic when it began to rain. Within minutes we were soaked and our fantasy was ruined. As quickly as we could, we packed up and flew out of there. We decided to return home and change our clothes before leaving for the coast.

In no time at all, we were on our way to the coast in Janet's green Ford Pinto. We started laughing about how miserable that picnic was for us. I do not know why I decided to try a picnic in the winter, as rain showers are constant that time of year. We figured we'd make it up to ourselves and try another picnic when the weather was warmer.

By the time we arrived at the Inn at Spanish Head in Lincoln City, we were both exhausted.

The Inn is a ten-story concrete structure attached to the side of a cliff that stretches down to the sands of the Pacific Ocean. From our room, we could open the sliding glass door, smell the salty air, and hear the roar of the ocean below. The waves crashed within 30 feet of the hotel's concrete wall during high tide.

We shared a candlelight dinner with a bottle of chilled white wine from our kitchenette room after cooking seafood bisque. Later, in a warm cuddle, we drifted off as the sound of the ocean gently faded into the background.

The next morning we awakened to the calls of seagulls squawking on our patio. After a stroll on the beach below the hotel, we had a wonderful breakfast in their tenth floor restaurant overlooking miles of ocean. Taking in the colorful westward expanse of the Pacific Ocean, I said aloud, "This is where life begins."

The ocean stimulates many human emotions and memories. Sometimes I look out over the ocean and feel sorrow. I send forth a silent prayer for the hundreds of thousands of sailors from Japan and America lying in its depths. I could not help but remember the stories my dad told us kids about his adventures in the Pacific and Hawaii during World War II. Those sailors buried at sea probably never enjoyed the sweet experience of a night with a lover, since most who fought and died out there were young men and teenage boys.

From Lincoln City, we drove through the Coast Range on our way to the Portland Airport. This scenic drive is breathtaking, with its curvy roads and endless forests of 150-foot tall fir trees lining the highway. In only two hours—on Western Airlines—we arrived in Las Vegas and checked into our room. We rested a short while, then wandered around the casino, astonished by the lights and sounds of the slot machines. We cautiously pulled out a $20 and exchanged it for nickels. Since I had never played poker or cards in my life, the only thing we did was put those nickels into slot machines for two days, and ate many fatty meals. Since I weighed 165 pounds and I'm six feet, three inches tall, I could eat all day and not gain a pound, or so I thought. Janet and I had a great time.

On the flight back to Portland, I looked at Janet and imagined that someday, maybe, she and I would have several kids. Then I wondered if we would make it to that point since my long hours interfered with our relationship. As usual, my attention was quickly diverted and I started talking to her about the investigation and problems preparing Columbia Bookkeeping for the upcoming tax season. Janet and Gary were my only sounding boards about Rod Addicks, the investigation, and business concerns.

Would clients return? Rod Addicks and Sam Moll had been the two highest-volume tax preparers, handling over 75 percent of all our clients' tax returns in the main Stark Street office. Only one tax preparer, Jan Hildreth, would be returning to the main office. I started fretting again as my mind went back into overdrive. Would the clients go somewhere else? Was the year-end tax tip letter I sent out enough to assure past clients that we still had their tax files and an experienced staff who could handle their tax preparation? We mentioned in the letter that their return would not cost one dime more than they had paid the previous year, no matter what.

With Janet sitting next to me, I began to review my checklists for the upcoming tax season. I knew I'd have to stay on top of all company operations since the options were certain: we would either lose the company, or survive, and the mold would be cast in the next four months. If we were successful, Columbia Bookkeeping would generate 90 percent of its annual profit between January and May 1. The business would be worthless if the clients did not return.

I began explaining to Janet the State of Oregon's CPA and preparer's licensing rules. As a CPA firm we could not advertise in the newspapers, on television, or on the radio, and there could be no large signs on our building. Due to those state licensing restrictions, my dad had decided to be a non-CPA accounting firm. Just last year, however, Oregon was the first state in the United States to grandfather in, without a test, all prior non-licensed tax preparers. They now require future preparers to take a written state examination before they are allowed to prepare tax returns for money. Because Gary had worked for H&R Block for two tax seasons and was entering the second year in his own tax accounting practice, he was grandfathered in. I explained we could use Gary's license temporarily, if we needed to, since we had let Rod Addicks go.

I told Janet that I would take the State of Oregon Tax Board Examination the next year to become licensed. Over half the tax preparers I interviewed for the upcoming tax season were grandfathered in as licensed preparers, but they had flunked my interview questions anyway.

"This conversation is not very romantic," Janet finally blurted out as we were flying home over the Cascade Mountains. So we returned to the subject of our future relationship, a topic Janet preferred. We spoke again about our concerns about a future together, specifically, would I have enough time for us. I was obviously preoccupied with the tax business and the investigation and Janet mentioned she might be transferred by her company to Seattle. It became apparent to us both that things between us might not work out.

Chapter 12: New Detectives Assigned

I went back to the office the day after New Years. By then I had already hired the tax preparers for the upcoming tax season to replace Rod Addicks and Sam Moll. I made sure the staff understood my new policies, which I developed with the help of Julie Syler and Peg. The one item I thought was missing from the files of past tax clients was a formal checklist. Previous preparers used a yellow pad and took handwritten notes. To remedy this, I created a basic checklist of questions to ask each client so that each of the tax preparers would need only to check boxes Yes or No, rather than take notes. Additionally, I had our lawyer Jim Auxier prepare an employee agreement form that included a covenant Not-To-Compete and a dress code for men and women. It was important that we really look professional when the new staff met with clients in our offices.

I became so wrapped up in getting everything organized for the tax season that my obsessions and office responsibilities doubled. I had to close down my aircraft waxing business completely since I had no time to handle those tasks. I was determined to stay focused on both Columbia's bookkeeping business and my dad's murder investigation. But I didn't want to sell the aircraft business in case I had to jump back into it if Columbia Bookkeeping failed.

The phones at Columbia started ringing for appointments. Many clients asked for Rod Addicks or Sam Moll to help prepare their tax returns. I wrote out a script for the receptionist to use when responding to those requests. 'I'm sorry. Rod Addicks left the company to handle personal problems up in Washington. However, all your tax records are here and we have other licensed and experienced professional tax preparers to assist you. May I make an appointment?' If that didn't work then the clients could talk to me.

While focused on the tax business, I incurred three vacancies in my personal apartment building, which I had no time to handle myself. I decided to just take the losses on potential rent and find someone who could clean them for me. After several weeks, I found a tenant who was behind on her rent and she agreed to clean the empty apartments and show them to prospective tenants in exchange for what she owed me. In January, the boiler of that apartment complex broke down and so the building had no hot water or heat. I had to use my personal credit line to arrange an upgrade. The boiler room looked like the inside of a submarine with all its pipes and pressure valves. I was becoming fatigued with too many competing worries.

On January 3, 1975, I received a call from a newly assigned homicide detective named Rod Englert who said he and Detective Joe Woods had taken over the case. "I'd like to go over all the information you've forwarded to the prior detectives and then bring you up-to-date on what we intend to do," Englert said. So, we set up a meeting at our office for January 8.

Before we hung up, I said, "Great, I'm glad you're on this case. Have you talked to detectives Blackie Yazzolino and Wells yet?"

"We sure have," Englert said. "And Blackie prepared a written summary for us. I can tell you straight out that Blackie agrees with you. Rod Addicks is hiding something and he may be involved in your father's murder. But don't worry, Stan, we aren't going to let you down. Have patience with us. We'll see you soon."

I feared the investigation was starting all over again from scratch, but Detective Englert's words gave me a glimmer of hope. At least he was asking the right questions.

Since I did not yet have a personal license to prepare tax returns, I made myself helpful by going into the lobby to greet the clients personally. I wanted them know the family was serious about carrying on my father's business. I even had a large framed photo of my father and my grandfather's lumber mills hung in the lobby of each office. I paid for a half-page advertisement in a local newspaper promoting the Turel Family History. The ad was designed to look like a news article, as opposed to an advertisement. It contained information that made our family and business appear stable. Most clients had to wait at least five minutes in the lobby, so they had the opportunity to read the article which I'd enlarged and framed. It was the only thing in the lobby for the clients to read, and people would comment positively when the tax preparers ushered them in. I had learned the value of advertising from my aircraft business   people want quality, reasonable prices, and fast service. If people feel connected to your business they are more likely to stay. History connects people.

I increased the number of phone lines to five and doubled the number of receptionists at the main office. I wanted to ensure that every incoming call did not ring more than three times, or I would pick up the phone myself. The phone started ringing off the hook by January 5. The system was starting to work, but I was still a nervous wreck because several clients mentioned that Rod Addicks told them he was forced out of the company. Was Addicks calling clients directly from his home in Kelso, Washington? Also, my lawyer sent a letter informing me that I could be removed as executor if Rod Addicks' lawyer really did file and win a lawsuit regarding my refusal to forward to him the title of the red Cadillac.

One client brought in a business card Rod Addicks had given to him with Addicks' home address and home phone number printed on it. That made me suspect Addicks was planning to prepare tax returns of some of our clients. It would be easy for him to make over $10,000 in three months from his home. This meant he might accumulate enough money to split the country.

On a Sunday in early January, the Columbia Bookkeeping office building was broken into again. Not much damage was done, although the desks in each office were ransacked. Since I normally went into the office on Sundays, I was able to assist the cleaning lady, Betty Smith, and help her straighten the disorder before we opened on Monday. The person or persons who broke in came through one of the back doors this time. The special reinforced steel bars I'd had inserted in the 20 file cabinets that held our client records were again effective in restricting unauthorized access. Plus, I'd had the safe's vault room entry reinforced, and the thugs weren't able to break it down. Immediately afterwards, I contracted with a company to reinforce all our doors with large stainless steel strike plates, based on police recommendations.

As I had been doing for the last four months, I sat calmly behind my dad's large oak desk while handling calls or moments of crisis even though my gut was tied up in knots. Quietly, out of sight of persons on the other side of the desk, I would press my fingernails against the outside edge of the desk. Without realizing it, I had been making numerous deep grooves in the wood. My nervous tic was destroying the perfect condition of the outer edge of the desk.

The very next day I moved my office upstairs to a corner of the large Processing Department. I took my locked file cabinet and the company checkbooks with me. This room was large enough to continue to be a processing center, where returns were checked and copied.

By then I also was responsible for the four apartment properties managed by Quality Financial Planning, oversight of Columbia Bookkeeping, and my own rentals. I had nine business checking accounts to oversee. I set up a routine that gave me three days a month to pay bills. I delegated payroll to Julie Syler, the bookkeeper. I felt safe up in my new office space, as there were no windows. Yes, I had become paranoid enough to believe that someone might try to shoot at me through a window. Whenever the detectives or someone else wanted to talk with me privately, I would still use my dad's office downstairs.

On January 5, the detectives called me again with more questions.

On January 8, Detectives Rod Englert and Joe Woods came to my office for the first time. When I first met Englert and Woods they appeared so young compared to Blackie Yazzolino; they were probably in their mid-thirties. Rod Englert was nicely dressed in his tan suit and did most of the talking. I was prepared with copies of all the items I had forwarded to Blackie Yazzolino in the last few months. The items I focused on, however, began with the signed receipts from Copeland Lumber, with Lee Cartwright's signature, proving that Dennis Lee Cartwright of Lee's Construction was in town the day Dad was murdered. I explained that Rod Addicks lied when he said Lee Cartwright had never worked for the apartments prior to Dad's death, and he may have lied when he said Cartwright had never met my dad. I was surprised that Blackie Yazzolino had not relayed to the new detectives the importance of these documents that connected Rod Addicks, Sam Moll, and Dennis Lee Cartwright.

The next few items I reviewed with the detectives was the $2 check that tied Rod Addicks to a possible house arson, checks to Sam Moll, and the transfer of property title from Sam Moll to Dennis Cartwright. Additionally, I pointed out that Addicks made it impossible for us to talk to Sam Moll when he said he did not have the man's phone number. I explained that my brother, Gary, had been to a tax update class in Eugene in late September or October where he sat with Rod Addicks and Sam Moll during the seminar. Before that seminar, whenever I wanted to call

Sam Moll, Addicks told me that he had not seen Moll, and did not know how to get in touch with Moll. I told the detectives that Gary and I decided not to delve into Rod Addicks' lies. I showed them the flip-up phone directory that had originally been in Addicks' office. As they examined the names scribbled in Addicks' handwriting, I watched their eyebrows rise. So I gave the directory to them, too. I suggested that the detectives go to my brother's office in North Portland to verify what I was saying. I heard back from Gary that they did come to his office the very next day.

Then I raised the topic of Addicks' refusal to take the polygraph test and from there, a review of Addicks' massage parlor accounts. I showed the detectives a summary showing a potential $103,000 loss to Rod Addicks if he left the company and was exposed for wrongdoing. I reminded them that my dad had been making background inquiries about Rod Addicks, following up on his own suspicions that Addicks had been involved in an arson. I explained my concerns that my dad may have stumbled onto an arson ring, and that was why he may have been murdered. I then showed Detective Rod Englert the first draft of the one-page $5,000 reward statement that my lawyer, Jim Auxier, had dictated to me over the phone. Englert asked me to keep the copy for now. I said I was planning to offer the reward if the police thought it would be appropriate.

I asked Detective Englert if they would go up to Washington to investigate Sam Moll and Dennis Lee Cartwright. I mentioned that Blackie Yazzolino could not get permission for the trips and that several times he had mentioned that his boss would not give him funding for trips to Tacoma and that he felt political pressure to back off the case prior to his retirement. "If you guys cannot get funding, I will be happy to provide the transportation up there. I'm tired of waiting. If the bosses will not let you go up there, maybe my brother and I will hire our own detectives to investigate Sam Moll and Dennis Cartwright. We do not want to interfere with the police investigation, but we need to get some movement on this case."

"Sheriff Lee Brown has approved our time to focus on the case," Detective Englert said. "Stan, don't worry about that anymore. One way or another we will investigate those guys up there. We will even go up there at our own expense, if we have to."

"No offense," I said, "but how much experience have you had with homicides?"

"This is my first job in this Homicide Department, but I worked for over six years in the Narcotics Department, and helped on several homicide cases." Englert said.

Oh, great, I said to myself, not only do these guys have little experience, but they look so green and young compared to Blackie Yazzolino. However, I could see they were eager to follow through with the documents and my list of suspicions, including the massage parlors.

"Mr. Turel, we are taking this case seriously," Englert said, "and we plan to put a lot of extra time and effort in to solve this case."

Detectives Englert and Woods seemed interested in Rod Addicks' written summary about D.B. Cooper. "Addicks probably considers himself of superior abilities and knowledge to everyone else," Englert laughed. "I've dealt with that kind of individual before and their overconfidence is usually their downfall." During this conversation, detectives Englert and Woods came across as very determined and quite personable. Rod Englert resembled Clint Eastwood, but with higher energy and more aggressive. I was hopeful he would be more pushy than Detective Yazzolino.

They even took the envelope that contained the $480 refund check from Lee's Construction and tested it for fingerprints to see if Addicks had been the one that sent the check. The detectives told me they wondered if Dennis Cartwright even existed at first. Was he a front for Rod Addicks? I explained that Blackie Yazzolino already confirmed that Dennis Lee Cartwright was on parole from the Washington State prison. I was surprised Blackie Yazzolino had not mentioned that piece of information to them.

I received a few follow up calls from Detective Englert the following week, asking for clarification on various documents. A few days later, he called to ask if I really had the money available to offer the $5,000 reward. I said, "Yes, everyone in the family has agreed to offer the reward, which would be funded through Columbia Bookkeeping."

And unbeknownst to me, the following week the detectives contacted Mr. Shannon, the head of all those massage parlors. They met with Mr. Shannon at his home in the presence of some of his "ladies" and associates. Then they quietly interviewed the ladies separately, away from Shannon, at which point it was confirmed the women were prostitutes. A few of them agreed to testify against Mr. Shannon if it became necessary. None of the people interviewed knew anything about the murder of Jim Turel.

Just days later, the detectives called me again and we carefully went over the checks and documents relating to Lee's Construction, including the $2 check that Rod Addicks wrote involving a property transfer between Sam Moll and Dennis Lee Cartwright, and the $400 check written to Sam Moll. I referred Englert and Woods to Jack Miller at First Interstate Bank, in case they needed originals from Addicks' personal checking account. And I asked them to talk to Jack Miller about my dad's suspicions about Rod Addicks' involvement with arson. I finally felt the detectives were determined to get to the bottom of the questionable actions regarding Sam Moll and Lee's Construction. They seemed to truly want to understand the little interconnections. Detective Rod Englert assured me he was working long hours, even on the weekends, following through on all details about Addicks, Lee Cartwright, and Sam Moll. This Englert guy seemed to be really focused on connecting the dots.

Gary and I continued to talk on the phone every evening to compare numbers on how many tax clients had come in that day. We were both working 60 to 70 hours each week. During that time, I kept Gary and my sisters informed on the new detectives' progress, but I gave them very little concrete information. On her own, my older sister called Rod Addicks and acted like she knew nothing, just to get a sense of his state of mind about the investigation. She said Addicks was still acting as if he cared about the family and tried to convince her that he was really our dad's best friend. Again Addicks had explained to her that he was only following the advice of his attorney, which was why he couldn't cooperate with the police.

My sister forwarded the details of her phone conversations to the detectives. Individually, each of us kids was doing things we hoped would help the detectives. I was asked repeatedly not to discuss what Rod Englert shared with me with anyone else, including my sisters.

On January 15, 1975, the detectives came by our office again to go over summaries and documents relating to Sam Moll and Dennis Lee Cartwright. They had just returned from Linfield College where Rod Addicks had graduated. There they discovered Addicks had an IQ of 120 and an evaluation had assessed him as having superior intelligence. The fact that the detectives were finally focusing on Rod Addicks and Sam Moll pleased me.

That was when I was contacted by my father's second cousin, Amy, who said she had information she wanted to share. I arranged for a meeting with her and the detectives at my office. Amy said she strongly believed my stepmother wanted my dad dead. She said Bernie had even prayed that my dad would die. She said Bernie had told her directly, in person, that she hated my dad because he had been seeing other women during the same period when they were talking about a divorce. Both the detectives and I assured Amy that Bernie had taken and passed the polygraph test several months ago. I appreciated Amy's straightforward information, as she knew my dad and Bernie very well.

The detectives left my office at 2:30 p.m. and headed for the office of my lawyer, Jim Auxier, to review the case. Detective's notes from that day stated Auxier told the detectives, "I seriously suspect Bernie of the murder, or Rod Addicks." Based on the $2 check I showed Auxier, he then agreed with the detectives that Rod Addicks was hiding something and may have been involved with arson. Jim Auxier reminded me that he was the one who referred Addicks to attorney Bill Hanson.

Detective Blackie Yazzolino had already explained to me that since Jim Auxier had been the attorney for both Addicks and my dad, I should not tell Auxier everything I was learning about the investigation. He said Auxier was the attorney who had handled the insurance claim on Sam Moll's house fire. But by then I trusted Jim Auxier totally since he'd been helping me engineer every aspect of getting Rod Addicks out of the business while avoiding a lawsuit.

I must clarify that in early September 1974, Jim Auxier broke off most ties with Rod Addicks. I was present when Auxier said to Addicks he could not represent both my dad's estate and Addicks. I felt comfortable with Auxier, but I continued to follow the detective's advice about not divulging too much information to him or anyone else in the family. These new detectives were interviewing everyone involved in the case again, as if the investigation was starting over from scratch. Detectives Englert and Woods were actually going deeper into the documents relating to my suspicions of Sam Moll and Dennis Lee Cartwright than Detective Yazzolino had ever done. I was impressed. Years later when I read over the detectives' notes of their first few weeks of the investigation, it turned out they had interviewed the managers of each of the apartments and some of the massage parlors. But no leads came out of those interviews.

Unbeknownst to me, detective notes from January 18, 1975 revealed an interesting connection. A realtor named Patricia had handled a few real estate transactions for Rod Addicks. During her interview, she said that at first the earnest money was in Addicks' name, but then it was transferred to third parties. The detectives' notes stated that Patricia seemed nervous and soon retained a lawyer. Later, she explained that Rod Addicks had taken her to the site where a house had burned down and he told her, 'Sam Moll and I were responsible for burning the house but the police cannot prove it because Sam and I have established iron clad alibis.'

On January 21, as the tax season ramped up, I had another call from my lawyer, Jim Auxier. "Rod Addicks' attorney called me again and is threatening to sue you for not following through with the Cadillac title transfer."

"Jim, please stall them until the middle of February," I said. "Promise Addicks money, but don't put anything in writing, and maybe some new leads will pop up by then. Rod Addicks is not going to get one damn dime from me until he is cleared of all wrongdoing!"

Then the inevitable conversation took place with Janet after one of my 12-hour workdays and a sleepless night. Janet said she had accepted the job in Seattle and was leaving the following week. Our relationship was over.

This news was expected, but it added to the stress I felt from the pressures of the tax season and worrying if Rod Addicks had put someone up to the breaking and entering. The next day, when I was preparing to sign some checks, I found that my hand was so shaky I couldn't sign my name. I couldn't believe it. I knew I was uptight, but I thought I was holding it all together. When I tried to write down a phone number, my handwriting was so wiggly the digits were unrecognizable. Was I on the edge of a nervous breakdown? I decided I needed to leave the office and get some fresh air right then.

I drove to Troh's Airpark, a secluded hilltop of trees near what had been my dad's home. As the wind blew through the trees, I made a prayer to God. I quietly said, "I have done my best and done everything possible to help solve Dad's murder. Dear God, I now place this in your hands." I went home that afternoon feeling exhausted, and I slept all night through.

The next day, January 22, I went to the office determined to step back and ease up on everything. The investigation was in police hands now and I needed to redirect my attention to make the best of Dad's business.

That afternoon, Detective Rod Englert called and delivered the best news I'd heard in a long time. First he said in a serious but calm voice, "The case is solved but don't tell anyone yet. Sam Moll has just confessed—with his attorney present—that Rod Addicks and Dennis Lee Cartwright killed your father." Then Rod Englert said it again, "You must keep this to yourself. Do not breathe a word of this, not even to your family. No one must know except you, other than the detectives and the District Attorney's office. And, Stan," Englert said, lowering his voice to a whisper, "if what Sam Moll told us is true, then Rod Addicks is much more dangerous than we could ever have imagined. I can't tell you all the details at this time, and we cannot arrest anyone until we investigate further. But I will keep in touch."

I felt as though a ton had just been lifted off my back. It was as though my prayer had been answered, and much more quickly than I ever dreamed. I thought, yesterday was the first day I had ever asked God for help in the investigation, and there it was! My Christian belief that good eventually triumphs over evil was reinforced.

Just as I hung up the phone with Englert, still reeling with what I had just been told, Julie Syler knocked and opened the door with a panicked look on her face. "There's a very angry client in the front lobby making a big scene," she said. "He doesn't want to pay our fee for his return!"

I walked to the front lobby and approached a short stocky man who was visibly angry. His face was red and his body was shaking. "Hello," I said. "I'm sure we can work this out. How can I help you?"

In a loud voice the man demanded to see the boss. I responded with a smile, "You're looking at him. Let's go into my office and figure this out." Actually, my goal was to get him out of the front office where the lobby was full of clients waiting for their tax interviews.

As we walked back to my office, I thought that solving this man's problem would be nothing compared to the murder investigation. I was still feeling a great exhilaration over the good news from Detective Englert.

Wow, the case is solved! I was grinning.

I asked the angry man what the problem was and within a few minutes I saw how we could work things out. "Even though the fee you were charged is correct," I said, "there seems to have been a misunderstanding about our fee structure. My policy is to make things right. So, I will reduce your $45 fee to $20."

The man looked at me in disbelief and said, "You know, I can't believe you're so nice and I apologize for losing my temper."

I walked backed out to the lobby with the now-calm man and said, in front of the waiting clients, "Have a good day. I'm glad we were able to work things out."

"Thank you," the man said, "I'll be back next year."

I wasn't concerned with the reduction of the fee. My policy is the client is always right, whenever possible, if we can afford it. A happy client will send referrals, but an unhappy client will tell 20 people what a rotten business you run.

Years later, when talking with Detective Englert, I learned that the detectives had travelled to Tacoma and interviewed Sam Moll at his place of employment. Moll said he wanted to talk to his attorney and the detectives accommodated. Englert said he told Sam Moll and his attorney that this was Moll's one chance to help with the case. The evidence he showed them was conclusive—Rod Addicks' $2 check transferring a house from Sam Moll to Dennis Lee Cartwright on a third planned arson.

"You should have seen the look on their faces when I mentioned realtor Patricia's testimony about Rod Addicks bragging about burning down the house with Sam," Englert said. "Sam and his attorney knew he was caught in the arson ring. All of a sudden Zderic and Moll were anxious to make a deal."

From Englert's notes of January 20 and 22, 1975:

January 20, 1975

1 p.m. We followed Sam and Francine Moll to his attorney's office, Ben Zderic. We laid out the whole case and Sam Moll denied any involvement in Arson. Attorney wanted offer of blanket immunity for Sam and then said he would talk to us again at 4 p.m.

January 22, 1975

4 p.m. Met again with Moll and his attorney and he said he wanted to talk to Multnomah District Attorney Schrunk about immunity. Sam Moll could have devastating evidence on the arsons and very important evidence on the Homicide. Learned that Addicks talked about hating Turel to Moll prior to the murder and planned on killing him. We left his office at 5:30 p.m. We called District Attorney Schrunk and Purcell and advised of Moll wanting immunity.

Detective Rod Englert called me at the office informing me about a possible immunity for Sam Moll. "Stan," he said, "do you object if we give Sam Moll immunity for arson and his knowledge of the murder if he agrees to become a State witness? We're going to meet with Sam Moll's attorney at 1 o'clock tomorrow afternoon on an offer, if Mr. Schrunk approves."

"That's okay with me," I said. "Immunity is fine, as long as Sam Moll wasn't involved in actually killing my dad."

That evening I left the office for my home around 10 p.m. I felt guilty leaving so early as there were still four tax preparers working when I left the building. I made myself a White Russian to relax, as I was exhausted with joy that something was finally happening in the murder case. I was fast asleep when the phone rang at 3 o'clock in the morning. Detective Englert was on the phone to verify that the $5,000 reward was still available. He told me that he had not mentioned the reward to Sam Moll or Moll's attorney yet.

"Yes, the reward money is just waiting there," I said. "If I can help out in any way please let me know." I also promised again I would not say anything to anyone.

As I continued reading Detective Englert's notes, I learned what had taken place in Tacoma back in January 1975:

Continuation Report, from page 5 of 8 pages
Case Number: 74-18471
Classification: HOMICIDE
Reporting Officers: RE/JW

January 23, 1975

3 a.m. Called Stan Turel and verified $5,000 Reward.

9 a.m. Called Mike Schrunk in Portland and he advised that he had talked to Sam Moll's Attorney, Ben Zderic, and arrangements made on immunity.

11 a.m. Went to Zderic's office and he came in at noon. Went to restaurant and he said Moll was involved in 2 arsons with Addicks where Addicks collected. Also he mentioned a fraud that we were unaware of. Sam Moll and Himself would come to Portland and talk to the D.A. Had to get everything in writing as to immunity. Etc.

January 24, 1975:

8:45 a.m. Called Zderic at his home. He said Moll lost his job over us interviewing him at his Job.

9:15 a.m. I called Mr. Gray at Gray's Business Service and got Moll his job back.

9:30 a:m. Called Zderic, Sam Moll's attorney, back and advised him of Moll getting his job back and that $5,000 Reward existed. Wanted to make sure that Moll wasn't influenced and inflated testimony over reward. Zderic said that he learned that Sam lived in Apt. in Portland and Addicks had Key made to Sam's apartment and planned to Burrow with Cartwright into next apartment to rip off a wealthy old man who kept money there. Sam said that they would have killed the old man if caught. Plans fell thru.

MOLL added that while he lived in the Parkview Apartments, Unit #67, in Vancouver, Washington, that he had a neighbor in Unit #68 who appeared nuts. this neighbor reportedly talked to himself, gave speeches in his apartment in a loud voice as though talking to a very large audience, and MOLL theorized that the man in Unit 68 was an heir to a large estate. Further that he had no family or close relatives and no visitors.

ROD and SAM MOLL cased apartment #68 and determined that there were several large trunks in the apartment and whenever the occupant would leave his apartment that everything was packed up as though ready to move – including all the bedding which was stripped from the bed and packed in the trunks. Occupant in #68 appeared tall, slim, avoided conversation, owned a 4 wheel drive vehicle white in color which he chained up on all 4 wheels during the slightest snow or icy conditions. Occupant of unit #68 also had extra locks on all doors and taped around the doors and windows as though he were attempting to keep out the slightest bit of dust. ROD ADDICKS and SAM MOLL decided to burglarize unit 68, and one evening, ADDICKS did burglarize the place by breaking the patio door with a crowbar. The burglary turned out quite unsuccessful as ADDICKS could not break the stronglocks on the trunk after he gained entry. ROD ADDICKS stayed with SAM MOLL in unit #67 last year and while he was there, he had a key made. Meanwhile, DENNIS CARTWRIGHT had come to the area and as late as December 7, 1974, ROD ADDICKS, DENNIS CARTRIGHT, and SAM MOLL had discussed using the key to enter unit #67 and then burrow through the wall to unit #68 to use some bolt cutters and burglarize the trunks. Additionally, they would use MOLL's walkie-talkies and MOLL would act as a lookout man while ADDICKS and CARTRIGHT went inside...

January 24, 1975 continued:

11 a.m. Called Patricia (the realtor) and she said she wanted to talk to attorney before talking anymore. I asked her to have her attorney call me and she said she would.

2 p.m. Attorney Zderic called and related that night before (1-23- or 1-22), Moll called Addicks and Addicks came to Tacoma next day. They discussed the arsons. Addicks made some incriminating statements like "well, you know nothing about the murder" plus others that Zderic didn't want to reveal at this time. Sam Moll wants to testify on the Murder but not on the Arsons if we can avoid that. Said they would still cooperate.

7:30 p.m. Called Patricia at her home and I mentioned or asked if Rod Addicks called her and she refused to answer saying that she wanted to consult with her attorney Sid Brockman before talking any further. Seems now that since Sam Moll talked to Addicks, Rod in turn called Patricia and is now intimidating her. I asked if she was being intimidated by anyone and she said that if she got hurt she hoped it would be on our conscience.

January 25, 1975:

8:45 a.m. Called Mrs. Moll at her home in Milton asking for her Attorney.

9 a.m. Called Zderic at his home. He said everything was set for Friday. I told him I felt Addicks had called and intimidated Patricia. He said that a case against Addicks was developing stronger and that we should consider intimidation and Arson proceedings against Addicks. Said that Moll still wanted to cooperate fully and would still testify on the arsons if really necessary.

1:15 p.m. Zderic called me and said Sam Moll had told him the murder was premeditated and that Moll was told that Addicks and Cartwright planned and committed the murder and Moll was aware of the whole thing and he would tell the whole story for immunity on the arsons and Murder. I told him I would call him back after talking to D.A. Schrunk et al. Zderic also wanted $500 for attorney fees.

SAM A. MOLL also related to the detectives that on December 10, 1974, that ADDICKS, CARTWRIGHT, and MOLL met at JOHNNY'S DOCK in Tacoma, Washington, to go fishing. No fish, so they drank beer, talked of murder and Police harassment. ADDICKS had remarked the Police were dumb, they hadn't talked to DENNIS CARTWRIGHT or ROD and inquired if the Police had talked to SI. SAM MOLL said, "No, but who did it?" With that, ROD ADDICKS said, "I did it," and there were no further details. Still, on December 10, 1975, ADDICKS, CARTWRIGHT and MOLL went to another tavern, Barnacle Bill's. They joked, drank beer, and played pool, and at one point in the evening, MOLL heard CARTWRIGHT say, "You better watch out, I'll take your wire away from you." SAM MOLL thinks this conversation was related to the murder. They then travelled to SAM MOLL's house and had dinner and ROD ADDICKS picked up the pistol that he had furnished to SAM MOLL to kill JIM TUREL (please note that this was December 10 and a later investigation revealed that ADDICKS applied for a pistol permit in Kelso on December 11.)

January 25, 1975 continued:

2 p.m. Contacted Schrunk and conference call was set up between Zderic, Schrunk, Purcell, Woods and I. Negotiations were set up for immunity and Woods and I are to meet Zderic in Tacoma at his office on Sunday.

2:30 p.m. I called Stan Turel for $600 to cover $100 for expenses and $500 to the Attorney.

4 p.m. Picked up Mike Schrunk at courthouse and he drafted a small informal immunity to Sam Moll and his attorney. Schrunk agreed to the emergency advance by Stan Turel. Stan Turel brought reward stipulation in plus the $600 for the Tacoma expenses. Went home, packed, and picked up Woods.

On January 25, Rod Englert called to ask if I had money he could use to advance to Sam Moll's Attorney. He said the County would return the money to us soon. I said the money was available and sure, I would meet with him immediately, anywhere, to advance the money. Detective Englert mentioned that District Attorney Schrunk was aware of the emergency need to fund Sam Moll's attorney plus some expenses. He said the reward money would be a separate thing.

"We need to get those funds now because our department has no process to get money at this short of notice or on weekends. We'll be meeting with Zderic on Sunday," said Englert.

I met the detectives in downtown Portland and gave Englert a business check for $600 made out to Mr. Zderic, along with a copy of the reward statement. Englert mentioned that he had told Zderic about the reward yesterday, but confirmed that Moll had already told him about the murder and arsons before knowing about the reward.

Englert said. "Stan, this information must remain secret because we don't want to spook Sam Moll." I made the detectives sign a receipt for the check with a note that the County would pay us back.

Detective Englert's notes, January 26, 1975:

Left for Tacoma office and met Sam Moll and Zderic in Zderic's office and gave them Sam's informal immunity. Sam Moll then gave statement implicating Addicks and Cartwright in the Murder. Said he was hired also by Addicks to kill Turel for $5,000 but backed out. He also admitted to the arsons with Addicks. See Report on his Statements. Investigation now to center more on Cartwright. Arrangements were then made for Sam Moll to take Polygraph in Tacoma at Police Department at 10:30 Monday.

Late on Sunday evening, Englert called me again and said; "Sam Moll has admitted that Rod Addicks made several failed attempts to have your father killed. Be careful, Stan. Don't talk to Rod Addicks or anyone in your family, no one at all, about anything I've told you. I want to remind you that he is very dangerous, more dangerous than we thought."

Detective Englert's notes, January 27, 1975:

8:30 a.m. Met Ronald Owens, investigating unit of Tacoma Police Department. Went over Polygraph questions to be asked of Sam Moll.

10:45 a.m. Zderic and Moll showed up and Owens gave Moll Polygraph. He passed exam and brought up new co-conspirator Maddock Tollocko who was offered $10,000 contract. Sam also said he was paid $400 down payment to do the job and Rod let him keep it. Sam was also going to do the job with Maddock in June. Sam Moll gave me the key that Addicks gave him to the door of the Columbia

Bookkeeping office so that he could open the door in order to get in and shoot Turel. Booked key into evidence for comparison to the Turel keys.

On January 27, I received a short update from Detective Englert regarding Sam Moll's polygraph test in Tacoma that verified two arsons and three attempts Addicks made to murder my dad. Englert also said Multnomah County agreed to give Sam Moll total immunity involving the arson and murder cases, as long as he was not actually involved in murdering my dad. I had some misgivings about this immunity because Moll had hid the information all this time, but I also figured that Sam Moll was finally helping to solve the case. It was the biggest break the detectives had since my dad's death.

I called my brother and sisters and told them that these new detectives were really digging in many directions fulltime. Also I mentioned that it was good we had all taken the polygraph test, which allowed the detectives to focus on Rod Addicks, the only person who had refused. I shared a few more details with Gary, but did not tell my sisters a thing. I again warned my brother and sisters—for the second time—that none of us should contact Addicks as it would interfere with the detectives' investigation.

Detective Englert's notes January 28 and 29, 1975:
Lined up reports from Pasco on Cartwright. Set up meeting with DA etc. Called Patricia ("Addicks' realtor); her husband said she was in Oregon City with her Attorney. He said he didn't feel she was really involved and I told him that all we wanted was her cooperation. And by her talking to Addicks she was only getting herself in deeper.

10 a.m. Called Sam Moll and got description of the gun that Addicks gave to Sam to kill Turel with. Said it was a .38 blue steel revolver with brown wood grips.

10:30 a.m. Had long meeting with Don, Schrunk, Norm Brown, Bearden, Woods, Yazzolino, Purcell, Wells and discussed whole case. We need to dig up more info on Cartwright.

2:30 p.m. Called attorney Sid Brockman back and he said he represented Patricia and he requested we not contact her anymore and she refuses to take the polygraph. I advised him she would be subpoenaed to court and a lot will be brought out.
January 29, 1975

Left for Kennewick, Washington. Contacted a person at 1912 S. Quincy and she said she has been receiving mail of Cartwright. Dennis has not lived there for a year and his wife left about 2 weeks ago with another man. A man named Billy Anglin and his wife looked after the Cartwright home at 1609 19th Street in Kennewick.

3:30 p.m. Went to Kennewick Police Department and got help from detectives to locate Anglin.

4:30 p.m. Went to Anglin's home. Not there.

11 p.m. Went back and talked to Anglin's cousin and got another address. Cousin called Anglin's home and she said we could come over.

11:30 p.m. Went to Anglin's home. They said they had control of the Cartwright's home because Mrs. Cartwright was in Oklahoma. Mrs. Anglin and I went to the Cartwright home about midnight to look for Dennis Cartwright. She showed me several pictures of Dennis. She then related that Dennis had put a ribbon around her neck quite awhile ago called it a wire referring to method of choking a person to death. She said that Cartwright's wife left 2 weeks ago and said for her not to tell police anything about Dennis if they came around because it would get him into serious trouble. Dennis Cartwright's wife told Mrs. Anglin that she was afraid of Dennis and Rod because they may kill her. She said that if she got killed, that Rod Addicks and Dennis would be the suspects.

Mr. Anglin said that Cartwright solicited him to kill Turel during the earlier part of 1974 and again about June of 1974. Dennis offered Mr. Anglin $5,000 to hit Turel in the pool of his home. Dennis told him that the man to be hit was on crutches, had a swimming pool, was a bookkeeper and had lots of money. Mr. Anglin also said that he knew that Rod and Dennis were also stealing cars and running them to Canada for $300 to $500, then they would fly back.

Mr. Anglin also said that Cartwright told him he pool-cocked a man severely (knocking him out), in a tavern in the Kelso/Longview area with a pool ball. Mr. Anglin told Lt. Turner of Richland Police Department of the offer to kill someone.

Continuation Report, from page 3 of 4 pages
Case Number: 74-18471
Classification: HOMICIDE
Reporting Officers: RE/JW

CARTWRIGHT said that he (Addicks) would pay $5,000 for the completion of TUREL's death. They further reviewed it in detail and CARTWRIGHT related that MR. TUREL possibly drank quite a bit and they thought it best if it could be arranged of an accidental drowning in the swimming pool. BILLY related an alternate method of possibly just sniping him with a rifle from a long distance away and CARTWRIGHT did not like that idea because he wanted the death to appear accidental or natural or robbery. CARTWRIGHT had told BILLY that he preferred the death to look accidental to the point that there would be no further investigation and that it would be ideal for TUREL to drown because people would naturally say that's what crippled people do when they drink and get near a swimming pool. They talked in detail about the neighborhood and about ROD's benefiting from the death by insurance and they talked about the possibility of BILLY being interrupted during the drowning by TUREL's wife. CARTWRIGHT stated that would be better yet and just go ahead and kill MRS. TUREL too.... BILLY could not relate exactly the words that were said but he understood that CARTWRIGHT appeared to have cased the neighborhood and knew the activities of the other neighbors during certain times of day so that there would be relatively little problems in coming and going during the time the actual murder was to take place...

In September of 1974 DENNIS CARTWRIGHT asked BILLY if he would torch his house for him for $500.00. They also wanted him to torch some apartments in the Portland area that ROD ADDICKS owned. The apartments reportedly had a bad foundation but were fully covered by insurance.

BILLY ANGLIN said he was asked a total of two times to kill MR. TUREL for $5,000. It was either to drown him and make it look like a robbery and the two dates were in the later part of June or early July.

My dad's house was secluded and someone could easily sneak in through the unfenced back acre. It was creepy to think that so many people were discussing ideas of how to murder him. Billy Anglin later passed a lie detector test regarding his statements to the detectives.

On January 29, Detective Rod Englert called again and wanted to go over still more details about Dennis Lee Cartwright and the invoices from Copeland Lumber that proved Cartwright had been in Portland on August 28, 1974, the day my dad was killed. Englert asked me to look up the names Billy Anglin and Maddock Tollocko in our files. Tollocko was Sam Moll's cousin. They wanted to know if Columbia Bookkeeping had ever prepared tax returns for those two men. I did the research, but found nothing. I learned later, during the trial, that according to Moll, additional men had been offered money by Rod Addicks to kill my father. Sam Moll had gotten within a few yards of killing my father in his office during the prior summer, but he said he couldn't go through with it.

"Addicks' motive was to take over the tax business after Jim Turel was dead," Englert said and reminded me again that I was to keep all this information secret for the time being, even from my family. "Just tell Gary and your sisters that I'm following up on leads."

Both the homicide detectives and the IRS investigators called regularly asking me to verify if certain individuals were tax clients. The strange thing is that most requests came up empty. Even the receptionist's list of prior-year interviews and client appointments showed no matchups with the names. Rod Addicks had apparently done a good job keeping those people separate from the company.

Detective Englert's notes, February 1, 1975:

> *10:15 a.m. Got call from Zderic that Moll is scared. I called Moll at 10:30 and calmed him down. He said he talked to Rod Addicks the night before last (1-30-75) and nothing much said. Everything seems cool. And Rod still thinks we are only hanging him on the arsons.*

That afternoon Detective Englert came to my office to pick up more documents connecting Rod Addicks to Dennis Lee Cartwright. He clarified even more details about the numerous securities fraud lawsuits that had been filed against Rod Addicks in Tacoma in 1969. Apparently, Addicks had formed several real estate partnerships that went bad and those parties had not been able to find Addicks in order to serve him the summons. Addicks had disappeared by moving to Kelso to live in his mother's home, while using his wife's maiden name for a phone account. His prior problems explain why Rod Addicks, the CPA, was utterly broke and had no credit cards when he came to work for my dad in 1970.

All this caused me to ponder. Perhaps he wanted to get rid of my father because Dad suspected Rod Addicks was involved in arson. I remembered the year before Dad died, he had arranged for me to take over check-signing authority on the main business account in the event he became too sick to function. When I asked why, my dad told me he didn't trust Rod Addicks to handle the check-signing. According to Julie Syler, Dad had insisted on reviewing every check Addicks wrote on the apartment accounts. Perhaps Addicks felt my dad had discovered his nefarious background and was going to kick him out of the business. The financial summary that I had drawn up months ago showed that if Addicks was forced out of the business and apartments, he would lose somewhere between $80,000 and $103,000 in net worth, which would have been the second time Addicks would have gone broke and his reputation destroyed.

My dad knew nothing about Rod Addicks' past, except that he had graduated from Linfield College and was registered as a Certified Public Accountant in the State of Washington. Addicks presented himself as a family man with two kids and a beautiful wife. My dad respected and admired Addicks, and had often said what a wonderful and smart tax accountant Addicks was. Only after my dad suspected Addicks might have been involved in arson, did my dad's attitude begin to change. According to later testimony by Sam Moll, Rod Addicks came to hate my dad.

After Rod Englert explained all this to me, he again made me promise I would not divulge any of this information to anyone else, at least not until the detectives were ready to arrest Rod Addicks and Dennis Lee Cartwright. "We're only half way there," Englert said. "We still have to get more detailed information on Cartwright before we can arrest anyone. But time is now on our side since Sam Moll is talking."

Detective Englert's notes, February 4, 1975:

Flew to Tulsa, Oklahoma and then drove to Muskogee. Following morning drove to Stigler and contacted Haskell County Sherriff and he drove us to meet Cartwright's wife. She said she had no knowledge of the murder. However Dennis told Mrs. Cartwright in Kennewick prior to the murder that Rod wanted to get rid of his partner Jim Turel. She didn't take it as meaning murder at that time.

Mrs. Cartwright also said Dennis wanted to have Rod burn down their home in Kennewick about a year ago and collect the insurance. Said they would go to Kelso and be with friends while Rod Addicks would travel to Kennewick and burn the home. Mrs. Cartwright didn't want to and Dennis said he would remove all the valuables first and then have old things put in.

Mrs. Cartwright did not like Rod and she fears that Rod committed the murder. Mrs. Cartwright said that Dennis said Rod was from the Mafia and that Rod could hire people to Kill. She mentioned that Dennis is now staying in the Trailer and Rod Addicks has stayed with him, especially after a fight with his wife.

During that trip to Oklahoma, the detectives talked for hours with Mrs. Cartwright while gathering numerous names and phone numbers of friends. Plus they discussed other crimes committed. When the detectives returned to Portland they spent a lot of time following up on those names and interviewing over 30 people. They also went through Rod Addicks' flip-up phone directory from Columbia Bookkeeping and interviewed 20 women who said they knew Rod Addicks personally. Four women admitted to having extramarital affairs with Rod Addicks.

By early February the tax offices were very busy. In fact, for January we had the same number of clients that had been there the previous year. I created a few half-page ads that appeared in the local weekly newspapers, which I designed to deliberately look like feature newspaper articles. I was trying to market the company in innovative ways, while reassuring all our existing clients that all was well. My goal was to develop the image of a family business, even though no one in the family worked fulltime for the business except me.

Sometimes my older sister would come in when we needed her, mostly on weekends and evenings, to assist us in copying the completed forms. Her help was invaluable in our effort to deliver returns within 48 hours after the initial client interview. In the back of my mind, I was worried that rumors about who killed my dad might keep clients from returning for tax preparation. But the positive marketing, with a story attached, seemed to work better than just plain ads. I also personally wrote and produced a few radio ads and designed a company logo.

I placed large A-frame signs on the corners of our office property proclaiming, "48-HR TAX," which my dad had done in the past. I did this even though the City of Portland and Multnomah County warned me I could receive a ticket for violating their sign ordnance. In fact, I received a citation for leaving an A-frame sign in front of our office, so I began placing them out on the street corner on Friday evenings and removing them after the traffic rush on Monday mornings, since I knew that the citation officer wasn't working during those hours.

I remembered when my dad and I, a couple of years earlier, drove my van all over the city, placing over fifty 4x4-foot tax signs on vacant properties located on busy streets. Laughing all the way, we did this without a permit. We felt it was similar to a political campaign and we used the signs to promote the company's location and 48-hour turnaround tax service. The City immediately fined dad, but he paid the fine and said the free advertising was worth the cost. My dad enjoyed that day so much. He'd laughed and said it felt good to get even with the City's sign ordinance, which restricted the color and size of the sign on his newly constructed office building.

Even though business at the beginning of 1975 was good, there were still lots of struggles. From the day Addicks resigned, I worried he would do something to ruin the reputation of the company or continue calling his past clients to tell them he'd been forced out of the company.

I had to pretend Rod Addicks was not a suspect to the tax office staff. "Don't worry," I told the staff, "the detectives think that the murder of my dad was the result of a robbery." Occasionally my younger sister, who lived in Los Angeles, called asking for details. I told her, "What I am about to say is confidential. You can't repeat it to anyone. The new detectives are following through on leads about Rod Addicks and making some progress, but I don't know anything more." I asked her not to call Addicks as it might interfere with the investigation. Eventually she became irritated with me because she thought I knew more than I was saying. "We're offering a $5,000 reward, which might help," I told her. "If I knew more, I'd tell you." I hated not being able to tell her more, but I knew anything I said, however unlikely, might jeopardize the detectives investigation.

In addition, I was so busy with the tax season that I really didn't have a lot of time to talk to her, which irritated her even more. She continued asking many pointed questions about the investigation and our dad's estate matters. She wondered if we could draw money out of the estate or Family Trust. It was a reasonable question, but the answer was no. "Families have the right to know everything," she said. I told her I understood her concern and referred her to Jim Auxier, our estate lawyer, who explained everything to her several times. Auxier had sent everyone a copy of the will and assured me that he would forward copies of any estate papers to my family members as soon as they were filed.

I could understand my brother and sisters' disappointment and resentment. It looked like none of us children would ever receive a dime since Bernie Turel would most likely use up all the money in the Turel Family Trust within seven years. Jim Auxier did a great job of convincing Bernie, Gary, and my sisters, that my running the company was the only solution. The Turel Family Trust might provide a chance of money eventually, if the Trust could last until the eventual natural death of Bernie Turel.

I continued working 70-hour weeks at Columbia Bookkeeping. I wanted to be on location all hours to assure the staff that everything was safe and okay. Deep in my gut, as a tribute to my dad, I knew I was going to do everything I could to make sure his company would survive, despite the tragedy. I vowed that the person who killed him was not going to destroy Dad's lifetime efforts. Over the phone each day, Gary and I would compare the numbers of clients interviewed the day before. I rarely saw Gary during the tax season. He was busy in his own separate business, preparing tax returns for his clients, without any help. However, with Detective Englert's permission I did advise Gary on some of the developments in the investigation.

Late on a Saturday afternoon, two friends of mine dropped by the tax office and talked me into going out on the town. I did not like going to nightclubs because of the smoky air and noise, but I needed a break and John Winters and Larry Myers were unpredictable fun guys who always had a good time. John had a rough construction worker's appearance. Larry Meyers was a tall skinny guy with a great sense of humor. We were all the same age and occasionally would go out and have a good time.

For instance, after a nice dinner one night, we went downtown to an upscale nightclub. Immediately John, wanting to impress me said, "Stan, watch this," as all three of us sat down at the bar. John, of course, sat next to a couple of beautiful ladies. He leaned over to the one sitting closest to him and said, "Hello. How are you doing? Can I buy you a drink?"

The woman responded with an annoyed smirk and said, "No!"

I laughed at the put down as John again leaned over and spoke to her. "Lady, I'd don't expect anything. I just want to be friendly."

The woman then bluntly said, "Don't you understand? F… off."

John, wincing, turned to our buddy, Larry, and whispered, "Okay. Plan B."

Larry left without saying a word, and then returned within five minutes. Moments later, an announcement came across the loud speaker. "We have an emergency call for a Doctor Winters. Please call your office immediately!" With that, Larry said loud enough for the ladies to hear, "John, you'd better return your call!" As John stood up and left, I watched the lady lean over and whisper to her friend.

Five minutes later, John returned and told Larry, "The staff has it under control now." Of course the lady next to John was now interested. She leaned towards John and said, "Are you really a doctor?" John said, "Yes," and they began a conversation which eventually led to her accepting a future date with him, on which he never followed through. John and Larry have a few moves like this worked out in case they want to get a lady interested in them. I was amazed that John and Larry set that whole thing up and that it worked so well. I found the set-up funny, but deceptive. I could never pull off such a stunt and I could never predict what John and Larry would do next. But I felt comfortable around them because they never touched drugs or smoked.

One day, my little sister came up from Los Angeles and invited me to accompany her to a dance club and I agreed. When we arrived, we ran into a friend from her school days. The last time I'd seen her friend was when she was 13 years old. But, my goodness, in the ensuing five years, she'd developed into a beautiful and kind young lady. Soon after, she and I started dating, which eventually lead to our marriage. Due to the nature of this book, I will not include any further information about her or our future family, which eventually included four children.

Chapter 13: Getting Away

In early February 1975, I had several meetings with Jim Auxier on a proposed settlement to clear up Rod Addicks' option to buy stock in the business. Addicks and his attorney, Mr. Hanson, were growing increasingly irritated because I still would not forward the title to the Cadillac. I kept saying an agreement was just around the corner and Addicks would be getting money and the car's title soon. I had to tell Auxier, confidentially, that I thought I had proof of Addicks' involvement with the arsons and that time was on our side.

But based on the detective's instructions not to tell anyone anything, I did not inform Jim Auxier about the murder investigation progress. "Just stall Addicks and his lawyer legally, as much as you can," I told Auxier. I felt bad that I was not leveling with him on the progress that Detective Englert had made.

"The last thing you need now is a lawsuit," Auxier warned. "A lawsuit will become public knowledge and cause harm to the company during tax season." Auxier was a good coach, but hesitant about taking a risk.

Also that same day I had another visit from Detective Rod Englert who requested copies of more documents. I had given those documents to Detective Yazzolino months ago, but no problem. Detective Englert and I went over the details again and the Copeland Lumber Yard invoices that definitely placed Dennis Lee Cartwright and Rod Addicks in Portland on the day my dad was murdered. The documents provided proof that Addicks lied when he said Cartwright wasn't in Portland on August 28, 1974, which tied Addicks to the case in at least a cover-up of the murder.

On February 4, 1975, at the request of Detective Englert, I forwarded more money to Sam Moll's attorney, Mr. Ben Zderic, in Tacoma. I'd had no personal contact with Sam Moll or Mr. Zderic. Soon after, Detective Rod Englert asked me to forward more funds to Mr. Zderic. The money was to be used to hire a bodyguard to protect Sam Moll. Englert reminded me that whether or not Sam Moll qualified for the reward, Multnomah County would reimburse me for all the money, including expense money I'd advanced to them. I had no problem providing the money, as I was pleased the police were making such great progress. I just hoped that Rod Addicks and Dennis Lee Cartwright would be arrested soon, as I feared that Addicks would become suspicious of the mounting case against him, and split the country. This was another reason why I was making sure he received no money from us. I also advised Jack Miller at First Interstate Bank that I had proof about Rod Addicks' involvement in arson, and suggested that he not loan Addicks any money. I also arranged with some of the apartment building partners to hold off buying out Addicks' interest unless they checked with me first. I wanted to keep Addicks as broke as possible.

February 15 was a peak day at Columbia Bookkeeping. We interviewed over 200 tax clients at the Stark Avenue and Beaverton offices. One client, Mr. LaRoug, who had an appointment at the Foster Road office, called to complain that our young accountant had refused to put out his cigarette in front of his pregnant wife while they were being interviewed. I was so angry when I heard this that I hopped into my van and drove right over there. But I took a big, deep breath outside. I waited for the preparer to finish the client he was with and then I walked in and fired him on the spot.

In an angry fit, the young accountant took off his wig (which I hadn't realized was not his own hair), slammed it down on the desk and said, "You can't fire me, I quit!" His long hair that had been tucked away under the wig cascaded down below his shoulders, and he left in a huff. Wow, I thought, that was the first longhaired, tax-preparing hippy I'd ever met. He always wore a white shirt and tie. Who would have guessed? The receptionist and I had a good laugh at the surprise of it all. And truly, other than the cigarette issue, this tax consultant was a very smart and gifted person. The quality of his work was excellent. I would have kept him on if it were not for his lack of respect for the client and the pregnant woman.

The client, from the LaRoug Jewelers family, never returned despite my personal call and apology. I informed Mr. LaRoug that I had fired the jerk and offered a free return, but the offer had no effect. That incident continued to bother me for years.

It angered me even more when the Oregon State Employment Department considered granting him unemployment benefits. I was already in the process of contesting their award of unemployment benefits to Rod Addicks, who wasn't fired and therefore should not have been eligible for benefits. I couldn't tip my hand to the Employment Department as to why Rod Addicks quit, other than to tell them he was a suspect in an arson investigation and had legal issues regarding charges of securities fraud in the State of Washington. The Employment Department told me that until proof came out that Rod Addicks was guilty of anything, it appeared as though he was pressured into resigning. I did not want him to have access to any financial support including unemployment benefits, if I could help it.

On February 15, 1975, my appeal to the Oregon Employment Department was heard. I met with the State reps and presented my argument and copies of the documents I had forwarded to them earlier. The documents proved Addicks had quit. Then, I was told that all his benefits would be cancelled if I could prove he had done something wrong. I had all the documents to prove he had mismanaged Quality Financial and had not kept client books up-to-date, which placed Columbia Bookkeeping in jeopardy. By the end of the meeting, the State's determination was that Rod Addicks was disqualified for benefits and as of that date, they were officially cancelled.

Detective Englert's notes, February 14 and 15, 1975 (in Kelso, Washington):

5 p.m. Contacted Rod Addicks' wife at House of Flowers. Mrs. Addicks said she couldn't believe her husband would do such a thing as murder and could understand why he wouldn't take the polygraph examination. She was very guarded in her answers. She stated she first heard of the murder 15 minutes after Rod left home on August 29 to go to work. She stated that the office (Columbia Bookkeeping) called her and told her of the murder even before the police arrived. Said Stan Turel had been calling a lot to talk to Rod after the murder.

5:40 p.m. Went to Rod Addicks' house and contacted Rod Addicks to introduce ourselves on the case. We said 3 times we did not want to discuss the case because he had been advised of his rights. He was very friendly and I asked him why he started carrying a gun. He said that he felt he should because somebody may try to hit him next. I asked to see the gun and he went out to car, and unloaded it on his way into the house. Addicks handed me the gun and it matched the one Sam Moll had described earlier as to the type, rust spots etc. I told him we were going to hold the gun to check it for stolen and to place the serial # on the permit. He became irate and called his attorney. I talked to the attorney who asked for a warrant etc. and if I knew the Constitution, etc. I advised him we were taking the gun and gave the phone back after telling him it was being checked and would be returned.

The gun was exactly as Sam described it as to rust and color and then polished off. The gun is a .38 blue steel. With break-open Iver Johnson.

7 p.m. Contacted Russell Cartwright, (Dennis Cartwright's father), *at Dennis' trailer. He normally lived above the Pastime Tavern apt in Kelso. He said that Dennis was in the Tri Cities area last August but he didn't want to commit himself to it. He said he didn't like Rod Addicks because Rod was too smart and he leads Dennis astray. 'He is too smart and a smart aleck.'*

2/15/75:

10:30 a.m. Drove to Kelso – interviewed Dennis Cartwright. He was extremely nervous and refused to take the Polygraph. Said he was in Sports Center Tavern (on the 28 of August 1974 when the murder took place) *from 6 p.m. until closing and was not in Portland at all during August 28.* (The detectives showed him a receipt from Copeland Lumber that he signed in Oregon City on August 28). *Changed story late and said he could have been. Said he was with friends, the Andersons (Gary and Norma), and his wife on August 28.*

3:10 p.m. Went to Rod Addicks' house. Gave Rod Addicks his gun back. Volunteered information (after we told him not to talk about the case). He never had any other .38 or other gun except for antique rifle. Said he really liked Turel and was his best friend. He gave receipt for the gun. Said he was not with Dennis Cartwright that day and didn't know if Dennis was in Portland. Said he bought the .38 7 years ago from Harry Morgan in Tacoma. Said he has shot the gun and has taken it Moose Hunting.

3:50 p.m. Went to Gary and Norma Anderson's and they slammed door in our face.

6:30 p.m. called Mrs. Cartwright to dispute Dennis' statement that he was in Sports Center Tavern on Aug. 28. Because he thought she

*was coming in on the 28th. She definitely told him she was coming in on
Aug 29. Said she may disappear.*

The detectives continued to interview more friends or associates
related to the suspects. Around that time, Forrest "Joe" Rieke was
appointed head prosecutor on the case. Many meetings took place in the
next few weeks between Joe Rieke, Rieke's assistant Norm Brown,
District Attorney Schrunk, and all the detectives. Prosecutor Rieke and
Norm Brown flew to Tacoma to take sworn affidavits from witnesses.
Witnesses were flown in from Kennewick and Oklahoma to get their
sworn statements. Most took lie detector tests and passed. Years later I
learned that if any of the witnesses were murdered, their recorded sworn
affidavits could still be used during a trial. The polygraph exams, however,
were not admissible.

Late one evening, Detective Englert called me and said he had talked
to Mrs. Addicks who had told them that I had called her husband a lot after
the murder and my phone intrusions really bothered them.

"Really?" I said. "I rarely called his home after he resigned because
the lawyers were negotiating the buyout of his stock and the title transfer
of the Cadillac. However, I did call him a number of times before he
resigned." No matter, it felt good that the detectives were putting pressure
on Rod Addicks. Detective Englert mentioned that they met Addicks at his
house and were surprised by how clean-shaven, professional, and cordial
he appeared.

On February 18, I attended another meeting at my lawyer's office
downtown. We finalized a proposed agreement to buy back Rod Addicks'
interest in Columbia Bookkeeping, including the issue of the bonus he was
entitled to. I knew that according to his employment agreement, Addicks
was entitled to more money, but I was still trying to hold off as long as I
could. I was delaying, quietly waiting and hoping that the police would
arrest him for the murder of my father. Jim Auxier couldn't understand
this, and I couldn't tell him why. Auxier was obviously becoming quite
frustrated and sent me several letters stating that I could be removed as
Trustee and sued by Rod Addicks for failure to pay. All I could tell him
was, "Please trust me. Time is on our side."

Before I left his office, Jim Auxier said, "Stan, since you are fairly
wealthy for someone your age, I need to advise you about preparing a

cohabitation agreement in case you end up sharing an apartment again with a lady. Depending on where you live, if you share living costs and space for long enough, it might be considered a common-law marriage and your girlfriend, if you break up, could be entitled to benefits."

"What do you mean?" I asked. "What benefits?"

"Plus, Stan, since you are also an employer, you need an agreement to protect you. If you date someone who is looking for a job, or works for you, it could be inferred under some recent court cases as sexual harassment. So be careful. We could type up a dating agreement for you that says your dating is a mutually consensual arrangement and is in no way connected to an offer of employment. This should be signed before your first date with the woman."

I laughed, "You've got to be kidding! No woman is going to sign anything before the first date."

Auxier smirked and laughed as he puffed on his pipe. "Maybe I'm being too cautious as your lawyer, but you should know some of the ground rules as an employer."

On February 25, I scheduled a meeting with Jim Auxier and Rod Addicks to take place at Auxier's law office. Then I called my banker, Jack Miller, and told him that Rod Addicks would be receiving $2,000 on February 25 from Columbia Bookkeeping. I suggested that he hound Addicks, pretending that the detectives wanted more information about whether or not there had been any problems between him and Jim Turel. Also, I suggested that Miller say to Addicks that the bank needed the full repayment of Addicks' past-due note for $2,000, or the bank would have to file a lien on Addicks' assets. Jack Miller called me back to say Rod Addicks had promised to pay off the $2,000 note the same day he received the money from Columbia.

Next, I went to Auxier's office downtown to sign the buyout agreement regarding Addicks' interest in the tax business. We would pay Rod Addicks $2,000 down that day on the contract, with the balance due at the end of tax season. I proposed this settlement although I had no intention of paying him one damn dime more. I had to bite my tongue when my heart started racing as Addicks came into the room. Jim Auxier did a great job in smoothing out the rough edges with Addicks and assured his attorney that he would force me to forward the title to the Cadillac in the next few days. "Stan has been so busy during the tax season that he just misplaced the title," Auxier explained. "I will personally go to the Motor Vehicles Department myself and file for a replacement title."

As he said this, I was thinking that my attorney has no idea I will never allow such a thing to happen! The stress of that meeting plus the problems at the office gave me a serious migraine headache.

But my plan with banker Jack Miller worked. As soon as Rod Addicks left Auxier's office, he went directly to the bank and paid them the $2,000. I was happy he did not get to keep a dime of that money. The only source of income Addicks had now was from preparing tax returns in his house and from his wife's small flower shop. By removing his signature from the four partnership bank accounts for which he was previously a signer, I was controlling the use of all funds to which he previously had access.

I also notified all the other banks where I suspected Rod Addicks had associations, advising them that Addicks was no longer associated with Columbia Bookkeeping. I suggested that they contact Jack Miller at First Interstate Bank. Miller was very helpful in shutting down Addicks' ability to get credit. I knew that Addicks had used Jack Miller as a credit reference in the past. I was still afraid that if Rod Addicks found out how close the detectives were to arresting him, he would skip the country, so I did not want him to have any money.

Then, the next day, February 26, 1975, I called Jim Auxier and told him not to pursue replacing the Cadillac title, as I would sign nothing. "I think Rod is going to have his hands full in the near future with the arson and security fraud cases in Washington State, so let's just hold off," I said. "Confidentially, I think Rod will soon be financially desperate and we can make a better deal. Or, perhaps we'll end up paying him nothing if it turns out he's connected to the murder case."

"Do you know more than you're saying?" Jim Auxier asked often.

"Time will tell," I always replied.

"Stan, you're walking a very slippery slope."

Auxier was a good, but a cautious guiding force for me. He'd sent me several letters explaining the consequences of my dealing with Addicks either way, if I was right or wrong. He also gave me great encouragement that I could be successful in Columbia Bookkeeping if I just stuck with it, which built up my confidence. He said my dad had always been hopeful I'd take over the company if something happened to him. Auxier even shared that my dad saw me as a sharp businessman and said I would probably be more successful than he ever could have been. Jim Auxier would put his arm around my shoulder, with his ever-present pipe in his hand, and say, "Son, you'll never know how important it is to me that you make something out of this business."

By the end of February, the tax accountants were exhausted and so was I. Most of the six tax accountants worked past 10 o'clock at night, or even later, to finish each tax return before the 48-hour turnaround time expired. I continued to work in the office upstairs, and keep track of the checking and processing department. The pressure I felt was due partly to the advertised 48-hour turnaround time for most returns. Back then, there were no computers to handle tax form preparation, so all 1040 tax forms were filled out by hand.

The one-page checklist I designed was definitely helpful in streamlining the interview process. On the busiest days, I would send out for food so the staff didn't have to leave. I was afraid that if they went out to eat lunch or dinner, they wouldn't come back until the next day. Some of the staff complained that I was a little pushy, but they respected me because I was working the same long hours they worked. I knew the workload would probably decline in March and I was relieved when we made it through the busiest weeks of the tax season.

I personally handled all client complaints and found that in my role as mediator I could efficiently resolve client and staff problems. If the clients were still not happy by the end of the discussion, I would offer to give them discounts on next year's return, or even reduce their fee for the current year. I continued to rely on the theory that the client is always right, as long as it does not cost too much. At first, some clients were leery seeing how young I was, but I handled myself well and ran the office professionally. I always wore a suit and tie to give a good first impression.

Our repeat clients asked, Where is Rod Addicks? Why did he leave? I still worried every day that something about Addicks would interfere with a smooth tax season. Also, I was afraid of personal reprisals from him. Was he planning something drastic to destroy the business because he felt forced out? I was told years ago that desperate people do desperate things. The fact that Rod Addicks was feeling pressure from the police and had scant access to money might push him right off his rocker.

I counted my blessings every single evening as the investigation neared a conclusion. I'd been told that the District Attorney and Sheriff Lee Brown approved funding for every move the detectives made regarding their investigation of Rod Addicks. The detectives finally had the freedom to travel to other states and follow through on all leads. However, I was shocked to learn from Detective Rod Englert that Addicks had offered a fourth man money to have my dad killed. Sheriff Brown encouraged the detectives to go for it.

Occasionally during the day, to reduce stress, I would walk outside to the back parking lot, look up at the sky and take a big deep breath of fresh air. I loved the rain and winter storms, as they reminded me I was still alive. It was as if God and Mother Nature were still in charge. Just the fresh air touching my face and the sound of the wind blowing through the trees made me realize that man cannot control everything. Nature is so pure and innocent in all its beauty.

For the first time in a month, I decided to go flying because broken clouds and blue sky beckoned me. It's a 15-minute drive from Columbia Bookkeeping to the Troutdale airport. After pre-flighting my little airplane, I flew east alongside the rocky cliffs of the Columbia River Gorge, leaving the Portland metropolitan area behind me. What an uplifting sense of freedom leaving the earth gives me! When flying, I experience a real separation from all my worldly stresses. Eventually I turned my little plane and I climbed southeast towards Mount Hood. The foothills and fir trees below me were still covered in a soft blanket of white snow, like a perfect Christmas morning.

After an hour, I guided my little yellow and white plane towards Estacada where Dad was buried. As I had done before, I flew over and circled Dad's cemetery several times. When flying away, I wagged my wings back and forth, as if to say goodbye to my dad. I found myself talking to him as if he could hear me. I said, "It's almost over, Dad, and the bad guys are going to pay for killing you." I know it's silly, but somehow I found relief for my grief by thinking his spirit was still with me.

Does a deceased person's soul and spirit hang around to guide us in the right direction? I have no idea. Anyway, the flight was good therapy for me. In the Christian way I was raised, I do believe in God's help and the destiny of mankind. Were there angels in the sky with me? I have no idea about that, either. I don't care which God one believes in, all religions have the same good intentions and general beliefs. Maybe different perspectives, but their God is good, too. I do believe we must look out for the extremists that twist religion to its limits.

Back at the office, upon entering the lobby, I heard the sounds of all five phone lines ringing at the same time. The two ladies at the front desk were swamped. There were twelve occupied chairs and two older ladies standing in the lobby. It irritated me that several young men were sitting in those chairs and they didn't have the decency to get up and offer their chairs to the standing women. It seems that most men today forget it's a gentleman's responsibility to be courteous and respectful of women. I went to the back room and brought out two chairs for the ladies and joked, "This must look like a dentist's office," I said. "But it won't hurt as much."

I often came downstairs when the reception area was busy just to offer some diversion and entertainment. On one occasion, I saw Mary Kay (that was my nickname for her since she sold Mary Kay products) in the lobby waiting with her boyfriend to have her taxes done. My dad had liked this young lady and even introduced her to me two years ago when Susan and I broke up. Mary Kay and I dated a few times and became good friends. That was when I was still afraid to make a commitment. It was nice to see her return to our company to have her taxes done.

Overall, I felt pretty good. I knew that soon Rod Addicks might be arrested and that Dad's tax company would survive thanks to the efforts of the people with whom I surrounded myself. Many of the clients told me what a wonderful man my father was and that they were glad to see me here. Their encouragement and comments meant a lot to me.

Detective Englert's notes, March 7, 1975:

Contacted Mrs. Jean Nelson at Montavilla Motel where the old phone # is registered to. Cartwright's wife said Dennis was living at the motel in August and that she helped him move out on Monday (1st Monday after the murder). Mrs. Nelson remembered Rod Addicks living at the motel from Jan 29 to April 28 of 1971. Said he was an accountant from Colorado or Arizona.

She checked the books and on 8-12-74 Ron Butler signed in to Room 16 and paid to 8-19-74. They had the license number and vehicle number of Cartwright's PU. Mrs. Nelson and her husband remembered Rod Addicks in the red Cadillac bringing Rod Butler (Cartwright) in and paying his first week's rent. Mrs. Nelson had a sheet filled out by Rod Butler. The address and name was phony.

Detective Engler's notes indicated Sam Moll explained that the Puyallup Indians had ownership of approximately 17,000 acres of reservation land and that Addicks and Cartwright indicated they had $50,000 to invest in locating a building and creating a whorehouse and gambling casino. It was their intention to set Sam Moll up as the front man because he was an Indian.

Chapter 14: Investigation Heats Up

On Friday, March 12, 1975, Detective Rod Englert called to say that great progress had been made since we had last spoken. "Rod Addicks might be arrested in the next few days by the State of Washington for securities fraud," he said.

I hadn't known Detective Englert and his partner were working 60 hours a week and traveling over a number of state lines. But apparently, Englert was instrumental in making sure the Washington Securities Department followed through with charges against Rod Addicks, and with his arrest. I felt bad that I could still not tell anyone in my family, so I asked Detective Englert to talk to my sisters and tell them what he could. I told him that my younger sister, the one in California, was upset with me because I would not disclose more details about the case. "I'll set up a meeting with them in the next few days," Detective Englert said.

On Sunday, back in the office, I found that we were way behind in the checking and the copying departments. Over 400 tax returns needed to be checked and processed before Monday. I called the checkers and the copy lady at 9 o'clock on Sunday morning. I pleaded with them to please come in. I begged them to commit to eight hours even though it was Sunday. I knew we had to catch up or we would not be able to make good on our advertising promise to process returns in 48 hours. I agree it was pushy of me to ask the staff to come in on a Sunday, but that is what it would take to keep the company on track. No one else, including Marvin Bridge, the general manager, seemed to understand the need for staying ahead of the workload. My older sister, who was by then working in our computer and processing department, bless her heart, came in and helped copy tax returns until midnight so the completed returns would be ready to pick up on Monday morning.

I reasoned that if the business was two or three days behind schedule, we would never catch up until tax season ended. Like I said before,

Americans expect quality, affordability and fast service for their dollar. America is McDonaldized. I also figured fast service would increase referrals. I pushed the staff to finish their work promptly. My theory was that by completing the tax forms while details of the client were still fresh in the accountants' minds, it would reduce the possibility of mistakes.

At that time I was personally short of cash since I had closed down my Air Auto Waxing business and I still wasn't taking a salary from Columbia Bookkeeping. Plus I had four vacancies in my own rental properties. So, I borrowed money from the bank and started visiting the apartments I owned to see if I could help move things along.

On March 15, Detective Rod Englert talked with my two sisters. "I gave them information about my investigative process," Englert told me, "without disclosing details. Please, Stan, I still must urge you not to discuss any details with anyone. We'll probably be arresting Rod Addicks in the next few days and we can't afford any leaks. There's still a chance Addicks will split if he finds out." I agreed to keep everything I knew to myself.

Detective Englert's notes from March 13 through March 15, 1975:

4:15 p.m. called Billy Anglin's home (in Kennewick) and talked to both he and wife, and learned Addicks and Cartwright were at their home. I said we would call back in an hour to see how things were. Possibly they intend to burn down the Cartwright home.

5:10 p.m. Called Anglin to see if everything was OK. Told them we were unable to come over due to distance and told them 3 times not to mention the case or solicit anything but just listen if you can't get rid of them. Don't Solicit. Talked to them 3 times on the phone because they were scared and wanted help. They said Rod Addicks and Cartwright left about 7:30 p.m. and they planned to meet them later at the Playboy Tavern to play cards.

3-14-75:

Called Anglin's home at 8 a.m. and everything OK. Said Rod and Dennis probably going to leave at noon or so.

11:35 a.m. Received collect call from Mr. and Mrs. Darwin (informant in Kennewick) that they just passed by Dennis Cartwright's house in Kennewick and that they saw Rod Addicks' red Cadillac.

3-15-75:

10:30 a.m. Called Anglin and everything OK.

5:30 p.m. Mr. and Mrs. Anglin called collect and said Rod and Dennis were still in town and they both felt threatened by Rod and Dennis, but said perhaps it was just paranoia.

Chapter 15: Arrests Made, Contract on Witness

On March 17, 1975 I received a call from Detective Rod Englert.

"We, and the State of Washington, have just arrested Rod Addicks on seven counts of securities fraud in connection to the money he took from his real estate investors. We've transferred him to a jail in Tacoma. We also filed charges against Rod Addicks for two counts of arson," Englert said. "I've personally talked to Addicks. He's looking pretty despondent. He has a moustache now. It's possible he was thinking of splitting the country. The rest of the charges for murder will probably come later, after the Grand Jury in Portland finishes its indictment."

Late that night Englert called me again. "Dennis Lee Cartwright just admitted he and Rod Addicks murdered your father together. It was just as Sam Moll said." Then Englert provided some details: according to Lee Cartwright, my dad put up quite a fight. They planned to knock him unconscious from behind, and at first they thought they had crushed his skull. But my dad fell to the ground and started swinging his crutches at them. Then they took his crutch away and beat him with it, but they had to finally choke him to death since the other injuries did not kill him. While Englert told me the details, I took a deep breath. I couldn't help but imagine the terror and suffering my dad must have felt during the attack.

It was horrifying to hear such details, yet I was so relieved to know that the culprits were now behind bars. I immediately called my sisters and Gary. Rod Englert said he would also call them the next day.

The next morning, March 18, 1975, I called the Portland *Oregonian* and asked for the crime reporter, Jim Hill, who I had previously met. I asked that he not print a full article about Rod Addicks' arrest in respect for my dad's lifelong efforts to build a business. I asked that if they were going to write a detailed article that they please mention and clarify that Dad was not involved in the arson or the securities violations. I explained that the business could be destroyed by unfounded rumors. I promised Hill that at the end of the trial I would help him in any way to make sure their information was accurate.

At the time, Jim Hill did not promise anything, but agreed to minimize the damage to my dad's reputation and business. He assured me he would not connect the arson charges to my dad or his business in any article until there was more information. I told Mr. Hill that my mother had worked at *The Oregonian* for over 20 years and the family always had a high regard for the paper.

The *Seattle Chronicle* printed a large front-page article about Rod Addicks being charged and arrested with securities fraud involving activities in the late 1960s. The photo in the paper surprised us as he had grown a mustache on that baby face of his. These charges had nothing to do with my dad's business, as those thefts occurred before my dad met Addicks. One of the securities fraud victims was an IRS agent from the Seattle area named Mr. White, who was the godfather of one of Addicks' children. This news made several of the partners in Addicks' apartment deals very nervous. They wanted out. Al and Mary Foglio agreed to buy out a few; the others agreed to wait and see what happened.

When I announced the information about Rod Addicks' arrest to the staff, most were shocked and dismayed. However, Peg and Julie Syler, the bookkeepers, were relieved that Addicks was finally in jail. Peg told me she couldn't believe two people were involved. She reminded me of the dreams I'd had just a few weeks after dad died, in which two men committed the murder.

The local district attorney, Forrest "Joe" Rieke, and his assistant, Norm Brown, set up meetings to update my family. I'd had several meetings with them downtown in the previous month and was so grateful for their understanding and backing of Detective Rod Englert. I called and congratulated Detective Blackie Yazzolino who, since the beginning, felt Rod Addicks was somehow involved. I respected Yazzolino's insight and patience in regards to this case. My dad's murder was Yazzolino's very last homicide case in a very long career.

Jim Auxier called and congratulated me on the outcome. He then told me that Mr. Hanson, Rod Addicks' attorney, had just called and wanted the title to the Cadillac, as Rod Addicks needed money for a lawyer.

"Tell Mr. Hanson to go to hell," I said. "And, I want the Cadillac back."

Ex-Tacoman accused of murder in Oregon

Roderick R. Addicks

March 17, 1975, the morning of Rod Addicks' arrest for securities fraud. The next day the Grand Jury indictments were issued for murder and two counts of arson. (photo © *Seattle Chronicle*).

Jim Auxier agreed to pass on my response since we no longer had to worry about Addicks skipping town. "But in the future," Auxier warned me, "we'll have to deal with Addicks' legal matters. He might be found innocent, so keep that in mind and try not to lose your cool."

"Are you kidding?" I said. "I can celebrate because the law will take care of it from here." I truly believed justice would prevail.

Then Auxier said Mr. Hanson seemed to have gone through a radical change in attitude. Hanson was now apologetic and said he'd been fooled by Rod Addicks' innocent appearance and swayed by Addicks' denial of guilt. Auxier said that Mr. Hanson told him he was refusing to represent Mr. Addicks anymore and was recommending that an experienced criminal lawyer take over.

I went home that night and said a Thank You prayer to God. In a way, I felt sorry for Rod Addicks' wife and his two kids.

I was told the next day that Dennis Lee Cartwright was being held in the Rocky Butte Jail in Portland, Oregon. Gary and I talked on the phone and decided we would try and get the Cadillac back from Addicks' wife. I wanted the Cadillac back so Addicks wouldn't benefit from its financial value. Gary and I drove to Addicks' house in Kelso but couldn't find the car. We called his wife to ask where the car was, but she wouldn't say. Finally, we got in my plane and flew all over Kelso looking for it, but to no avail.

I was pleased that Jim Hill, from *The Oregonian,* wrote only a very short article about Addicks' arrest.

During that week, Detective Englert called asking if we had ever prepared taxes for a certain individual by the last name of Munson. According to Cartwright, five years ago Rod Addicks felt he had been ripped off in a real estate deal by this man. To get even, Addicks arranged for one of his friends (maybe Cartwright) to take the realtor on a drive to the mountains, supposedly to look at some timber property. Addicks' friend then told Ross Munson to get out and left the guy stranded on the mountain in the middle of nowhere.

I also learned that after they murdered my dad, Sam Moll, Lee Cartwright, and Rod Addicks made a pact that if one of them ratted on the others, the remaining two would kill the rat.

Since the arrest of Addicks and Cartwright, the detectives still had over 30 interviews to follow up with in preparation of the upcoming pretrial hearings. On March 20, 1975, they traveled to Kelso to clear up the ambiguous alibi that Gary and Norma Anderson had given Cartwright on August 28, 1974, the day of the murder. The detective's notes below reveal a lot of the behind-the-scenes information collected about Addicks and Cartwright.

Detective Englert's notes, March 20 through 22, 1975:

3:20 p.m. Contacted Mrs. Addicks at her House of Plants business and she refused to talk and escorted us to the door.

4:50 p.m. Contacted Gary and Norma Anderson at their home and both were crying and remorseful for Turel and very unyielding toward Cartwright at this time.

Norma said Cartwright called her at 1:30 on 3-18-75 after confessing and said he did the "Job." Norma asked what he meant and Dennis cried, saying he did the job on the old man in Portland.

Gary said that a couple of months ago Dennis said he had nothing to worry about in the murder but that the Police probably had been to Kennewick and the only person that could hurt him would be Billy Anglin. Dennis didn't explain that statement.

Gary said that Addicks had a fascination about the Mafia and Godfather stuff. Read the book about a Fat Guy "My Life in the Mafia" and always talked about being that way. He seemed over-infatuated with that kind of stuff.

Norma said that Cartwright filled her with ideas and stories during the past months since the murder to set up an alibi. Norma said Cartwright called her confessing he had used her and Gary as an alibi.

Gary Anderson said that approximately two months ago Rod Addicks gave him a .38 with a 6" barrel and he wanted Gary Anderson to make a silencer for it. He gave Gary the gun after Elk season and said they wanted him to make a silencer in order to shoot elk according to Dennis Cartwright. Gary said he made a silencer but it didn't work. Rod Addicks picked up the gun approximately 2 days after we took his other gun away from Rod Addicks. He told Gary that he had made the police really mad.

In Rod's alibi, he told Gary Anderson that Turel was keeping books for massage parlors and the Gangster had Turel killed because he knew so much about the gangsters.

3-21-75

10:40 a.m. I called Rocky Butte Jail and arranged to talk to Cartwright. Asked about the silencer and whether or not it was for Elk hunting like Gary Anderson said. Dennis said "No" it wasn't for Elk and Rod had it for other reasons. Said he wanted to talk to me and I told him he should contact his attorney first for permission. Said he didn't know where the gun was at this time.

3-22-75

11:30 a.m. Met Mr. Ross Munson at Luv's Restaurant and he said he was held up (robbed) during hunting season in 1970 by a man telling him he had timber for sale. He was taken in the woods and robbed of his ring and approximately $175. He made a report to Pierce County Police Department. And that while checking their files for the report Mr. Munson said he would testify if his attorney said it was OK. He said the person that robbed him had a front tooth missing. He could not identify the mug shot of pictures of Cartwright but recognizes Addicks. Didn't give him a lay down because of Statute of Limitations. But we only wanted to corroborate Cartwright's earlier story of what he and Addicks had done to the man.

Munson stated the man who held him up cocked the gun he was carrying and was possibly going to shoot him. Munson said Addicks did business with 3 banks.

2:30 p.m. Called Mrs. Cartwright and asked her if Dennis ever had a tooth out and she said he had his bottom tooth out.

6 p.m. Met with Cartwright in the Rocky Butte Jail at his request and he wanted to tell us that Blackie Yazzolino had a $25,000 contract on him from some other prisoner. Cartwright spoke freely about still wanting to help us and said Rod had a "Hit List" of people he wanted to knock off but he never saw the names or the list. Said that the bank Rod conspired to hit was the Puget Sound National Bank in Downtown Tacoma. Rod hated them because they seized his nice home and furniture on the lake in Tacoma and he wanted to get even. He said Rod was probably now in 7th heaven in Jail because he wanted to be a Mafia Figure and will always be even better when he gets out, according to Dennis.

As I mentioned earlier, Paula Travington, the manager of Woodstock Apartments, had resigned over $3,000 in missing rental receipts and moved out of the state. Soon after Rod Addicks' arrest, the detectives went to Idaho to interview her. She and her husband admitted they had stolen around $2,500 from the apartments. However, she denied having an affair with Addicks. I was glad to see that even with Addicks in jail, the detectives continued their long-distance travels to follow up on leads from the scenarios presented by Dennis Lee Cartwright and Sam Moll. They were still wrapping up details in preparation for the prosecution's upcoming case. The detective's discoveries and their pursuit of leads in the case seemed endless.

Detective Rod Englert discovered that Addicks had rented a hotel room just down the street from our Stark Street office under a fake name so Lee Cartwright could live nearby prior to dad's murder. Also, Englert had followed up on how Gary and Norma Anderson, from Kelso, Washington, had gotten tricked into claiming that Cartwright had been in a Kelso bar after 6 o'clock the night Dad was killed. They said Addicks was in the bar by 9 p.m., but their alibi for Addicks failed when the detectives found proof that Addicks had made a call from Columbia Bookkeeping at 9 o'clock the night Dad was murdered. The call was to a woman Addicks had an affair with the year before.

Apparently, Addicks had pretended to arrange a blind date for my dad as a setup for the murder, to ensure he'd return to the office after they ate dinner. Dad and Rod Addicks waited quite a while in the front lobby of Columbia Bookkeeping, expecting his "date" to show up any moment. Addicks made the call to the woman from the phone in his own office asking why she hadn't shown up yet.

When questioned, the woman who received the call told Englert she thought the call was strange since she had not dated or even heard from Addicks for over a year. She told the detectives she called her best friend right after she hung up with Addicks—to share her uneasiness about the call. The next day she was shocked to hear on the news that Jim Turel had been murdered the night before.

To prove that Dennis Lee Cartwright and Sam Moll were telling the truth, Cartwright took the police to the Columbia River to show them where he and Rod Addicks had thrown my dad's flight bag into the river. He said that after the bloody murder took place, they decided to make the crime look like a robbery rather than take his body up to Mt. Hood or a location in North Portland, as they planned. Since Jim Turel was left waiting so long in the front lobby, their timeline must have been screwed up and the murder did not go off as planned.

The Multnomah County sheriff's scuba divers dove into the Columbia River where Cartwright indicated. They found the flight bag half buried in silt. In the bag were my dad's shaver, overnight clothes, and various other personal items. It proved that what Sam Moll and Dennis Lee Cartwright said was true. Cartwright said he was offered $5,000 by

Addicks to help him kill my dad.

During the same week, Rod Addicks was put in solitary confinement at the Rocky Butte Jail for offering someone else $15,000 to murder Dennis Lee Cartwright. Dennis was transferred to the Oregon State Prison, 60 miles south, for his protection. Officials also discovered that Addicks had a plan to escape from the jail. While inspecting Addicks' jail cell, prison guards discovered a fork that had been modified into a knife.

By March 25, District Attorney Rieke and his assistant Norm Brown met with me again to review documents in preparation for the trial hearings scheduled to start in three or four months. There were pretrial hearings, depositions taken, and games played between Rod Addicks' attorney and the District Attorney's office. My brother Gary and I gave up on looking for the Cadillac, but at least no one was bothering me about the title any more. Blackie Yazzolino stopped by with Detective Rod Englert at the meeting downtown and we all congratulated each other on the success of their investigation. Gary and I offered to take them out to a special dinner, but they refused since they thought it might represent a conflict of interest. They mentioned that they were not allowed to socialize with witnesses.

In the meantime, Rod Addicks sold his interest in the Big Spruce Trailer Park through his attorney to Mr. and Mrs. Foglio. It was my understanding that all the money went to his attorney and as far as we knew, he was still totally broke. We knew Addicks' wife had a flower shop in Kelso in her name, but we decided not to pursue a lawsuit against their joint assets since Addicks had so little left. Addicks' wife wasn't involved, so why make her more miserable than she was? I really did feel sorry for her.

Out of the blue, I ran into complications regarding the preparation and filing of my dad's Federal Estate tax return and forming the Turel Family Trust. I was surprised when I received a bill from the Oregon Welfare Department for money they had given our family during our welfare years. They had a rule that they could receive back from an estate any funds advanced to a welfare recipient in the event the recipient had money when he or she died. It had been 15 years since my family had been on welfare. Dad had already paid back the student loans the government advanced him for college. The bill surprised me, but I did appreciate that they helped us during a dire time for our family.

We had already filed for Workers Compensation Insurance on

Bernie's behalf since Dad was murdered at work. By doing this, Bernie would receive $750 per month for the rest of her life, or until she remarried.

The staff at Columbia Bookkeeping had performed well during the tax season. We had proven to the bank and the State Tax Board that we could run a good operation. I received a call from the head of the local IRS office, Mr. Ralf Short, congratulating me on the outcome of the investigation and our cooperation. I told him, "Without the dedicated help of the entire staff and the authorities, we could not have pulled it off."

The head of the massage parlors, Mr. Shannon, came into the tax office in late March for a consultation. He was a nice looking, well dressed, executive-type man in his mid-30s. I noticed his flashy gold watch and necklace right away. He wanted to know who would be in charge of his account now that Rod Addicks, who used to oversee his accounts, was gone. I looked at him and said, "Do you realize that some of the women that worked for you during the past three years are missing or were found beaten?" I looked him in the eyes and said, "I do not like the business you're in. The police tell me you're just a front for prostitution."

"You sure are young and cocky," the man said. "Keep in mind that I'm one of your company's biggest monthly accounting clients.

"I don't care if you are. You need to take your business somewhere else. I do not like you and I don't respect the business you're in."

Within two days, all his accounting business went elsewhere. I had been waiting for a chance to do this ever since Dad died, but decided not to run him off until after the case was solved. As he left, I still wondered if he and Addicks were involved in arson.

During the next few weeks, I stayed focused on the tax business because the end of the tax season was fast approaching. By late April we held a dinner party for the tax staff at the River Queen Restaurant. I felt like a kid when school has been let out for summer vacation. What a celebration! Addicks was in jail and we had a very profitable tax season! The Turel Family Trust and Columbia Bookkeeping would survive!

Detective Rod Englert's notes, April 8 and 9, 1975

5:05 to 6 p.m. Called Addicks' wife at House of Flowers and advised her that Stan Turel told me she may be interested in talking to us. She opened up and I gave her info on which houses were burned etc. Based on the newspaper clipping, she asked several questions and said she would be seeing Rod tomorrow. She admitted that Rod read a lot of Mafia books and was infatuated with that kind of thing. Said she remembered Rod coming home late the night of the murder and it was 10 p.m. or sometime thereafter. We talked about Rod's clothes and his shoes and she couldn't offer anything about them being missing. She said she would try to find the gun that I told her we were looking for. She asked several questions about Rod's extramarital affairs and houses he owned that she was unaware of. Said Stan Turel told her most of this and she feels like she has been a fool to believe in her husband.

4-9-75:

4:10 p.m. Called Addicks' wife at House of Flowers and she said she had a long talk with Rod and feels she doesn't want to talk to us anymore.

Detective Rod Englert filled me in on more details about Dad's murder. Apparently, the murder plan had been to knock dad unconscious with the first blow to the back of his head from the cue ball, then choke him to death without leaving a trace that anything took place. They would then haul Dad's body away to a remote location. But because there was such a bloody mess in the hallway, it would have done no good to move his body somewhere else. It was obvious the attack had occurred in his office.

So, Rod Addicks and Dennis Lee Cartwright decided to make the murder look more like a robbery and leave the body where it lay. They removed cash from Dad's wallet and placed the wallet next to Dad's body. They opened the safe vault with Dad's keys and took $25 from the cash register. But, as Blackie Yazzolino had first indicated, the scene was way too neat for a robbery.

Englert explained the solicitations to kill leading up to the actual murder: Sam Moll and Rod Addicks had planned to use part of the $50,000 life insurance money to pay Sam Moll $5,000 for murdering Jim Turel in the first murder plot. When Sam Moll could not complete the murder, Moll's cousin, Maddock Tollocko, was offered $10,000 to kill my dad. Sam Moll and Maddock Tollocko were both members of the Puyallup Indian Tribe.

Sam Moll and Rod Addicks had collaborated on burning down a house in 1973. The house was owned by Addicks and located in southeast

Portland. It was 1973 when my dad first mentioned he'd become suspicious of Rod Addicks' involvement in an arson incident. That was also the time, according to Julie Syler, my dad insisted on opening all the mail that came to the office before forwarding it on to the appropriate parties. And that was when my dad had registered a new business name, "All Year Tax Service." This name was used as a descriptive subtitle under all of Columbia Bookkeeping's letterhead, envelopes and building signs.

The year before my dad died, he said that if Rod Addicks ever took over the business, he would be permitted to use the name "Columbia Bookkeeping," but if he had to let Addicks go, Dad could change the name of his business to "All Year Tax Service" as a backup. He said he would be able to do this because he was the sole owner of the office building. I thought my dad was overreacting or paranoid about the possibility that Addicks was involved in arson. But obviously I was wrong.

According to Sam Moll, Rod Addicks came to hate my dad because he was exerting more and more control and monitoring all of Addicks' business activities. Apparently, Addicks may have figured that if Dad died, then he could buy the remaining stock from the family, using the balance of the $50,000 life insurance money as a down payment. Addicks was right; no one would want to buy a tax business after the owner was murdered. Addicks would be the only logical buyer. Also, maybe Addicks knew Dad was investigating his background or possibly discovered Addicks' lawsuits in Washington. Addicks may have feared he was going to be forced out of Columbia Bookkeeping.

Since Addicks was now in jail, I turned my attention to who was going to get the reward money. I did not like that Sam Moll would get full immunity after I heard the full details of his involvement in the plots that almost killed my dad. It riled me that Moll knew so much and was willing to work with Rod Addicks in the business after plotting to take over the company when Dad was dead. Okay, Sam Moll did help break the case, but he was not going to get any reward money from us, if I could help it. There were others deserving of reward money, such as Billy Anglin from Kennewick, Washington, who had provided valuable information to the police about the fourth attempt to murder my dad. But according to Jim Auxier, I couldn't pay Billy Anglin until the trial and all appeals were concluded in case others came forward to claim a reward, too.

By then, Rod Addicks had been formally charged with seven counts of securities fraud in Pierce County, Washington. Additionally, he was charged with two counts of arson and grand theft. However, the murder trial would be scheduled first. Addicks changed attorneys from Mr. Hanson to Mr. Michael Kohlhoff of Portland, Oregon. Jim Auxier was in the final stages of submitting the Estate tax return, but decided we should hold off and not file until we knew if the Turel Estate was going to be sued by any of the Portland apartment complex investors regarding the deals Addicks had put together. All of these partnerships were showing losses and some partners just wanted out.

With the lessening of the tax business workload, I began focusing again on the problems with the partners of the three apartment buildings and the Mobile Home Park in Florence on the Oregon coast. By then it was apparent I needed to push for better control over operations.

The Oregon City partnership, a 14-unit apartment building, was losing money and could hardly make its mortgage payments. Al and Mary Foglio approached me with the idea that they would help me buy out the other partners if I would also invest. I reviewed the books and decided that with some help from my older sister, we could operate the apartments if we had better onsite management. At that time my sister and her husband lived in a rented duplex and both had good jobs, so they were looking for a house to buy. I talked them into putting up a down payment of $4,000 for a 20 percent interest in the apartments. They would live in one of the apartment units free, and act as the managers. Gary, my brother, also put up $4,000 for his 20 percent interest in the partnership. I invested $8,000 for a 40 percent interest. The Foglios would hold the remaining 20 percent.

Jim Auxier, my lawyer, was concerned that this arrangement might be a conflict of interest unless we held a meeting with my stepmother first, explaining why this was being done. So, prior to the transaction being finalized, we held a meeting of the Turel Family Trust and included Bernie Turel. We explained that the some of the partners were threatening a lawsuit against the company and wanted out. We said, "Here's a solution." The new partnership would pick up the $120,000 first mortgage, plus some of the past-due bills. I suggested that Bernie, as secretary of the Corporation, take notes of the meeting and she agreed to the transaction. Ken Marts, who held the mortgage, also agreed to the transfer of debt to the newly formed partnership, as long as I personally guaranteed it. We paid full fair-market value for the apartment complex based on what properties were going for at that time.

Within one month of buying the apartment building, my older sister and her family moved in. Two weeks after that, we had the three empty units rented out. The building could now pay its own way. The pride of ownership with my sister and brother-in-law efforts showed up right away. This was a positive development that briefly took my mind off the tax business and upcoming trials of Addicks.

Chapter 16: Pretrial Hearing, Jail Escape Foiled

By late May of 1975, Rod Addicks had been transferred back and forth from the jail in Olympia, Washington, where he was held regarding his securities fraud charges, to Rocky Butte Jail in Portland, to face a charge of murder and two counts of arson. I was told the pretrial hearings and discovery process was estimated to take at least four months. During this process, Mr. Kohlhoff, Addicks' private defense attorney, had access to all the detectives' notes and all the tape recordings of the confessions of Sam Moll and Dennis Lee Cartwright. Additionally, he was given copies of all documents that might be used by the prosecution.

Addicks' new lawyer demanded payment from Columbia Bookkeeping for the balance of Addicks' contract and the title to the red Cadillac he had hidden away. I still refused to do anything of the sort. I thought if I pushed on the issue, the trials would allow the Turel Estate rights to counter-file with a wrongful death civil suit against Rod Addicks.

I made a number of trips downtown to the courthouse to review all the documents and notes from conversations I'd had with my family and Rod Addicks. I went through every detail on each and every document the prosecuting attorneys felt was important. They were confused regarding the Stock Purchase agreement Addicks had with my dad regarding Columbia Bookkeeping. And it took hours to explain in detail how all the apartment deals Addicks put together tied in with the investigation. My brother, Gary, and my older sister were also interviewed to determine if they had any information of use in the trial.

The Grand Jury and District Attorney's office approved the money to fly various witnesses to Portland from as far away as Oklahoma. Four individuals had knowledge of, or had been indirectly involved with plans to buy and sell another home Addicks intended to burn for its insurance money. Sam Moll was cooperating directly with the detectives and District Attorney. Five additional people involved with my dad's murder and attempted murders were providing testimony via depositions. Three of the men who had been asked to murder my dad, but turned down the deal, were afraid that Addicks or Cartwright would kill them if they told what they knew. I was amazed how many people came forward after Addicks was arrested, offering their bits of information.

During the pretrial hearings, defense attorney Kohlhoff moved to have the court throw out over a dozen documents I had turned over to the police. The defense alleged that I was an agent of the police and that if I had not turned over the bits of information to the police, they would not have suspected Sam Moll of being involved and he wouldn't have turned State's evidence. Apparently, in January 1975, the detectives applied pressure on Sam Moll. The detectives told him he would probably be charged with arson since they had proof Rod Addicks and Sam Moll had been involved in an arson ring. Attorney Joe Rieke did a great job defusing the issue. He said, "Stan Turel acted on his own without instructions from the detectives." About five hundred pages of testimony were devoted to these issues alone.

In the months following Rod Addicks' arrest, but before the actual trial, Addicks attempted to spin a media extravaganza by claiming that all the witnesses coming forth did so in hope of collecting the $5,000 reward offered by Columbia Bookkeeping. Fortunately both *The Oregonian* and the *Portland Journal* did not play into his hands. But in May 1975, a reporter from *Willamette Week* interviewed Addicks who made it appear as though money I advanced to the detectives was used to buy witnesses. The reporter called me after she had already interviewed District Attorney Rieke and his assistant Norm Brown.

I had the chance to talk to the reporter and explained that money was needed over a weekend when the County's office was closed. The money was used to pay Sam Moll's attorney to be present while the suspect was interviewed. Time was of the essence because the interview had to be conducted before Addicks found out his friend Sam Moll was a person of interest. I told the reporter that funds were also used to cover travel expenses and protection when a witness was moved to a secret location. Addicks claimed that if the money hadn't been made available for Sam Moll's attorney, then Sam Moll would never have talked. Maybe Addicks was right. Maybe the pact Moll made with Rod Addicks and Dennis Lee Cartwright to kill anyone who snitched would have kept Moll from talking, due to fear of retaliation.

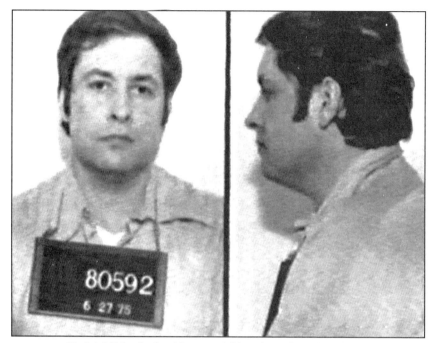

Rod Addicks during his pre-trial hearings, June 27, 1975.
Portland Police Department, Multnomah County, Oregon.

I also showed the reporter the document where the County signed for, and promised to reimburse Columbia Bookkeeping for all the emergency money I had advanced to the detectives. The total sum was only $1,300 and that money had nothing to do with the Reward Fund. I told her that Jim Auxier, my lawyer, had instructed me that I, personally, could not decide how much, nor to which witnesses the reward money would go until the trial and appeals were over. But no matter what I said, the reporter had already been swayed by Rod Addicks and his lawyer and tried to discredit the detectives and the District Attorney. In the end, the paper printed very few details of the allegations of murder, arson or securities fraud facing Rod Addicks. Most of the ironclad evidence was missing from the article.

To escape on Memorial Day weekend, I stopped by Bernie's house to pick rhododendrons from Dad's yard before driving to his gravesite in Springwater Pioneer Cemetery south of Estacada. I wanted to place the flowers from his own yard, flowers he loved, on his grave. I went early in the morning. I also placed flowers on Uncle Jack Marrs' grave, right next to him. Dad's gravestone was so small and lonely, with an American flag stuck in the ground for veterans. It offended me that my stepmother did not want to spend any money on a larger gravestone. She didn't even visit him. I can understand why, since their relationship had crumbled at the end, but I vowed that someday I would arrange for a better gravestone.

By July, prosecutors Joe Rieke and Norm Brown invited me down for another meeting to review a list of witnesses the defense planned to call. I took the list back to the office and typed up a 20-page summary with details on the names I recognized, about two-thirds of the people on their list. I included a simple outline of why I thought Addicks would call them as defense witnesses, their connection to Addicks, and the topics on which I thought the defense would have them testify.

In the pretrial hearings Addicks claimed he was being railroaded by the detectives and that the information they obtained from me gave them leads to witnesses that would testify against him. Despite the hard evidence, Addicks denied his involvement in the murder and the arsons. During his bail hearing, Addicks' attorney moved for a reasonable bail or dismissal of all charges on the grounds that Addicks was a Certified Public Accountant and a pillar of the community. But Judge Jones refused to drop the charges. An insanely high bail amount was suggested, which was impossible for Addicks to raise.

By then, Addicks had been placed in solitary confinement at the Rocky Butte Jail due to his alleged escape attempt and alleged proof of the murder contract put out on Cartwright. Addicks protested and, without the help of his lawyer, began preparing a lawsuit he later filed against the County and the jail supervisors for violation of his civil rights and abuse of process. Meanwhile, the State became concerned about the safety of Cartwright, their primary witness, since he, too, was still being held at the State Prison in Salem. To play it safe, Multnomah County transferred Cartwright out of there.

When Addicks was removed from solitary confinement he met with his lawyer, filed a complaint against the jailers and tried to paint a picture of himself as the victim. He presented himself as a man unjustifiably being singled out. He could not understand why the detectives and jailers were picking on him. After all, people like Sam Moll were given immunity.

During numerous pretrial hearings, the detectives and witnesses, including myself, were asked to remain outside the courtroom as the hearings took place so one testimony wouldn't influence the next witness. My real mom attended most of the hearings when the public was allowed in. She did not relay details of the testimony, but did mention Addicks' demeanor throughout the hearings. I was thankful *The Oregonian* never sent a reporter to attend the trial and that they apparently decided not to write anything until it was all over.

A great deal of the courtroom time was spent with the defense trying to exclude prosecution witnesses and evidence. According to the trial transcripts, District Attorney Joe Rieke spent a lot of time defending the State's right to include all their witnesses and evidence. Rieke was 36 years old, six foot four, tall, and stocky and had a deep voice, which gave him a strong, commanding presence. His assistant attorney, Norm Brown, was in his late 50s with graying hair. Brown had a good handle on all the details and was relentless about making sure everything they needed was organized in advance.

Gary and I took pleasure in seeing Rod Addicks walking the courthouse halls in shackles on both his feet and wrists. Looking into his dark eyes as he walked by, I still could not understand how a man of his intelligence—and supposedly a friend to my dad—could do what he appeared to have done. Yet, the facts were overwhelming. There was no doubt in my mind now that he had arranged to have my dad murdered.

Chapter 17: Oregon Murder Trial Begins

I was still worried about negative publicity reflecting on the tax business from Addicks' upcoming murder and arson trials. I purchased a word-processing typewriter so that I could send a personalized letter to the three thousand Columbia Bookkeeping clients. Each letter included a Gold Seal Guarantee using an actual gold-colored seal, and offered free audit assistance and guaranteed accuracy, or we would pay the IRS penalty and interest if the mistake was ours. I signed every letter in blue ink.

All too soon it was time to plan and prepare for another tax season. I arranged for all our tax preparers to take classes for updates on tax law. The preparers had worked too many long nights last season, most putting in over 70 hours a week. I decided to add more tax accountants to the staff for the upcoming season. I had pushed the staff too hard during the prior tax season and decided to do better this time. I was also disappointed that clients had to wait in the lobby, sometimes over half an hour, for their tax interviews. If I could hire a few more preparers, I could speed up the process. Marvin Bridge, the general manager, was almost a month behind on his work. Marvin was a nice man, but I became concerned that he was overworked beyond reason during the last tax season. He needed more help, so I began interviewing extra staff to catch him up.

My dad was in the practice of using plain manila envelopes to deliver clients' completed tax returns. To me, that looked cheap. I decided to spruce up our image. I designed a new logo on full-size, colorful, foldout packets. The company policy and guarantees were printed on the cover. When I had worked with employees of the local aircraft distributors, I had been impressed with the way they marketed their products. Western Skyways remanufactured aircraft engines and gave their customers a one-page Gold Seal Guarantee statement upon completion. It emphasized their professionalism. Al Kempin, in charge of their marketing, had also been my printer since I first started in the aircraft waxing business. Whatever I designed for marketing over the years, he was the one I hired to print it. I could always count on Al to make whatever task I assigned him just a little better. The finished product, with his help, looked professional and upscale.

I took a weeklong vacation to visit my little sister in Los Angeles. My sister had a flower business and her husband worked as an art director for movies. I really enjoyed the time with them, especially when we went to Catalina Island in the Pacific Ocean, west of Los Angeles. Addicks' murder trial was set to begin when I returned home. The good news was that over a year had passed since Dad died and the accounting business was definitely not going down the drain as Addicks said it would.

After the vacation was over it was back to business. My goal was to focus on the existing clients, streamline the business and expand it if possible. I wanted to improve our image during the upcoming tax season with brochures, advertising and a new look. In fact, Gary and I negotiated with a competitor, Granning & Treece Financial Company, about buying out their tax business. I'd become involved with that company six years prior, through my Air Auto Waxing business. I had been detailing the cars and airplanes of their top executives. Granning & Treece had several financing, furniture leasing, and insurance offices in the Portland area. They contacted us. My brother acquired their clients located in North Portland, and Columbia Bookkeeping took over the remaining 1,500 clients. We paid very little for the accounts as they wanted to shut down their tax business. Our operations met their needs. So, between Gary and me, we had four offices located throughout Portland. We were careful to structure the deal so we paid only a small amount down, with the balance due at the end of the following year's tax preparation cycle.

With business preparations settled, my attention returned to Rod Addicks' murder trial.

Mr. Michael Kohlhoff, Rod Addicks' lawyer, entered a plea bargain request just before the murder trial began. District Attorneys Harl Haas and Joe Rieke refused. They said if it was up to them, Addicks was going to jail for life since—at that time—there was no death penalty in Oregon. They would try him first for the murder of Jim Turel, then for the arson cases, and after that he would be transferred to Tacoma, Washington, to stand trial in the securities fraud cases.

**Rod Addicks, entering Judge Dale's courtroom during 1975 murder trial.
Note his smile. This is the baby faced, professional look that he normally wore in
the accounting practice.** *(photo © Stan Turel)*

The murder trial started on September 26, 1975. Presiding was Judge
William Dale of Multnomah County. Over 100 witnesses were scheduled
to speak and they'd logged in over 190 exhibits. The defense attorney said
it would take over three weeks to present his side. Even before the jury
was selected, they spent at least a week dealing with motions to suppress,

motions to exclude witnesses, and motions to throw out testimony. First to be interviewed were Detectives Wells and retired Detective Yazzolino. As the days went by, the prosecution, jurors and Judge Dale appeared exhausted by the delays. Kohlhoff again claimed that Rod Addicks' Miranda Rights had been violated, that I was an agent of the police and therefore all the documentation I forwarded to them should be thrown out. At the end of the week, Kohlhoff filed a motion to dismiss the case. That motion was denied by Judge Dale. Then, ten motions were filed by the defense to dismiss ten of the State's witness, all of which were denied.

Days were spent arguing whether or not I had violated Addicks' Fourth or Fifth Constitutional Right. The prosecutor's argument was that I was running my own investigation within full compliance of my authority as overseer of that company. The defense's argument was that I was an unemployed agent working under the direction of detectives Yazzolino and Wells. The detectives testified that I acted on my own and turned over documents or forwarded leads when I felt it was crucial to the investigation. Out of the presence of the jury they said Rod Addicks had refused to take a polygraph examination although he was the last person to see Jim Turel alive. And they explained that they had not talked to Rod Addicks since they read him his rights on September 16, 1974, eighteen days after the murder took place. Except one brief incident when Detective Englert talked with Addicks about his gun.

Before the jury was called into the courtroom, several days' worth of testimony from vital witnesses was heard. Over 470 pages of court transcripts, tape recordings of confessions by Dennis Lee Cartwright, Sam Moll, and others who had been offered money by Rod Addicks to murder my dad, were introduced. Judge Dale forbade the prosecution from bringing up the arson and Washington State securities fraud charges pending against Addicks. In the end, hundreds of documents were accepted; only a few were excluded.

Jury selection began on October 2. The day after the jury selection was completed all the jury members visited the Columbia Bookkeeping office at 139th and Southeast Stark, accompanied by policemen, defense staff, and the District Attorney's staff. I had arranged for my staff to cancel all client appointments, and I gave all our employees, except for one, a few hours off. I wanted the office environment peaceful, without commotion or staff interference during the site visit.

Next, several small buses were used to transport the jurors, attorneys, and court staff to the location on the Columbia River where sheriff's detectives recovered the overnight bag that Rod Addicks and Dennis Lee Cartwright threw into the river the night of the murder.

After the caravan returned, the prosecution called its first witness to the stand—Julie Syler, our bookkeeper and secretary, who discovered Dad dead in his office. District Attorney Joe Rieke asked her to confirm that she, Peg, Jim Turel, and Rod Addicks were the only people who knew where the key to the vault was located, which she did. Julie verified that the doors to the tax office were locked and lights were out when she arrived the morning Dad's body was discovered. When Julie was asked, 'Who went through the mail each day?' she said, "In the year prior to his death, Mr. Turel insisted on going through all the mail first and then he would direct it to the proper recipient. He was making sure all bills for both Columbia Bookkeeping and Quality Financial Planning were paid on time." During defense questioning, they tried to imply that the murder was due to a robbery gone wrong, but they could find no weakness in the witnesses' answers.

The next witnesses were the Firefighter Emergency Medical Technicians who had been the first to arrive at the murder scene. They confirmed that Dad was dead when they arrived, and that they did not disturb the crime scene. The prosecution questioned the Medical Examiner's office personnel and the Scientific Investigation team, which included officers Lucas and Winslow and team leader, Detective Lewis Rice. The defense tried to trip up the witnesses as to their arrival times and who moved the body and when, in an attempt to show that the crime scene was contaminated or disturbed. But again, no serious issue was raised that could destroy the prosecution's handling of evidence.

The prosecution witness from the coroner's office set the time of death between 8 and 10 p.m. on August 28, 1974. The defense lawyer contested the validity of this information in an effort to insert doubt into the minds of the jurors. Kohlhoff tried to imply the murder took place as late as 11 o'clock that night, which would clear Rod Addicks since he had an alibi that placed him at home at 10 p.m. or just a little later. However, the coroner's office confidently asserted that the condition of the body, when discovered by Julie Syler the next morning, indisputably placed the time of Jim Turel's death between 8 and 10 p.m.

The next witness called by the prosecution was homicide Detective Blackie Yazzolino who had been the first detective on the case. Yazzolino was asked about his years of experience. He explained he'd been on the police force for over 30 years and was the senior homicide detective at the time of Jim Turel's murder. He confirmed that he retired in the middle of this murder investigation.

When Blackie Yazzolino was questioned about his first interview with Rod Addicks the morning of August 29, he said Addicks told him he had last seen Jim Turel out in the parking lot at 8 or 8:30 the night of the murder. Addicks said that as he drove off he saw Jim Turel talking to a young, blond man about a car that was illegally parked in the office parking lot.

Next up was Detective Stewart Wells who spoke of his initial private interview with Rod Addicks. He said he came away with a different story than the one Rod Addicks told to Yazzolino. Wells said Addicks told him he last saw Mr. Turel at the door of the tax office, walking into the building. Wells said Addicks didn't mention a blond man. When he and Yazzolino returned to their office on August 29, they compared notes and saw they had conflicting information from Addicks.

All the detectives were cross-examined about how and why they were receiving so much information from me. Kohlhoff, Addicks' defense attorney, again tried to imply I was a police agent, particularly emphasizing the reward money my family offered. I hoped that the jurors would understand my behavior; it was what any son of a murder victim would do.

Under cross-examination, without the jurors present, the detectives were asked when they first contacted the Fire Department regarding Addicks' possible involvement in arson. They replied that I raised the topic during my first visit with them, which I said was based on my dad's suspicions. They said the following day Fire Department investigators also confirmed their suspicions regarding Addicks' house fire.

The defense tried to distort the focus on Addicks by diving into Blackie Yazzolino's investigation of the massage parlors. I was surprised to learn the detectives had acted on my concerns regarding the arsons and massage parlors within a day of my first interview with them. Since it appeared as though Rod Addicks oversaw those accounts without my dad's involvement, the detectives originally felt Addicks was hiding information about who killed Jim Turel. The D.B. Cooper hijacking manuscript was never brought up.

Lengthy arguments between the defense and prosecution took place while the jury was excused from the courtroom. Kohlhoff continued to move to exclude numerous documents I had turned over to Blackie Yazzolino during the investigation. The doodles and sketches I made on notes and documents were objected to by the defense. Yazzolino confirmed that I submitted about 90 percent of the evidence that was turned over to them; 10 percent was from my brother, Gary.

Both Gary and I spent four days at a time, on alternating weeks, waiting in the hallway outside the courtroom with the other witnesses while the trial continued. Periodically, Rod Addicks was escorted out into the hall and it continued to be gratifying to see him in those ankle chains and handcuffs. Frankly, I was surprised at how well this man, accused of murder, kept his composure. He was always dressed in a suit and tie and walked along with a confident step and that arrogant, snickering expression on his face.

Murder victim's sons, Stanley and Gary Turel, as they wait their turn to testify outside Judge Dale's office during the murder trial of Rod Addicks, September 1975.

Gary and I were scheduled to appear as witnesses on several occasions, but due to legal motions and challenges to documents our testimonies were delayed. We were told that the jury had been excused three-quarters of the time that court was in session, while legal challenges by the defense took place. On the days we were scheduled to testify, Gary and I would stand in the hallway or sit on hard benches for hours watching as the witnesses for the State came and went.

At last I was called into the courtroom as a witness after detectives Yazzolino and Wells were excused. Gary was on standby, to be called in only if the prosecution needed him. Rod Addicks, however, listed Gary as a defense witness, for what reason we could only guess. When I entered the courtroom I saw two dozen people in the gallery. The room had 20-foot ceilings. The walls, finished with marble, had beautifully decorated dark oak panel inserts.

When I sat down in the witness stand, Rod Addicks and his attorney were just 25 feet away, on my left. To the right sat prosecuting attorneys Joe Rieke and Norm Brown, and another young man. The twelve jurors were poised, watching me from the jury box. I had butterflies in my stomach as I was sworn in. The judge asked if I wanted water, which I declined. Looking at Addicks, with his dark black eyes staring back at me, made my temper flare. Okay, you bastard, I thought. You can keep playing this game only so long, but soon it will be over. There may not be a death penalty in Oregon, but I hope you rot in jail for the rest of your life.

The prosecution began by asking my name, address, and connection to the case. I was asked about my business relationship with Columbia Bookkeeping, Quality Financial Planning, and with Rod Addicks. 'Who had control of the business after your father died? Explain Addicks' offer to buy the business. Explain your father's insurance policy,' Rieke said.

Then the questions turned to how I acquired documents and when I forwarded them to the detectives. The jurors were excused several times during my testimony when the defense asked for a mistrial. The defense repeatedly objected to questions and my answers. The attorney kept asserting that I had obtained documents illegally and those documents had led the detectives to the witnesses who eventually testified against Rod Addicks. Motion Denied. Some documents the defense attorney objected to were discounted because the person who actually prepared them was not present. Copies of some documents were not allowed as evidence, but they would have been if it were a civil proceeding.

The topic of the money I thought was missing from the Woodstock Apartment account was raised, but I had no proof. The defense again tried to inflate the importance of our offer of reward money and the loans I made to the officers for their travel to Washington State.

In all, my testimony lasted about an hour. I was disappointed in myself because my answers to the questions were spoken at a rapid-fire pace. Addicks, looking directly at me, smirked and grinned a few times which caused my adrenaline to race with anger. I was asked by the judge to slow down as the information was complicated and they needed to hear it clearly. Once I calmed down, the clarity of my responses became more effective.

The next witness called by the prosecution was Norma Crane, the waitress who served dinner to my dad and Rod Addicks just hours before the murder. She verified that Dad and Addicks had three drinks each that night, and there appeared to be no arguments between them. Surprising to me was that her boyfriend, Officer Dennis Fitz, just happened to be one of the Multnomah County scuba divers who retrieved Dad's overnight bag from the Columbia River. Six months later, Norma and Dennis were married.

Nora Banks, the woman who accompanied my dad to Hawaii, was called as a witness for the prosecution. She verified that she and my dad had an affair and that Rod Addicks knew about it. According to the notes from Detective Wells' first interview of Rod Addicks the day my dad's body was found, Addicks claimed he did not know any of the women my dad dated.

Next to testify was Bernadine Turel, the widow of the deceased, my stepmother who went by the name of Bernie. She testified that Rod Addicks came by her home to offer his condolences the day the murder was discovered. He gave her $200 in cash, saying lawyer Jim Auxier told him that she'd need some cash. She said my older sister was at the house when Addicks arrived. Bernie said Addicks told her the last time he had seen Jim Turel was the prior night. She said Addicks mentioned he and Jim had been out for dinner and a few drinks and that he'd dropped Jim off at the tax office just after 8 o'clock. He said the last time he had seen Jim Turel was when he drove away and Jim was standing outside talking to a young man about cars being illegally parked in the office lot. Bernie testified that she asked Rod Addicks why he would leave Jim there alone to confront the man by himself. Addicks had no answer. Bernie said that when my sister asked Addicks specifically what time he'd last seen her dad, Addicks said he left about dark; he remembered he'd had to turn on the car lights. The prosecution placed the time of onset of darkness at 8:45 p.m. or later, since it was a clear day. This timeline would have placed Addicks at the crime scene later than he had originally claimed during his initial interview with the detectives.

The prosecution asked Bernie to go into more detail about the conversation between my sister and Rod Addicks. Bernie said my sister told Addicks that she was driving home from church the night of our dad's murder and had to turn on her headlights as it was dusk, but not yet dark, at 8:10 p.m. Bernie said Addicks and my sister got into it, meaning they had a minor argument about the time, and that Addicks finally stopped talking. Addicks left the Turel house and as he walked out he said, 'I guess I will go back to the office and hold the policemen's hands.'

Defense attorney Kohlhoff asked Bernie if she was aware that her husband had gone to Hawaii with his girlfriend. At first she said no, then later admitted she'd found four baggage claim checks from a Hawaii trip when he was supposed to be at a computer training class in San Diego. She admitted going out to a singles club after Dad died and said yes, she had confided to a cousin prior to Jim's death that she had prayed and wished Jim would die. When asked if she killed her husband, Bernie said 'No.' There were also questions about her rocky marriage and the $10,000 she was offered to leave the marriage, which she had declined. The jury was not allowed to know that Bernie had passed a polygraph examination shortly after the murder was discovered.

When Detectives Rod Englert and Joe Woods testified, they laid the foundation for the four people who had either been offered money to kill dad or participated in the murder. Most of their testimonies related to how and when the detectives contacted the various witnesses. Defense attorney Kohlhoff tried to discredit the detective's methods, specifically concerning the offer of reward money in exchange for testimony. The topic of money advanced by me to the detectives for advances to Sam Moll's attorney was raised again, but the detectives clarified that emergency funds were needed on a weekend when their office was closed, so they approached me and I offered to help. The detectives said they were afraid that unless the money

Jim and Louise Turel's wedding photo in San Francisco, California, 1945, after World War II, following his tour of duty on the aircraft carrier Yorktown.

Rod Addicks, "Jailhouse Lawyer," prepares paperwork on one of his numerous frivolous lawsuits (photo during *60 Minutes* episode "Plague of Justice").

Police drawing made by a Lake Oswego psychic in 1974, after handling bloody crutches and the watch James Turel was wearing the night he was murdered. Note resemblance between this drawing, and the convicted mastermind of the murder. The psychic had never met Rod Addicks.

Sheriff Lee Brown (center) presenting special awards for this murder case to Detective Joe Woods (left) and Detective Rod Englert. (photo from *Official Detective Stories* article by Andy Stack)

Detective Joe Woods (left) and Detective Rod Englert.

Stanley Turel in his early twenties, before his father was murdered 1974.
(photo © Ernesto Santos)

Stanley Turel interviewed by Morley Safer during shooting of *60 Minutes* episode,
"Plague of Justice." Note stacks of legal papers regarding frivolous lawsuits.

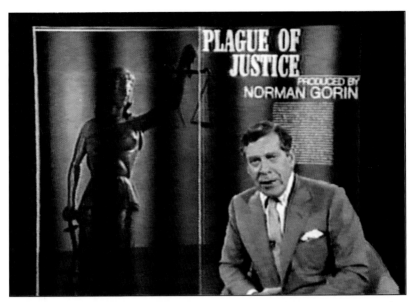

Morley Safer introducing the *60 Minutes* episode aired on December 12, 1982. He opened the show by saying, "Rod Addicks has exhausted the legal system with his appeals and lawsuits. There was no doubt in anyone's mind then, nor is there any doubt now, that Rod Addicks is guilty of murder."
(See entire episode on youtube.com. Search "Plague of Justice")

Columbia Bookkeeping complex and front parking lot, August 29, 1974.

Convicted murderers left to right: Dennis Cartwright, Floyd Forsberg, and Rod Addicks with moustache. (photo © *The Daily News*)

Oregon State Attorney Scott McAlister defended the Oregon State Prison System in response to numerous frivolous lawsuits filed by Rod Addicks. (photo during *60 Minutes* episode, "Plague of Justice")

Many lawyers say this library, inside the Oregon State Prison, far exceeds the resources available to most private law firms. (photo during *60 Minutes* episode, "Plague of Justice")

The Sunday O

VOL. 136 — NO. 45,137   PORTLAND, OREGON, JUNE 14, 1987

Up, up and away

Zachary Hudgik, 2, of Tualatin compares his helium balloon with some of the 23 hot-air balloons launched Saturday in the PSA/Willamette Savings Hot Air   Balloon Classic at Sunset High School. The continue beginning at 7 a.m. Sunday at Sun

Hot air balloon used by Columbia Bookkeeping to give free rides to kids and promote the company in an innovative marketing move.
(photo © *The Oregonian,* June 14, 1987)

was advanced to Sam Moll's attorney immediately, Sam Moll would refuse to be interviewed about what happened the night of Jim Turel's murder. They said Moll was afraid of retribution from Rod Addicks. The implication was that the detectives—or I—used the reward money to buy witnesses was offensive to me. The detectives clarified that Multnomah County reimbursed me for the advances.

The detectives explained that a $1,200 emergency fund was in place for the Narcotics Department, which was a separate department from Homicide. When emergency money was needed on a weekend for the Turel murder investigation, no such fund existed for the Homicide Department.

The fact that the Homicide Department had no funds available on an emergency basis embarrassed the County Commissioners and a short time later Multnomah County developed an emergency fund policy in order to avoid future situations where private citizens advanced money during murder investigations.

Detective Englert then testified that after Dennis Lee Cartwright confessed and was arrested, Cartwright was asked what happened to Jim Turel's overnight bag. Cartwright told the detectives where it was, and how he and Rod Addicks disposed of it as part of their attempt to make the crime scene look like a robbery. He explained how Cartwright accompanied the detectives and the Sheriff's River Patrol to a site east of Portland on the Columbia River and described how he and Addicks had weighted down the overnight bag and threw it into the river. Englert said that after an hour searching the area identified by Cartwright, diver Officer Dennis Fitz noticed the white handles of the overnight bag sticking up from the silt. The bag was recovered with the items Bernie Turel claimed it contained. The disintegrating bag was a lucky find as it tied in the testimony of Sam Moll with Dennis Lee Cartwright.

Because the evidence was so conclusive, the defense attorney attacked Detective Englert's limited experience with homicide investigations. Several witnesses were interrogated hoping to imply that Englert was new to that type of work. However, it turned out that Englert had been a detective with the Los Angeles Police Department for more than six years and spent five years working as a detective for Multnomah County Narcotics Division. Englert had assisted in three homicide cases prior to this one.

The jury heard how the detectives traveled throughout Oregon, Washington, Idaho, and Oklahoma to secure testimony from various witnesses. Some witnesses said they were afraid Addicks and Cartwright would kill them prior to Addicks' arrest. Most of the witnesses were provided with tickets, or reimbursed for travel expenses by Multnomah County.

Again defense attorney Kohlhoff implied that reward money had been used to pay witnesses. But no reward money had yet been given out, and no promise of reward money had been made to any witness for their testimony. After Rod Addicks was arrested, one potential witness contacted me to find out if he would receive reward money after he testified. I did not recall meeting the person and all I could say was, "You need to go through the District Attorney's office for that. It's up to them to determine what information led to the arrest and conviction of the murderer. My understanding is that I will not pay any reward money until after the trial and appeals are over."

Chapter 18: Murder for Hire; Conspirators Testify

Next to testify was Sam Moll, the tax accountant who worked part-time at Columbia Bookkeeping for three years. During Moll's testimony, when the jury was excluded, Moll was asked to provide further details surrounding conversations in 1973 when he and Rod Addicks began talking about burning down a few houses for the insurance money. Moll said that at first it was just in jest and then they came up with a plan to torch one house. Moll described in detail how they bought a house, made sure it was empty, provided an alibi for each other, and then torched the building. They figured that because Rod Addicks was a CPA, no one would suspect him.

The jury was called back in, but a lot of the details involving the arsons were not allowed by the judge. During these arguments, the jury would be asked to step out of the courtroom and wait in their jury room. They missed a great many important details of the case.

Moll said their plan was carried out the year before by renting a hotel room in Ilwaco, Washington, and letting others know they would be going on a fishing trip together the next day. After renting the room, they drove to Portland with three five-gallon cans of gasoline and burned down a single-story, three-bedroom rental Addicks owned. The structure had been insured for three months at a very high value. The prosecutor asked Sam Moll to explain how they did it and Moll replied that while Rod Addicks drove around the block, he went inside and started the fire. They drove away slowly and watched a giant explosion in the rearview mirror as the gas cans detonated. Then they quickly drove back to Ilwaco, Washington, a two-hour drive, went to a local bar, and made sure the bartender and a couple of ladies noticed them. Sam Moll and Rod Addicks spent the rest of the night in their Ilwaco hotel room. They were up at 6 o'clock the next morning for their fishing trip and made sure they were noticed. Their alibi was provable.

The insurance company paid off the claim even though they knew the fire was an act of arson. Their alibis at the bar, hotel, and fishing trip seemed airtight and the insurance company chose not to dispute it. Jim Auxier, their lawyer at that time, handled the case.

The prosecuting attorney prompted Sam Moll to describe other acts of arson he committed with Rod Addicks. Moll said they set up subsequent incidents of arson to get the insurance money, except he and Addicks intended to arrange it in other people's names. Moll said that two incidents were successful and they collected the money.

According to Sam Moll, neither Jim Turel nor the lawyer, Jim Auxier, were aware of the second fire but Jim Turel was suspicious that Addicks may have been involved in the first. When asked how he knew, Moll said Jim Turel began taking over more control of business details, which irritated Rod Addicks. Addicks complained that he and Moll were doing most of the work, but Jim Turel was making the profits. Addicks said he hated and despised Jim Turel.

That's what led to talk about killing Turel. If Jim Turel were dead, Moll said, they figured his family wouldn't be able to continue the tax business, especially since his sons were too young and didn't have enough experience to handle the clients. Sam Moll and Rod Addicks planned to own the business together after arrangements were made to buy out Jim Turel's remaining interest.

Then Sam Moll went into details of how Addicks planned the first murder attempt, a year before the actual murder was accomplished. This first plot was set up in 1973 as a phony tax interview on an evening when the office was closed. Moll said that Jim Turel would occasionally meet clients late in the evening or on weekends if the client was unable to come in during normal office hours. Addicks gave Sam Moll a 38-caliber Iver Johnson revolver with the serial number scratched off. Moll said the gun had a few rusty marks on the outside of the barrel. The police in Kelso, Washington, verified that a few months after Turel was murdered, Addicks received a permit to carry that gun with him. The court showed a shiny black gun to Moll to verify that this was the same gun given to him by Rod Addicks. Moll said he didn't recognize that one.

Sam Moll then described what happened the evening he set out to shoot Jim Turel. As he drove slowly into the office parking lot and saw Mr. Turel sitting at his desk through the window he decided he couldn't go through with the plan. Also, he noticed three men standing across the street talking. Jim Turel was just sitting there in his swivel chair with his back to the window. "It would have been easy," Sam Moll said on the witness stand, "but I never killed a man before and I just didn't have the nerve to do it."

When he was asked by prosecutor Rieke, "What happened after that plot failed?" Moll said, "Addicks and I decided that was okay. We thought maybe we could find someone who might kill Jim Turel for us." Addicks and Moll discussed that his cousin, Maddock Tollocko, might do the deed for $5,000. Shortly after that, Moll said he met Addicks' friend Dennis Lee Cartwright, who already had a criminal record. Addicks said Cartwright lived in Kennewick, Washington, and he might do the murder for $5,000. So, Moll, Addicks, and Cartwright went on several fishing trips together to discuss murder plans.

"When did Addicks tell you he arranged for someone else to murder Mr. Turel?" Rieke asked.

"Just before I found out Jim Turel was dead, Addicks mentioned he'd found someone else who could do it. I was told that after the murder was done, we should go fishing again. On the fishing trip, when Cartwright, Addicks, and I were together, we made a pact that if any one of us ratted on another, the others would kill the rat. We shook hands on that. Then Addicks and Cartwright told me how they murdered Mr. Turel in the hallway."

I was surprised that so much information from Sam Moll's testimony was not allowed to be presented in front of the jury. I understand that you cannot ask anything that may damage the defendant's image, but the arsons and robbery and other information Moll knew about was prohibited from being discussed during his testimony. I guess it's only fair if hearsay rules protect the accused from malicious prosecution. But I would think it fair that crimes for which there is documented proof would be allowed, but not so in today's courts. This does show however, that the accused is given every protection allowed in an effort to be fair.

Maddock Tollocko, a cousin to Sam Moll, testified next. Tollocko lived on the Puyallup Indian reservation near Tacoma, Washington. At 24 years of age, Tollocko was a rough-looking character with long hair. His build was short and stocky. Tollocko verified all of Sam Moll's testimony and admitted that he had originally seriously considered committing the murder for the money.

Tollocko explained that the initial contract offer to kill Jim Turel was made at a party in late December 1973 or early 1974, when both Sam Moll and Tollocko were fairly drunk. "So we got to talking about it. I told him, 'Okay, tell you what. I'm broke. I'm hurting real bad. You tell the guy $10,000 and I'll do it.' I said I'd need half the money up front and the balance when the job was done."

"Did the subject come up again another time?"

"Yes, in July 1974, when I first met Rod Addicks. I met Rod Addicks a second time and we discussed the situation in more details. We agreed that I would be paid $5,000 to do the job. At our third meeting, Mr. Addicks told me how he wanted it done. He said he would supply a key to the back door and that he would pay me the $5,000 before the job was done. Also, he would give me a gun to use. We decided that we would do it soon, once everything was set up. About two weeks after that meeting, we were having some problems with the Council at the Puyallup Tribe regarding fishing rights. Addicks offered to take out, to murder, three Council members in exchange for killing Jim Turel." Tollocko said Addicks also encouraged him and Sam Moll to set up a gambling casino at the Puyallup Indian reservation near Interstate-5.

Multnomah County Senior Deputy District Attorney Rieke asked, "How were you going to get Mr. Turel alone at his office?"

"Rod supplied me with a name and phone number of a business associate at a construction firm. The guy was a tax client. So, I called Mr. Turel, pretending to be this guy, and tried to set up a late-night appointment. But Mr. Turel said, 'No, I'm busy and can't meet you.' Meanwhile, I got a job at the Nichiro Fish Company running the cannery and got tied up with that, which is why I wasn't the one that did the job."

Next, Billy Anglin was called to the witness stand. Anglin was a thin, slight man in his mid-30s who had worked with Dennis Lee Cartwright in the constructions industry years before and had remained friends. Anglin testified that he was approached by Cartwright to murder a crippled Portland accountant. Anglin was aware that the target was a business partner of the man paying for the hit. The murder contract fee would be $5,000. Rod Addicks' name was never mentioned, and Addicks never approached Anglin directly.

Anglin said he was told the target had a swimming pool in his backyard and to make the hit look like an accident or drowning. Anglin had never met Mr. Jim Turel and no other details were given to him about the proposed victim. Later, Cartwright told Anglin the job had been done and he wasn't needed.

Anglin testified that he considered doing a murder for hire because he needed the money for a fresh start. But Anglin talked with his wife, then forwarded what he knew about the murder contract to the Spokane Police Department. According to the Spokane Police, they called Portland in March 1974, five months before Mr. Turel was murdered, to warn about a possible hit planned on a Portland accountant. Anglin said his wife warned him not to get involved. Anglin said his wife was available to testify also. No record of the call was found in Portland police records.

Anglin said that after he told the detectives what he knew, the detectives mentioned reward money had been offered by the Turel family, but that wasn't the reason he was testifying. "After all, I told a local policeman in Spokane about the proposed hit before the murder had ever taken place."

After the murder investigation began heating up in January 1975, Rod Addicks and Dennis Cartwright made several trips to Billy Anglin's home in Kennewick, Washington. During one of those visits, Addicks told the Anglins he had a gun in the red Cadillac parked outside.

I figure that Addicks probably wanted a tighter relationship with Billy Anglin because Cartwright had approached Anglin earlier regarding a separate murder contract on Turel. Since the intended murder victim was now dead, Addicks must have thought it important for the Anglins to know that he had a gun nearby and thus was capable of murder. Billy Anglin testified that he and his wife, who had already met with the detectives two weeks prior to meeting Addicks, were afraid of Addicks.

My family was shocked to learn that information about a plot to murder my father might have been forwarded to the Portland police months before our dad was killed. What if the local police had followed up on the tip from Spokane? My dad would still be alive and Rod Addicks would be in jail. But Anglin said that at that time he did not have the name of the person the hit would be on.

Again, the defense objected to the bulk of Billy Anglin's testimony, citing that Rod Addicks never talked directly to Anglin before the murder. At best, Dennis Lee Cartwright would be the co-conspirator. However, the jury didn't buy that line of reasoning since Billy Anglin never met Sam Moll or Maddock Tollocko. The only connection among all these co-

conspirators was Rod Addicks. The prosecutor pointed out that Rod Addicks went to the trouble of meeting Anglin after the murder took place, when the investigation was heating up, which implied Addicks was trying to control any leaks that might take place within the circle of people who were aware of a murder contract on Jim Turel.

The prosecution then introduced the hotel manager of the Montavilla Motel, located a few blocks from the murder scene. The manager verified that Rod Addicks registered Dennis Lee Cartwright under the alias of Ron Barton. But Addicks was the one who paid for the room with cash. The manager of the old motel had a clear recollection because Addicks drove a brand new red Cadillac.

The hotel manager's testimony verified that Dennis Lee Cartwright was in town the day of the murder. I was impressed at the amount of evidence and extensive details detectives Englert and Wells had uncovered.

Transferring Dennis Lee Cartwright from the Oregon State Prison in Salem to the Multnomah County Courthouse in Portland to testify was done very carefully because the police were still concerned Rod Addicks had a contract out on Cartwright's life. Prior to testifying, Cartwright was held upstairs in the District Attorney's office. Just before bringing him in, two security guards double-checked the hallways to make sure nothing suspicious was going on.

The defense had spent months in pre-trial and discovery without the jury present, trying to put a different slant on Cartwright's confession. But their motions to exclude the testimonies of the other men who had been asked to kill Jim Turel were defeated one by one. The time had finally arrived for the damaging testimony of Dennis Lee Cartwright. Addicks and Cartwright had been lifelong friends since the third grade, but that day in court they looked at each other with long blank stares as Cartwright took the stand.

Dennis Lee Cartwright's demeanor was that of a defeated man. In his plain clothes, he looked thin, frail, and rough. Cartwright was in his mid-30s, had dark brown hair and a thin mustache. His pockmarked face gave him the appearance of a man who had led a rough life.

First, the prosecution had Cartwright describe his lifelong association with Addicks. Then they verified that Cartwright had purchased items at Copeland Lumber the day Jim Turel was killed. Receipts showed Cartwright signed for material bought that day.

Defense attorney Kohlhoff asked to have the jury sent out of the room. He suggested that if the prosecution would first go through all the questions, the defense could challenge without the jury present for any testimony. This jury going in and out was wearing everyone down.

Dennis Cartwright incarcerated at the Oregon State Prison
(photo © *The Daily News*)

When the jury returned, Cartwright was still in the witness chair ready to testify. District Attorney Joe Rieke looked like a football coach, ready for the game to begin. Rieke spoke fast, in a deep voice that was calming to the witness. Several times the judge asked Rieke to talk slower as people could not keep up with him. Rieke asked Cartwright:

Q. Mr. Cartwright, when was the first time Addicks brought up the suggestion to kill Mr. Turel?

A. Sometime in February 1974. Rod Addicks and I were talking about a number of things, and then he asked me if I would help him kill Mr. Turel.

Q. Mr. Cartwright, can you recall specifically what was discussed, what words were said?

A. He just told me he wanted to get rid of Mr. Turel. He asked if I would do the job. I told him, yes.

Q. Did Addicks mention any amount of money?

A. Five thousand dollars. And that he wanted it done as soon as possible.

Q. Could you tell us any more about the specific arrangements made at that time?

A. Well, he just wanted to get rid of him because Rod was buying into the business, and he had another payment coming up and he wanted it done before that.

Q. What plans, if any, were made at that time?

A. Well, we didn't have any specific plans at that time, and he told me he might have another man do the job. I told him that would be great.

Q. You really did not want to do it?

A. No.

Q. When was the next time the subject came up?

A. I think it was in May 1974, and he said that the man he had to do the job couldn't do it. He had it all set up, but it fell through. He asked me if I would still go ahead with it. I told him I would. He said he would let me know when.

Q. When did you start doing work with the apartments for Addicks? Was that when you formed the plan to kill Mr. Turel?

A. I think it was sometime in late June, but soon after that we started working on a number of plans, and just picked the best one at the time that would suit the situation.

Q. Can you tell the court and jury, please, what it is that Mr. Addicks told you about why he wanted to do this?

A. Well, he was going to get the business, keep it for awhile and then liquidate as far as I know. There was a $50,000 insurance policy on both Mr. Turel and Mr. Addicks. He told me I'd take over the management of the apartments and maintenance.

Q. What did he tell you about Stan and Gary Turel?

A. Well, that they would probably get part of the business or get into it, but he could handle them because they didn't know that much about CPA work.

Q. What was the specific plan that you picked, sir?

A. Well, hit him on the head and knock him out and strangle him. I was given a key so I could come in the back door of the office while Mr. Turel and Addicks were out for drinks at the end of the day.

Q. How did you come up with that idea?

A. We'd watched a movie where a gangster used a cue ball to knock out a victim prior to a murder.

NOTE: Cartwright also told others he had cold-cocked a man with a cue ball in a previous dispute.

Q. Had you ever met Mr. Turel before, and did you ever receive any money from him?

A. No, I never met Mr. Turel. I only dealt with Mr. Addicks.

Q. Mr. Cartwright, did you have any conversations about how you would get rid of the evidence or anything of that nature once you committed the crime?

A. Well, we had a talk about taking Turel's car and credit cards down into the skid row area of Portland and leaving them there and letting somebody else steal them up. Let's say somebody steals the credit cards or maybe they get found with the car. That would turn the suspicions on other people.

Q. Where did you get the key to the office? And what did you bring with you?

A. I got the key from Rod. I brought in a cord, cue ball, a sock, and gloves. Addicks gave me an attaché case to put those things in. I put the cord in my back pocket.

Q. What time was it when you snuck into the office?

A. About a half hour before they returned.

Q. Please explain to us and the jury, and point to the location on this map of the office, where you were and where Mr. Turel and Addicks were.

As Cartwright pointed to the spots on a large map of the office he said,

A. At first they were sitting here in the reception room talking. Rod was trying to get Mr. Turel back into his office. When Addicks went to the back of the hallway to make the phone call to the woman who was supposed to be there, Mr. Turel went into the bathroom, here. When Mr. Turel came out, I came around the corner, behind him, and hit him.

Q. Where were you hiding when Mr. Turel came out of the bathroom?

A. I was hiding in the back of the office when Mr. Addicks and Mr. Turel came in, and Mr. Addicks got Mr. Turel to go to the back of the office to make a phone call. Mr. Addicks had it set up that Mr. Turel was supposed to meet a girl there and take her out on a date. And when Mr. Turel passed by the door, I hit him on the back of the head.

Q. What did you hit him with?

A. A cue ball in a stocking.

Q. And what happened?

A. Well, he didn't get knocked out like he was supposed to. I swung at him again for the second time with the cue ball. The sock broke, and the cue ball went flying. I grabbed Mr. Turel's crutch and beat him over the head with it.

Q. How did you happen to grab his crutch?

A. He was still standing and turned on me in the middle of the hallway. He was trying to hit me with his crutches. He turned on me and was swinging his crutches at me.

NOTE: The Multnomah County Coroner's office testified that James Turel had extremely strong neck muscles, larger than a wrestler's, most likely due to having to lift himself on crutches for over twenty years. Apparently, these muscles protected the victim from an immediate knockout and this strength unexpectedly thwarted the murderers' efforts.

Q. And you grabbed one?

A. Yes, and I hit him, I don't remember how many times, several times. Mr. Turel appeared to be semi-conscious and fell down on his back.

Q. Where was Addicks during the time this beating was taking place? Did either of you get blood on you?

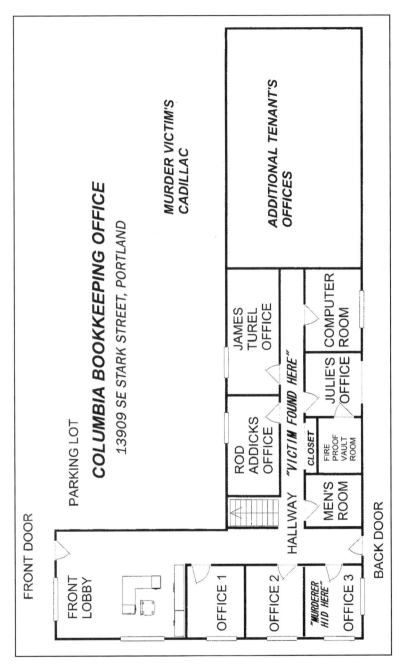

First floor of the Columbia Bookkeeping building showing where the murderer hid and where James Turel's body was found.

A. Mr. Addicks was standing in his office doorway far enough away so he wouldn't get any blood on himself.

Q. What happened after that?

A. Well, Addicks took the cord from me and straddled Mr. Turel. Addicks' feet were wide apart trying to stay out of the blood. Then he put the rope around Mr. Turel's neck and tightened it as he pulled up on his head. After he was sure Mr. Turel was not breathing anymore, Addicks pulled the cord off him and put it in that attaché case we brought with us.

Q. What happened after Mr. Turel died?

A. We went into the vault room and opened it to take out some cash. Then we put the key back in the desk that Addicks had taken it out of. Also I turned Mr. Turel's body over so I could get his wallet out. We took out his credit cards and some cash.

Q. What else did you do and how long did you stay at the office after that?

A. We stayed about ten minutes. We put my gloves, cue ball, cord, and credit cards in the attaché case. Then Addicks put Mr. Turel's overnight bag and the attaché case in Addicks' trunk and we drove to the Columbia River where we threw both into the river.

Q. Did you weigh them down?

A. Yes, with rocks. It took about 15 minutes to drive to the river.

Q. What time was it when you left the murder scene?

A. It was almost getting dark.

Q. After you dumped the stuff in the river, where did you and Addicks go?

A. He drove me back to my truck, which was parked down the street from the tax office. I then went back to the Montavilla Motel and took a shower and changed clothes. Rod Addicks drove back to Kelso, Washington, and I joined him after that. He was in the shower at his home, and he had already put his clothes in a bag on the back porch. I then threw our clothes in several dumpsters in the Kelso area.

Q. What time was it when you got back to Rod's house in Kelso?

A. It was about 11 p.m. Rod told me when he got home he changed the clock in the back to 10 p.m. so it would look like he got home earlier.

Q. Mr. Cartwright, it is our understanding that you checked into the motel under a false name and also used Lee's Construction as a business name. Why was that, can you explain?

A. Well, since I was on parole, I was supposed to be restricted to Washington. It was a violation for me to be in Oregon. By my using a false name and Rod Addicks paying for my motel room, I thought no one would know I was here in Oregon. I opened a bank account in Vancouver, Washington, for Lee's Construction with the help of Rod Addicks. The account was at the First Interstate Bank.

After that, the prosecution went through a long list of exhibits, including Dad's overnight bag recovered from the Columbia River, and checks written to Lee's Construction. No checks were written to Lee's Construction until after the murder took place.

Chapter 19: The Defense Calls Its Witnesses

Throughout the trial, Addicks' attorney, Mr. Michael Kohlhoff, filed motions to suppress, motions to dismiss all charges, motions to dismiss indictment for a fair trial, motions for a mistrial, renewed motions for a mistrial, motions to dismiss witnesses and exclude testimony, motions to exclude all evidence of the conspiracy, motions for directed verdict, and several others. The legal debate between the attorneys on all of these motions was done out of the presence of the jury, which was waiting patiently in the juror's room. Every motion was denied, one by one, after lengthy arguments between Addicks' attorney and the prosecution.

Next up to testify was lawyer Jim Auxier, who verified the authenticity of Jim Turel's will and confirmed that Rod Addicks was present in his law office downtown in 1973 when Dad discussed the proposed provisions, terms, and conditions of the will. Addicks was also present when the will was drafted on June 1, 1973.

The defense attorney, Kohlhoff, objected, as he did not see any relevancy of the will in this case. Then the jury was asked to leave the room before any further testimony by Auxier could be given.

Prosecuting attorney Rieke was asked by the judge to explain the relevancy of the details of the will. "Your Honor," Mr. Rieke said, "the fact that Mr. Addicks had knowledge and was present at its creation and at the formation of its initial provisions is important. The individuals, both Moll and Cartwright, indicated to Your Honor the low esteem in which Mr. Addicks held Stanley Turel and Gary Turel, and that he felt the takeover of the corporation was going to be accomplished due to Addicks' ability to manipulate those two individuals.

"Your Honor," Rieke continued, "The testimony of Stanley Turel with respect to the financial condition of the estate after his father's death, and making this clear to the jury is going to be difficult, but I wish to try using this will as a document. The condition of the estate was that it had a low cash or liquidity situation. It was not liquid. It needed money to pay estate taxes. A number of offers were made by Mr. Addicks, which relate to his efforts to take over the corporation, and relate both to this document and to an insurance policy with respect to getting the money out of the corporation and into the hands of the estate."

"This is another one of these instances where I don't understand why you are both fighting so strenuously about the document," Judge William Dale said. "Most of what is in there has been said already, but without objections."

"Your Honor," said Rieke, "the ownership of the corporation in terms of maintaining or holding ownership was the objective of the defendant."

The judge overruled the objection from the defense and accepted the will and Auxier's testimony.

Both Jim Turel's will and the business life insurance policies were in effect prior to the arson fire that took place in July 1973. The judge ruled that any discussion about the arson could not take place in front of the jury, since it was a separate crime yet to be tried. I was never allowed to mention my dad's suspicions about Addicks' involvement in arson in front of the jury.

Next to testify was Joe Huber, the agent for Wausau Life Insurance Company, who said that on June 19, 1973, a $50,000 life insurance policy was written on both Rod Addicks and Jim Turel. Not mentioned during the trial was something Joe Huber told me privately—that Rod Addicks approached him with the idea of taking out a Key Man life insurance policy in case something happened to Dad or himself. Key man life insurance is used as an instrument to fund the buyout of a deceased partner or to supply necessary cash flow in a company following the death of a partner. Joe Huber met my dad through his close association and friendship with Rod Addicks.

Defense attorney Kohlhoff called in my cousin who had told detectives she suspected Bernie Turel committed the murder. But there was no evidence to support that theory.

The list of a hundred witnesses included Rod Addicks' wife, his mother, and various friends.

Defense Attorney Michael Kohlhoff asked Addicks' wife if she recalled what time Addicks returned home the night of Jim Turel's murder:

A. Around 10 p.m.

Q. What time does he normally come home?

A. Around 6:30 p.m.

Q. Why is your home phone number listed under an alias?

A. Because we were getting a few crank calls.

Mrs. Rod Addicks was a well-dressed lady who looked like the perfect wife trying to protect her husband. However, by the end of the trial she had learned of her husband's numerous affairs, including one woman who testified at the trial. I continued to feel sorry for her; the stress of finding out the truth about her husband concerning the murder plots and infidelities must have been difficult for her and her kids to handle. Shortly thereafter she divorced Rod Addicks.

Ten other defense witnesses were called to testify to the fact that they never saw Mr. Turel and Addicks quarrel. It appeared as though the men were friends and worked together just fine, most said.

Then three State witnesses were called in to testify that they saw Dennis Lee Cartwright, Sam Moll, and Rod Addicks together at their restaurant or bar on numerous occasions. This backfired on the defense as it showed that the three had known each other and associated together on numerous occasions.

A former college roommate of Rod Addicks was called in as a defense witness. The man testified he and Addicks shared a room while they attended Linfield College years ago. He said Addicks was one of the most intelligent people he had ever met. He said Addicks' memory was excellent.

Several tax clients were called to the witness stand to document that they had never seen my dad and Addicks quarrel.

A witness named Mr. Piccallo was flown in from New Jersey. Mr. Piccallo was also a CPA and had his own tax firm on the east coast. He testified that he, Rod Addicks, and Jim Turel had a great time for over a week when they attended a Burrough's computer seminar in San Diego just a few weeks prior to Dad's death. He said that Rod Addicks and Jim Turel appeared to have a father-son relationship. There was no sign of any problem between the two men. Mr. Piccallo testified that all three of them went out together several evenings to Tijuana, Mexico. There may have been ladies involved. They all had a great time.

"Did you ever hear Jim Turel talk about his son, Stan?" asked Kohlhoff. But prosecutor Rieke objected, based on hearsay. The judge asked the jury to step out so he could hear the questions and answers without the jury present.

Mr. Piccallo testified that Jim Turel complained he was having a difficult time getting along with one of his sons, but he didn't know which son Mr. Turel was referring to. Mr. Turel mentioned that this son had taken over one of his offices plus a few of his clients, but he was not getting along with him at all."

Rieke objected again, saying the information was hearsay, especially since Mr. Piccallo didn't know which son Jim Turel was referring to.

The jury was still out of the room when Kohlhoff tried to make it appear as if my brother, Gary, with his separate small tax business, had a motive to kill his father. The jury was not allowed to hear the lengthy argument that ensued between the prosecution and defense. Several times the defense tried to prove that my dad had quarrels with my brother, Gary. In fact, my brother didn't find out why Rod Addicks used him as a witness until the trial was over.

Next, the defense called Gary Turel. The first question to my brother was, "Did you work with your father in the Columbia Bookkeeping business?"

"No," said Gary. "Although I am a Licensed Tax Consultant."

Gary was asked a few more questions and then dismissed. The defense's efforts to smear my brother and his relationship with Dad was never allowed to be heard in front of the jury. The judge and Rieke did a good job putting a stop to it. Gary had waited in the hallway for four days before being called as a witness for his ten minutes of testimony.

Also, the defense dug into Bernie and Dad's marital problems including the fact that she had hated my dad, and prayed he would die before he was murdered. They also repeatedly brought up suspicions about the massage parlors in an effort to dilute the prosecution's focus on Addicks.

Rod Addicks, in an act of extreme self-confidence, took the witness stand to speak in his own defense. But few of the questions asked by defense attorney Kohlhoff had to do with the substance of the trial or the allegations. At first, rather than focus on the murder case, the questions were geared to creating a positive sense of Addicks' good character, while casting doubt and lack of sympathy on the prosecution and the victim. Later, Addicks' testimony seemed primarily an effort to discredit the prosecution's witnesses and to confuse the jury with extraneous facts outside the topic of the murder. As before, neither I, nor any of the other witnesses, were allowed to hear what was going on in the courtroom. My information came after-the-fact from the court transcripts.

In answer to defense attorney Kohlhoff's promptings, Addicks answered question after question about his past, his knowledge of business operations, and his work history. When he said he'd worked for the LaSalle CPA firm in San Francisco, it impressed the jury. On the stand, Rod Addicks looked like a professional and spoke well. One question brought up the topic of a scorpion tattoo on his upper leg. Addicks was very proud of the image, with claws that pointed up, and a stinger that curved backwards then up again. His answers were lengthy, descriptive, relaxed.

When the prosecution cross-examined him, the tone and manner in which he answered the questions changed abruptly. Prosecuting Attorney Joe Rieke asked the following of Rod Addicks:

Q. Mr. Addicks, you are a Certified Public Accountant in some states, is that true?

A. I'm sorry?

Q. Mr. Addicks, you are a Certified Public Accountant in some states?

A. Yes.

Q. Do you have a CPA license in the state of Washington?

A. Yes.

Q. Prior to working at Columbia Bookkeeping, where were you employed?

A. Prior to working at Columbia Bookkeeping?

Q. Yes, that's the question, Mr. Addicks.

A. The last position I had was with my own company.

Q. Did you have the same kind of investing organization similar to

Quality Financial Planning going on up there in Washington as well?

A. Pardon me?

Q. Did you have the same kind of investing organization similar to Quality Financial Planning going on up there in Washington as well?

A. Not really, no. Not similar.

Q. Did that go well?

A. Pardon?

Defense lawyer Kohlhoff objected as the topic was outside the scope of this trial and was not relevant. He did not want the jury to hear about the fraudulent investment schemes and charges against Addicks in Washington State. The judge let the questions continue.

Q. Did those investments go well up there?

A. Some of them went well, and some of them did not go well.

The judge interrupted, called the lawyers to his bench, and quietly warned the prosecution that it could not bring up the securities fraud cases pending in Washington. I found out later, from Rieke, that Addicks started squirming in the witness chair when these questions came up. Joe Rieke continued the questioning:

Q. Did Mr. Turel know about your experience in Washington?

A. No, he did not.

Q. Did you develop the books for the property investments you were overseeing?

A. Pardon me?

Q. What were the books developed for the Big Spruce Trailer Park?

A. Umm, a checkbook was kept. The general ledger was not prepared until after Jim was killed.

Q. Are you aware of any reason why Mr. Dennis Lee Cartwright would kill Mr. Turel?

A. Pardon me?

Q. Are you aware of any reason why Cartwright would kill Mr. Turel?

Rieke later told me that this type of game is played when someone needs time to think up an answer. The prosecution spent much more time interviewing Addicks than the defense attorney had. What Rieke found interesting was how easily Addicks impressed the jury and judge with his intelligence. But what he failed to realize was that by using those stalling tactics, he was hurting his own credibility.

The jury had an either/or case on their hands. If Rod Addicks was telling the truth, all the other witnesses in the murder conspiracy were lying. Addicks denied or twisted all prior testimony, while continuing to say he and Dennis Lee Cartwright were good friends. "I have no idea why my friends would say I offered them money to kill Jim Turel," Addicks testified.

Addicks explained at length about how he, Sam Moll, Dennis Cartwright, and Maddock Tollocko spent a lot of time and research on building a gambling casino at the Puyallup Indian reservation. I'm sure the jury remembered Sam Moll and Michel Tollocko's testimony about Rod Addicks' offer to kill uncooperative Tribal Council members in exchange for them killing Jim Turel.

The trial ended when the defense called the last of their 35 witnesses. The jury was given eight pages of instructions, including the statement that even if they found that Rod Addicks had not been directly involved with the blows and strangulation that killed Mr. Turel, they could still determine that he was instrumental in soliciting and hiring someone to do it for him. If they determined Addicks had any involvement whatsoever, they would need to find Rod Addicks guilty of murder.

Chapter 20: The Jury Returns a Verdict

On a beautiful fall morning in early September 1975, after six months of motions, pretrial hearings, and two weeks of testimony with the jury present, the jury members were ushered into the jurors' room for deliberation. At 4:30 p.m., after only seven hours of private discussion, the jurors notified the court that they had reached a verdict. Present when the verdict was read was my mother, my older sister, my brother Gary, Rod Addicks' wife, and a few others. Bernie, my stepmother, was not there. Judge William Dale questioned the Jury spokesman:

Q. Mr. Goodall, I notice you have what appears to be a verdict form. Are you the foreman of this jury?

A. Yes, I am, Your Honor.

Q. Has the jury arrived at a verdict?

A. Yes we have.

Q. Will you stand and tell us what the verdict of the jury is?

A. The jury finds the defendant guilty as charged.

Q. All right, sir. Will you hand it to the clerk, please?

Mr. Goodall did so.

Q. The verdict form is signed 'Theodore Goodall?'

A. Yes.

Q. We will poll the jury. When your name is called, if you voted for this verdict of guilty as charged, would you respond with the affirmative, yes. If you did not, would you respond with the negative, no."

Thereupon the roll was called and all jurors responded, yes.

The judge gave instructions about removing Rod Addicks and he was led out of the courtroom in chains. My spirit soared as I took a big deep breath of relief. All of us in the family went and congratulated District Attorney Joe Rieke and his staff. We told the detectives how much we appreciated all their work. We invited them to join us for dinner, but they said it would be a conflict of interest.

My mother, brother, sister, and I went out to celebrate. The stress I'd been internalizing during the entire past year started to dissipate. I'd developed great respect for how well the officers and District Attorney's personnel functioned, even amid all the bureaucracy and a hand tied behind their back.

During the previous months, a few people told me they would kill the person if someone murdered their dad. My feeling is, if I were going to kill Addicks because he killed my dad, then I would be lowering myself to his barbaric standards. However, if someone attacked me or my family in my presence, I could easily kill someone in self defense to protect my family. The legal process of catching and convicting Addicks reinforced my belief that justice does prevail, if given enough time. I trusted that the System and God would punish a convicted murderer.

Many clients and friends, when learning that I had worked side by side in the office with Addicks for over four months, asked how I could keep my cool during that time. Well, all I could say is if someone murdered your dad, you would adapt and do what you had to do in an effort to find out what really happened. I had a driving force inside me to find out who committed the murder and why. Even though Addicks became my prime suspect, I felt I could learn more by working with him while conducting a covert investigation. My hands were not tied behind my back as the detectives' had been. However, when Detective Englert took over he knew how to make things happen, which lead to the solving of the crime. The pursuit of justice takes time. Even though I had strong suspicions, I did not have conclusive proof that Rod Addicks killed Dad. Not until after detectives Englert and Woods determinedly followed up on all leads was the case solved.

Rod Addicks was sentenced to life in prison.

This was a moment of justice and great relief.

I wish I could say, 'That was it. End of the story. ' But it wasn't.

Addicks' murder conviction was just the beginning.

I returned to work the day after Rod Addicks was sentenced to life in prison for the murder of my father. I felt relief and exhilaration. It was like the bell had rung and summer vacation was out there waiting for me. But hey, it was already fall and the leaves were turning bright yellow. To see the change of seasons and feel the cool breeze after a hot summer is something that always excites me.

With the murder trial over, it was time for Addicks to face a court for the arson charges, so we were not done with him yet.

As I walked down the hallway of the tax office where Dad had died and I could still see faint gouges under the newly painted walls, I have to admit the murder still bothered me. The gouges reminded me of the struggle Dad must have gone through. I'll have to refinish the wall again in the near future, I thought to myself.

I entered my private office, which had once been my dad's kingdom, with a sense of determination. I would do my best to make something of Dad's business. Peg, Julie, and Marvin Bridge came into the office with their cups of coffee and sat down. I suggested a toast to all of us. Julie said, "Wait a minute, since you don't drink coffee, I'll get you a glass of water."

Sitting at my dad's desk, I could see the relief and mutual respect in their faces. As a team, we'd worked through what seemed impossible and we made it through. "I couldn't have done it without all of you," I said, raising my glass. "I'm not going to sell the company. With your help, we can really make something out of this. This company will support all of us, and it will be here for my family's future. This company will be a tribute to my dad."

Chapter 21: Bernie Turel, the Widow, Remarries

My stepmother met a man named Roger when she attended a dance at the Top of the Cosmo restaurant, one of Portland's finer dining establishments. My brother and I began referring to him as "Mr. Cosmo." The man was 57 years old, had red hair, and a thin, short stature. A few weeks after they met, Mr. Cosmo started seeing Bernie almost every night. My stepmother was gaga over him.

Gary and I did a little background research on Mr. Cosmo. Our limited investigation showed he was divorced and living in a poorly maintained apartment downtown and drove an old Ford Pinto. He appeared to have little money. I was worried about Bernie because she did not have much in the way of street smarts. I thought she was a vulnerable widow and must have looked like a good catch to a man close to retirement with no savings. I reminded Bernie that according to the state, she would lose her $750 per month SAIF workers compensation payment if she got married to Mr. Cosmo.

"Stan, his name is Roger and the Turel Trust and Roger's wages are enough for us to get by," she told me.

A month later she announced that she and Mr. Cosmo had gotten married and he was moving in with her. Okay, great, I thought, knowing the estate would already be short of money needed to pay off the estate taxes. After her marriage and several conversations about Mr. Cosmo, Bernie stopped returning my calls. She did come into the tax office to pick up a check once a month, however. I must have insulted her by trying to talk her out of getting married to Mr. Cosmo.

A few months later I received a call from our attorney, Jim Auxier. "I received a call from Bernie's attorney," Auxier said. "She and her new husband are going to file a motion in court to remove you as a Trustee of your father's estate. They think you're mismanaging it."

That call left me feeling as if a rock had dropped into the bottom of my stomach. "What now?" I asked Auxier. "What's the real problem?"

"Bernie is accusing you of having a meeting, without her knowledge, where you, your brother, and your sister bought out some partners in the Magnolia Apartments without her knowledge. They say you should have contacted your stepmother, as this is a clear conflict of interest in your position as executor of the estate. Also the lawsuit is going to assert that you are too young and inexperienced to handle the business. They think maybe you should sell the business."

"Wait a minute! Are you saying she did not attend that meeting?"

"Yes," Auxier replied. "That's what the lawsuit will allege."

I had Auxier read me the complaint that was to be filed in court by my stepmother in the next few days. "However," Auxier continued, "her attorney said if you choose to resign, Bernie and her husband will not file the lawsuit. Also, Stan, her lawyer mentioned that she might want to make Mr. Cosmo—I mean Roger, herself, or maybe her attorney, the trustee of the Turel Family Trust."

"What!" I shouted. That little pimp was only using her money and living off her. I breathed in deep. I took the time to exhale. "Jim," I said calmly, "Bernie did attend the meeting and I can prove it. A number of months ago, before we bought the other partners out, I had her write down the minutes of our discussion. Let me pull out the file and I will get right back to you."

"Julie!" I shouted.

Julie was there in an instant, but before I could say anything Julie asked, "What's wrong?"

"You will not believe what my stepmother is trying to do!" I explained the situation and Julie just shook her head and sighed. She went out and was back immediately with the folder for the Magnolia Apartments, which I had renamed the Elizabeth Court Apartments. I opened the file, fearful that Bernie had removed the notes, but luckily there they were; Bernie's handwritten notes from our hour-long meeting. Everyone had been present. I was relieved to have the truth in writing, in Bernie's own hand. But I wondered what should I do with it? I decided to have some fun. I'd show her and her new husband what fools they were.

I called Jim Auxier back and told him I'd found the meeting notes proving Bernie was present. "Without saying anything about these notes, let's set up a meeting in the Columbia Bookkeeping office. Have Bernie bring her lawyer and Mr. Cosmo. And Jim," I said, "I want you to tell her lawyer that I will resign if, after our meeting, they still feel I should resign. Tell them I've had enough pressure; that maybe they're right. Do not tell them that we have her handwritten minutes to prove what happened. I want to see the look on their faces when they see this. Tell them this meeting should take place before they waste money going to court. And Jim, please make sure the meeting takes place in the next few days. The last thing I need is for the staff and clients to see this type of squabble going on in the papers. We have enough problems with the press and the Addicks trials. I don't want the press to get a hold of this."

That same day I met with First Interstate Bank to expand and renew the business credit line. I needed $70,000 to make it through the upcoming tax season. I showed them a good-looking profit and loss statement, which even indicated improvement from the year before. The banker was impressed, but what he did not realize was that I was taking a salary of only $800 a month to make sure the company could meet its expenses. As I sat there talking to the banker I thought to myself, Oh, my God, if only the banker knew what I was going through with my stepmother at this time, he would never approve the credit line. The bank insisted that I personally guarantee the loan for the family business.

Two days later, the meeting Jim Auxier set up with my stepmother, her lawyer, and Mr. Cosmo—Roger—came to order at the Columbia Bookkeeping office. I sat behind my dad's desk with my hardcopy proof in one hand while biting my tongue and pressing my fingernails into the outer edge of the desk. Jim Auxier opened, "Thank you all for coming. Please tell me why you feel Stan should not be executor and Trustee."

Bernie's lawyer thoroughly and professionally explained their complaint. That sleaze ball Mr. Cosmo piped up and said, "Since I've had experience as the manager of a Fred Meyer's hardware department, I am capable of helping Bernie in handling the Turel Trust and other things in your stepmother's best interest." I sat there, looking right at Mr. Cosmo, while continuing to run my fingernails in the expanding grooves I was creating in the desk in an effort to reduce my stress. I tried to appear calm and poised in front of everyone, despite my frustration.

I looked at Bernie and asked, "Do you recall attending a meeting where we talked about potential lawsuits from the apartment partners against Columbia Bookkeeping and the Turel estate?"

Emphatically, Bernie said, "I was never invited and knew nothing about it until I heard through the grapevine that you bought it from the partners."

I could hold my tongue no longer. "I see," I said. "Do you remember that we were worried about having enough money to pay the estate taxes and make it to the next tax year?"

"No," she said. "I was never told about this and I really think you're too young to run this business."

"Well," I said, "maybe you will remember these!" I handed two pages to her lawyer first, then copies to the rest of them. "Those two pages are copies of Bernie's handwritten notes from the meeting that she supposedly never attended. Look at the date."

My stepmother looked at them and blurted out, "I knew I should never have taken these notes. I thought I had thrown them away!"

I laughed to myself thinking, this is a real Perry Mason moment! I waited a few moments. No one spoke. Then Bernie's attorney looked at my attorney and said, "Maybe we should talk about this a little more."

"I think Stan is willing to put this behind us," Auxier said. "And there is absolutely no reason for your lawsuit to be filed. If you will drop this right now, I am sure Stan is still going to work with everyone and move forward as if nothing has happened here."

Bernie's attorney said, "Thank you for clearing up this matter. I'm sure Bernie just forgot about the meeting due to the stress she's been under."

I thought, sure, Bernie just sat here and lied to us all. It angered me that she lied and then remembered so quickly about writing the notes. However, I stood up and shook hands with her and her lawyer, but not Mr. Cosmo. "Call me if you have any problems, Bernie," I said. She and Mr. Cosmo had shown their true colors. I could not trust them, and in the future I would document every interaction with that duo. When Mr. Cosmo got into my Dad's golden Cadillac I thought, that scumbag is even driving Dad's car!

But as my temper receded, my mood improved. I knew Bernie wasn't really to blame. She's gullible and way too willing to please. No match for Roger's manipulation. Mr. Cosmo took advantage of her.

Later that day Norm Brown, from the District Attorney's office, called to set up a meeting downtown to discuss the upcoming arson trials, scheduled to begin in December.

When I went home that night, I had a few white Russians, to relax, while I spoke with my brother by phone.

"I don't know how you keep your cool when confronted with things like that," Gary said.

"It's easy," I told him. "Compared to dealing with the man who murdered our dad."

But the stress of my day had really gotten to me. After that, I told the staff I needed to take a few days off from the tax business before the arson trials began.

Chapter 22: The Arson Trials

It was sunny the next day when I drove downtown. But the cool morning breeze was a reminder that winter was on its way. Before I ascended the courthouse steps, I took the time to scan the beautiful trees on the downtown street, look up at the sky, and take a big deep breath of that fresh air for which Portland is so famous. I love the way the air smells as the seasons change in Oregon.

As I walked up the cold marble steps of the old Courthouse, I thought, here we go again. I took the stairs to the fourth floor, where District Attorney Joe Rieke had set up a private meeting with Norm Brown and me.

We reviewed a number of exhibits I had forwarded to the police almost a year ago. One of particular interest was the $2 check written by Rod Addicks regarding a house targeted in an arson scheme, for which Addicks denied involvement.

That check was the one item that provided the detectives with a pressure lever to get Sam Moll to talk. The check, number 237, written in 1973, came from Addicks' personal checking account. It was addressed to Clackamas County. Issuance of that $2 check transferred ownership of a house located on Oak Street in Milwaukie, Oregon, a suburb of Portland, from Sam Moll to Dennis Lee Cartwright. The house was supposed to be burned down shortly after the transaction took place. When the police first confronted Sam Moll with this piece of evidence, Moll opened up and became a witness for the State. That house was their third arson plot, after successfully torching the first two houses.

"Where did you find this check?" asked Norm Brown.

"In Rod Addicks' desk drawer," I said. "Rod had left over two years' worth of his personal bank statements in his left-hand drawer and one evening I spent four hours, after the office closed, going through hundreds of his checks. This one looked suspicious since it had the names of

Addicks, Moll, and Cartwright on it. I turned the check over to Detective Blackie Yazzolino since I thought it might involve a property transfer of some kind. The county confirmed it did, so that is why you have it now."

At the time, I had no idea that the check would end up shedding light on three possible arson deals, not just one. The houses affected by arson or arson schemes were located on Oak Street, 18th Street, and Knapp Street. Each arson target was located in a different county.

Brown, Rieke, and I also reviewed the paperwork from earnest money deals I had photocopied or removed from Addicks' desk and file cabinet, which I had turned over to Detective Yazzolino. I spent a few hours in the Court House, then left.

A week before the first arson trial was scheduled to begin, the District Attorney called and said Addicks was going to defend himself without an attorney. They wanted to know if I could control myself on the witness stand, with Addicks himself asking the questions and twisting the information so it would seem as if I worked for the police and bought Sam Moll's testimony.

I reasoned that Addicks hated detectives Englert and Yazzolino, not me. But now that he had been convicted of murdering my dad, I wondered if I could keep my cool. It was different when I had no proof, only suspicions that he killed my dad, and spent my days working with him one-on-one while he was still employed by Columbia Bookkeeping. I told the District Attorney I would try my best.

I said, "It was Detective Rod Englert's pressure and excellent tactics that worked with Sam Moll, not me. If it wasn't for Englert's effective manner in handling Moll, the murder would never have been solved."

Rod Addicks' first arson trial started on December 9, 1975.

Detectives Yazzolino and Englert, and Gary and I waited in the hallway. Blackie Yazzolino was the first witness to testify. Most of Yazzolino's examination centered on how he received the documents relating to the case. First, Prosecutor Rieke asked Blackie Yazzolino the following questions.

Q. During the period from August 29 to December 3, 1974, did you receive a number of documents from Stan Turel?

A. Yes. Mr. Stan Turel was examining the books of the company and whenever he came up with something that didn't look right, he would call me and I would go out there and he would give me a Xerox copy of it. We didn't always know how something was connected, but if it looked a little fishy, we'd file it with the Special Investigations Department.

Q. Tell us what this is.

A. That is the bank statement with regard to Addicks' checks.

Q. Who gave this to you?

A. Stan Turel.

The identification process went on for quite a while and the jury was sent out of the courtroom when Yazzolino was asked the details of what he discovered in the Jim Turel murder investigation. And then it was time for Rod Addicks, acting as his own lawyer, to cross-examine the witness. Addicks slowly stood up and looked at the jury box. He was dressed in a sharp, dark suit. He was cool and collected. He appeared to enjoy the limelight. Remember, Addicks is the one asking the questions and acting as his own defense attorney.

Q. Mr. Yazzolino, in the suppression hearing during the murder trial, you said you heard Mr. Addicks, meaning me, tell Stan Turel in your presence that he had the authority to take anything out of his office, out of his filing cabinet. Is that correct?

A. Yes, we were getting ready to leave after we had questioned you in your office. Stan Turel came in and you told him you had nothing to hide, that he was free to look in your cabinet and files. You said, 'You can look at anything because I have nothing to hide.' You did that right in front of me. I heard it.

Q. I said you could look at anything in my office. That's your recollection?

A. That's right.

Q. Did you encourage him to give you copies of my personal documents?

A. I didn't have to encourage Mr. Turel. In fact, I had to hold him down.

Q. You held him down. Did you discourage him?

A. I told him, 'Take it easy.' I told him a lot of things not to do.

Addicks appeared to enjoy taunting the detective.

Q. That's your statement and if I catch you later, you won't change your story again?

A. I will not.

Q. Did the arson investigation begin on August 30, 1974?

A. I didn't have anything to do with the arson investigation.

A series of questions followed that implied evidence was forwarded to the arson investigator, Mr. Hillgaertner. Addicks attempted to trip up Yazzolino by causing confusion regarding dates when certain conversations took place and when Rod Addicks was read his Miranda rights. Addicks raised the issue of whether he should have been served a subpoena before the detectives received his personal documents from Stan Turel.

Finally, Blackie Yazzolino was excused from the witness stand and then it was my turn. First, Prosecutor Rieke asked me a lot of questions and when finished it was the defense's turn.

Rod Addicks, still acting as his own lawyer, was a pit bull ready to go after me. My heart raced for the first few minutes after I was sworn in. I could feel my blood pressure rising just thinking about answering this asshole's questions. I felt like jumping him. Okay, I thought to myself, let me just get through this. Soon he will be back in his cell, being treated like the animal he is. Here are the questions Addicks asked when I was on the witness stand:

Q. Are you still the president of Columbia Bookkeeping?

A. Yes.

Q. How much money does Columbia Bookkeeping owe me?

A. How much do you owe my father for murdering him?

I fired back my answer. I admit I was not keeping my cool.

Q. I asked you, how much money does Columbia Bookkeeping owe me?

A. It's debatable.

Q. How much money is in the signed notes and documents that Columbia Bookkeeping owes me?

A. Pending the wrongful death action that will be coming against you? Zero.

Q. Is there a signed note for Columbia Bookkeeping for repayment of my stock?

A. For $9,000?

I was already so pissed off I could hardly keep from shouting. It was obvious that Addicks was rattling me. He began to smirk.

Q. Is there a signed agreement for the payment of my bonus?

A. That's right, but that was signed before you were proven guilty of murder.

I had raised my voice, but caught myself. Get a handle on it, Stan! I admonished myself.

Q. Did you refuse to pay me the notes before I was found guilty of murder?

A. Prior to your arrest, yes, but anything coming is subject to the lawsuit against you.

Q. Your Honor, would the court please instruct Mr. Turel to answer the question?

Judge Jones looked at me and said, "I can fully appreciate your emotional feelings. But this is not going to accomplish anything."

A. Unlike the defendant, I get a little emotional when I think about this.

Q. Mr. Turel, did the corporation owe me $14,000, which was due and payable before I was tried for murder and which I never received payment for?

A. Before the trial, but not before the arrest.

Prosecutor Rieke then addressed Judge Jones, "Your Honor, we've got a problem here. If Mr. Turel answers that question with a yes, he jeopardizes any cause of action that might be pending against Addicks."

Judge Jones looked at me and asked, "Was that amount due and owing prior to the arrest?"

A. Before the trial, but not before the arrest.

Addicks continued his questioning:

Q. Was there an installment due that was not paid before the arrest?

A. No, there was not another installment due before your arrest. The next installment was due on March 20, but you were arrested on March 17. For murder.

Q. When was the date we signed the agreement regarding the Cadillac? How many times did I ask for the title?

A. Mr. Addicks, under the circumstances when I signed the agreement to give you the Cadillac as part of your bonus, at that particular time I had not come up with conclusive evidence on my own part to indicate that you had committed corporate fraud. After we signed the agreement I found evidence that indicated you were not honest when we signed the agreement, that indeed you had committed corporate fraud and subsequently you've been arrested. You've been charged and been found guilty of corporate fraud through that channel and I am saying it's true, you signed an agreement. When I signed an agreement then find the other party has not been honest, I am not bound by that agreement.

I felt better after getting some of that anger off my chest. Right then Judge Jones asked Addicks: "What is the relevancy of this? What does this line of questioning have to do with your motion to suppress?"

"Your Honor, it does relate." Addicks said. "I want to first show the client's prejudice against me. And secondly, I want to show his close cooperation with the police department. He didn't pay me because he had insider information that I would be imminently arrested."

"Go ahead with your questions, Mr. Addicks," Judge Jones said.

Q. Mr. Turel, did the police tell you during January and February 1975, that they were going to arrest me sooner or later?

A. I was personally convinced, through the information I had given the police and through your own actions that sooner or later you were going to be arrested, whether it be for murder or something else.

Q. Mr. Turel, I asked you, did the police tell you during January and

February of 1975 that they were going to arrest me?

A. Detective Rod Englert didn't say they were going to. He thought maybe they could, sooner or later. So did I. Nothing was for sure.

Q. Mr. Turel, I'm asking you specifically, were you working in cooperation with the police to have me arrested?

Judge Jones, interrupted, "Mr. Addicks, the witness was responsive to that question. You can address another question to the witness at this time."

Q. Mr. Turel, did I ever give you permission to turn any of my personal papers over to the police?

A. You said you had nothing to hide in your personal office, which is owned by Columbia Bookkeeping. Because of my position in the company, I was free to go through anything in your office because you had nothing to hide. You said so in front of witnesses.

Q. Did I ever give you permission to turn my personal records over to the police?

A. I didn't tell you I was doing a lot of this stuff because I suspected you of being involved in something illegal. I was investigating this on my own. I didn't tell you because I didn't want you to kill me, too.

I felt a bit of personal satisfaction each time I could put a little dig into my answer. Still, I was overly emotional and uptight. I'd like to believe my emotional response was understandable, though.

The questions and answers went on and on. Addicks spent a great deal of time arguing that I had no right to turn over to the police evidence I collected from Addicks' office. Finally, after what seemed an eternity, I was allowed to step down. As I left, I looked at Addicks and frowned back at him even though I was quietly upset at myself for not doing a better job of answering his questions. Rieke was correct in objecting to many of Addicks' tricky questions—if I admitted I owed money to him, we might have to pay him off. There was something nightmarish about the experience of being cross-examined by the man who murdered my dad. I left feeling frustrated because it seemed like this murderer was having too much fun.

Next, Detective Rod Englert was called to the witness stand.

Joe Rieke, the prosecuting attorney, began by questioning Englert about how he collected information on the case, which included the items from the offices of Columbia Bookkeeping. Addicks moved to have all the documents thrown out of court. He was setting the stage for a mistrial by excluding all evidence that lead to Sam Moll's testimony. Rieke asked:

Q. Mr. Englert, would you explain to the court where it was that you first came into contact with Sam Moll?

A. Yes, sir. That was January 21 or 22, 1975. When I contacted him at Gray's Tax and Business Service in Tacoma Washington.

Q. What arrangements were made with Ben Zderic, Sam Moll's attorney, with respect to Mr. Moll's testimony?

A. The arrangement was Mr. Moll would be transported down to Multnomah County and brought before a magistrate so that he would be given formal immunity, and for that grant of immunity, he would testify for the State with regard to the activities between himself and Rod Addicks regarding a conspiracy to commit murder and arson.

Q. Was money paid to Mr. Zderic with respect to Mr. Moll?

A. Yes, sir. To Mr. Zderic a total of $950 was paid in three installments. This was for Mr. Moll's protection and for Mr. Zderic's attorney's fees. This was all receipted and accepted by the attorney, Mr. Zderic.

Q. Explain to the court why protection was necessary.

A. For the safety of Mr. Moll who was going to be our witness. He was in fear of his life, and had taken several precautions including hiring a bodyguard and wiring his house with firecrackers and keeping a loaded 12-gauge shotgun next to his bed to prevent him from being harmed.

Addicks sat there listening to the prosecution and made notes on a yellow legal pad. He was anxiously waiting his turn to cross-examine the detective who was the cause of his actual arrest. Finally it was Addicks' turn to act as his own attorney in his defense. Addicks asked Detective Englert:

Q. When you went to Tacoma to talk to Mr. Moll, and Mr. Moll told you he wasn't involved in any of this stuff, did you tell Mr. Moll you were going to prosecute him for the arsons?

A. Yes.

Q. Did you have lengthy discussions with the attorney for Mr. and Mrs. Moll, as far as giving him immunity to prosecution and paying funds before he finally agreed to do it?

A. No. That is not correct. We discussed the case at length before the part about reward money came up. That came up later in the conversation.

Q. Mr. Moll had already agreed to testify against me and to be given immunity before the subject of reward money came up?

A. Yes, sir. That was the second day. We received a phone call in our motel room, or we called from our motel room to the Moll residence, and he asked that we accompany him to his attorney's office, that his attorney wished to talk to us, which was quite a surprise to us.

Q. Who furnished the funds to pay Moll's attorney?

A. Those funds were furnished by Stan Turel and reimbursed by the Multnomah County Commission office.

Q. Mr. Englert, did you encourage Stan Turel to turn over any records or documents that he had in his possession?

A. These items were volunteered. The checks were given approximately a month later. Stan Turel had a thing about going through all the rooms of that office and any time he found even a little thing that could be important, he turned it over to us. We never did encourage him or coerce him to give us anything out of that office.

Q. You told Mr. Cartwright that you were going to the parole board for him, or that the district attorney's office would go to the parole board for him if he testified against me and pleaded guilty to murder? Is that correct?

A. Yes, sir.

Q. On the evening when you interviewed Mr. Cartwright, after my arrest in the Kelso Police Department, did he maintain his innocence when you were interviewing him, when you started to interview him?

A. At first he did, yes, sir.

Q. Did he ask you to call an attorney for him, and did you call the attorney for him?

A. Yes, sir. After he gave me the name of an attorney, he said he was reluctant to call, so I said I would place the call for him and I talked to the attorney on the phone. Mr. Cartwright then talked to the attorney on the phone. The attorney recommended some public defenders, two of them whose names I wrote down on a piece of paper and gave to Cartwright. He declined to call anyone.

Q. How many hours did you talk to Mr. Cartwright before he confessed to you?

A. Approximately three and a half hours.

Q. Did you intimidate him?

A. No, sir.

Q. He maintained his innocence for a couple of hours, and then all of a sudden he changed his story?

A. No, I would not say he maintained his innocence. We had a long conversation. He was free to leave at any time he desired. He had Mr. Lansing, sort of like his foster parent, with him. He asked that his father be called, and when his father arrived his whole story changed. He broke down.

Q. He broke down in front of his father?

A. Yes, sir.

I have to admit, Addicks was doing a good job cross-examining the detective. An interesting side note is that Cartwright and Addicks both bore a resemblance to the police artist's drawing made from a description provided by the Lake Oswego psychic after she touched my dad's watch. The drawing was never mentioned during the trial. The second man in the drawing resembled Rod Addicks.

Numerous witnesses were sworn in and testified about their knowledge of the arsons. Out of the presence of the jury, Addicks tried to find holes in the testimony of each of the witnesses who had been called to speak at the murder trial. The arguments that Rod Addicks presented before the court were confusing, but with the jury out of the room during most of it, little damage was done to the outcome of the arson trial. Addicks tried to find holes in the way Rod Englert had interviewed four people who eventually admitted to a conspiracy involving murder and arson. It became apparent that Englert's follow-through on leads is what solved the case. Judge Jones did a great job keeping the murder case out of the testimony heard by the jury.

As the prosecutor, Joe Rieke slugged through the testimonies of many witnesses, the arson scheme was carefully revealed item by item. Earnest money checks on at least three homes showed that Addicks was the first person to have made the offer. Then prior to escrow or closing on the transactions, Addicks would put someone else's name on the title. Each house purchased was empty and no attempt was ever made to rent them out, which was at odds with Addicks' statement that these were all investment properties.

After the houses were purchased, the insurance taken out was double the value of the home's purchase price. With the exception of one house, Addicks' name did not appear as owner. The scheme backfired since many of the people inside the arson ring testified that Addicks was the brains behind the operation. Also the earnest money agreements in Addicks' file cabinet at Columbia Bookkeeping connected the dots. The property agreements lead to five people located in Portland and Vancouver, Washington, who were aware of, or involved in possible arson schemes. Three of them were also connected to the murder or conspiracy to murder my dad.

Prosecutor Rieke pointed to Addicks' personal check for $2, written to Clackamas County for the transfer of title on the Milwaukie house from Sam Moll to Dennis Lee Cartwright. He apparently did not want the same name to pop up on two different property fires.

In the closing arguments to the jury, Addicks did a good job of presenting and twisting the facts. When I compared transcripts of the murder trial with the arson trial, I thought Addicks did a better job of interrogating witnesses than his lawyer had. The judge and jury were impressed that such an intelligent man was capable of carrying out such an elaborate scheme, but in the end Rod Addicks came across as being dangerous.

The jury deliberated about four hours before returning to the courtroom to declare a verdict of guilty. Judge Jones required a physiological and psychiatric profile and analysis be done on Addicks, at the State's expense. He said, "Well, Mr. Addicks is a very perplexing problem, and I'm not in any hurry to jump to justice, so to speak, and I was really impressed with the way you handled yourself during this trial, Mr. Addicks. You had complete control of yourself. You had a great grasp of the law. You conducted yourself professionally. You made one of the better closing arguments I have heard, and it's just a mystery to me why a young man of your obvious intelligence can become so immoral and psychopathic as to become involved in these things, and I think that rather than send you back to a penitentiary where they do not have any adequate diagnostic facilities, that as long as I have jurisdiction of the case, I intend to do a complete job of it."

The trial took one week.

As Addicks left in chains he stared at me with those dark eyes of his. I stared back and shook my head, while biting my tongue. Since it was just a week or so before Christmas, Judge Jones said that the sentencing would take place on January 5, 1976.

Once again, back at the office, Julie Syler and Peg greeted me with big smiles and said they were glad it was over. We gathered in my office and, as usual, they had their coffee while I sipped my ice water. We started going through a checklist for the upcoming 1976 tax season.

"We're not going to allow smoking in the office this tax season," I said. "It's unhealthy."

"Most all our employees smoke, Stan," Julie reminded me. "They might have a problem with that new rule."

"I'll put some chairs out back and they can smoke there."

"What about when it rains?" Julie laughed.

I didn't have an answer for that. Our talk shifted to the holidays.

That Friday, we gathered again to stuff and mail out 3,500 Happy New Years letters to current and past clients. I included a tax checklist for the clients in every letter, so they could review what they would need to bring with them, before they came in for their appointments.

I wanted each letter to look personal. Again, I hired a young lady, this one named Amy, from the Church of Christ, to prepare individual letters on our word-processing machine and I personally signed each letter with blue ink. I thought that due to possible negative publicity from the trials, we should put our best foot forward to save the clients we had.

I found that Amy could type 100 words a minute. She was very cute and very professional. Soon she was dating, then engaged to one of our tax accountants, Bill Jameson. They wanted to be transferred to our Beaverton office, rather than stay at the main office in southeast Portland, which is where we needed her. Okay, I thought, maybe they will work well together and the long hours of tax season will be less of a problem since they'll be together. Both were excellent employees. Within a year, they became a happily married couple.

Peg came into my office on the Friday before Christmas and said, "Stan, Jim Auxier is on the line and needs to talk to you now, if possible."

What now? I thought as I picked up the phone. "Hi, Jim, what's up?"

"Stan," Auxier said, "I hate to talk to you about this now, but Mr. Kohlhoff called me several times on behalf of Rod Addicks. He wants to work out a settlement on the stock option deal we made before Addicks was arrested."

"Are you kidding me?" I said. "Tell them to go straight to hell. I do not want to give Addicks one dime!" My blood pressure must have hit the ceiling.

"Let's talk about this, Stan. We might have an opportunity to get this man out of our lives forever. Addicks has already signed over his rights to the Cadillac, and all the contract money is owed to his attorney, Mr. Kohlhoff, as payment for his legal fees. Kohlhoff said they would file a lawsuit against the Turel Family Trust and Columbia Bookkeeping within a week if we don't settle up. If you like, we can avoid any more publicity by settling it quietly without a public trial. The last thing we need is for the newspapers to print a large article about all the trials just before tax season. It might scare away clients."

Shit, I thought. "Jim, if we just let them sue us, Addicks and Kohlhoff will look like jerks," I said. "We still have the right to sue Addicks for wrongful death, even if they win the suit over the money and title to the Cadillac. Besides, if Addicks transferred his rights to the attorney, then it would be just avoidance by Addicks to have his assets attached." I was really mad and usually do not talk this way.

The past sixteen months had been stressful, to say the least. I found myself still habitually running my fingernails along the outside edge of my dad's desk as I spoke on the phone. The grooves were already a permanent flaw on his beautiful oak desk.

"Stan, you're right," Auxier said, "but do you want to continue to deal with Addicks in court? Besides that, the cost of me filing a response to his lawsuit and a lawsuit against Addicks would be at least $10,000. Yes, we would probably prevail but what does Addicks have? Nothing at all. He is broke. Except, we might prevail in going after the assets of his wife and mother since years ago Addicks put everything he had in their names. Is it worth the drama for you and your family to go through all this stress again? You know Addicks hates you already and blames his conviction on you, Yazzolino, and Rod Englert."

"What do they want?" I asked. "If it costs me one nickel besides your fee, I will not settle with that asshole attorney. This just sucks."

"If they sue us," Auxier said, "then you will have to pay me $10,000 to defend it. I'm just advising you to do what is best for you and your family now, even though it feels wrong in your gut. It's what I would do if I were you."

"Jim," I said, "I do not want Addicks to get one dime. However if all we have to do is give the Cadillac title to his damn attorney then we can make a deal. I don't want anything to do with Rod Addicks ever again. Columbia Bookkeeping and the Turel Family Trust cannot afford any bad publicity. So, okay, I agree. But I want to see all the details in writing before I sign my name to anything. I will call my stepmother, Gary, and my sisters to see what they think."

I then called my siblings and stepmother. After some discussion, all of us, except Gary, agreed to the deal. He said we should sue Addicks anyway. The agreement we decided on would release Rod Addicks from our right to sue him, and Addicks attorney was going to get the title to the Cadillac. This agreement meant the rest of the contract regarding what we owed Addicks was null and void. I felt the same as Gary, but decided to do what was best for the family and company finances. If it were not for the chance that the lawsuit would be reported in the press during the upcoming tax season, I would have told the attorney to shove it where the sun don't shine. I was still mad about everything having to do with Rod Addicks.

Despite my feelings to the contrary, I called Jim Auxier back and told him to make up the settlement agreement. "Jim," I said, "what are you going to charge us and do I have the right to sign on behalf of Dad's estate and Columbia Bookkeeping?"

"I'll charge you $1,000 for my time," Auxier replied. "And yes, Stan, as executor, you have the right to sign on behalf of the estate. I'll set the signing date for January 5. Let's get this done before tax season gets into full swing."

What a way to start the holidays, I thought, as Jim Auxier and I talked. He had a way of calming me down with his long chats and fatherly advice.

Company policy at Columbia Bookkeeping was to give all of our employees and all the tenants in the apartment buildings I managed the gift of a ham just before the Christmas holiday season began. For Thanksgiving, I usually gave each of them a turkey. I saw it as a small way to say thank you. I had started out as a tightwad, but after watching the movie *Scrooge*, I thought the least I could do for my tenants was to buy them turkeys to let them know I cared about them. We also gave the year-round employees a small cash bonus. And we provided turkeys to my sisters, brother, stepmother, mother, and mother-in-law. My van came in handy for these holiday deliveries.

By then we had 25 employees and 40 tenants in the various rentals I had an investment in. The cost of buying turkeys for each employee and tenant was expensive, so I had my staff negotiate the best price and I drove down to Safeway to pick up 65 turkeys.

The staff truly appreciated this small gesture and it showed the people I counted on know how much I appreciated them. I think giving something to my employees to take home and cook and eat with their families means more to them than receiving just a gift certificate or cash. The tenants in our rentals seemed to appreciate it even more. I would give the turkeys to the apartment managers, with holiday notes, and the managers would distribute the food to the apartments. Also, many times in early fall months, I would drop by the rentals with a vanload of potatoes, beans, or other vegetables from local farms, which the managers then gave out to the tenants. Yes, it was good public relations, but I always remembered times past, when relatives or friends helped us or brought food to our family when we were on welfare.

Think positive, I would say to myself. I have a nice girlfriend at the moment, a nice home, my family is healthy, the company is stable, and Rod Addicks' trials, at least for now, are over. The Rat is enjoying himself in prison, hopefully as someone's favorite honey. I thought again about Rod Addicks' poor wife and kids. I could only imagine how bad they felt during these holidays.

On January 5, 1976, Jim Auxier called to set up a meeting with me at his downtown office to sign the agreement with Rod Addicks' attorney. I did not want to see or be around Addicks' attorney and was assured he would not be there. After I signed the five-page document, Auxier took me to an expensive restaurant to celebrate the fact that Rod Addicks would be out of my life for good now.

"Stan, the way you're going," Auxier said, "you're going to make Columbia Bookkeeping into something bigger than your father ever imagined. He would be so proud of you. If you play your cards right, your brother and sisters might see a lot of money out of this. Just keep your stepmother happy. Roger is a loose cannon and I predict Bernie won't stay married to him much longer. She's already having problems with him."

"What do you know about that?" I asked.

"I can't say much. All I'll say is that I received a confidential call from Bernie's attorney to discuss some problems."

I had noticed that Bernie was calling me more frequently. We seemed to be on fairly good terms with each other now, even if the others in the family were not feeling much warmth towards her.

On January 6, 1976, I was back in court again for Rod Addicks' sentencing. Judge Jones asked Addicks to stand as he read Addicks a 10-page summary of Dr. Constantine Columbus' psychiatric report from the Department of Human Resources, State of Oregon.

"First," said Judge Jones, "the diagnostic impression according to the doctors who examined Rod Addicks wrote that he is a Psychopathic Personality. According to their tests, and I quote, 'Mr. Addicks functions in the superior range of mental ability, full scale I.Q. 120. Mr. Addicks' long-term antisocial behaviors appear to be deeply ingrained and at the present time he seems to be hostile, defensive, self-righteous and overly manipulative of nearly everyone he comes into contact with. He shows no remorse of guilt for his offenses, but appears to have been concerned only with fulfilling immediate and long-term self-gratification. The defendant is seen as dangerous in most social settings including his present incarceration and probably will continue in his efforts to misuse his environment for self-gain. In summary, Mr. Addicks has demonstrated a history of aggressive and manipulative activities, which will probably continue the remainder of his life.'"

After a few words of instructions to the district attorney, Judge Jones sentenced Addicks to another 20-year sentence for Arson 1, five additional years for Theft 2, and another ten years under the Dangerous Offenders Act. The Dangerous Offenders Act ensures that super-dangerous convicts will not be granted parole based on good behavior. Addicks' sentences were to be served consecutively—after his life sentence for murder was completed. He would serve until death and beyond, without the chance of parole.

Years later, I asked the Parole Board for a copy of the doctor's statements on Addicks. When reviewing the 11-page report, I learned more details of Rod Addicks' escapades while incarcerated at Rocky Butte Jail. During an interview with Commander Stanley Kerner, the director of Rocky Butte, several significant facts were revealed. I had known that prior to Addicks' conviction of murder, jail staff had conducted a routine inspection of Addicks' cell and discovered a fork that had been converted into a knife-like weapon. What I hadn't known is that he'd also taken bed sheets, wrapped them into a cord, and hidden them on a ledge above his bunk.

Jail staff had also discovered that several steel bars had been sawed through in Block A, the maximum security unit at the jail. The bars had been held in place with toothpaste. And they found out Rod Addicks had approached another inmate, due for release, and offered him considerable money if he would obtain a pistol and hide it in a bathroom of the courthouse prior to Addicks' court appearance.

Commander Kerner's summary described Addicks as a very cool, calculating, intelligent person who was trying to escape. He characterized him as a very dangerous individual who needed to be constantly watched.

At that point District Attorney Joe Rieke dropped the second arson charge, which surprised me. I asked him why they wouldn't prosecute Addicks on that arson case, or any of the other crimes the detectives discovered he'd committed in the State of Washington and in Canada. Rieke's response was, "He's in jail for life plus thirty-five years already. He'll die in prison. There's no possible way he will ever be released. I don't want to waste taxpayer money."

Chapter 23: Taking Care of Business

New Years 1976 started off with a bang. Literally.

Again the Columbia Bookkeeping tax office was broken into on a Sunday night, but this time it was through a shattered back window. Our desks were ransacked but nothing was missing except a few adding machines. Thank God I had previously paid to have stainless steel bars put through all the file cabinets. The invaders tried to use a crowbar to break in through the back door, but we had reinforced plates on the door jams, which were screwed deep into the framework of the building.

The burglar actually took a dump, defecating like a dog right in the middle of the office area upstairs where I had set up my Tax Season Desk. We called the police and reported the break-in, but I never turned in an insurance claim, as I did not want it to affect our future business policy ratings. I strongly suspected Addicks was behind the break-in. Most likely someone recently released from jail.

What a scumbag the burglar must be, I thought. A bathroom was six feet from where the shit was piled. Okay, now I was really pissed. I called a specialist on wrought iron fixtures and had all the windows in the back reinforced with jail-like bars to end that type of entry. But I didn't have bars installed on the front windows facing the street. I did not want the place to look like a prison to customers. Eventually, I had an alarm system installed.

Even with this incident, I still felt a sense of relief and a fresh commitment to improving the company. I did not see my brother very often, as he was devoted to running his own tax office, College Crest Tax Service. But I arranged a family meeting to update them all on my plan to not sell Columbia Bookkeeping. Even though it was my sole choice as Trustee of the Turel Family Trust, I wanted them to know I wasn't doing anything drastic without their blessing. They all agreed that we should keep the business going in an attempt to create wealth for the remainder of us beneficiaries.

It was time to get ready for the additional staff coming in for the next tax season, so I set up a process for each room. Each tax preparer's desk had a set of tax form files and all the checklists I designed for small businesses and rental properties. By now I had passed the State exam and was licensed to prepare taxes.

In the prior tax season, several clients had become upset that they weren't getting a larger refund. Sometimes a client would throw a fit about the money they owed the IRS—or us—right in the lobby, in front of others. I knew it was bad policy to try to handle outbursts in front of other clients, so I expanded the waiting room into a separate suite next door. I posted a sign that said, "Pick up finished taxes here." That way, I could keep problems separated from the front lobby. Also, it gave the staff a chance to spend more time in private, explaining to clients a few details about their finished tax returns. However, I had to add the cost of hiring another person for that room.

By then, I figured we had around 3,800 clients and tried to estimate how many total cups of coffee the staff and clients would use in four months. I bought the coffee in bulk and cases of cups from a local supplier at a great discount. I'd noticed during the prior season that cans of coffee seemed to disappear too fast. Even the cases of toilet paper seemed to disappear. I'd purchased enough coffee and cups for 10,000 cups of coffee, but where did it all go? Shortly thereafter I learned that an employee was taking some of those items home.

"Okay," Peg laughed, "you're even tighter on the budget than your dad."

I dropped in on all three tax offices and went over company policy, prices, and checklists with the staff at each location. Some of the tax preparers balked because they'd never used a checklist before. They said they were smart enough to use the 1040 form as the checklist.

"How are you going to prove to the IRS that you asked questions?" I said to the most hardheaded. "Also, you might miss something that would help the client. And if a client asks you to do something illegal, just say no."

During the two tax seasons before Dad died, according to staff, the IRS sent in phony clients who had talked tax preparers at other firms into taking illegitimate deductions, or to not report tip income. Several other firms had been shut down because the IRS put them out of business. "Think of it," I told my staff, "that guy in blue jeans who you're tempted to help with a phony tax deduction could be an IRS agent in disguise."

I was very firm about the No Smoking policy in the office, which caused an older taxman to quit before the tax season had even started.

I made sure the front lobby of each office had similar marketing materials and pictures on the walls. One item I added was a framed Satisfaction Guaranteed Policy, followed by a price list for our services. I picked up most of the frames at a garage sale during the previous fall for less than a dollar each.

And since the company no longer had any company cars, I was still using my red Ford Econoline van to deliver equipment and furniture for the offices. I compared the process of preparing for Tax Season to preparing an aircraft for a cross-country flight. Checklist: condition of the office, rules, supplies, staff.

When the phones started ringing, I considered myself lucky. Here we were, going into a second season with all those legal problems behind us. Rod Addicks would soon be transferred to the Salem State Prison. I relaxed some, figuring I could now focus just on the tax business and property management oversight. It seemed like everything was going to run smoothly from here on. Boy was I wrong. Our problems with Addicks were just beginning. I'll get to why in just a minute.

Several of the Quality Financial Planning clients wanted out of their investments since they had never seen a dime of profit and here I was, making a capital request from the partners to cover delayed repairs and essential upgrades. Some apartment deals had been created purely as tax shelters. Also, I had to go to court—without a lawyer—three times in two months to evict tenants who had not paid their rents.

Not all the relationships were strained, however. I became friends with a number of the investors, such as Joe Rand. Joe was a doctor at Kaiser Hospital who often came to my office for advice regarding his investments in several projects I was managing. Joe was a remarkable man in his late 30s who died of cancer a few years later. His death bothered me, since he had worked so hard to become a doctor and had such a short time to enjoy the fruits of his labor. In the last six months of his life, Joe took his VW Van packed with camping gear and a canoe, and made the best of his remaining months. His death reinforced my private drive to make the best out of life while I am here, as only God or destiny knows how long we will live.

One building deal that Addicks put together, the Going Street Apartments, was in really bad shape. The manager called me over to look at the vacant apartments. These had been beautiful units in Northeast Portland, on Going Street, where it leads down to the Swan Island Industrial Park. When the manager led me down to the basement units, she showed me where the cement floor had broken, and when she cleared out the broken pieces, she found garbage buried under the concrete slab. Wow, I thought. What a mess with no simple solution.

A little research revealed that the property had been a city-owned garbage dump. The land had been covered, and later the property was approved for the building of apartments. When I disclosed this to the investors, they were astonished and felt that Rod Addicks should have known the history of the property. We got rid of that investment and the partners lost some money, but not much. Eventually the City of Portland took the property back and the buildings were all removed by Emmert International's house-moving company.

Shortly after meeting Terry Emmert of Emmert International, he told me that the Oregon State Building Department was going to demolish 12 nice homes on a street near the State Capital building in Salem, unless someone would move them. Terry and I drove down to evaluate whether the houses could be moved by his company. After serious consideration, I decided not to proceed since the risk and cost would be too high for me. I was always on the lookout for a good deal. It was a shame that the State just demolished those sound buildings. I was impressed by Terry Emmert's independent drive for his young age.

Al and Mary Foglio always had a positive attitude about their investments and agreed to fund any shortages. They bought out Addicks' interest in the Big Spruce Trailer Park in Florence, Oregon, and bought out several partners in the Woodstock Apartments in southeast Portland. It was my understanding that those partners' money went to Addicks' lawyer.

My apartment building in Camas, Washington, was doing well. I drove over there twice a month to check on things. One week, I knocked on the door of an old retired sailor who was ten days late on his rent. It turned out he was in the process of moving out all his stuff, taking the last of his belongings as I stood there. When he was gone, I entered his apartment and was overwhelmed by an awful stench. Something had died in there. I held my nose and traced the smell to the underside of the kitchen sink. Three bloated mice were floating in a bucket of water. I cleaned the apartment the best I could, then repainted the walls and ceiling.

Six years earlier, in 1970, after I broke up with Susan, the woman who shattered my heart, I had lived in this unit. To handle my depression regarding the end of that relationship, I painted a three-by-four foot angry seascape on the back of new paneling used for the apartment's upgrade. The panel had been nailed over a badly damaged door, the painting hidden on the backside. With the help of a tenant, I refurbished the unit and when we removed the dark paneling we both had a good laugh. I used to paint for fun. Over the years I've been told I could have made a living as an artist, but I still consider it just one of my moody hobbies.

Okay, back to the legal proceedings.

On March 17, 1976, Rod Addicks was convicted on one count in a plea bargain deal regarding the seven securities fraud charges in Tacoma, Washington. One of the charges involved $75,000 collected from 15 individuals on a real estate deal that Addicks never transacted. He used the investors' money for his personal expenditures. Addicks was sentenced to ten years imprisonment for violation of the Washington Securities Act. This sentence was to be served after the conclusion of the time he would serve in the Oregon State Prison, which was life plus 35 years. We thought that meant no chance for parole.

But by March 29, 1976, barely three months after his arson convictions, Addicks had arranged a parole board hearing at which his mother and sister testified that he was a good person who could have never done such a thing. By April 8, Addicks appeared before the parole board to test the waters. The parole board denied the request to set a parole date until after, and if, his appeal on his cases was upheld. I was astounded that he was already working the system, but in fact, I expected no less from him.

The tax season went smoothly, without the stress I suffered in the prior year. As the weeks went by, it appeared we had a 20 percent increase in clients. We were advertising in *The Oregonian* and on KEX radio. Some of the employees at KEX became clients. All the tax signs and A-frame signs were brightly painted to maximize our service. I even designed some banners that said, "It's Not Too Late," and posted them at each of our locations just a few days before the April 15 filing deadline. The staff wasn't thrilled about doing more returns in the last few days, but I insisted that we needed to serve last-minute clients. Plus, it improved our profit.

I remembered when Rod Addicks told me that someone could have robbed the business because we would have a lot of money on site Saturdays and Sundays during tax season. I had a low-grade fear all during tax season that someone, encouraged by Rod Addicks, would rob us on the last day of the season. I made sure I collected all the deposits from all the offices and took them home with me every weekend and on April 15.

I was home by 10:30 p.m. on April 15. The tax preparers had interviewed over 170 clients that final day. Last-minute clients were still waiting in the lobby, but we locked the door at 8 in the evening and began a brief staff celebration. We even offered the waiting stragglers some champagne.

On April 16, I was at the office at 9 o'clock sharp to review how the two other Columbia Bookkeeping offices did as far as client count for the year. I called my brother, Gary, at his College Crest Tax office to compare numbers. We both counted our blessings that it had been such a positive tax season. Columbia Bookkeeping had prepared tax forms for over 4,500 clients. Gary had hit 350 clients that year. For a sole proprietorship with only one helper, Gary was doing quite well, and he decided to celebrate by purchasing a Datsun Z sports car.

In late April 1976, a client brought in a copy of a nationally-recognized magazine called *Official Detective Stories*. The story was a long and detailed article about Rod Addicks' murder conviction. The eight-page article was exact in its details and the accompanying photos were shockingly graphic. There was even a picture of my dad's dead body at the crime scene. It was the first time I had seen a photo of my father lying in a pool of his own blood. Actually, I was impressed how the author, Andy Stack, described Addicks' numerous crimes and convictions. I was glad to see that detectives Rod Englert and Joe Woods received special commendations for their outstanding investigation of the Turel murder. It bothered me, however, that the author used a fictitious name when describing Sam Moll's involvement in the arsons and murder scheme. Shortly after this article appeared, Addicks filed frivolous lawsuits against the publication and the writer for libel and defamation of character.

When tax season ended I decided to visit my grandparents and Uncle Ray and Aunt Lorraine in Seattle for the weekend. My Aunt Lorraine was a registered nurse who watched over my grandparents, who had relocated from their farm in Grandview, Washington, to live in a house across the street from Ray and Lorraine. I loved visiting them and felt right at home there. Granddad George was in his mid-80s and still driving an American-made car. He said he would never buy a foreign car as American citizens should buy American products. I believe a lot of my work ethic came from my Granddad and from working on his farm. As a kid, I had worked beside the Mexicans in the fields picking asparagus, peaches and potatoes. There is something grounding about working with the earth. I also learned to drive a tractor before I was 12.

Granddad was an avid hunter, but sitting in his backyard he enjoyed watching the squirrels and birds playing in his trees. Tears streamed down his cheek as he told me how bad he felt about killing animals for sport in the past, and how he could never kill again as God's creatures are all too beautiful. He had never been a drinker, but he started imbibing wine for his health when his doctor advised it. We talked about the good old days when Granddad developed one of the first vineyards in the Yakima Valley in connection with the University of Washington's Farm Research Program. He always denied growing grapes for wine. In fact, he sold his grapes to Concord for grape juice. It was a joke in our family that he could never drink alcohol.

I had a long talk with Uncle Ray as we played our traditional two-hour chess game. I told him how upset I was that Sam Moll received total immunity for his part in the murder and arsons. I wondered aloud if perhaps Sam Moll would get in trouble with the tribe for something else, since several of the men living on the reservation had been involved in the murder plans. Uncle Ray said that since the Puyallup reservation was only 30 miles south of Seattle, he would keep his eye on the papers for anything that seemed a bit odd.

The next week I met with my older sister and her husband, who were still living at, and managing the Elizabeth Court Apartments in Oregon City. We talked about apartment improvements and what a wonderful job they were doing. Ever since they took over management, we had remained at 100 percent occupied. We were planning to raise the rents, but decided to first landscape the courtyard with 30 new plants, plus replace the carpeting in the interior courtyard walkways with more colorful rugs. Occasionally I went over there to help on weekends. They really did a great job with the landscaping and the tenants were delighted with the improvements. Whenever a vacancy came up, my sister's husband and I installed the new carpets ourselves, which kept costs down. Believe me—laying carpet is hard on the knees. And through trial and error, I learned that the best time to raise rents is during the wet winter months when people are less likely to contemplate moving out.

I had a minor argument with my sister about a beautiful mermaid fountain for the courtyard. This 200-pound, water-gushing concrete mermaid wasn't wearing a bra. After I had a good laugh, we installed the lady anyway, which gave the main courtyard a sense of tranquility.

My older sister began working at Columbia Bookkeeping after she left her job at ADP. For several years she worked for us helping to coordinate the processing and secretarial staff. She was very helpful and dedicated to putting in the extra effort on whatever needed to be done. After a few years, she received an executive position with Precision Cast Parts, which paid a lot more than we could afford.

That fall, I bought a twin engine Cessna with my own personal money. I designed an all-black paint job with colorful stripes. It was my poor man's Lear Jet. I could meet a large prospective accounting client 200 miles away in less than one hour. This tool gave me a great first impression when meeting clients.

Throughout 1976 and early 1977, Rod Addicks continued to file numerous appeals on all cases related to the crimes he'd committed in the states of Washington and Oregon. I didn't get involved because the District Attorney's office assured me he stood no chance in hell of getting his convictions overturned. "This process can take several years," they said.

On July 24, 1977, the Oregon Court of Appeals upheld all of Addicks' convictions.

On July 27, the Supreme Court of Oregon denied Addicks' Petition for Review.

Rod Addicks was represented free of charge at State expense in the above appeals, since he claimed he had no money or income. In addition, Multnomah County had to cover the cost of the prosecutor. It was all such a waste of money. However, one must remain open-minded as the man in jail, if falsely accused or convicted, should have the right of review by an appeals court. Due to the overwhelming testimony, however, there was no doubt as to Addicks' guilt in all these cases.

In late 1977, I start receiving letters directly from Rod Addicks wherein he insisted that I change my testimony or else "you and your family will suffer serious financial consequences." I called the State Prison to protest their allowing an inmate to harass witnesses and family members of the man he murdered. The warden's office replied, "I'm sorry that you're in this situation, but prisoners have the right to send letters to anyone they want." I couldn't believe what I was hearing. I felt a rock land in the pit in my stomach each time I received mail from him. I forwarded Addicks' letters to the local District Attorney's office but they, too, said there was nothing they could do about it.

Near the end of the year, I received a call from my stepmother, Bernie Turel, saying she needed help in getting her husband, Roger—Mr. Cosmo—out of her house. He had been living off her and spending her money on ridiculous things. As an employee of Fred Meyer, he received a discount on all the store's products.

Bernie said that, for instance, after Christmas 1976, Fred Meyer had a super sale on shirts. Mr. Cosmo had used her money to buy thousands of shirts, which had been sitting in her garage for almost a year. He bought old perfume bottles for ten cents on the dollar, but they were out of date and no longer could be sold legally. Bernie said she thought the man was crazy and would not move out. She was afraid to kick him out.

I accommodated her request to get him out of there with great pleasure. I went to her home and helped Mr. Cosmo pack that very night. He came back to her home only one more time to haul all his special deals out of Bernie's garage. Mr. Cosmo ended up with just his Pinto and an apartment downtown.

A month or so later, Bernie said she was worried about living alone out in the country on the two-acre property she had lived in with my dad. I found this out when she came to the Columbia Bookkeeping office for a visit and spent an hour detailing her health problems and fears of living by herself. Bernie's appearance was neat and tidy, as usual, and I noticed the gold Cadillac was still in perfect condition. "I've already listed the place with a well-known realtor," Bernie said.

Bernie set the price for the 900 square foot ranch-style home on two acres at $60,000, a high price at that time. She mentioned she had her eye on moving into a mobile home park where a few of her friends lived. A used manufactured home was for sale in that park and she asked me to check it out and give her some advice on whether she should buy it. I drove out to the mobile home park with her and noticed it was only five blocks from Clackamas Town Center, Oregon's largest and most modern indoor shopping mall with over 100 stores.

Bernie was 60 years old and wanted to live near police, a fire station and emergency medical care in case problems came up. Bernie was very healthy and slim for a woman her age, but I could see her point. Gradually, over the last year, Bernie had begun confiding in me and said how much she appreciated the help I was providing. She expressed her confidence in what I was doing. I helped her with budgeting and made sure she was provided for, as I felt bad about the way my dad had treated her at the end.

In early July 1977, I sold my red Ford Econoline van and bought a used Chevy Ranchero pickup for Columbia Bookkeeping. This was the first vehicle the business owned since my dad's death. I proudly painted the Columbia Bookkeeping name and logo on the side of the pickup. The plan was to let the staff use the Ranchero during the day as a delivery vehicle between the various offices. During tax season, we generally had two runs every day between offices in an effort to keep the processing of returns on schedule. I would drive the Ranchero home each night.

Chapter 24: Frivolous Lawsuits Flow from Inside Prison Walls

Convicted murders left to right: Dennis Cartwright, Floyd Forsberg, and Rod Addicks with moustache (photo © *The Daily News*)

During the past year at the Oregon State Prison, Addicks had been making friends with numerous other prisoners. In a strange twist of fate, he re-established a friendship with Dennis Lee Cartwright and developed a close association with Floyd Forsberg, a convicted murderer and bank robber, when they were both incarcerated in the same cellblock.

Forsberg had a mean reputation and the other prisoners tended to avoid him. But with Addicks working with Forsberg, they started manipulating the other prisoners to obtain favors. In 1978, Addicks and Forsberg were implicated in a prison-break plan, but they both passed lie detector tests in their attempt to prove they had no such plan. (Two years later Addicks testified how he and Forsberg fooled the lie-detector tests).

Addicks and Forsberg made sure to eat meals with Dennis Lee Cartwright in an effort to protect Cartwright from the other prisoners. Word was out among the prisoners that Cartwright was a snitch for the police in Addicks' murder conviction. Why Addicks was doing this was a puzzle at first, but later the truth came out.

On January 13, 1978, a Petition for Review to the Supreme Court of Appeals upheld Rod Addicks' conviction for murder.

On March 28, 1978, Rod Addicks signed a Complaint for Injunction, Declaratory Relief and Damages, against 11 individuals, including me, for a total of five million dollars. I didn't know about it until I was served with the paperwork a few months later.

On July 9, 1978, I received another letter from Rod Addicks saying I had one last chance to change my testimony. He wrote: "I have proof that I did not kill your father. If you wish to change your testimony and work with me, I can save your family from financial loss." That week, I'm sure by pure coincidence, my Ranchero pickup was broken into.

On July 25, Rod Addicks contacted The Court of Last Resorts, a nonprofit organization in San Francisco, and asked them to review his murder conviction. This nonprofit organization will conduct an investigation, at no charge to a convicted murderer, if he claims he is innocent. Apparently, they spent a lot of time and money reviewing the histories of Rod Addicks and Floyd Forsberg. They reviewed the transcripts of the murder trial testimony and interviewed witnesses that Addicks mentioned might help his case. They had Addicks take a lie detector test, which he failed. After three months of research on the Addicks and Forsberg cases, the Court of Last Resorts concluded that Rod Addicks had tried to deceive them and that he was guilty of murder. Shortly after *The Oregonian* received the results of Addicks' polygraph test, they published an article about his case. Rod Addicks sued The Court of Last Resorts for defamation of character. He also claimed he was not properly represented in his murder trial. It made me laugh to think his own attorney was now being discredited by the convicted Rod Addicks. Addicks also sued *The Oregonian* for publishing that information.

On August 11, 1978, Addicks sent me another two-page letter explaining again that he would drop the lawsuit against me if I changed my testimony. Of course, each time I saw a letter or package coming from the State Prison, I felt a gut ache all over again. In this letter, he apologized for including me in the lawsuit, '…but it was just a formality due to the nature of how the investigation was run,' he wrote.

"What an intimidating way to harass me," I said to Jim Auxier. "That shithead is making a mockery out of the legal system. Is there nothing you can do to stop this?"

"No, I'm sorry, I can't," Auxier said. "It's just the way it is. Addicks is obviously getting his jollies by harassing you and the other witnesses by making everyone spend money defending themselves against these lawsuits."

One week later, on August 18, 1978, Dennis Lee Cartwright and Floyd Forsberg filed an affidavit with the United States District Court in Portland, Oregon, claiming that they were the ones who murdered Jim Turel. Forsberg was already a convicted murderer and bank robber, and Cartwright was a convicted murderer. In their affidavit they claimed Rod Addicks was innocent and that he was not involved in any way with the murder of Jim Turel. By mere coincidence, Forsberg and Cartwright had been residing with Addicks in the same cellblock.

That same week, Rod Addicks filed a writ of habeas corpus with the United States District Court in an effort to get his conviction reversed and thus, his freedom. Addicks had been spending a lot of his time in the law library typing up numerous legal complaints and lawsuits.

After Floyd Forsberg's confession to Dad's murder, which I assumed was false, Forsberg contacted numerous newspapers in Oregon and Washington offering his services to solve six unsolved murders in the state. Forsberg explained to the press that he was doing this to convince the authorities that his confession to the Jim Turel murder was credible.

In late August, less than two weeks after Cartwright and Forsberg's affidavit, I learned that a small tabloid, *The Innocents,* had begun publication in Longview, Washington. The August edition contained an article that went into full detail about how Floyd Forsberg murdered Mr. Jim Turel. An interview with Forsberg by the author Andy Stack contained the wording and grammatical mistakes that Addicks had made in some of his other writings. I suspected that Addicks' sister, who showed up at his parole hearings, was helping with this project.

Copies of that tabloid were sent out all over the country and it found its way into various newspapers and prison literature. Apparently, Addicks started using the pen name "Andy Stack," pretending he was the editor who had written the long, accurate article about the murder trial that appeared in *Official Detective Stories* in 1976. Just to remind you, Addicks had sued the real Andy Stack and the magazine shortly after that article had been published.

On August 30, I was served with a lawsuit from Addicks for five million dollars, claiming I was a police agent in disguise who violated his Miranda rights. In it, Addicks asserted that he would never have been convicted if I had not—illegally—turned over his personal information that I found in the tax office.

I called Jim Auxier to complain about the lawsuit. Auxier said, 'You're in good company." Also named in the lawsuit were the District Attorney, County Commissioners, the detectives, and almost everyone else who had been involved with the trial. "Stan, I know this is a frivolous lawsuit, but we must fight this in court anyway," Auxier said. "I agree with the District Attorney; each person sued must obtain his or her own attorney. That's the law."

Since I was being sued personally, I had to make a decision as to whether or not Jim Auxier would be my attorney, or if he would continue to represent Columbia Bookkeeping. After a long discussion we decided that I should have a separate attorney representing me. I was given the name of Robert Koplegard.

I held a short corporate meeting with Bernie Turel and Julie Syler. I requested approval for Columbia Bookkeeping to pay for my attorney. "This is not going to be cheap," my attorney said.

I contacted the State Attorney General's office and was referred to Assistant Attorney General Scott McAlister in Salem. McAlister was in charge of all the lawsuits and pleadings filed by Addicks against the State of Oregon, so I made an appointment to see him. This whole process of justice seemed totally upside down.

I flew down to Salem in my own plane to meet with McAlister. On my final approach to land on runway 16, I flew low over the Oregon State Prison where Addicks was incarcerated and advanced the props to make a lot of noise. I thought, next time I'm going to drop a thousand flyers in their courtyard saying that Addicks is ratting on his fellow prisoners.

McAlister was a nice young man in his early 30s, athletic, and full of confidence. He appeared to be very well versed on the shenanigans of Rod Addicks. McAlister and I agreed that the Forsberg fabrication was probably Rod Addicks' scheme to get himself out of jail, and to get his hands on a lot of money—if he collected on the lawsuits. We agreed to work together in coordinating our respective information. McAlister assured me that he was working with the Multnomah County District Attorney's office on these lawsuits.

McAlister also said the civil cases had to be heard individually, one-by-one, no matter how frivolous. I had hoped we could get a quick court date for a summary dismissal hearing, but he said that wasn't an option. "It will cost us—and you—thousands of dollars in legal fees, but Addicks is able to file all his court documents for free because that's what the law allows prisoners to do. Sadly, it's the taxpayers who are paying for all of Addicks' frivolous lawsuits. But you, as a private citizen, will have to pay for your own lawyer, no matter how frivolous."

On September 1, 1978, I paid $2,000 of the reward fund money to Billy Anglin of Kennewick, Washington, for his testimony in the murder trial. I don't think I had ever met the man in person, although I may have passed him in the hallway during testimonies. But, because all three appeals to the State of Oregon upheld Addicks' conviction, Anglin was entitled to part of the reward money. Billy Anglin was the man who had originally been solicited to murder Dad, but instead went to the Kennewick Police Department with the information before the murder took place. Anglin was not involved in Dad's murder. I received advice from Jim Auxier on how to handle this and made Anglin sign a document that I had never offered him a reward before he testified in Addicks' murder trial.

On September 15, 1978 *The Oregonian* and the *Portland Journal* printed stories about Forsberg's background and his confessions. The District Attorney's office went overboard defending its conviction of Rod Addicks. They included the FBI's proof that Forsberg was not even in the State of Oregon the day my dad was murdered.

On September 22, 1978, Floyd Forsberg led the press and State police to a hidden gravesite that contained the bones of a young woman who had disappeared in 1976 near Tolantino, Oregon. Forsberg refused to take the police to the location unless the press would accompany him there. Forsberg told police he had been told of the location by fellow inmate Mr. Godwin. Godwin had been arrested in 1977 on a parole violation. Godwin pleaded innocent and later claimed that Floyd Forsberg and Addicks coerced the information out of him.

That's when excerpts of *The Innocents* articles began cropping up in the state's major newspapers. The *Albany Herald* published a series of articles that included verbatim sections of the fabrications from the *Innocents* articles, playing right into Addicks and Forsberg's scheme. In the articles, Forsberg claimed to have killed Jim Turel in an effort to get tax information on an FBI agent named Renning. Forsberg said he believed the agent had his tax return done at Columbia Bookkeeping. But Agent Renning never had his tax return prepared at Columbia Bookkeeping, and neither Forsberg nor Dennis Lee Cartwright had ever met Jim Turel or had their taxes prepared at Columbia Bookkeeping. Agent Renning denied Forsberg could have been involved since he had proof Forsberg was in Reno, Nevada, planning a large bank robbery at the time Jim Turel was murdered in Portland.

Ignoring the denials, a series of long articles came out in *The Oregonian, Portland Journal, Willamette Week, Eugene Register Guard*, and numerous other papers during the following month. The press was eating it up. Forsberg also made himself available to all the TV stations.

Up through 1979, Rod Addicks, Dennis Lee Cartwright, and Floyd Forsberg sued over 70 individuals for many millions of dollars. Addicks even sued Rocky Butte Jail and was allowed to present the case in front of a jury. That trial was the follow-up to his claim that the prison put him in solitary confinement without a hearing. Never mind that the reason he was put in solitary was because of his attempted jailbreak and his solicitation of a fellow prisoner to murder Dennis Lee Cartwright just prior to Addicks' murder trial. [In the back of this book you will find a chart that lists each lawsuit, who was sued, and for what.]

Most all the lawsuits were initiated by Rod Addicks and Floyd Forsberg. They had free access to the State Prison's air-conditioned legal library, typewriters, copiers, office supplies, and postage. According to other prisoners, it appeared Addicks wasn't content filing just his own lawsuits; he began an in-prison business of filing lawsuits for others in exchange for favors or a percentage of whatever was collected. His transformation into a legal expert gave him a reputation as a jailhouse lawyer. When interviewed by the press, the other inmates said payment for such services could be cash, cigarettes, or drugs in exchange for preparing the paperwork. In one instance, Addicks won a worker's compensation lawsuit and the prisoner received $16,000. It was suspected, but not proven, that some of that money made its way into a checking account Addicks opened with the help of a person outside the prison.

In another case, Addicks prepared the legal filing for an inmate who claimed he was insane. Addicks prevailed in getting that inmate a settlement for back Social Security payments based on his disability. I hadn't realized that a prisoner in jail could collect and keep Social Security payments. Shouldn't the State be able to deduct the cost of room and board from the payments the prisoner is receiving?

During that time I became active in Crime Victims United, campaigning for reinstatement of the death penalty in Oregon for convicted murderers in aggravated cases. Bob and Dee Dee Kouns, co-founded the organization in 1983 with other members of Parents of Murdered Children. I appeared a number of times on Channel 2's Town Hall programs prior to the general election, in support of a Yes vote. On Tuesday, November 7, 1978, the new law passed with over 70 percent in favor. Of course, the new law wouldn't affect Addicks' life sentence since it wasn't retroactive. But once that victory was in place, I switched my focus to helping Crime Victims United draft legislation giving relatives of victims the right to attend parole hearings, which in 1978, victims of crimes did not have.

I also got involved with a group called Concerned Oregonians for Justice, founded by Dedi Streich and Mr. and Mrs. Cohen. Many people were volunteering full-time to improve victim's rights. The dedication of other crime victims was amazing. I felt sorry for rape victims and parents of murdered children whose cases had not been solved yet. Norm Frink from the Multnomah District Attorney's office helped guide us in legal matters.

The November 8 edition of *The Oregonian* and *Portland Journal* had nice articles explaining Addicks and Forsberg's allegations, but the District Attorney's office again denied that there was any connection between Floyd Forsberg and the murder of Jim Turel. They said it was an attempt by Rod Addicks to get out of jail. Forsberg had nothing to lose by admitting to another murder; he was already in prison for life. Was it possible, I wondered, if Addicks' murder conviction was overturned due to Forsberg's confession, that Addicks would be set free? And would he remain free even if Forsberg later rescinded his confession to the murder? Was it really possible that Rod Addicks could never be re-convicted once Forsberg's confession was proved false?

Rod Addicks and Floyd Forsberg were playing a hard game. In some of their discussions with prison officials, they wouldn't even begin talking until the press got there.

There is more to the Floyd Forsberg story. According to newspaper articles, in January 1975, Floyd Forsberg had been arrested near Woodland, Washington, for robbing a bank in Reno, Nevada on September 17, 1974. He got away with $1,044,000. Forsberg escaped from the Washoe County Jail in Reno while awaiting trial. Forsberg's accomplice, a woman named Denise Catlin, drove the getaway car. Catlin was 20 years old and from Merced, California. Her body was found in a shallow grave south of Bend, Oregon, on October 1, 1975. She had been shot in the back of the head at close range. Forsberg pleaded guilty in June 1976 to killing her.

Forsberg's alleged reason for supposedly killing Jim Turel—to obtain tax records of FBI Agent Renning who had been instrumental in Forsberg's capture—did not hold up. In the midst of Addicks' flurry of lawsuits, Floyd Forsberg took a moment to sue the FBI and Agent Renning, just for good measure.

At the trial in which Rod Addicks won his civil lawsuit against the Rocky Butte Jail, Floyd Forsberg was allowed to testify in front of that jury that he, not Addicks. had killed Jim Turel. The jury that heard this testimony awarded Addicks $5,000 based on the testimonies of Addicks and Forsberg. The jury did not hear about Addicks' conviction of arson, nor about the securities fraud conviction in Washington. I could not believe what I was reading in the papers! Rod Addicks was accused of an attempted jailbreak and his response was to claim he was improperly placed in solitary confinement without access to his lawyer. With all due respect to that jury, they were misled to believe that Addicks was an innocent man behind bars due to Floyd Forsberg's phony testimony.

More lawsuits were filed in 1979 and 1980. Some were dismissed in a summary dismissal filing in 1980. Addicks then appealed the local courts findings in the United States Court of Appeals for the Ninth Circuit in San Francisco. The appeals sat in those courts for months and in some cases, over a year, before they were heard.

In the meantime, I was running the tax business as if everything was normal. However, when I applied for a credit line at the bank, I had to reveal all these legal wranglings. It took a lengthy explanation to convince the bank that the lawsuits were frivolous. Since I was personally being sued, bank policy prevented them from extending my personal credit line, but they did approve the Columbia Bookkeeping credit line. They still made me personally guarantee the credit lines as in the past. No beneficiary of the Turel Family Trust, except me, was required to guarantee anything.

That fall, I was flying my twin engine Cessna 310 to clients' offices throughout Oregon. Even though I was flying it on company business, I asked for reimbursement only for gas. I often had to go to Salem and whenever I made my final approach to the Salem Airport runway, I would advance my props full forward to make as much noise as possible because the prison was right next door. I would look down at the prison football field and think, at least that son of a bitch is still down there and I am enjoying life as a free man.

In August 1979, I wrote a letter to the FBI at the U.S. Department of Justice, referencing a recent lawsuit filed against them by Rod Addicks. In that lawsuit, Addicks indicated that the Turel Family Trust was a participating claimant, that my family was suing the FBI. This was obviously not true. After talking to Charles Turner of the US Attorney General's office, FBI Agent Hansen dropped by the office assuring me that they were aware of Addicks' frivolous lawsuits and would make sure I was dropped from that action with the help of my attorney. Jim Auxier did not charge me for his help on that legal matter.

Addicks continued filing lawsuits, making outrageous claims, and involving others without their knowledge. Why couldn't the warden at the jail do something? Warden Culp's response continued to be that they had no legal authority to stop any prisoner from filing a lawsuit against anyone, no matter how ridiculous it was, based on a 1963 Supreme Court ruling.

By this time I knew I was dealing with an intelligent, but deranged man who was obviously enjoying his right to file frivolous lawsuits and write articles in his defense using the names of other people to make it look like he wasn't the author. All Addicks' other rights had been taken away. Most of his schemes were backfiring, although reporters occasionally printed his articles and allegations without checking out the facts. I could have sued Addicks for damages, but it would have given him pleasure knowing that even if I prevailed, Addicks had no assets against which to file liens.

Meanwhile, I had to defend myself against the second lawsuit Addicks filed against me personally. In this second scenario, Addicks alleged that I was a police agent in disguise and guilty of buying witnesses. My attorney, Robert Koplegard, explained we would have to file another summary motion to dismiss. Since Koplegard was too busy, he assigned the case to a lawyer named Mrs. Kelly. The process would take months to complete.

When it finally came time to present our argument in court, I felt like standing up in front of the judge and yelling, 'Why do you even allow this farce to continue? You know it's been through the court system three times already!' I got into an argument with Mrs. Kelly in the courthouse hallway when I told her what I wanted to do if she did not present a more forceful oral argument and presentation against Rod Addicks' phony allegations. She threatened to quit right then and there. I sometimes think lawyers are too reserved. Their courtesy to each other and to the judge hinders their ability to do justice to their clients. They seem to feel safer filing papers. Based on my observations during the past few years, I believe many lawyers have stage fright when it comes to presenting oral arguments in front of the judge and jury at a trial. However, I backed down and followed her advice. I did not feel her written responses to the frivolous lawsuits were detailed enough. Her theory was that we should answer Addicks' complaints in written form only. Just hand the written response to the judge with no oral presentation. From a legal standpoint, I am sure she was right and just following protocol.

I was nervous that Addicks' continuing outrageous and unfounded allegations would hurt not only my reputation, but that of the tax business. How could reward money eventually paid to someone I never met be construed as me buying a witness? Obviously, the facts had nothing to do with the charges. Nevertheless, unfounded allegations published in the newspapers definitely could have hurt Columbia Bookkeeping's public image. Every time Rod Addicks sued the State, district attorneys, or me, another article would appear in the paper. I made a point of staying away from the press and let the district attorneys defend themselves.

When Federal agencies—IRS, FBI, or other government entities—are sued, their internal policy prevents them from appearing on TV or radio talk shows to address the accusations. But, I could. I was already giving about 80 speeches each year on taxes and appearing on 20 call-in radio talk shows, which had given me a great deal of practice in public speaking. I found I could make people laugh about taxes, which was a relief to many.

As my confidence grew, live appearances got easier for me and I began getting invitations to speak about crime issues. I even received a few invitations from political groups and individuals who encouraged me to run for office. "Are you kidding?" I said, flattered at their confidence in me. "But half my clients are Democrats and half are Republicans. I don't want to lose any Columbia Bookkeeping clients. Thanks, but no thanks!"

But whenever I explained my predicament concerning Rod Addicks during interviews, the viewers and listeners could hear the anger in my voice. I could not make people laugh about murder and injustice when convicted prisoners were allowed to file frivolous lawsuits. I appeared on several Town Hall programs broadcast on Channel 2. At one of the shows, I noticed a suspicious-looking man hanging around me before and after the Town Hall show was taped. As I drove away from the studio I noticed he followed me most of the way back to my office in his faded green Thunderbird. I saw that same car driving slowly by my office a few times the following week. At that time I figured the man was just a nutcase. A week after the show aired, Addicks wrote me a letter saying that an ex-con friend of his overheard me say at the Town Hall show, 'I'm going to hire a hit man to kill Rod Addicks.'

That kind of outrageous statement really got to me. I had worked so diligently to go through the proper procedures of the legal system in order to keep Addicks in jail. Of course I never said I would hire a hit man to kill Addicks. I went back to the State Prison to have them do whatever was necessary to stop him from writing me letters. But no matter how many times I complained, the Prison officials said there was nothing they could do—Rod Addicks had every right to contact me with direct threats and false accusations. My attorney, Jim Auxier, was also receiving letters from Addicks saying he was going to sue me again if I didn't stop saying bad things about him on these talk shows regarding crime victim's rights and the death penalty.

I never responded to any of his letters.

When Addicks lost his second lawsuit in the Oregon Court—on a summary dismissal since there were no facts to back up his allegations— he immediately filed an appeal with the Oregon Court of Appeals trying to reinstate his lawsuit once again. This now meant that I had to spend even more money to fight the appeal. The guy is nuts, I thought, but what else does he have to do but play the system? It's pure entertainment for him.

Chapter 25: *The Innocents* Begins Publication

Rod Addicks, with the help of his associates, set up RANDF: the Rod Addicks National Defense Fund, which raised the money to cover the cost of continuing to publish his newspaper, *The Innocents.*

In 1979, *The Innocents* printed the gory details of the murder of Jim Turel, supposedly described by Floyd Forsberg and Dennis Lee Cartwright. According to the article, Rod Addicks was completely innocent. I was told, and have to assume, that Addicks wrote the story himself, using the alias "Andy Stack."

According to the later sworn testimony of Floyd Forsberg, Rod Addicks and Dennis Lee Cartwright told Forsberg exactly what happened during the violent murder so that *The Innocents* article would be a plausible match to the actual murder scene. Since Addicks and Cartwright were the only ones at the murder scene, this probably is an accurate reflection of how Addicks and Cartwright, not Floyd Forsberg, killed Jim Turel. I'm including an excerpt from that article here. Remember, Floyd Forsberg was most likely stepping into Rod Addicks' shoes as he describes the murder scene:

HOW THIS MURDER WAS PLANNED
by Andy Stack
Innocents Publications, August 1979
Funded by RANDF: The Rod Addicks National Defense Fund

NOTE: The article begins with Andy Stack (probably Rod Addicks) interviewing Floyd Forsberg.

Andy Stack [Rod Addicks, contributing editor]: Maybe we should jump ahead to 1974 and the events preceding the Turel Murder.

Floyd Forsberg: Shortly after our greeting, Cartwright asked me if I would be interested in making $5,000. I said, 'Sure, what's the score?' He wanted me to help him kill someone. I said, 'Oh,' in such a manner that he could see my hesitation. 'Who?' I inquired. He said I would know that when I declared myself in. I explained I wasn't really hurting for money and that $5,000 wasn't enough for something that heavy. He was disappointed, but he didn't push it. Dennis [Cartwright] called me again on August 14, 1974. I remember the date because I was getting married on the 16th. He called me and said he really needed to see me and would meet me wherever I wanted. I suggested Delta Park.

After exchanging a few pleasantries, Dennis commented that everyone he knew was either too scared to handle anything this big or interested only in arson and forgery. He offered me $5,000 again. I told him that I really could use the money now because I had just lost almost that much in Reno while on my honeymoon. I asked him where the money was coming from. He said the intended victim always carried $5,000 on him, or he kept it hidden in his office. He also said the victim was crippled.

Since Dennis knew that the FBI had been hassling me over a bank robbery, he asked me if they were still hassling me. I said yes, that it was worse than ever. Next, Dennis assured me, that if I helped him he could get me the addresses, telephone number, and all relevant personal information about each FBI agent in Portland. I thought he was trying to con me, and told him so. I asked him, 'Did it include Agent Renning's address?' Dennis began bragging that Turel did the tax returns for all the FBI agents in town and half the police force.

I asked Dennis if I'd get the addresses the same time I got the money. He replied that I would get the money the night we killed Turel, but that I'd have to wait for a month or six weeks until things settled down so he could get into the files.

I asked how and where we would do it. Dennis said we would take him out in the woods somewhere and make him disappear without a trace by shooting him and burying him. The bait for setting Turel up would be a date with a woman. He revealed how Turel had even taken one woman on a Hawaiian vacation just to have a good time.

I told Dennis I liked it and from then on there was never any doubt in my mind that I was in. We then went up into the Mount Hood area to find a place to bury the guy. On the way back towards Portland Dennis started to discuss stealing a car to haul Turel in. I suggested that we simply use Turel's Cadillac, which Dennis had pointed out to me when we had first driven past the office.

Dennis, however, expressed a concern several times that this hit had go down soon, that it had already gone undone too long, and that he was going to be out a bundle if we didn't get rid of the creep posthaste.

The Perfect Crime

We made a dry run on Tuesday night, and on Wednesday we did it. Dennis had already set Turel up with a promise of a date with a young chick. Turel expected Dennis and the girl at 8 p.m. As I entered through the door, I could hear a toilet flushing. We entered a reception area. We walked up the hall into another hallway. Turel was coming out from the bathroom. He had a funny walk, kind of waddled like a penguin. He turned and saw Dennis and said, 'You're late.' Then he noticed me for the first time and said, 'Who's this?'

I stepped around Dennis, and drew my .38 snub-nosed from my right pocket and a pair of handcuffs from my left. I planned on playing like a cop and arresting him, but for some reason I forgot and said, 'Don't move, M*****F****r!'

For a second, Turel seemed confused about whether to attack Dennis or me, but only for a second. Like an acrobat, he swung himself around to face me. He began to raise his right crutch to hit me. I was flabbergasted by his fearlessness. I took half a step back with my left leg, raising the gun to his eye level. He was the most fearless man I had ever seen, not a coward like Agent Renning who merely pretends to be brave. I raised the gun quickly and pointed it directly at his eyes and with a quick snap, I jerked the hammer back and said, 'Don't do it.'

I saw Dennis swing his sock with full force. He had a sock with a cue ball in it. The only person I ever saw not go down beneath such a blow was Mr. King at the Diagnostic Center at Fort Warden, Washington. Turel took the second blow. Not only did Turel not go down, somehow he pulled his raised crutch back down, the one he had been raising to hit me, then flipped himself around with such grace and speed that I was amazed. I have little doubt that had he not been a cripple, he would have overpowered both of us, my gun notwithstanding. Turel was raising his crutch to hit Dennis when Dennis again hit him full force with the pool ball. The force was so great that the sock split open and the ball flew down the hall toward me.

Staggering as the blow was, Turel still did not go down. The last blow stunned him and while trying to recover enough to swing the upraised crutch, Dennis quickly jerked it right out of his hand. Then Dennis began hitting Turel over the head with his own crutches. Over and over Dennis hit him, driving him down slow, like driving a large stake into soft earth. What held the cripple up, I do not know; just the sheer power of his will to live, I guess. The fifth or sixth powerful blow finally put him all the way down, but this did not seem to satisfy Dennis who had become enraged at Turel's refusal to die.

263

Over and over Dennis smashed the crutch into Turel's head. Blood was flying everywhere. I stood there as if in some sort of trance. It was like watching a movie with things running in slow motion for me. I wondered if Agent Renning would fight so hard to save his miserable life. I can't say how many times Dennis lifted and swung that crutch into Turel's head. As a rough estimate I would say 10 to 12 or more times when he was already on the floor. I was looking down at Turel's head and saw the top of his head give away and a piece of skull opened up. I was actually able to see gray matter from his brain oozing out of his head.

I told Dennis that Turel had had enough. He had been unconscious for quite some time. Dennis heard me and tossed the crutch down on the floor to the side in one fluid motion. Dennis seemed totally consumed by his rage. Blood was still coming out of Turel's head. While Turel was being hit, blood was flying out of his smashed-in skull. It was hitting the wall and shooting out onto the floor.

I opened the briefcase I had dropped, unfolded the tarp and placed it under Turel's head to catch some of the blood that was still flowing out. Then I stood up and looked at Dennis who was still breathing very hard and sweating profusely. He looked at me and between gulps said, 'That son of a bitch died hard.'

As if on cue, and in one last act of resistance, Turel began to make this funny noise deep from his throat. It was like someone snoring very loudly, but it was more than that. To this day when I hear someone snoring or making a similar noise, it chills my spine. I glanced at Dennis who shook his head from side to side in disbelief. Neither of us would have been surprised if Turel jumped up and took a swing at us. He was that tough. I noticed a length of rope I had brought laying on the floor. It must have fallen out of the attaché case when I pulled the tarp out. I did not wish Turel to suffer any more so I picked up the rope and wrapped it around his neck and pulled it tight. He quit making the noise so I released the rope, leaving it around his neck, and stood up facing Dennis. 'You okay?' I asked.

Before Dennis could answer, Turel started making that ghastly noise again. I again leaned over Turel, this time I wrapped the rope around my hands and pulled with twice as much force as I had before. I felt embarrassed that I hadn't been able to shut him up the first time. I pulled for what seemed forever. My hands began to get numb.

Suddenly, as if in one last defiant gesture, Turel began making those horrible noises again, it seemed louder than before. Was his soul screaming in rage from his throat, cursing his two immobile killers? The last vociferous rage from Turel's throat seemed to reactivate

Dennis who leaped down on Turel saying, 'I'll kill the bastard yet!'

NOTE: According to the coroner's office report, James Turel's neck muscles were so strong from walking on crutches that strangling him was considerably more difficult than it would be on an average man.

Dennis told me we should wrap Turel up and get out of there. 'We can't take him now,' I said. 'There's blood all over the place.' Dennis wanted to get some cleanser and clean up, but I explained to him that all the Comet cleanser in the place couldn't remove those stains. Dennis then suggested, with a shrug of his shoulders, that we burn the place down. 'They will still be able to tell that he was murdered. We'll leave him here and make it look like a burglary.'

So I emptied Turel's wallet and a small register and hurriedly went through his office trying to make it look like a burglary. 'Let's pick up the stuff and get out of here,' I said. Dennis walked over and picked up the pool ball. I hadn't noticed it had rolled into the big office after the sock had broken. We went out into the hallway then. I pulled the tarp out from under Turel's head. It was covered with blood. As I pulled the tarp out, a big congealed mass of blood slid off onto the floor. It looked kind of like a jellyfish. I put the tarp and the rope back into the attaché case.

Back into the hallway, we started to leave when I noticed the attaché case was leaking blood. 'Shit,' I said. Were we never going to get out of this place? I said, 'Let's get.' I told Dennis the first thing is we had to get rid of all of the bloody stuff since it was class A evidence. So we drove down to the river to dump it. The tide was out and the river was low so we had to walk out quite a ways to the water. I found a heavy rock, put it in the flight bag and heaved it in. To my surprise it didn't sink, but began floating away. I watched it float off toward the boathouses, hoping it would sink before it got that far. We got rid of the other things. Next, we went to the motel room Dennis had reserved, and counted the money in a white envelope we found at the office that had $100 bills in it.

End of Section.

At first, I couldn't make myself read these details. When I finally forced myself to read the article, I was so upset I couldn't sleep for days. Reluctantly I have included this excerpt here because it is important to the story. Please understand as you read it, that it was Addicks and Cartwright at the murder scene, not Floyd Forsberg.

Detective Englert also said *The Innocents* article was accurate, just more detailed and more horribly graphic than what had been disclosed during the trial, except it was Rod Addicks and Dennis Lee Cartwright doing the killing, not Floyd Forsberg and Cartwright.

Remember, Rod Addicks sued the real Andy Stack in January 1977. Andy Stack was the author of the article in *Official Detective Stories* magazine that explained in detail the actual investigations and Addicks' convictions for murder and arson. It's strange that in Rod Addicks' *Innocents* article, Andy Stack is falsely listed as a contributing editor. This may show Addicks' continuing efforts to get even or harm anyone who has thwarted or exposed him.

In fact, Englert said Addicks' claim that he did not kill Dad might be psychotically correct in Addicks' sick mind because, although Addicks tried to strangle Dad, it may have been Cartwright who did the final, third, strangling of Dad, which caused his death.

A psychiatrist, after examining this written summary by Addicks, said it was typical of killers with large egos to enjoy talking about exactly what went down during the murder scene. Detective Blackie Yazzolino confirmed that theory. He said, "killers and bullies need to tell someone about the dramatic act they performed. Like a hunter describing the moment-by-moment action when killing their deer after a hunt. Remember, Addicks is a hunter."

I was astounded at how easy it was for Rod Addicks to send out so many articles to the press, all focused on Forsberg's false confession. He was showering the courts with numerous motions, depositions, and lawsuits, and at the same time he and Forsberg were working with the press in numerous directions. The prison had no control over this. It was like a paper war with no solid base, and yet everyone on the other end had to get his or her own lawyer.

Chapter 26: The Deposition of Co-conspirators

While Addicks and Forsberg were carrying on their propaganda machine with the press, Addicks was still involved in numerous legal proceedings regarding his frivolous civil lawsuits. In 1978, 1979, and 1980, dozens of witnesses, detectives and other government officials were deposed in Addicks' frivolous lawsuits and his attempts to challenge people's previous testimonies. The State, meaning taxpayers, paid the cost for attorney Robert Donaldson to represent Addicks in his claim that Forsberg killed Jim Turel, not him. Also, in association with Lewis and Clark College, young aspiring lawyers became engaged with this process. The estimated cost for the State to handle each lawsuit and depose relevant witnesses was around $50,000, according to the Oregon State Attorney General's office. Multiply that by the number of frivolous lawsuits filed by these men and we are into millions of dollars in legal costs.

The following excerpt from the deposition of Sam Moll provides a perspective on how a man with no criminal record can become involved with a psychopathic criminal such as Rod Addicks. It also serves as an example of how the United States justice system works. In reviewing the following testimony, you will read a lot more detail than was revealed during Addicks' trial. It displays how serious crimes are played out without a defense lawyer objecting to the facts or testimony.

Frivolous lawsuit
Case No. 107834

RODERICK R. ADDICKS
   Petitioner
     vs
HOYT C. CUPP, Superintendent,
   Oregon State Penitentiary,
DEPOSITION OF: <u>SAM MOLL</u>

At the request of Roderick R. Addicks, the deposition of SAM MOLL was taken by the Petitioner, before Robin Reger, a Notary Public for the State of Oregon, on Friday, the **12th day of October, 1979**, commencing at the hour of 9:00 o'clock a.m., at the Doric Hotel, 242 St. Helens, Tacoma, Washington.

APPEARANCES:
    MR. ROBERT W. DONALDSON
    For the Petitioner; Rod Addicks

    MR. J. SCOTT McALISTER
    For the Defendant. The State of Oregon
    - - - - -

NOTE: Scott McAlister is defending the State's right to keep Addicks in jail. Rod Addicks is suing the State for early release due to Forsberg's false testimony claiming that Addicks was not the murderer.

SAM MOLL
is called by the Petitioner, and having been first duly sworn by the Notary, was examined and testified as follows:

DIRECT EXAMINATION
BY MR. DONALDSON:

NOTE: This deposition was taken five years after the murder of Jim Turel.

Q. I'm Bob Donaldson. I'm an attorney that has been appointed by the Marion County Circuit Court to represent Rod Addicks in a legal proceeding which he has before that court known as a Petition for post conviction relief.

As you probably know, Mr. Addicks was convicted of the murder of James Turel. And Mr. Addicks now has filed a Petition in which he challenges violations of certain constitutional rights.

And we are here trying to present his case to the Marion County Circuit Court. We are here today in this motel room taking your deposition. It's a rather informal atmosphere here, but this is, essentially, the same as a courtroom. You have just been sworn in.

Your testimony is going to be presented to Judge Ertsgaard in Marion County by way of a deposition, by way of a transcript. It will be considered by him along with other testimony that's going to be presented to the court.

Q. For the record, would you give us your full name and your address, please?

A. Sam A. Moll. (address omitted).

Q. At one time you were an income tax --

A. Preparer.

Q. Did you ever work for Columbia Bookkeeping?

A. Yes.

Q. And during what time periods did you work for Columbia Bookkeeping?

A. I worked there approximately three years, approximately '74, '73, '72, I believe.

<snip>

Q. Did you ever know Rod Addicks?

A. Yes, I did.

Q. Did you work with him?

A. Yes.

Q. What was your relationship to Mr. Addicks?

A. He was one of my bosses.

Q. Was he working for Columbia Bookkeeping when you first went to work there?

A. Yes.

Q. You testified at Mr. Addicks' trial?

A. Yes, I did.

Q. Now, there has been a bit of discussion in this proceeding, and prior to this proceeding on behalf of Mr. Addicks concerning sums which were paid to certain people, either in the form of rewards or for other purposes. As a result of your being a witness against Mr. Addicks, were you paid any sums?

A. No.

Q. Were you paid any expense money?

A. I was given expense money when I first started, yes.

Q. Tell me about that. What did you receive, and when, and how much, and what was said, and why?

A. Well, I believe it was approximately three or four hundred dollars. They helped pay my lawyer's fees when I first started, the State of Oregon, through the county, Multnomah County.

Q. You received payment from Multnomah County?

A. Yes.

Q. Did you receive that payment directly or was that through your attorney?

A. Right to my attorney.

Q. So, they paid your attorney. Your attorney was Ben Zderic?

A. Yes.

NOTE: Addicks' goal was to try and smear key witnesses' testimony and to imply that they received money for their testimony.

Q. Were you promised any other sums for your testimony?

A. I was told there was a reward of $5,000. But I never received it.

Q. Did you make a claim for it?

A. No.

Q. Did you think you were going to get it?

A. No.

Q. Did you receive any promises or deals of any kind for yourself for your testimony; was there any kind of immunity granted to you or anything of that nature?

A. I was given immunity; yes, sir.

Q. Have you ever been convicted of a crime?

A. No.

Q. Have you ever been charged with a crime?

A. No.

Q. Did you feel at that particular time that you could be facing any sort of criminal charges?

A. Well, yes, I did.

Q. And, specifically what charges would they have been?

A. Fire fraud, insurance fraud.

Q. And was this the immunity that you were granted on the fire business?

A. No. Well, I was given immunity on fire, also. But the

main immunity was on the murder.

Q. <u>Were you ever promised a $5,000 reward if you testified?</u>

A. <u>No.</u>

Q. You obviously must not have been afraid of Rod?

A. No.

Q. But sometime later you became afraid of him?

A. I was worried about what he might do, yes.

Q. When did you begin to worry?

A. I was worried at that time what he might find out.

Q. As I recall, some of the money in reading the statements, some of the money paid to Mr. Zderic for you was for a bodyguard; is that correct?

A. For protection. That is right.

Q. Whose idea was it to have this protection?

A. Mr. Zderic's.

<snip>

Q. I've read your testimony. I understand what you said and how it fits into the case. But, I guess, what I want to know, <u>was there any particular event or happening that triggered your fear that made you afraid?</u>

A. <u>Well, it was an understanding with Rod and Dennis that before any of this stuff happened, that if any one of the three of us ever squealed, the other two would get them. This was always on my mind.</u>

<snip>

Q. Do you know whether or not Rod had a gun?

A. Yes. He had several.

Q. Did he have a pistol?

A. Yes.

Q. Do you know where he kept it?

A. No.

Q. Did he carry it?

A. Different times he had a pistol with him, yes.

Q. Did you ever see him put the pistol in the glove compartment of his Cadillac?

A. I think during all the time -- I knew at different times he had it in his car, yes, glove compartment.

Q. A little bit earlier you said you made some of your living by being on the tribal council. What's that, what does that entail?

A. I was elected to the tribal council by the people of the tribe. I'm one of five people that run our tribe.

<snip>

Q. Did you and Rod Addicks ever have discussions about starting a casino on the reservation?

A. We talked about it, yes.

Q. Did it ever get off the ground?

A. No.

Q. Now, you indicated that there was an immunity offer prior to your testimony in the Addicks' trial. And this was worked out by your attorney, Mr. Zderic, correct?

A. Yes.

Q. Do you know who was making the offer of immunity, who was Zderic dealing with, or do you have any idea?

A. With the police officers from Multnomah County.

Q. Was the District Attorney's office involved in the discussion?

A. Yes. I had given testimony before I had immunity. They came up to take -- had taken my deposition beforehand.

Q. Would you have testified at Rod Addicks' trial if you had not been given that immunity?

A. Yes, I would have.

Q. If you were given the opportunity to testify at the murder trial today, would you testify any differently?

A. They had nothing I could be convicted of on the murder trial.

Q. In other words, was your testimony truthful when you talked about Rod Addicks soliciting you to murder Jim Turel?

A. Yes, it was.

Q. Was there any part of your testimony in the murder trial, but not the arson trial, that was either untruthful or incomplete in any way?

A. No.

Q. Do you know whether Jim Turel had some mad money he kept in a secret place?

A. No, I don't know.

Q. Did you ever know about a fund that he would keep in an office drawer or glove compartment of his Cadillac?

A. No, I didn't.

Q. Never see anything like that?

A. No.

<snip>

Q. Did Jim Turel ever talk to you about divorcing his wife, or attempting to divorce his wife?

A. He told me a story about it one time, yes.

Q. Did this involve a payment; do you recall any story about him writing her a check and that sort of thing?

A. I believe so, yes.

Q. What was that story as you recall?

A. I don't know. They were having a fight. I believe he just said he sat down and wrote her out a check for $10,000 and told her to leave. She didn't leave, didn't take the check. He thought it was humorous.

Q. Why do you suppose he thought that was humorous?

A. I don't know. Kind of put her in her place. I don't know.

Q. Did Detective Englert ever tell you that they weren't really interested in you, but they wanted Addicks, that was their goal?

A. They wanted whoever did the crime.

Q. Did they tell you that they were after somebody other than yourself?

A. No, not really.

<snip>

Q. Tell me what it was that Rod Addicks asked you to do? As I recall now, it's been some time, but as I recall concerning the murder of Jim Turel, what was it that Rod wanted you to do? And, then, what did you do?

A. He wanted me to commit the murder.

Q. What was the arrangement?

A. Well, we both, like I said before, were drinking very heavy at this time. And I feel that booze had control of a lot of my life anyway, but I could do it. I could commit a murder.

<snip>

Q. What was the arrangement?

A. Well, during the first couple years we got to be close friends, talked about it. We always kind of joked about Jim. Like I say, we were pretty heavy on booze. And he was a very hard man to work for. I know Rod didn't get along with him at all.

Q. I didn't hear the last part.

A. Rod, they were partners in their business. And they didn't get along very well. And we talked many times about doing him in or something, somebody getting caught on it. He could make it look like his wife did it or a jealous husband or somebody. The more we talked about it, the more we built ourselves up to actually doing it. I don't know that at one time I could do it, and I did plan on doing it at one time.

Q. Did he give you a gun?

A. Yes, he did.

<snip>

Q. What happened to the gun that Rod Addicks gave you?

A. I gave it back to him -- well, he had given me two guns. One that he gave me for fishing that I returned.

Q. One was a fishing gun, one was the one you were supposed to use in the murder and, then, there was the one the police officer showed you?

A. I don't recall the one that I was going to use to commit the crime if I kept it and gave it back to him after fishing or what. I don't recall on that. The one I was going to use to commit the crime, he told me it was not registered. He bought it from somebody, and he imagined it was hot.

<snip>

Q. What sort of occasions would prompt you and Rod Addicks to get together during August of 1974?

A. Well, I had moved up to Tacoma in July. And we kept in contact with each other.

Q. How?

A. Called each other. He would come up.

Q. He would come up and visit?

A. Yes.

<snip>

Q. What sort of activities did you do together?

A. When he came up?

Q. Yes.

A. Drink.

Q. So, the thing you had in common was to drink together?

A. We would drink a lot, yes.

Q. Did you do anything else?

A. Go play pool.

Q. Did you ever go down to Kelso and drink with him down there?

A. Several times, yes. A couple times.

<snip>

MR. DONALDSON: That's all I'm going to ask you at this time.

CROSS EXAMINATION by the State
BY MR. McALISTER:

Q. Mr. Moll, most of the questions you answered were asked about a time which was admittedly a long time ago. And you were never really given a point of reference when you were trying to answer them. So, I'd like to start out with a date as a point of reference, the August 1974 murder of Stan -- Jim Turel -- I'm sorry; Stan is his son. Do you recall that date at that particular time?

A. No, I don't.

Q. Were you working for Columbia Bookkeeping then?

A. No.

Q. And do you recall how much earlier than that you left Columbia Bookkeeping?

A. I'd only worked at Columbia Bookkeeping January through April 15th.

Q. So, you would have worked probably up to or through April of 1974?

A. Yes.

Q. Had you ever met either Mr. Addicks or Mr. Turel prior to going to work for Columbia Bookkeeping?

A. No, I hadn't.

Q. Did you work directly under either one of them during your first tax season?

A. Under both of them, yes.

Q. Now, how did you become acquainted with Mr. Addicks on a social basis? That was during that first year?

A. During that first year, yes.

Q. Were you married at that time?

A. No.

Q. Kind of liked to go out after work, have a drink and have some fun?

A. Right.

Q. Mr. Addicks was sort of the same way?

A. That first year we would stop on the way home and have one or two drinks. We worked till ten, eleven, twelve at night.

<snip>

Q. What about Mr. Turel that first year, did you get to know him very well?

A.   No. Not really.

Q.   Did that ever change during the subsequent years you worked for them, did you become better acquainted with Mr. Turel?

A.   I knew him better, but we never got to be friends.

Q.   You didn't particularly like Mr. Turel?

A.   Like I said before, he was hard to work for.

Q.   Could you describe in what ways?

A.   He was very untrusting. I felt my tax knowledge was greater than his. And he questioned a lot of the things I would do, and I would have to go show him in the books that I was right.

Q.   Would you describe him as a demanding individual and somewhat abrasive?

A.   Yes.

Q.   Did the amount of time you spent with Mr. Addicks in that next couple of years increase?

A.   It increased, yes.

Q.   And how was that?

A.   Well, that first year after tax season, we saw each other maybe once or twice. And I went back to work. They kind of kept in touch and wanted me to come back to work.

Q.   Did both of them keep in touch, or Mr. Addicks?

A.   Mr. Addicks more than Turel. The second year our drinking increased. We stopped more and more after work.

Q.   Were you still stopping in the Vancouver area or did you begin drinking in the Portland area?

A.   In both, yes. We, the second year, we started to go have dinner. The office opened at eight in the morning to eight at night. We had to have our work done before we went home. So, the last year or so, we would work till four or five in the morning to complete it. The second year, his business increased, and we had more and more work to do. We would go out and have dinner and come back and finish our work after the office closed.

Q. Did you see more of Mr. Addicks that next year?

A. Yes.

Q. Socially?

A. Right.

Q. How much more would you?

A. Quite a bit more.

Q. Would you say you started drinking together on, at least, a weekly basis?

A. Yes. I would imagine.

Q. Doing a little, if you will pardon the term, womanizing, hustling?

A. Yes.

Q. And, then, the third year you worked for them until April, and this would be -- now we're up to 1974?

A. Yes.

Q. You were really good friends by then?

A. Right.

Q. And was it during this period of time that Mr. Addicks asked you about killing Mr. Turel?

A. Yes. Uh-huh.

Q. Could you describe briefly how that conversation came up?

A. Well, like I said, we would talk about it several times, not just all at once. It wasn't --

Q. Mr. Turel was a source of irritation to both you and Mr. Addicks, wasn't he?

A. Yes, he was.

Q. And, so, if you were out drinking, you would be getting drunk, it wouldn't be uncommon for his name to come up in the derogatory sense?

A. Right.

Q. And would you say that the conversation turned into killing him was sort of a natural flow from what you were saying about him in the other senses?

A. I think so. At first there was more joking than anything. It went from there.

Q. Did Mr. Addicks offer you money to kill him?

A. Yes, he did.

Q. How much money did he offer you?

A. Ten thousand dollars.

Q. Did he subsequently agree to that?

A. Yes, he did.

Q. And Mr. Addicks provided you with a weapon?

A. Yes.

Q. And you accepted the weapon?

A. Yes.

Q. And did you at any time take any steps toward accomplishing your mutual goal?

A. I had driven over to the office and was going to do it until I come to my senses. I had driven into the parking lot.

Q. You had the weapon?

A. I had the weapon. I was disguised and had a different car. I saw the man sitting in the window, and I woke up and left.

Q. Did you subsequently tell Mr. Addicks you couldn't do it?

A. Yes.

<snip>

Q. Were you ever present when Mr. Addicks offered anyone else money to kill Mr. Turel?

A. I believe I was, yes.

Q. And who did he offer money to?

A. Maddock Tollocko.

Q. Who is Maddock Tollocko?

A. My first cousin.

Q. How did you happen to be together?

A. We were out drinking with him.

Q. Mr. Tollocko is also a drinking associate of yours as well as a cousin?

A. Right.

Q. When he made that offer, do you recall how much money he offered Mr. Tollocko?

A. I believe it was ten thousand dollars.

<snip>

Q. Had you been drinking at that time?

A. Yes.

Q. As had Mr. Tollocko and Mr. Addicks?

A. Right.

Q. When is the first time you recall hearing about the fact that Mr. Turel had been murdered?

A. Mr. Addicks had called me one evening like two, three weeks after it had happened and told me.

Q. That he had been murdered?

A. Yes.

Q. Did Mr. Addicks tell you at that time who did it?

A. No.

Q. You didn't ask?

A. No.

Q. Did you have a pretty good idea?

A. I thought he had done it, yes.

Q. You really weren't particularly wanting to find out directly from him that he had done it, were you?

A. No, I wasn't.

Q. When was the next time you were required to contemplate the Turel murder?

A. When is the next time?

Q. Yes.

A. Couple weeks later.

Q. And what were those circumstances?

A. I believe it was in September or October I had to go down to Portland. It was either Portland or down to Eugene to attend a tax conference to keep my license active.

Q. And what happened then?

A. It was at that time I met with Rod, and we talked about it.

Q. You were subsequently contacted by the police?

A. Later that year, yes. I believe it was the next January or whatever it was.

Q. Do you recall who contacted you?

A. It was Rod Englert and Joe --

Q. Where did they contact you?

A. My place of employment at that time.

Q. At that time, what did you tell them?

A. Told him I didn't know.

Q. Anything?

A. Anything, right.

Q. Did you have another contact with them after that?

A. They talked to me the next day, yes.

Q. Did you tell him anything different then?

A. No.

Q. Still told them you didn't know anything?

A. Correct.

Q. You subsequently decided to talk to them?

A. Yes, I did.

Q. Why did you do that?

A. Well, mainly, because of the crime.

Q. The fact that it was a murder?

A.   It was a murder, yes. I had seen pictures of the murder itself. And it was pretty hard to live with.

Q.   Who showed you those pictures?

A.   The police officers.

Q.   What steps did you take to let the police know what you knew about the crime?

A.   I talked to my lawyer about it.

Q.   And your lawyer was Mr. Zderic?

A.   Yes.

<snip>

Q.   You had used him previously?

A.   Yes.

Q.   So, you went to talk to him at this time. Do you recall what time of year that was?

A.   The police officer suggested at the first meeting if I wanted to talk to a lawyer, I should talk to a lawyer about it.

Q.   So, you did?

A.   Yes.

Q.   Did you disclose to Mr. Zderic the facts that you have described about Mr. Addicks approaching you to commit a murder?

A.   No. Not at first.

Q.   Did you ultimately tell him what you knew about the case?

A.   Yes.

Q.   During the time that you were having these meetings that we're now talking about with Mr. Zderic, did you talk to the Portland Police or wait till you had advice from Mr. Zderic?

A.   When I met with them, he was with me.

Q.   You told Mr. Zderic everything?

A.   Right.

Q.   What did he advise you to do at that time, what did he tell you to do once you told him what you knew about the murder case?

A. To tell the police.

Q. And you subsequently met with Mr. Woods and Mr. Englert and told them the story you have earlier described about the offer of money to kill?

A. Yes.

Q. At that time was there any discussion of money or rewards?

A. No. Uh-uh.

Q. Do you know what discussions Mr. Zderic might have been having with the police about money or rewards?

A. No.

Q. Did you ask Mr. Zderic to obtain any money for you on your behalf?

A. Not at that time, no.

Q. Did you subsequently ask Mr. Zderic to obtain any money for you?

A. I believe after everything was over, I asked him to check on it, on the reward. It was offered, but, then, the police thought I should have it because I helped to break the case for them. But the family had offered a reward, and refused to give it to me. And I didn't push it.

Q. You didn't ask about a reward until the case was over?

A. Yes.

Q. You would have testified without the reward?

A. I testified before I knew there was a reward offered.

Q. Now, during this time that you were talking to the police and prior to the arrest of Mr. Addicks, to your knowledge, did Mr. Addicks know that you had told them about this particular incident?

A. No. No, he didn't know.

Q. Subsequently, your attorney did obtain money from the Portland Police; is that your understanding?

A. Yes.

Q. What was the reason for obtaining this money?

A. Part for his fees and part for protection for me.

Q. Have you ever asked him to get protection?

A. No.

Q. Was that his idea?

A. Yes.

Q. Was it also his idea that his attorney fees be paid by the Portland Police?

A. I believe it was offered that first meeting.

Q. You also obtained immunity, was that also your attorney's idea?

A. Yes.

<snip>

Q. Do you know a man named Dennis Cartwright?

A. Yes.

Q. How do you know him?

A. He is a friend of Rod Addicks'.

Q. When did you first meet him?

A. Met him through Rod.

Q. Before the murder?

A. Before.

Q. Before or after?

A. Before.

Q. Did you meet him during that first tax season you worked for Rod?

A. No. I believe it was the last tax season.

Q. Did you ever go out drinking with Mr. Turel?

A. Not really. We had a couple times. We stopped and had a drink afterward, but that was not what I consider going out drinking.

Q. When you go out drinking, you like to drink a few rather than one after work?

A. Use to.

Q. That was back in your single days?

A. Right.

Q. To your knowledge, did Mr. Cartwright ever go out with Mr. Turel?

A. Not that I know of.

Q. To your knowledge, did Mr. Cartwright even know Mr. Turel?

A. I don't believe so.

Q. When you indicated in response to Mr. Donaldson's question about your expenses being paid, did you receive any expense money other than your attorney's fees?

A. I don't believe so.

Q. Did you ever actually get one nickel out of this thing?

A. No.

Q. All right. You indicated, I believe, that no part of your testimony was false; is that correct?

A. That is correct.

Q. There is a second case, Mr. Moll, involving Mr. Addicks' conviction of arson. And that's a separate proceeding. And Mr. Addicks is represented by a different attorney in that case. I'd like to ask you some questions about that arson case.

A. Okay.

Q. Were you also a witness against Mr. Addicks in the arson case?

A. Yes, I was.

Q. And what was that involvement? I mean, how were you and Mr. Addicks involved in the arsons? Just briefly so we have it background-wise on the record.

A. We committed the crimes.

Q. Could you explain to me what the set-up was, how you did it?

A. Well, there was two fires. And the first one happened the year before, the second year I worked there. At one time he asked me if I would mind driving him to Portland and driving him back. And I really didn't know what he was up to. I knew it was something illegal. But he said, "Just drive the car." He paid me $50 for that.

Q. What did he do on that trip, set a fire on one of his own pieces of property?

A. Yes.

Q. What about the second one?

A. It was after the first one. He got paid off and received all the money. It went so well that he decided to do it again. He told me how smooth it was, how he could beat the insurance companies. And we went out and bought -- he went out and bought houses, and put one in my name, which we burned down.

Q. He paid the money and, then, he put it in your name. And, then, who burned it down?

A. We both did.

Q. You both did?

A. Uh-huh.

Q. How much did you get paid for that one?

A. $17,000.

Q. You did a little better than your first $50 job?

A. Right.

Q. Did you ever burn one by yourself?

A. No.

Q. Ever burn one with Dennis Cartwright?

A. No.

Q. Did you ever engage in any business of that kind at all with Dennis Cartwright?

A. No.

<snip>

Q. On the house that you burned down with Mr. Addicks in Portland, the one that was under your name, was there anybody in the house at the time?

A.   No.

Q.   Was that a home which you were supposedly living in?

A.   Yes.

Q.   Did you make sure there was nobody in it when you had it burned down?

A.   Yes.

Q.   How long had it been since anybody had lived there?

A.   Two, three months.

Q.   And who lived there at that time?

A.   I don't know.

Q.   You bought the house two or three months ago and, then, removed the people more or less?

A.   Right.

<snip>

Q.   Did you get any payment at all for testifying against Mr. Addicks in the arson case?

A.   No.

Q.   You did receive immunity for your own arson involvement in order to testify against him; is that correct?

A.   When I received -- when my lawyer suggested I get immunity on the murder trial, the police officer not knowing my involvement, said if there was anything I was worried about, to include that. At that time, I included the arsons.

<snip>

Q.   Did you ever sign title of the street -- I'm sorry, of a house in Portland on Oak Street over to Dennis Cartwright?

A.   Well, at the time we were planning to commit all these arsons, Mr. Addicks bought several houses. And he went and put a bunch of names on there.

Q.   You didn't do it?

A.   I didn't do it, no.

Q.   Was the basic Addicks plan that he would buy a group of houses, put other people's names on them and, then, burn them down?

A. Correct.

Q. And take a piece of the action?

A. Yes.

Q. It doesn't make much sense for him to keep buying houses and burning them down in his own name, would it?

A. No.

Q. Did you have any involvement with Dennis Cartwright other than with Mr. Addicks in these arsons?

A. No.

Q. I believe you have already been asked this in the context of the murder case, but would you have testified against Mr. Addicks in the arson case if you hadn't been promised immunity?

A. Yes.

Q. Were you promised any cash or any other benefit other than the immunity for testifying against Mr. Addicks?

A. No.

Q. You indicated that the reason you testified in the murder trial was because of the brutality of the murder?

A. Yes.

Q. Why did you testify against Mr. Addicks in the arson cases?

A. Why?

Q. They weren't particularly brutal, were they?

A. No. They weren't.

Q. Once having testified against him, you figured what the heck, may as well clear yourself completely?

A. I could see the man was a criminal, habitual criminal. He needed to be put away for a long time.

<snip>

Q. Did you ever attend a meeting with Englert and Stan Turel where cash payments for testimony were discussed?

A. No.

Q. Did either of those people independently?

A. No.

Q. Have you ever discussed cash payments with Mr. Rieke?

A. No.

<snip>

Q. Let me take a minute and make sure I've asked all the questions he wanted to ask.... Mr. Moll, did you take a polygraph examination with respect to the information you provided on the murder in the arsons?

A. Yes, I did.

Q. Did you pass that test or those tests?

A. Yes.

<snip>

MR. McALISTER (Attorney for the State): I don't have any further questions.

(DEPOSITION CONCLUDED)

When I read this deposition and Rod Addicks' article in *The Innocents* publication I called attorney Jim Auxier to ask him what I could do. I had to think of something that would expose Addicks for what he was, despite Addicks' propaganda machine operating from behind bars.

Jim Auxier wrote back and said that it would not be worth the effort to retaliate; responding would only entertain Addicks and add to his inflated ego. "Besides, Stan," he wrote, "If you win, he has no assets. It's not worth the family's money or emotional trauma to proceed."

I reluctantly agreed. It seemed like the nightmare of the out-of-control Rod Addicks would never stop and the toll it was taking on my nerves was huge. But my personal life and Columbia Bookkeeping had to go on.

When Addicks filed a second $5 million lawsuit against me in which he claimed the Forsberg plot had nothing to do with his records being taken out of the Columbia Bookkeeping office without his permission, I called the parole board and insisted that his latest prison plot should be enough proof that Rod Addicks was still operating with a malicious and criminal mind. "Can't you do anything to stop these frivolous lawsuits?" I asked.

Hoyt Cupp, the warden of the prison, again said he was sorry, but there was nothing he could do. Addicks had the right to sue and mail letters to the victim's families. I arranged to meet with Cupp at the airport restaurant in Salem, since he was also a pilot. Cupp was an honorable man, heavy built, who again said his hands were tied as to what he could and couldn't do.

My letters to politicians did no good; it was out of their jurisdiction, but they understood my plight with the justice system and wished me the best. Included in sincere responses, which I appreciated, were Ron Wyden, Gordon Smith, Mark Hatfield, Bob Packwood, and the Governor of Oregon. Since they could not do anything, I considered writing a letter to the TV show *60 Minutes* to ask them to expose how the legal system was being abused.

Chapter 27: Home, Mountains, and a Gold Mine

I wasn't happy with where I was living. My house was located on the corner of 157th Avenue and Southeast Stark Street in Portland. The noise of the traffic never stopped and large commercial jets would fly low on their base leg to Runway 28, aiming for the Portland airport. The airplane noise and vibration would wake me up. I decided to look around for another place to live. I wanted to move for another reason as well: Rod Addicks knew where I lived. I decided to leave the metropolitan area and find something on the outskirts of town.

I had a $70,000 equity in my home and if I rented it out, the money I collected would cover my mortgage payments and provide a little extra profit. Inflation was still working in our favor, so why sell it? It was easy enough to buy another home for $4,000 down.

By then, the real estate listing for my stepmother's home had expired and she was eager to unload the property she'd lived in with my dad and Mr. Cosmos. Bernie invited me to lunch and asked if I wanted to buy her home. She had kept the yard immaculate and I have to admit I was tempted. As we talked, I was quietly doing the math. Bernie had the property listed for over a year, but the agent couldn't find a buyer. If the house had sold through the realtor, she would have netted $56,400.

I thought the 900-square-foot house with an indoor pool on the two-acre site had potential, besides it was part of the family. I offered Bernie $57,000. She refused even after I showed her how I came up with that figure. I explained how she'd net more from me than she would have received using her realtor.

Around that time, I sold my interest in one of my rental properties so that money was available for a down payment on a home loan. After thinking the matter through, I agreed to Bernie's $60,000 price and helped her move to that fancy mobile home park in southeast Portland. Bernie felt much more comfortable with neighbors her own age. I could really understand her concern about living alone, in an isolated locale, especially with what the family had been through in the past few years.

As we approached the end of 1979, I started preparing for another tax season. Columbia Bookkeeping had grown to 15 offices because we'd taken over a few more one- and two-man tax businesses. We had already acquired Granning & Treece, the Meier & Frank Tax Offices and five locations inside Lincoln Savings Banks. In most cases we incorporated the offices into our existing business. Columbia Bookkeeping agreed to pay 25 percent down on a contract, and then another 25 percent on the contract balance at the end of the following tax season. By structuring the deals this way, we could usually make enough profit during the tax season to pay off the balance in three years.

Finding new staff for the offices was an ongoing nightmare, so to attract more qualified tax preparers, I offered continuing education seminars free to our existing staff and invited outside practitioners from Salem, Eugene, and Portland who had to pay. We had over 100 people registered for most classes, which allowed us to cover our own costs for continuing education hours. It also gave us access to trained people who were looking for tax preparation jobs, and the chance to entice smart accountants away from other accounting firms.

In the first few years of holding seminars I prepared and gave most of the class presentations, but would sometimes hire professionals to provide specific training in areas where we all needed more education. I wrote and produced an 80-page Tax Planning Book, and used that as a marketing tool in every seminar I gave, whether it was for continuing education or presentations for business groups. My brother, Gary, even though he could have been seen as a competitor, was allowed to attend free. I noticed that he, too, would work the room looking for applicants to hire for his firm because his business was expanding, too. Gary and I made a pact that Columbia Bookkeeping would not move into his side of North Portland, and he would not open an office near Columbia Bookkeeping.

After Bernie moved out of Dad's house and I moved in, I had to readjust to living there. I enjoyed mowing the lawn and doing things that my brother and I used to do. But I was careful to put the telephone number in someone else's name as I still feared reprisals from Rod Addicks.

The tax business continued doing well throughout 1980 and I was again looking forward to January. It was my custom to meet with business clients during the last few weeks of the year to go over their year-end tax planning.

On December 31, 1979, I met with Ray Halphide, a friend of my dad who had remained a client. Halphide owned Sell's Marine service. I thought the meeting was for a consultation on taxes, but he wanted to talk about how he and his partner were losing their gold and silver mine property in Arizona. They were in default on mortgage payments for their unpatented mining claim, an area that covered over 160 acres. The amount owed was only $24,000.

At that time gold had reached over $600 per ounce and the Hunt Brothers were cornering the silver market. Ray Halphide asked if I would be interested in investing in his mine. I told him I would have to wait until early January before I could leave to go check it out. In college, the classes I enjoyed most were Geology and Geography, so I was intrigued.

In the middle of January 1980, Halphide and I hopped in my little twin engine plane on a Saturday morning and flew to Prescott, Arizona. Our flight plan took us from Portland to Redmond, Oregon, then south toward Lakeview, then to Reno and Las Vegas, and finally to Prescott. I love that type of flying. Just getting out of town was a great stress reliever long overdue.

Looking down from 10,000 feet, I tried to visualize what the pioneers must have gone through crossing that rugged terrain during Gold Rush days. Here we were, traveling at over 200 mph, covering the distance in four hours what had taken those adventurers most of a year. I didn't have to worry about food, water, or Indian problems. The only problem with my plane was it didn't have a bathroom.

During our approach into Prescott, I was awed by the giant, jutting, ragged rocks. I was told by Ray Halphide that there was no phone service in those mountains, so I called my office from Prescott to see how things were going at home. They said freezing rain was falling and ice coated everything. More freezing rain was expected over the next few days. I was worried that the ice storm could knock out power while I was away. It was definitely not flying weather up in Oregon. Halphide and I had left just before the storm hit.

The gold mine was a one-hour drive to the foothills of the Black Canyon Mountains, near the little town of Mayer, which had 85 residents. Oregon's lush green vegetation is so different from the barren, rocky hills of Arizona that I was thoroughly captivated by the passing landscape. When we left Highway 69, we took a dusty dirt road that traversed numerous gullies until we finally drove to a bluff and looked down at a low, dry valley. Within 30 minutes, we were down in that valley, approaching an abandoned gold mine.

The closer we got to the mine, the more amazed I was to see the size of the operation. The buildings included an old stone cabin with a real copper roof and a cement floor that covered a large basement. It had its own giant 10,000 gallon water tank which was supplied by an artesian well located on the mine's property. The natural artesian well, which could generate 30,000 gallons of water per hour, was like something you'd see in a movie. It created its own creek right there in the middle of the desert terrain. In past times, the stone cabin had been a stagecoach stop.

The old mill was still intact, but the guts and machinery were long gone. Across the creek from the stone cabin was a gold-colored, mountain-sized pile of sand tailings from the mill's prior operations. Surveyors later estimated there were over two million tons of these tailings and that a Canadian business consortium had expressed an interest in reprocessing them. The old mine was called the "Golden Turkey Mine."

Halphide introduced me to his partner who lived on the property. The old man's body shook as he stood or sat, but he was very talkative, with an incredibly foul mouth. I could smell alcohol on his breath from the moment I met him. We spent three days there and the man had a beer in his hand from morning until night. Many neighbors visited the site during the hot part of the day, to sit under the tree in the courtyard. The old mine was a natural meeting site for all the other broke gold miners in the area. Hanging out with them, I found myself truly relaxing for the first time in years. I forgot to worry about Columbia Bookkeeping and Rod Addicks. I really liked the place. But I was antsy about the Pacific Northwest ice storm and shutting down the tax office. I knew I needed to return to Portland as soon as the storm broke since tax season was starting. I was anxious to stay focused on the office, but found being out in these mountains was seductive.

I did a lot of research at the Mining Historical Society in Phoenix, and found abundant history about this gold mine's production that verified its early success. In fact, the foothills of the Black Canyon Mountains are pocked with gold mines. Ray Halphide's mine had been productive for over 40 years, but it, along with all the other gold mines in the area, ceased producing during World War II when the United States government declared all non-essential mining operations be closed down. Gold was not considered essential to the war effort.

Before heading back home, I enticed a professor of geology from the University of Arizona to join me in investigating deep into the mineshafts to determine if the 8-foot wide, 2-foot deep gold and silver veins were actually what everyone said they were. At the end of several mile-long tunnels and stoops were large veins that were tested and assessed as gold and silver. The professor determined the ore was really still there. When the bats started flying, however, I got spooked. I have a thing about bugs, spiders, snakes and bats. Plus the shale rock ceilings looked very unstable.

Was yes my answer? The mine definitely had large gold and silver veins at the end of the tunneled shafts. Some carved-out rooms down there were the size of a gymnasium, the result of the mining operations from 40 years ago.

Yes, the endeavor would be risky, but if I could be patient, the mining claims and the value of the land—with its steady source of water—would be worth a fortune even if we never made a dime from the gold. There were over three miles of underground tunnels and ample water supply for mining, but would the safety and mining regulations be affordable? Of course, everyone around those hills thought there was a fortune of gold waiting in that mine.

I agreed to buy out the defaulted mortgage from the lady who was repossessing the mine, and I formed a Sub-Chapter S-Corporation. This would allow Ray Halphide and his partner to keep a remaining interest in the mine. By the fourth day, the weather in Portland had improved enough to fly back home. The ice storm had ended and tax season was ramping up.

Gary and I called for a Turel Family Trust meeting to be held the Sunday after my return from Arizona. We all met in the lobby of Columbia Bookkeeping's office and had a long discussion about the status of the Turel Family Trust and Addicks' lawsuits. Then Gary asked why the family Trust didn't invest in the Golden Turkey Gold Mine. "You met Ray Halphide as a client of Columbia Bookkeeping," Gary said. "And as such the Turel Family Trust or Columbia Bookkeeping should have been the entity to invest, not you by yourself."

I explained the parameters of the corporate opportunity doctrine, which allowed me to invest my own money since it was a different business. "Also," I said, "an investment in a gold mine is extremely risky and totally unrelated to Family Trust business. As a trustee of the Turel Family Trust, I would be derelict in my duties if I invested our money in something that risky."

It was a very productive meeting, and maybe if I were in Gary's shoes, I would have asked the same question.

I headed back to the grind and the long hours of tax season and figured I would focus on the potential of the Golden Turkey Mine after the April 15 tax deadline.

I also started building an addition to Dad's old Turel family home—from the ground up—with the help of my friend, John Winters. We did our own excavation, foundation, and framing under John's direct supervision. John steadfastly refused to take any remuneration. 'It's what good friends are for,' he would say. My design, without an architect, turned the small ranch style home into a Spanish hacienda with three courtyards. I wish Dad could see his home now.

In early May 1980, Mount Saint Helens started a series of small earthquakes. By the second week of May it began venting ash plumes that were drifting to the east and blackening the top half of the volcano. On Sunday, May 11, my pilot friend John Frank invited my wife and me, and Gary, to join him on a flight around the mountain to take a closer look. John also had a twin engine Cessna. We met John and his wife, Lona, at the Hillsboro airport and he joked that he would consider trading his wife for mine. I said, "No way. Mine's not ready to retire yet."

John was 60 years old and the owner of Frank Electric, which serviced the DC electronic drive systems for the timber industry. When Gary and I were teenagers, we use to bum free rides with him all over the place. In one day, Gary and I could end up in Marysville, California, or at a mill in Idaho, and be back before nightfall. John was full of encouragement and the funniest man I ever met.

Both John and I checked the weather with the FAA, even though it was a beautiful day. The FAA had just placed an eight-mile No Fly Zone around Mount Saint Helens, warning pilots that it might spew ash in that vicinity. As we approached the mountain at its summit, around 10,000 feet, we were startled to see dark black ash covering the whole east side of the mountain. The west side of the mountain was pure white in stark contrast.

With our cameras rolling, a black blast of ash and rocks shot straight up in the air about four thousand feet above us. We could see rocks the size of cars falling out of the ash cloud back down the east side of the mountain.

"Wow," said John. "It's lucky we're still eight miles away!" The ash cloud was drifting eastwards, towards us, and the ash was falling like black snow.

Our aircraft circled at 10,500 feet to the north side of the mountain so we could look down at its 10,000-foot-high peak. We saw a small black hole on the top where steam and black ash was still shooting straight up. "What a sight! But let's get out of here before some idiot in a small plane flies the wrong way," I said to John. The pilots had established a specific direction for aircraft to circle the mountain. There were at least ten aircraft nearby communicating about the size and force of the eruption we had just witnessed.

A week later Mount Saint Helens blew its entire top to smithereens. When I looked north from my home in the Portland countryside, I could see a dark, thick cloud of gray ash billowing up 50,000 feet in a mass that must have been three hundred times the size of the mountain. I said to a friend, "Let's go to the airport right now! We need to fly south immediately! Just in case the winds shift direction! If it does, the air here will be full of all sorts of deadly stuff to breathe! We can return as soon as the mountain settles down."

Within 45 minutes, a few friends and I were in my plane headed 80 miles south to Albany, Oregon, for breakfast. We could still see the plume from that far away. We returned later in the day after it was evident that the entire ash cloud was headed northeast. I felt sorry for the people in the Yakima Valley of Washington who were inundated with darkness and covered in a snowstorm of dark grey ash.

Chapter 28: The Murderers Turn on Each Other

In late October 1980, Floyd Forsberg, co-conspirator in Rod Addicks' lawsuits, got angry because he had not yet received his one-third share of the $5,000 Addicks had been awarded from his lawsuit against Rocky Butte Jail. Forsberg's one-third share was supposed to be payment for his false testimony at that trial, claiming Rod Addicks did not murder Jim Turel.

So much for honor among thieves.

The alliance of Forsberg and Addicks began to unravel publicly when Forsberg informed Oregon State Prison officials and the press of an alleged escape plot involving six long-term convicts, including Rod Addicks. Forsberg led the prison officials and reporters to a restroom in a cellblock recreation area where he dramatically kicked a hole in the wall to reveal a cache of escape tools. In front of reporters and prison officials, Forsberg also admitted his phony confession to the Turel murder. He explained in detail how Addicks and he worked up this scheme in an effort to free Addicks, so Addicks could get money from a lawsuit and then split it with him. Forsberg said the plan was Addicks' idea from the start.

After Forsberg destroyed Addicks' frivolous lawsuit schemes to get out of jail, Addicks turned on Forsberg during a meeting with prison and State officials. Addicks also provided a sworn statement on November 4, 1980. I'm including an excerpt of that statement below because of how well Rod Addicks reveals the mental machinations of a criminal mind and an insider's view of how the prison's 'boss system' works. Addicks admits moral responsibility for his criminal acts, including having been responsible for the murder of Jim Turel. I've underlined statements I think are most important; a few non-relevant sections have been removed. Some of the names you will read about have not been mentioned thus far. They belong to other prisoners caught up in Addicks and Forsberg's Boss Convict activities.

SWORN STATEMENT OF RODERICK R. ADDICKS,
November 4, 1980

The sworn statement of the above-named RODERICK R. ADDICKS was taken **Tuesday, the 4th day of November, 1980**, commencing at the hour of 1:45 p.m., at the Oregon State Penitentiary, 2605 State Street, Salem, Oregon. Mr. Gorham is Addicks' Attorney which is paid for by the State of Oregon. Scott McAlister is with the States Attorney General's office. Several other persons were there too at Addicks' request.

- - -

RODERICK R. ADDICKS
was thereupon produced as a witness and, having been first duly sworn on oath, was examined and testified as follows:

MR. GORHAM: I think, Mr. Addicks -- somebody should advise him of his rights before you go further.

MR. McALISTER: You're Addicks' counsel, you can advise him.

<snip>

MR. ADDICKS: I am willing to accept any responsibility that I had and bring in these things to the point where they are now or where they were before Mr. Forsberg made his statement. And I have already notified and informed all the authorities. I'm going to do that. I'm going to cooperate in any way with them to see that nobody is convicted on any disciplinary charges or any criminal charges because of false or perjured testimony.

<snip>

MR. ADDICKS: I have informed Mr. Whitley and Mr. GrosJacques and Mr. Keeney that I am willing to be tested by the very best polygraph experts and/or the very best sodium pentothal expert. I suggested a Dr. Abram who is nationally renowned and who presently is in Portland and has written several authoritative books on polygraphs. And if anybody wants to test me on anything I say here today, I am making that open offer right now.

NOTE: Later in this testimony, Addicks states he is unwilling to discuss details of the Turel murder or to take a polygraph test about the Turel murder, even though he admits moral responsibility for James Turel's death. Addicks had previously failed a polygraph test when questioned about the Turel murder.

I think we eliminated the possibility this morning of a polygraph test. This was another grand scenario of Forsberg's I'm involved in, because that was one of the questions that was asked by the State Police. And the police office was concerned there may be an ongoing conspiracy, some flimflam behind this, and there is not.

<snip>

MR. ADDICKS (CONTINUED): For what I'm doing today and for what I've done so far and in my offer of total cooperation with the authorities on this, I don't want anything. I'm not asking for anything. I'm accepting any consequences that come out of it. If I'm subject to institution disciplinary consequences, I'm going to accept them. If I get something that's unreasonable, of course, I'm going to appeal it. I'm going to accept anything that comes out of this. And I really believe in what I'm doing.

I'm not bitter towards Forsberg. In some respects, this is really a blessing, it forces me to do something I should have had the courage to do a long time ago. I hope he's able to find peace with himself.

To show you that I'm serious, you already know I talked to the police about the Little case and passed the polygraph test. I want to tell you, I accept the responsibility for James Turel. I don't feel I have the same physical capability as the co-defendant, but my moral capability is much greater, and I accept that responsibility.

There is no escape plot that I'm aware of. I have never talked to Atterberry about escaping in my entire life. Even if I was inclined towards escaping, I would have never talked to Atterberry, because he has a history of being a rat. Forsberg included Atterberry in the escape plot because Atterberry owed him money, he was in debt. And I'm sure that Forsberg was obsessed with the fact, like he gets obsessed with the facts, that -- he was going to get Atterberry one way or another. And I think this is one way of getting him.

And by Ron Kalama, he's the only one in that whole group I've ever trusted. I've never discussed an escape plot with him. I don't believe there is a current escape plot. I'm willing to take a polygraph on all these questions as I said before.

NOTE: Previously, Addicks had failed a polygraph test wherein he claimed no participation in Jim Turel's murder. But in the interim, he seems to have gained enough experience to pass, by learning from mistakes while taking several additional tests on other prison matters. Addicks still refused to take another test regarding the Turel murder.

Cartwright and I never made any overt act toward an escape. There was no current escape plots. I don't believe Forsberg went to him because I think Cartwright would have told me if he did.

The upshot of this is that it's possible that Forsberg went to each of these individuals individually and told him something about some escape plot and planted it in their minds there was going to be an escape plot, because he knew what I was doing. But I think that was a rather last-minute decision of Forsberg. I think he didn't have time to do that, and I think that when all this is said and done and everything becomes known, you will find there was no escape plot.

<snip>

MR. ADDICKS (CONTINUED):

I'm going to tell you about my responsibility, and what I did in these things -- some of them, all of them that I was involved in. I guess the first place to really start, that would be in about 1977, during the summer of 1977, actually during the spring of 1977. Forsberg discussed with me the possibility of escaping from the institution. And I didn't make any kind of commitment one way or another. But I listened to his suggestion. And during the period of the summer of 1977, Mr. Forsberg accumulated some tools and some weapons and secreted them in the group living offices. Mr. Forsberg did all the accumulating of the weapons. I never accumulated any weapons. Mr. Forsberg did all the secreting of the weapons. Mr. Forsberg paid for the weapons. Mr. Forsberg was in the group living office doing this prior to the time that I actually worked in the group living office.

But I believe some of them were also secreted after I went to work in the group living office. Mr. Forsberg told me of three different locations where these weapons may be secreted. They were secreted in the group living office. I don't know for sure whether I believed or knew where they were, that was -- where they were according to my write-up, one of those places Mr. Forsberg said they were -- the other two places he said they were was in the eaves and behind the wall of the storage room. So, I believe to the very best of my knowledge, the only person who knew exactly where the weapons were for sure was Mr. Forsberg. To my knowledge, no one else besides he and I even knew that there was a stash of weapons. I did know he had a stash of weapons.

I'm told by hearsay, but it was from Keeney, so I believe it's probably true, that Kalama and Dennis Cartwright were charged with accumulating weapons for Mr. Forsberg. This is totally erroneous. Mr. Forsberg's weapons were procured by a friend of his who's left the institution. And I am rather reluctant to give his name, because he is on the streets now. And I don't want to cause him any trouble. However, if Mr. Forsberg won't tell the truth, I'm going to give his name because I'm not going to allow Mr. Cartwright and Mr. Kalama to be framed for obtaining weapons they didn't obtain.

I know the details of how Forsberg accumulated the weapons. I'm willing to divulge them if Forsberg becomes unwilling to do so. To do so now would be -- since the statute of limitations has run on them and the institution can't punish the man who actually did. I want to hold that up. I want you to understand I'll freely do that if it becomes necessary, if Mr. Forsberg won't admit what really did happen.

Before the 1977 alleged escape plan could go into effect, Mr. Forsberg had some people he knew from the outside investigating the possibility of picking the proposed escapees up outside of the walls of the penitentiary after they went over the wall. And the people that he had look into it told him it was a bad plan, and they refused to go along with it. And the escape plan was abandoned.

I had actually abandoned any type of escape plan prior to Forsberg abandoning the plan because -- I'm not going to make this a boxing match or shouting match, because of some of the things Forsberg wanted to do when he got out of here, and I was totally morally opposed to it, and I refused to go on with it.

Sometime after the plan was abandoned, the institution got word of the plan, which was basically the plan, and we were taken to the hole. And Forsberg and I both passed polygraph tests that we weren't involved in any current escape plan. The reason for us being able to pass the test was because the plan was already abandoned at that time, and there was no plan.

After the hole incident, it may have been before the hole incident, I think it was -- it's hard to put things in proper perspective, the retrospect, it's been almost three years ago. Mr. Forsberg asked me what I thought would happen if somebody came forward and confessed to the Turel murder being a participant with Cartwright. He said he wanted to throw a monkey wrench in it. I said, do you think it would help, and he said probably at least get people looking at it. So, Mr. Forsberg decided that he would become a participant in the Turel murder. And, basically, it was his idea to do. I'm not denying any responsibility.

Obviously, he couldn't have done it if I wouldn't have gone along with it. I wholeheartedly went along with it.

The next step was to talk to Mr. Cartwright about it. I talked to Mr. Cartwright about it, and Mr. Cartwright was in agreement with going along with the plan. And I think the reason why Mr. Cartwright would go along with it so willingly is obvious to everybody. Mr. Cartwright had a difficult time at first, because people thought he was a rat and he was very bad for implicating me in the Turel murder. He was willing to do anything to redeem himself in the eyes of the other convicts and himself. And I don't blame Cartwright a bit for anything that's happened.

The way that we set the plan up is, we went over the -- all the details of the facts of the Turel murder. And the details that Cartwright lied about at trial, we straightened out. And we basically prepared an affidavit -- Frosty prepared an affidavit of how he was involved with Cartwright in the Turel murder. It's a 56 or 58-page affidavit. I don't know if Frosty still has one, but I still have a copy somewhere in my legal papers of the papers he prepared. And if you want it, Mr. McAlister, you are welcome to it or a copy of it.

MR. McALISTER: Thank you.

MR. ADDICKS: Then, shortly thereafter, after the affidavit was prepared and the stories were straight, we got ahold of Mr. Babcock. Mr. Babcock looked it all over, listened to Forsberg and Cartwright. He says, 'Hey, that's really something.' He says, 'There is only one problem in the case,' he says. 'You have got to corroborate the fact that Forsberg and Cartwright knew each other when they were kids, you have got to find somebody that can establish that fact. So, we found somebody that could establish the fact that Forsberg and Cartwright knew each other when they were kids, which ironically enough, they were close enough to each other when they were kids at one stage, we were able to do it. They had never personally actually met before. I'll clarify that. But they had enough common friends and common acquaintances that it was able to be done.

I guess the next big move was -- his name is Richard Godwin, came to the institution. And when Godwin got here, there was an article in the newspaper about a sculpture found in Mr. Godwin's trailer house. And when Frosty saw that article in the newspaper and saw what kind of criminal case Mr. Godwin has, he said, 'We can get this guy.' I says, 'What are you talking about?' He says, 'We can get this guy to confess.' I says, 'Well, it might be pretty tough, the police haven't got him to confess.' And he says, 'Believe me, we can get this guy to confess.' And I says, 'Well, what will it do for us?' And he showed me how at the very least we could get a lot of publicity and increase his credibility and possibly force the authorities to speed things up on my case.

So, when Mr. Godwin got to the institution, we befriended him. And what happened shortly after he got here is, people were picking on him, pounding on him, beating on him, threatening him out of the commissary, like refusing to let him eat in the cafeteria. So, Forsberg got him moved onto the tier where he was. We let him eat with us in the cafeteria, went to the yard with him, and talked to him. And believe me, that was even regarded -- sometimes people would come up and say, Do you know who you are sitting with. We would chase him on. Godwin respected that. A couple times people would get on him, and I asked them to not beat on Mr. Godwin, something far worse was going to happen to him. He says, 'Are you going to strangle him? And I says, 'No, far worse than that even.'

So, anyhow, we -- Mr. Godwin wasn't even going to the cafeteria to eat until we let him sit with us. We talked to him over a period of time. And we convinced him we were his friends and got him to loosen up to give us a lot of background details to us about his history and his case and a little bit of progressive admittance regarding the current case.

And on or about the first part of July of 1979, Mr. Forsberg wrote an affidavit up. And as of this time, Mr. Godwin had not confessed. We wrote an affidavit up and sent it to the Lane County District Attorney, which was a confession of Richard Godwin. And shortly after that, the County people and State Police came to talk to Frosty. He started negotiating with them regarding the Andrea Tolantino case. As it ended up, all that Forsberg was going to get for leading the authorities to the remains of Andrea Tolantino was the opportunity to have a press conference and some newspaper reporters that he selected present on the scene and a TV reporter. And during this period of time, there was several meetings between Forsberg and the State Police and the Lane County authorities. And they slipped little things out that we didn't know about Richard Godwin before, which Richard Godwin hadn't told us. And one of the things was the fact that he was an artifacts collector. And we had confronted him about the sculpture in his trailer house and asked if he was collecting other artifacts. He said, no. State Police said there was a frozen fawn in his freezer. When we confronted him with that, he just about fell apart.

Another thing the State Police said, another thing is they had identified him at a bar where the little girl was picked up. His motivation for confessing was to us, number one, that each of his children would receive $25,000 from a fund that would come from my winning a civil suit against the authorities for incarcerating me for all these years. As you can see, his motivation was rather farfetched. And, number two, that after I was released -- before I was released, it didn't matter, but after the authorities met our demands, that Forsberg's friends were going to come and take him and Richard Godwin out of the institution, going to escape to Mexico. And that was bogus, too. But that was what Mr. Godwin was led to believe.

After we got the confession which he wrote out in longhand, and which was a true confession, and which -- and the map which he drew out in his own hand, which is a beautiful map, and after we obtained those items, Mr. Forsberg contacted the Lane County District Attorney and had him contact the press official, and he led them to the site of Andrea's remains. When they first got there, they searched for several hours and didn't find anything. Forsberg was very depressed when he got back to the institution. He said that little puke lied to us, blah, blah, blah. Within a couple hours, they came and told us they found the remains. So, shortly after that, Godwin was indicted. We talked to Godwin about then the possibility of cleaning up a couple other murders that we knew he was suspected of.

And during the period of time -- in fact, this was before that period of time when we were talking about the Andrea Tolantino case, he drew the other map which I'm going to give you. I'm not going to attest there is a victim there anywhere. You can do whatever you want with it. It's yours. And they were pretty serious about him being involved in the Kay Turner murder and, also, the murder of her little boy that disappeared from his neighborhood -- didn't disappear, but drowned, from his neighborhood. And there is another case that I don't think the authorities even know about that he told us. And that was he had a little nephew, I believe, who died because he wouldn't go in the car, and the car rolled up and crushed his neck. We never pursued that, because he refused to talk very much about it, which made us pretty suspicious.

The Carouso (phonetic) and Kay Turner murders, we basically did the same thing we did on the original Godwin confession, we took the newspaper clippings, and we took the information that Godwin had given us and the information we knew from the State Police, and we put together confessions. We told Godwin that we had these basically put up and asked them if he would write them out in his own handwriting. And I guess that's really when, seriously, they -- we were all talking about what he was going to get out of it, the $25,000 for his kids. And he and Forsberg were going to escape. That was his inducement for writing out the Turner and Carouso confessions.

When he got to Eugene, and his attorney got ahold of him, his attorney told him that these flimflam guys in the penitentiary are just using you, you are never going to get anything they say you are going to get. He confessed to the Tolantino murder and pleaded guilty, which enraged Mr. Forsberg. And he issued a 2,000-word statement, supposedly, which I never seen, which said we had coerced him into the other two murders, and they were bogus, he had nothing to do with them, knew nothing about them.

At that time Mr. Forsberg wanted to proceed with trying to get the authorities to pick up those other two murderers anyhow. He dropped any demands, he turned the information over to the authorities. I was reluctant to go along with it. I didn't want to go along with it. Forsberg's wife didn't want to go along with it. We tried to talk him out of it. He gets rather vindictive and bitter about things. He pushed it. Not to downplay my part in that any either, because I could have backed off, said I don't want anything to do with that, but because Mr. Forsberg asked me to, because we believed I could pass it, I took a polygraph test as to whether or not Godwin had confessed to me the Tolantino murder, the Carouso murder, and the Turner murder -- I failed all three of those questions according to the polygraph operator.

The polygraph was in error, I respectfully submit, because I was present during all of the Tolantino confessions, and Mr. Godwin will support me on that, because there were two or three occasions when he was confessing and I was there. The polygraph was probably right on the Carouso and the Turner murders, because even though he did confess them to me, they were concocted confessions. So, I can understand how I can fail those questions. And I dropped it after that.

Forsberg still pursued it a little bit. He wrote to newspapers and asked them why nothing was being done and so forth.

About this period of time, Mr. Forsberg made a statement to the newspapers that he had six murders to solve in exchange for six questions for FBI Agent Renning to take on a polygraph test. And those six murders were the supposed Godwin murders, the Kalama murder, the Shawn McGrew murder, and the Timmons murder, the one Forsberg was involved in. Now, Mr. Forsberg says that those murders included the four Little murders, and that is totally false. Mr. Forsberg had never talked to Dwayne Little in his life until 1980.

<snip>

MR. ADDICKS (CONTINUED): Regarding the tools that were discovered in the office and the weapons and the devices and so forth, I'm guilty of knowing for more than three years that there was such things. I think -- I really believe my only guilt is not turning Forsberg in for hiding them. I never personally would have ever used them. If I thought that he was personally going to use them, I believe I would have done something about getting them out of circulation. But after the plot was abandoned in 1977, they were just left there, they were totally abandoned. I think when they were found, at least Forsberg told me this, he had somehow cut them loose from anywhere he could get them. I think the only way they could have gotten them is tearing the wall down or kicking the wall in. I'm not sure about that, but that's the understanding I have.

<snip>

MR. ADDICKS (CONTINUED): I imagine there is a question as to why Forsberg is doing this to me. And I think it boils down to three things. Well, another question I didn't deliberately overlook is, Why was Forsberg willing to accept the responsibility of the Turel murder, and why was he willing to put himself in that position to take another life sentence if he had to, or an additional setup from the parole board? And the reasons for that ultimately was if I was to win, and if I was to receive a settlement or civil suit damages from the authorities for being wrongfully incarcerated, he was to get a third of it. And the reason -- that's the ultimate reason.

There was some preliminary discussions about the possibility of me helping him in an escape plot. Quite frankly, we both thought that was a futile effort, that he knew that I wasn't excited about being involved in any escape attempts. And I don't think there is really a realistic way of escaping from this penitentiary, quite honestly, I honestly don't.

Anyhow, the reason I bring that up now, I'm sorry I forgot it earlier, that one of the reasons Mr. Forsberg is probably mad at me is because when I won the $5,000 suit against Rocky Butte Jail in Portland, he thought $1,666 of that should belong to him. That was not what our agreement was. $1,666 doesn't belong to him. When he asked me for it, I refused to pay him.

NOTE: With this testimony it appears that Addicks continued to lure in convicts and others with the promise of big money in exchange for them carrying out or assisting in his crimes. After his plans backfire, Addicks can pretend he was not the center of the activities. I find it interesting that most of the schemes were based on Addicks convincing others that he has, or will have, access to money.

<snip>

MR. ADDICKS (CONTINUED): Another reason, this is kind of a heavy reason, he sort of admits in his letter, these three gentlemen knew I had it -- it gleams out in my mind before I got the letter, is my wife. And the way that I met my new wife was because during the course of the Godwin events, she saw Forsberg on TV. She wrote to Forsberg, and she says, basically, 'I saw you on TV, you're an exciting personality, and why won't the authorities look into what you're claiming?' And they started correspondence. And during the course of their correspondence, Forsberg got the hots for her. And she didn't particularly for him. And Dee was very jealous, Mrs. Forsberg, because he sent her copies of the letters both coming and going. And she could see it was leading to something that was threatening to her. So, Dee told Forsberg he was going to have to drop writing letters to this girl. In the meantime, Forsberg had a plan of, perhaps, using this woman at some future time in some schemes of his own, some activities of his own. And about December of 1979, he wrote the woman an ultimatum letter. And the ultimatum letter was, basically, she was going to become a robot for him, become his slave, or else he didn't want anything to do with her and so forth. In the course of reading letters to him and his to her, I saw she was a very intelligent and caring person.

307

This may sound a little corny, but I was a little bit in love with her before I started writing to her. When he wrote her the ultimatum letter, I at the end of the letter said, when you drop this creep, you can start writing to me if you would like to. And she did. And we started corresponding. And we started visiting. And we really did fall in love. I really believe it's love. And we got married.

And during the period of time when Forsberg thought I had her wrapped around my finger, he wanted me to ask her about doing some little things that bordered on the verge of being criminal. I refused to do it, because anybody involved in my cases knows I never ask my wife or loved ones to do anything ever. And I'm not going to bend my morals for anybody in that respect. And he was mad about that, too. And probably just a little bit jealous because he felt I took her away. I don't know how he felt about that.

I'm open to any questions you gentlemen want to ask me.

EXAMINATION

BY MR. McALISTER:

Q.   I've got a number of them. Some of them make a difference, some of them don't. Forsberg said while he was making his statement, you approached him about this plan to get you off by having Forsberg confess.

A.   The first time that this comment was ever made, and you can write down my exact words on this, because I will take the polygraph on it. When we circled the track on the far corner when we were running one afternoon by the baseball screen out there, he says, 'What would happen if I confessed to participating with Cartwright in the Turel murder?' That's where it started. Basically, it was a joint -- basically, it was a joint plan, don't get me wrong. I'm not knocking out any responsibility. But the basic first mention of it was he mentioned to me what would happen if that happened.

Q.   And then you approached Cartwright?

A.   I talked to Cartwright about it, yes.

Q.   Then it was agreed. The three of you worked it out?

A.   Yes.

Q.   Now, is basically Forsberg's Confession simply a statement of your involvement if we skip the trip to Reno, the van, and that sort of thing?

A.   Well, I've talked to my attorney before we had this session, and he's agreeable with me in accepting responsibility. He asked me not to get into any detail on the Turel murder at this time until we sort out where my appeals stand, as far as details on the Turel murder. I would like----

Q. You will answer those when your appeals are over?

A. I'll have to talk to my attorney and find out what future positions, you know, what we're going to divulge as far as that. I'm going to leave it -- I'm accepting responsibility for Mr. Turel's murder.

Q. So, we won't hear any more claims of innocence as far as your appeals are concerned or post-conviction?

A. My appeals and post-conviction, I will file joint motions with you to take out Forsberg and Cartwright confessions, yes.

Q. You indicated that almost everything Forsberg talked about was made up. I've had the opportunity to read both your letter and Mrs. Forsberg's letter. And both the letters exchange information concerning an alleged informant in the Federal Prosecutor's office who was to be saved for a witness in a federal habeas corpus proceeding. Is that made up or correct?

A. I'm not going to divulge this information if it would hurt anybody. I don't hate Forsberg. I hope I made this clear. I'm not going to get into a mud-slinging contest with him. He may want to get into a mud-slinging contest with me. That's perfectly all right. I'm not a bitter person. I don't want people that are not guilty -- at least not told him the things he says they have. That's my primary purpose.

<snip>

MR. McALISTER (CONTINUED):

Q. For your convenience because you made a reference to the letter, it's only fair that I tell you Mr. Forsberg approached me on Monday or Tuesday to find out when your case was going to be decided. He said I would have to let him know what the result was, because he had big plans after that date. He has told the prison authorities the escape was for November 1, 1980, or later, and that the reason he had to come forward was because you would no longer allow him to stall.

A. No longer allowing him to what?

Q. The other people involved in the escape plot would no longer allow him to stall and hold you off from escaping, and so it was necessary for him to come forward at that time. Based on that, do you have any kind of response to what you said earlier about his letter?

A. Well, I'm sure, knowing Forsberg, there is some things that he's -- as I said earlier, there was some things he told me were different from things that he had in here. But I think I can shoot that theory down pretty handily, because the first knowledge I had of the denial of my post-conviction was 15 minutes before I was in the hole. I think you very well know I would never have gone along with any escape plot or gone along with one while my post-conviction was pending. And, secondly, as you well know, the habeas corpus is pending for this winter sometime. And, of course, the primary issue is really a heavy issue, whether I'm successful getting it out or not, I don't know, but I would certainly never go on an escape plot until that was heard. And the third thing, I had some previous hope for parole at some reasonable time. I had a fairly favorable psychiatric report. And I had a couple pretty decent discussions with the parole board. And I don't think they are going to be totally out of line. I might be mistaken. I would have stayed around to hear that if I was interested in anything. And I think the evidence, circumstantial evidence, is pretty conclusive, there is no way in the world I would become involved in an escape plan this winter. And that's certainly open to polygraph examination and any other examination.

Q.   With respect to Cartwright, right now I think you would have to agree, he is sort of holding the bag as far as that post-conviction -- three people lied, basically yourself, Forsberg and Cartwright. Two of them have now recanted those lies. Is Cartwright free to do the same?

A.   I saw Cartwright for a second this morning when they brought me down here. And he said that you had told him to talk to me. And I says, 'Well, where do we talk?' I told you last night, as far as I'm concerned, Mr. Cartwright can do whatever he wants to do. I'm no longer involved in the manipulation business of any person at any time. And he is fully free to do what he wants to do.

NOTE: At least Addicks admits that he has been in 'the manipulation business' of other prisoners. Boss Convict System Exists *was the headline news of an* Oregonian *article by reporter Rolo Crick.*

Q.   Just so it's clear on the record, in the event I want to take this transcript to him, show him some sentences, the direct question is, is Mr. Cartwright free to admit that he was involved? And, in fact, that you lied in your post-conviction?

A.   Well, as far as I'm concerned, Mr. Cartwright can do whatever his -- he wants to do, yes.

Q.   Now, you talked about the pressure that was put on Godwin because he was, one -- I'm sure because he's a sex offender, and you have also talked about some things generally that happened to snitches.

How is it Mr. Forsberg was busy collecting and snitching, and he had no problem in the institution?

A. There was nobody that was going to pick on Forsberg. He would have killed them. It was as simple as that. Everybody knew what his background was.

NOTE: It appears nobody was going to pick on Addicks since Forsberg and Addicks were close buddies and co-conspirators in numerous prison schemes and possible jailbreak plans. Forsberg appears to be Addicks' enforcer.

Q. Forsberg described you as a small-time organized crime figure in Portland.

A. He did? It's news to me.

Q. This would be another one of those confessions that aren't quite accurate?

A. I'll take a polygraph on that one.

Q. <u>You have your attorney here on the post-conviction proceeding regarding the arson. Are you also dropping those?</u>

A. <u>I haven't said I dropped any post-convictions.</u> I said I would join with you in a motion to dismiss the Forsberg confession part of the post-conviction and so forth.

Q. Are you dropping your claim with respect to allegedly other people, and I think you at one point said Cartwright and Moll were the people involved in burning those buildings rather than yourself and Cross.

NOTE: Observe how cleverly Addicks responds below. He does not admit to anything and in fact, avoids answering the questions. Yet his testimony appears to confirm he is the center and maybe a major planner of these events.

A. Mr. McAlister, I'm not going to involve anybody in any crime that doesn't commit a crime. And I can't tell you exactly what I'm going to do yet until I talk to everybody that's involved. I'm not going -- I will assure you that -- and I promise you nobody that wasn't involved in a crime is going to become involved in a crime that has anything to do with me.

Q. That means you will decide whether or not Mr. Cartwright was actually involved, and if you decide he wasn't, he cannot participate on the post-conviction proceeding, that claim will be dropped; is that right? You have alleged an innocent person has done something when, in fact, they didn't, and we can expect that to be forthcoming?

A. If I've alleged in the arson post-conviction that Mr. Cartwright burned the house down and Mr. Cartwright didn't burn the house down, then I would drop that issue from the post-conviction for sure.

MR. McALISTER: Anybody have any questions?

<snip>

MR. WHITLEY: Will you tell us how Forsberg got the weapons up to the group living office? You said you didn't want to divulge who brought them up for him.

MR. ADDICKS: Well, as you saw in his letter, I've given him the opportunity to tell who did bring them. And if there is some compelling reason if he doesn't tell, I'm going to tell you for sure. Otherwise, if you have some compelling reason, yes, I'm going to. I'll tell you, too. But I can't see a compelling reason right now for the simple fact that you have my assurance the man has been gone for a long time that brought them. And, number two, the statute of limitations has run on it. You have my assurance that they have been there for more than three years.

MR. BLALOCK: What kind of weapons are they?

MR. ADDICKS: They are -- well, I honestly don't know all of what they are. But I heard Mr. Whitley describe some of them yesterday. And you can tell him, I guess.

MR. WHITLEY: Couple of knives, wrenches, hammer, couple iron bars.

MR. BLALOCK: No revolvers?

MR. ADDICKS: No. Is there a compelling reason for knowing who it is particularly?

MR. WHITLEY: I want to know how it got up there so it doesn't happen again.

MR. ADDICKS: How he got them there?

MR. WHITLEY: How he got them from the shop or wherever they were made, into group living.

MR. ADDICKS: I'll be happy to give you the background of how he did it. The guy he knew worked in the yard, and he hired a guy that was the head of the biker's gang at the time or was in the biker's gang at the time who hired various -- subcontracted bikers to bring them out to the yard. The guy he knew in the yard brought them in to him in the group living office. And he stashed them. That's the basic mechanics of it. If he's unwilling to admit that Kalama and Cartwright didn't do it, I will tell you who did do it. And we can proceed that way. I don't want them to be framed for something they didn't do.

MR. GROSJACQUES: How about Little? He's down on the write-up on this escape plot too.

MR. ADDICKS: Who?

MR. GROSJACQUES: Little. There was some dealings between Forsberg and him about possibly taking him on the escape. Is this true?

MR. ADDICKS: There was no serious escape plot that was discussed with Little. And obviously Little hadn't even become involved to the extent of writing out a confession. That was part of the thing. And I think you were present when I told you when Forsberg was discussing the alternative possible escape plots and wanted to show Little a 30-foot ladder, Little didn't want to see it. It never proceeded to the stage where there was any culpability on Little as far as there was no fixed plan or anything like that. It was just BS.

MR. GROSJACQUES: Do you know anything about any weapons that Little had on the outside?

MR. ADDICKS: Little?

MR. GROSJACQUES: Yes.

MR. ADDICKS: I thought we went over this last night. He discussed the fact he had 200 guns buried in barrels in the Portland area -- or outside of the Portland area or something like that. He said he was going to give Forsberg a map of where one of those stashes was. But to my knowledge, he never gave Forsberg a map. Forsberg's letter says he did have a map. I'm not aware of it if he did. As a matter of fact, when I asked Forsberg if Little was willing to give him a map, that same afternoon Little was taken out. I assumed there was no -- this was during this last week when things were getting hectic. The reason we wanted that map, we felt that was corroborating to Little's total story, that was why he wanted it.

MR. WHITLEY: He said one time during this he had another map he was going to give to you. Of a body?

MR. GROSJACQUES: We're talking about Godwin now? Godwin made that map?

MR. ADDICKS: Right.

MR. WHITLEY: You said you had another map?

MR. ADDICKS: Just the Godwin map. And the Little map, as far as I know, is nonexistent.

MR. BLALOCK: I'm a little concerned about Cartwright. Was he coerced into this, you felt like -- I don't recall or I thought you were -- we gave him a finding of mitigation which resulted in a variation from a range below the range because he cooperated with a criminal justice agency in your prosecution. And he stands to lose that finding obviously. How did he get involved in -- how was he coerced into cooperation? Was he afraid of Forsberg?

MR. ADDICKS: Actually ----

MR. BLALOCK: Or is everybody afraid of Forsberg?

MR. ADDICKS: To a certain extent. But you can't use that as motivation. This is a penitentiary. There is a lot of people afraid of a lot of other people. I can't say that Cartwright is afraid of Forsberg. I certainly can't say I was afraid of Forsberg. I'm not going to try to mitigate my responsibility in any way. I'm willing to accept it.

As far as Cartwright goes, I sincerely hope that he isn't hurt from a parole board standpoint over this. Basically, he got involved in this fabricated story of the Forsberg, Cartwright confession because he felt so badly about what he did to start with about implicating me.
MR. BLALOCK: I was trying to regard what you said about that.

MR. ADDICKS: He was having a tough time in the pen because people were calling him a rat. I told people to get off of him and stuff. I forgave him, various things. He just felt he had an emotional feeling about it. That's basically why he got involved.

MR. BLALOCK: I had just lost that. I remember now.

MR. McALISTER: Thank you.

- - -

STATE OF OREGON
    County of Multnomah

Years later, when I received a copy of this transcript, I realized that Addicks, by offering to take polygraph examinations numerous times in the span of this interview, was boasting. He admits in this testimony how he had learned to fool the lie detector technology. He'd failed the test performed by the Court of Last Resorts and had avoided taking another until he'd had the chance to practice. There were now approximately four lie detector tests taken by Addicks who admits he knows how to fool a polygraph test by now.

A few weeks after Forsberg exposed Addicks' schemes and this interview was recorded, Forsberg had the unlucky experience of being severely beaten in a prison yard. Addicks, who was coincidentally nearby, claimed that Forsberg was lying face down in a deep pond of water moments after that beating took place and, according to Addicks, thanks to his quick action, Addicks was able to pull Forsberg out of the water meaning he thereby saved Forsberg's life from drowning. In subsequent statements provided to the parole board and doctors who evaluated Addicks, this event was used by Addicks to demonstrate that he was not a violent man! No motive was discovered for the beating, but Addicks insisted that it was certainly not arranged by him as revenge for Forsberg's ratting him out.

Detective Englert's investigative reports indicate that Addicks has repeatedly shown a propensity to get even. Examples are the robbery of the realtor who was taken into the woods and abandoned out there, which he had someone else carry out, and his scheme to rob the bank that repossessed his home in Tacoma.

Call me crazy, but I have private suspicions that Addicks might have arranged or encouraged the beating of Forsberg in retaliation for Forsberg's snitching on him. And that Addicks' effort to save Forsberg's life may have been merely a ploy to make himself look like a hero. After all, in Addicks self-perception, he is not a violent man. In fact, affidavits submitted by Addicks at his parole hearings suggest he is 'a gentle soul who cannot stand the sight of blood.' The fact that he was a hunter was never brought up at the parole hearing. According to his testimonies, Addicks never plans anything; the crimes are never his ideas. He is just a bystander. There is an old proverb: genius is laying the blame for one's action on someone else.

Chapter 29: Disasters, Too Close for Comfort

On August 23, 1981, a nice sunny Sunday morning, I drove to towards Astoria, Oregon, in anticipation of a relaxing day. I had been invited by Ray Halphide, of the Golden Turkey Mine connection, to go deep-sea fishing on his 40-foot yacht in the Pacific, off the mouth of the Columbia River Bar. I was reluctant to go.

On my last fishing expedition with my dad and my brother, Gary, we almost capsized. The date was August 21, 1967, and our boat's only engine quit while going through rough seas where the Columbia River meets the Pacific Ocean. And because we were headed to that very same spot, I made sure to ask if Halphide's boat had two engines. It did. And since Ray Halphide was the owner of Sell's Marine, a yacht maintenance yard in Portland, I figured, what better skipper than a man with all his experience?

When I arrived at the Warrenton Marina near Astoria, Halphide and a lady I at first thought was his wife met us at the dock. He introduced the woman as a friend who oversaw the care of his yacht in Astoria, a two-hour drive from Portland.

We left the dock and headed out to sea. The day remained cloud-free and the ocean stayed fairly calm. About two miles out, we stopped and began fishing. I was surprised that hundreds of little boats were out there with us. Most of the people on the boats held beers in their hands. It concerned me that Halphide had imbibed a few drinks himself. I was growing increasingly paranoid that something bad was going to happen.

After an hour, we saw three men in an open 15-foot aluminum boat. I said to Halphide, "What idiots they must be to come way out here in that little boat." As we drifted and bobbed closer to the three men, we had a good laugh. They held up their trophies—four large salmon. We'd caught nothing.

Soon after that, the wind picked up and we heard a Coast Guard warning announcement on the marine radio. "The entry to the Columbia River Bar is too rough to cross, and it will be closed until further notice."

Wow, I thought, as I checked the fuel gauges on Halphide's boat. He looked at me and laughed, "Don't worry, Stan. We have seven hours of fuel on board and lots of food. When the tide change is over, the entry to the Columbia River should calm down. We just have to be patient."

Ten minutes after the Coast Guard warning, an emergency Mayday call was broadcast over the radio. We heard a panicked voice say, "Oh my God, this is the Yellow Jacket! A yacht just flipped over and people are in the water! Can someone get in there to help them?" We listened as the Coast Guard asked for more information, and the voice again warned people not to attempt to enter the Columbia Bar. Five minutes later the Yellow Jacket announced they were attempting to recover five people. That was followed by a sad announcement when the captain of the yacht, Yellow Jacket, announced, "We just picked up another person, the rest all appear to be dead." All the drowned were people in their 80s. It brought tears to all our eyes to hear the drama going on over the radio.

Five minutes later another boat near the Ilwaco, Washington, side of the river capsized and a few more had drowned. In less than 15 minutes, three boats had capsized and numerous people had lost their lives. It was chilling to hear the marine conversations between radio observers and rescuers detailing their efforts to retrieve the survivors plus the bodies.

We continued to bob for two hours, until the tide changed and the sea calmed, then we returned to port without incident. I vowed that if I ever owned a yacht, it was going to be a bigger boat that the one owned by Ray Halphide. According to the Coast Guard, over a thousand boats were fishing outside the Columbia River Bar that day. The Coast Guard said it responded to 12 vessel breakdowns caused by the extremely high seas. The maximum ebb tide around noon had caused swells and large breakers that buffeted the boats where the Pacific and Columbia River meet.

The incident reminded me of my first experience on the sea. In 1965, as an adventurous teenager, I had been invited by a pilot friend, Warren Vaughn, to join him on a shakedown cruise aboard his new yacht in the Puget Sound. We planned on yachting from Seattle to La Push, Washington, during the last week of August. He had just bought a 36-foot yacht, named Pinzon, after Christopher Columbus' navigator. I jumped at the chance since I'd always had a love affair with boats and airplanes. On that two-week cruise, we sailed numerous waters and inlets throughout the beautiful Puget Sound.

The weather forecast was for beautiful skies as we headed out to sea through the Strait of Juan de Fuca between Canada and the United States, but we couldn't help but notice that the ocean was getting rougher. As we headed south for La Push, a storm hit with waves large enough to break clean over the top of the bow and cabin. For hours I shared the task of steering the yacht directly into the large waves, which was fun, but scary. We stayed out longer than we'd intended because the storm and wave action was much stronger near shore. I learned that the safest way to ride out that storm is to wait farther out at sea until the storm passes. As we waited, Warren taught me to use a radio directional finder (ADF): where radio signal lines cross from two different stations, that is the spot where you are. Even though we could not see land during the storm, we always knew exactly where we were.

After a long and tumultuous night, dawn brought a calm sea and we headed back towards the coastline, but stopped where we saw birds swarming and small fish jumping out of the water. We caught our limit of salmon and continued on our way. We pulled into the port of La Push that evening, but the lighthouse was barely visible; it was surrounded by a ghostly fog.

I loved that whole trip, but gained a great respect for the sea, which is like a lover who becomes your worst enemy when she's angry. The sea is a sleeping beauty, always ready to wake up and swallow you into her deep, cold arms forever.

After that fishing trip with Ray Halphide, I became superstitious about going on any adventurous trips in late August. That sad fishing trip was the fifth time I skirted danger the last week of August. In 1965, I was stuck in that storm with Warren Vaughn off the Washington Coast. I was a passenger in a twin-engine plane crash on Sunday, August 21, 1966. Gary, my dad, and I were on a charter fishing boat that almost capsized on August 21, 1967 when its only engine quit. On August 22, years later, two days after my brother, Gary, bought his first airplane, he was flying it back from the east coast when the plane caught on fire at 3,000 feet. He attempted an emergency landing and escaped the fiery plane crash without a scratch. Dad was murdered on August 28, 1974. And there I was, helplessly standing by, watching people drown on August 23, 1981. I said to myself, "I think I will just stay home the last ten days of August from now on."

Chapter 30: CBS and *60 Minutes* Get Involved

Without mentioning my plans to my brother, I made a deal with Lincoln Savings & Loan to expand our tax offices in ten of their locations. The bank had 16,000 clients we could reach directly by including a flyer about our tax services within their mailed bank statements. That new association gave Columbia Bookkeeping a total of 20 locations. My brother, Gary, mentioned that he was planning to buy Larry Scheer's small tax office located four blocks away on the same main street from our branch office in Beaverton. At first I was upset since we originally agreed not to move in on each other's territory. But Gary discussed the purchase with me first before he bought that practice and I realized it was a good opportunity for him. I agreed not to contest the location. As the years passed, however, that move caused some competitive issues between us.

For the fourth year, I was invited back to be the tax expert on "Tax Tips," a call-in radio show on Oregon's largest radio station, KEX. As part of my marketing program, I'd sent out my Tax Planning Book, which I wrote and updated each year, to all the area networks and to most professional organizations and offered them all a free tax seminar. Over the years we distributed over 200,000 of these books. That book gave me many opportunities to promote Columbia Bookkeeping including appearances on local radio and TV stations in the cities where we had offices. I always kept Gary in the dark as to how I was marketing the business since I considered him a competitor to Columbia Bookkeeping. I knew that some day he would eventually benefit from his interest in the Turel Trust, even though he was its rival.

Around that time I had to make a difficult decision regarding the Golden Turkey Gold Mine. I took my Uncle Bob, an avid gold prospector who had tinkered with inventions to separate gold from sand, on a flight down to Arizona to get his opinion. He, of course, was thrilled with the project and thought I would be nuts to sell. I truly loved that property and its nostalgia. On our flight back home I had to navigate around a towering thunderstorm with cumulonimbus clouds in our little twin engine plane, but the beauty of the sky's display was a reminder of how powerful Mother Nature is. I was once again reminded that if you don't respect Nature, she will tear you apart!

A few months later I decided to negotiate with the U.S. Forest Service to exchange the acreage of the Golden Turkey Mine for forestland in Oregon. Various governmental bureaucracies had stifled our ability to develop anything with the mine and negotiations with the Forest Service fell apart. After spending $25,000 in fees for lawyers in Arizona and Oregon, I decided to just write off my losses and get out of the project. The $50,000 investment in the Golden Turkey Gold Mine was one of my biggest financial losses ever. Even though our claim was free and clear of any liability, the cost of lawyers was eating me alive. No one else in the partnership had any money to continue paying its bills except me.

By late 1981, the constant harassment of lawsuits filed by Rod Addicks was having a seriously detrimental effect on my life. I was edgy, anxious and withdrawn. Addicks was having a gay old time suing everyone for everything, and there were never any repercussions for him. So, I continued working with Bob and Dee Dee Kouns of Crime Victims United, and with Dedi Streich of Concerned Oregonians for Justice, the ringleaders of their respective organizations. My involvement led to participation in additional public forums, radio, and TV talk shows.

I was convinced that the FBI, the State of Oregon, and Multnomah County could not, or did not have the time, energy, or desire to stop these lawsuits. The time had come for me to do something big to expose Rod Addicks to the world. "I'm tired of letting things happen," I told Wanda Fuller, my new executive assistant, and Judy Krussow, who I had recently hired as my general manager. Wanda and Judy had been helping manage and organize Columbia Bookkeeping while graciously putting up with my micro-management style. Marvin Bridge had left to form his own practice a few years back.

When Gary and I were teenagers, Norm Winningstad gave us a pep talk that I still remember vividly. We'd just returned from a quick roundtrip flight to San Francisco in Norm's Cessna 320. "Boys," he said, "there are three kinds of people. Those who make things happen, those who wonder what's happening, and those who never know what's happening."

Keeping that premise in mind, I had been considering contacting the most popular TV show in the world, *60 Minutes*. Maybe *60 Minutes* would expose the maliciousness of these jailhouse lawyers, which might encourage the legal system to do something about the problem. "It's a long shot," I told Wanda and Judy that day. "I've got nothing to lose."

In early January 1982, I called Scott McAlister at the State Attorney's office to see what new outrage Addicks was up to. I learned that Addicks' latest administrative appeal had been denied. The parole board, in their written response, stated, *"The board does not want to reward the various schemes and falsehoods you engaged in during the first few years of your incarceration. To do so might encourage others to engage in manipulations based on falsehoods to serve their release. Finally, the occupational background and educational advantage that you enjoy could well be used in the opposite manner. Those to whom much has been given in the way of talent, education and occupational advantage may well owe more, not less, to society. Advance degrees and 'professional' status are not included in the matrix calculations that you come under."* McAlister and Norm Brown of the Multnomah County Court promised to protest any future parole date.

I spent two weeks summarizing all of Addicks' frivolous lawsuits and wrote a one-page letter of introduction for my submission to *60 Minutes*. In the cover letter I pointed out that the public was paying all the legal bills related to these numerous lawsuits filed by Rod Addicks, as well as those filed by Lloyd Forsberg and Lee Cartwright. I attached a five-page summary of 70 separate lawsuits filed against individuals and governmental agencies by Addicks and his cellmates. I placed the letter and attached documentation in a large odd-shaped, red envelope. I figured if the size and color of the envelope were unusual, my proposal would stand out brightly in a stack of mundane mail. By mid-March I had the package ready to mail and obtained the address by calling the *60 Minutes* office at CBS headquarters.

A week after I sent the letter, I received a call from an assistant of the executive director for the show. She made me promise that I would keep our discussion and their interest in the story absolutely confidential. If I let the local newspapers know *60 Minutes* was interested, it would ruin their ability to conduct an investigation and would be a deal breaker. "Don't even tell your family or business associates until after the interviews have been done," she said. "We have not decided yet to take this on."

Ten days later, they sent out a young investigative reporter who did the preliminary workup of details regarding Rod Addicks and his lawsuits. In preparation for meeting the reporter, I gathered all the court papers and documents relating to the case. I didn't know what to expect and was nervous as a cat on a hot tin roof. The reporter, an attractive, well-dressed lady in her 20s had a cute New York accent. She was all business. We spoke for an hour, after which I referred her to detectives Rod Englert and Forrest "Joe" Rieke who had also been sued by Addicks. I also suggested that she speak with Oregon's Assistant Attorney General Scott McAlister. Since I had met with McAlister several times, I thought he'd be the best person to organize the reporter's interviews at the State penitentiary.

I asked *60 Minutes* to please not run the story until after the United States Supreme Court threw out Rod Addicks' final appeal regarding his lawsuit against me. I was afraid that if they ran the story before the U.S. Court of Appeals for the Ninth Circuit in San Francisco had the chance to refuse the case, Addicks would use the *60 Minutes* story to file still another lawsuit. I knew Addicks wouldn't be able to resist the opportunity to be on television. Thankfully, *60 Minutes* agreed to my request.

The show's investigative reporter left town a few days later, but called me back to put Norman Gorin on the line. Gorin, the show's producer said, "Do you know how lucky you are that we moved on this? We receive thousands of letters weekly and your story stood out immediately. It's a good issue and we want to bring the judicial inequity to the forefront. Be patient, and keep all this to yourself. Stay in touch, and when the time gets closer to the San Francisco Court's decision, we will proceed and bring out our crew."

By then it was fall 1982 and I was dealing with problems relating to the rental properties. I had to put *60 Minutes* out of my mind for the time being. Then something else came up.

In September of 1982, my Uncle Ray and Aunt Lorraine called me from Seattle. "Remember when you asked us to watch out for strange dealings on the Puyallup Indian Reservation? Well, according to newspaper articles from the Tacoma paper, the U.S. Attorney General and State of Washington authorities are contesting attempts by the tribe's leaders to open a gambling casino on tribal lands." One article said Sam Moll was the chairman of the Tribal Gaming Commission. Another article mentioned that arson took place on the reservation."

It sounded too familiar. "Does the article include the name of any government official to contact?" I asked. I was curious to know if the authorities were looking at Sam Moll.

I called the U.S. Attorney General's office in Seattle and got through to an agent familiar with the Puyallup situation. I explained how Sam Moll and Maddock Tollocko had been given immunity in the arson and murder trials in Oregon. The agent said Sam Moll was on the Chief Tribal Council and in the center of everything going on down there. The agent was unaware of Sam Moll and Tollocko's background in the Portland trials.

"Originally, I thought about just contacting the papers to destroy Sam Moll's reputation," I said to the agent. "Sam Moll was deeply involved in the murder of my dad, and arson, and besides that, Moll and his cousin, Maddock Tollocko, are on record in trial transcripts as having discussed killing Tribal Council members in exchange for my dad's murder."

The agent was interested in talking with me further, but first I got a guarantee from the Washington State Attorney General's office. The deal I made, if I worked with them, was that I would remain anonymous. I did not want to have any reprisals coming back at me. "No problem," said the agent. "We'd like to see the transcripts and let's see what we can do together."

"Everything is already in writing," I said. "It's in sworn testimony from the arson and murder trials."

I arranged to send copies of all the transcripts to him. I highlighted in yellow the testimony I thought would be vital to presenting Sam Moll and Maddock Tollocko as the scheming conspirators they were. I also gave the agent the phone number of Detective Englert in case they needed more information.

The agent called me back the same day he received the packet of trial testimonies. He was excited that so much information was already available. He said he couldn't believe that Sam Moll, a man so immersed in crime, could be so influential in the tribe. "The press will love this story," he said. "But let's wait for the timing to be right before going public. If you could hold off for a few weeks, we'll have an easier time exposing the nefarious deeds of these two men." Two weeks later, the agent called back and gave me the phone numbers of two reporters eager to meet with me in person. One reporter was from the *Seattle Times*; the other was from the Tacoma *Tribune*.

I called the reporters right away and gave them a brief rundown of what I intended to discuss with them and explained that I'd be meeting with both papers the same day. I promised to bring them copies of the transcripts, and arranged back-to-back meetings at the Tacoma airport, located just west of the Tacoma Narrows Bridge.

I was feeling very preoccupied and figured I'd be too tired to fly alone, so I hired my instrument flight instructor, Del Hendrickson, to accompany me on the trip to Tacoma. I landed, then taxied to a small restaurant located at the airport, which was our prearranged meeting place. A young reporter from the *Seattle Times*, a man about my age, greeted me first. I gave him the condensed trial transcripts where I had again used a yellow marker to highlight the most destructive testimony against Sam Moll and Maddock Tollocko. I also included a contents sheet in an effort to help organize the reporters' thoughts. From experience with reporters, I felt it was important to underline the subject matter you wanted them to focus on, or they'd totally miss the important parts. Obviously, they would not have time to read all 5,000 pages of transcripts. I had both reporters agree that I would remain an anonymous source.

I had scheduled the reporter from the Tacoma *Tribune* to meet with me 30 minutes later. My hope was that the two reporters would see each other and want to be the one to break the story first, which would speed up the process.

After my meeting with the second reporter I was energized beyond words that maybe some late justice would be served on Sam Moll. Whether or not he did anything wrong at the Indian reservation, I was hopeful that his criminal background would be exposed. When we took off southbound from the airport and headed home, I was so excited that I forgot to retract my landing gear. After a few minutes of trying to figure out why we were flying so slow, I realized the landing gear was still in the down-and-locked position. I quietly raised the landing gear lever, hoping Del Hendrickson wouldn't notice my mistake. The airplane started flying a lot faster. Del looked at me and grinned. "I wondered when you would catch that," he said. It was a good wake-up call. I told myself that I was just too preoccupied with this Sam Moll stuff and I needed to focus on flying. The rest of the 35-minute flight back to the Troutdale airport was uneventful.

Two days later my Uncle Ray called, his enthusiasm evident. "You won't believe this," he said. "Both papers have articles about Sam Moll on the front page! The articles make Moll and Tollocko look like dangerous thugs. According to the papers, the tribe has begun a full investigation!"

By the end of that week I received a call from Detective Rod Englert. He was laughing. "Stan, Sam Moll and his attorney came down to Portland and accused me of trying to destroy him," Englert said. "I told them I didn't know who sent the press all that stuff about Sam. They are really pissed off and wondering who to go after next. They tried talking with the reporters, but the press wouldn't divulge their source. And by the way, the Tribe fired Sam Moll and they may press charges to have him arrested for mismanaging funds." Also the articles printed quotes from court transcripts about Sam Moll and Maddock Tollocko's involvement in the murder-for-hire scheme involving tribal council members.

Both Englert and I had a good laugh. "Stan, you really got him in trouble now."

"Those guys are getting what they deserve," I said. "Sooner or later their scum was going to rise to the surface like oil from a sunken shipwreck. I just can't believe that after all the crimes they've committed and all the trials and convictions that have taken place, that the authorities and the Tribe knew nothing about them." Sam Moll had been given a chance to go clean, but he threw it away.

Within two months, Sam Moll was arrested then convicted for embezzling funds from the Puyallup Indian Tribe. He was sentenced to ten years in a Federal penitentiary in the State of Washington.

Sam Moll's new trial uncovered a situation where a man named Peter was paid more than $4,000 for consulting work, but his signature on the paper was a forgery and he received the money without having performed any service. Newspapers reported that two Puyallup tribal leaders, Robert Muni and Sam A. Moll, were convicted of embezzlement schemes that netted $80,000. The money paid to Peter Esquiro was to keep him quiet after he discovered their activities. The money came out of tribal health funds but it was used for personal excursions, expensive cars, and the purchase of frivolous items.

All this legal jockeying of Moll and Addicks was leaving me overwhelmed and the stress of getting ready for another tax season was doing me in. I had just finished presenting a series of 10 tax-planning seminars for various Portland real estate companies in a three-week span, plus I was juggling the tax office's daily obligations.

I decided to incorporate Judy Krussow, my general manager, into the seminar presentations to help offset my obligations. At first she refused because she was too shy to try. I kept encouraging her and gradually included her for a few minutes during question and answer sessions in front of groups. Judy eventually gained enough confidence to speak in front of groups by herself. Her participation became increasingly helpful as it gave me an occasional break, plus we could work off each other to entertain the audience. Judy Krussow worked tirelessly behind the scenes, quietly helping organize lists and mailing the invitations and tax planning books to the press. One of our goals was to ensure we received positive press. I was always paranoid that negative publicity relating to Rod Addicks would hurt the business.

I also began taking Judy to the KEX Radio talk shows. We worked as a team. When a sticky question came up, she would verify tax regulations while I started talking. The more adept Judy became, the more I saw how crucial it was that I learn to delegate responsibilities. The company was growing and I couldn't handle the business alone anymore.

I also installed eight computers in the upstairs central processing room. I was a fan of Star Trek, so I plastered murals of Mars and Saturn on the walls to create a spacious atmosphere. I wanted the room to appear as high tech as the Star Trek Bridge, which it was for its time. The murals and all those computers made a perfect space-age background when holding interviews with the TV crews and reporters who filmed news segments during tax time.

In one tax season alone, film crews from different stations came to our office 14 times. With each client's permission, reporters were allowed to film, interview, and take photos of clients going through our tax consultation process. You cannot buy this kind of free advertising. Over 200,000 people might see one news segment in one night. Competitors, including my brother, Gary, would ask, 'How come they interview you all the time?' But I never divulged the techniques I used to attract free press. After all, that's what separated Columbia Bookkeeping from our competitors. Most accountants stick with reporting financial history and are so deep into the books that they rarely step back far enough to develop a progressive marketing plan.

I applied the lesson I learned from Norm Winningstad, "Be the one that makes things happen." He taught me to become organized by keeping a little notebook in my pocket for people's names, phone numbers, and ideas. I also applied Granddad George and Dad's theory that long hours and hard work pay off. There is no such word as 'can't'!

In October 1982, while making my periodic check-in on the status of Rod Addicks' appeal of his lawsuit against me, I found out the Federal judges in San Francisco were about to consider the case. I notified Norman Gorin, the CBS producer for *60 Minutes* who had expressed interest in covering the story. Within a week, Gorin and his assistant flew to Portland and scheduled personal interviews with numerous people involved in the case.

Gorin was a slender, middle-aged, energetic man who explained that the cameras would not be showing up during this trip; he was there to organize who, where, and what kind of material they would include in the TV episode. I explained to Gorin, "My hope is you will expose the legal system's failure which allows prisoners to file frivolous lawsuits." I had no idea what angle he planned to take.

"Stan, we do not know what direction the segment will take," Gorin said. "But we will see what comes out after I talk to everyone."

Would he concentrate on the failure of the legal system, or focus on Addicks' backfiring schemes to get out of jail? What if they decide to take the prisoners' side and support a prisoner's right to sue anyone he wants? From that day on, Norman Gorin or his team would slip in and out of town without saying anything to me about who they were meeting with. Assistant Attorney General Scott McAlister called and said some of the judges in Salem were talking about the Addicks case and were shocked and pleased to know that *60 Minutes* might film a segment there.

Scott McAlister indicated that arrangements had been made to allow entry of the TV crew into the prison law library and grant access to inmates, including Rod Addicks. Mr. Gorin and his staff seemed overly concerned that the local press not be informed about their presence in Oregon. As instructed, I kept my mouth shut. I didn't even mention what was going on to my family. I didn't tell anyone except Wanda Fuller, Jim Auxier, and Judy Krussow—the people I brainstormed with and sought advice from regarding my approach to *60 Minutes*. Without their support and encouragement I would not have been so organized.

In early November 1982, I called *60 Minutes* and told them the hearing for Addicks' final Supreme Court appeal was coming up soon. I was surprised when the *60 Minutes* staff said they were already aware that the U.S. Supreme Court office in San Francisco had set a tentative date to consider the case and that Gorin's staff was getting ready to schedule interviews. Gorin's secretary called back and said Norman and his camera crew would be showing up with Morley Safer at Columbia Bookkeeping's office within the week.

Sometime during the first week of December, my lawyer Jim Auxier, called to say the Supreme Court was supposed to come out with their decision before Christmas.

When Norman Gorin arrived the next week, he and I agreed to hold the interview in the front lobby at the receptionist's desk. The black tax books and the legal binders on the shelves behind the filing cabinets made a professional backdrop. We arranged to film the interview after 5 o'clock, when the office was closed. I was nervous and so were Judy, Wanda, and Dorothy, our bookkeeper. At the last minute, Judy and I decided to gather up all the court documents related to the Addicks case and have them stacked neatly in a two-foot high pile on the desk. Also, I had learned during earlier TV interviews that I needed some makeup to cover a few blemishes and those tired bags under my eyes. Judy did the best she could, but I was still self-conscious about my looks.

Jim Auxier, my ever-cautious lawyer, called and reminded me to be careful about what I said on camera, as he did not want me to give Addicks cause for another lawsuit. He added to my paranoia when he said, "You never know what direction the liberal press will take. They are anti-business, so be careful!"

I had to trust my instincts that no rational person could make us look bad, besides I had watched *60 Minutes* for years and the show always seemed to be on the correct side of justice.

I stood at the window looking out as a white panel truck without any identifying insignia showed up and parked. It was a cloudy, overcast day. A few minutes later a sedan pulled in and a nondescript man in a long, tan overcoat got out. Morley Safer walked over to the camera crew, who were setting up their equipment in the parking lot. I decided to greet Safer outside where he stood chatting. "I've heard a lot about you, Stan," Safer said in his deep voice, "and I am really glad to finally meet you." His handshake was firm and made for a solid impression. Before Safer entered the building, he stood in the entryway and faced the cameras. When the bright white lights came on, Safer began describing the murder scene.

Norman Gorin and his head cameraman entered the building with a three-member camera crew. They rearranged some of the furniture to film several angles of the interview simultaneously. Between their light fixtures, camera equipment, staff, and general assistants, the lobby was packed. Judy and Wanda stepped back to watch the interview and gave me two thumbs up.

I was visibly uptight and way too excited about the interview. Okay, I admit I was nervous as hell. Was that pimple on the side of my face going to show? Was my hair too long? It's funny the things you think of when you're about to shoot a commercial or be on the news or do live TV interviews.

As the equipment was being arranged, Morley Safer chided, "Relax!" and explained in general how the interview would go. We made sure that the phone lines were all tied up after that, so calls would not interrupt the interview. When the cameras were ready and the hot lights came on, Safer began asking me questions and I forgot to worry about my looks. "Tell me how all this came about, regarding the lawsuits," Safer said.

I launched into a summary of the investigation that led to the arrest of Rod Addicks. I suggested that he should talk to Detective Rod Englert, since he was the one who really solved the case. I spoke about my brother and sisters, my stepmom, and how the estate owned the business and the building after Dad died. Then we got into the murder, investigation, arrest, convictions and lawsuit details. I also explained how my Dad was crippled and worked hard to start and build this business. I was thankful that Safer's questions kept me focused on Rod Addicks and the lawsuit. He was very kind and professional in how he kept redirecting my focus.

"What did you do that is causing Rod Addicks to claim you violated his rights?" asked Safer.

"After my dad died, I let Rod work here for four months while I was investigating him and came up with information that led the police to some of his accomplices."

"You mean you worked side-by-side for four months with a man you suspected might have killed your father?" Morley said and chuckled in his friendly, disarming manner.

"Yes," I said. "Addicks was one of three people I originally suspected. My brother and I agreed that if Addicks were around, we would have a better chance to learn if he was involved in anything criminal. I kept him here until I had enough evidence to prove to myself that he participated in the arson, the murder, or both."

Safer asked about working with the police.

"I turned evidence over to the police during the murder investigation," I said. "But I had the right to investigate anything in the building since my family owned the business and building. Addicks even said I could go through anything in his office. He said that when the detectives were present. I wasn't a police agent in disguise, as Addicks alleged in one of his lawsuits."

I could tell I was talking too fast and Safer asked me to slow down a little. "Let's go over that question one more time, Stan," Safer said. "Why did you take it upon yourself to become so involved?"

"Morley," I said. "What would you do if your dad was murdered and you had several suspects? You would naturally follow your instincts and look into everything possible, especially if the police had to restrain themselves due to legal restrictions. I was not restricted by Addicks' Miranda rights. I even asked some family members to take lie detector tests, which they did. I checked with my lawyer all the time to make sure I was doing nothing wrong."

"What would happen if you just said, 'The hell with it! I am not going to respond to his lawsuits!'"

"Well my lawyer told me that if I did not fight these ridiculous lawsuits I would lose by default. In other words, I would have had to pay out ten million dollars so far. Addicks would automatically win if I did not fight him in court."

My on-camera interview took twenty minutes. When the spotlights were turned off, Morley Safer said, "Son, I cannot believe what you have been through. It's surreal, you should write a book."

Gorin, Safer, and their crew spent another day in downtown Portland, then headed south to Salem and the Oregon State Prison. The evening after the crew had been at Columbia Bookkeeping, I called my brother, sisters and other family members to let them know about the interview.

A few days after that, Assistant Attorney General Scott McAlister called. "The prison was very cooperative. Even Addicks and I were interviewed. Everyone down here wonders, how in the world did Stan Turel talk *60 Minutes* into covering this issue?"

"So, how did the interviews go?" I asked.

"You don't have to worry," McAlister said. "The questions Morley Safer asked were focused on frivolous lawsuits, which was your intent."

On December 7, 1982, I received a call from my lawyer, Jim Auxier, who said the U.S. Supreme Court had thrown out Addicks' appeal in his lawsuit against me. Once again I was totally elated. I called Norman Gorin's staff in New York and let them know the good news. "Great!" they said. "Our staff already knew and we were getting ready to call you! So, Stan, we'll run the story this coming Sunday."

I had a hard time believing that CBS would broadcast the story so soon! Gorin's staff asked if any of the local press had found out about their interest. "Not that I know of, except a small paper in Salem that ran a five-paragraph article saying that the *60 Minutes* crew had been in Salem to interview a few prisoners about frivolous lawsuits." Norman Gorin called to thank me for all my assistance and said, "I think you'll like the show."

I called my brother and sisters to let them know the segment would be on TV that Sunday, December 12, 1982. Gary was shocked and upset that he hadn't been invited to participate. "The show is focused on frivolous lawsuits only, not the murder and not our family," I said. "I'm the only one being sued by Addicks, not you, not the rest of the family. Besides, they didn't want a crowd hanging around and they preferred I not invite any family or friends to attend the interview."

I called Dick Winningstad and asked him to let his parents and family know to watch CBS on Sunday. Dick invited me over for dinner to watch the show with his family. He wanted to celebrate with us by opening a 50-year-old bottle of wine purchased at an auction in support of the Oregon Museum of Science and Industry.

On Sunday, December 12, we arrived at Dick Winningstad's new home and watched the *60 Minutes* show together. The show didn't include any of the information I'd shared with Morley Safer about my family, my brother, or my dad's efforts to make something out of himself despite being crippled—but that was okay. My hope was that the *60 Minutes* focus would be on the failure of the legal system. One must remember that we do not control the press. They will shoot 20 minutes of tape and only a few minutes of what you say will be in the final version of the segment. In fact, my part in the segments was only 5 minutes. The frivolous lawsuit issue was made very clear.

Morley Safer opened the segment by saying, "It will not come as news to anyone in the judicial system that a plague of justice has fallen over the land. Suing is rapidly becoming America's favorite indoor sport. And the result is a court system that has become, in some cases, hopelessly clogged with important and frivolous lawsuits all mixed up together, that under our democracy get the same thoughtful and serious consideration. So pervasive is this plague of justice that it may be leading to a major injustice...."

While standing in the parking lot of Columbia Bookkeeping, Safer explained the attack and murder of James Turel, and how the police investigation led to the arrest and conviction of Turel's business associate, Rod Addicks. Safer states that Rod Addicks appealed his conviction to the State Court of Appeals and the State Supreme Court, which upheld his conviction. "There was no doubt in anyone's mind then, and no doubt in anyone's mind now, that Rod Addicks is guilty of murder."

I was happy *60 Minutes* made that very clear at the opening. It was a relief to know that the show left no shadow of a doubt. Morley Safer said it better than anyone else, and he said it to a national audience on one of the most widely watched TV shows in the world. "Rod Addicks is guilty of murder."

Safer then introduced Addicks as an inmate of the State Penitentiary in Salem, Oregon: "Meet Rod Addicks. He is no longer a practicing accountant. He has become a full-time jailhouse lawyer, a writ writer extraordinaire."

The scene shows Addicks in front of a typewriter, working on a case. Safer says, "Addicks does not deny his guilt ... and he showers the courts with the fruit of his labor." Safer asks Addicks, "How much money have you sued for over the years, the total sum?"

"I'm not trying to (he laughs) back off or to lessen the impact or anything like that, but I just honestly don't know. It's in the millions, maybe ten or fifteen million, maybe more. You know, I don't know."

"Don't you feel it is an outrage for you to sue the son of the victim of the murder?" Safer continues.

"Not under the circumstance of what I believe the son did," Addicks replies. "He went into my personal briefcase that had nothing to do with family business."

"What was found in the brief case or the files in his father's business became evidence that convicted you of the murder of his father. Correct?"

"Without the data, yes that's correct. Without the files there would be no conviction," Addicks responded.

Morley Safer is then shown interviewing me. "What has all this cost you in time and money, and whatever?"

"Time, money, and mental hassle," I say. "I'm approaching $15,000 in total legal fees as a private citizen defending myself in these lawsuits."

The scene returns to the jail and Safer asks Addicks, "Why do you file these lawsuits? Is it a hobby?"

"No it's not."

"You're a trouble maker," Safer says.

"Some people would say that to some degree," Addicks replies with a grin.

An interview of Scott McAlister follows. McAllister was the assistant attorney general for the State of Oregon who defended public officials in suits brought by prisoners. Safer asks, "How can a man like Rod Addicks sue the son of the man that he, Addicks, admitted killing, for slandering and libeling his good name?"

"It's hard to believe but that's the state of affairs that the courts are in right now. Normally, what Stan Turel could have done was bring a suit against Mr. Addicks for abuse of process, or something along that line, for filing a purely frivolous lawsuit. But it doesn't work against prison inmates because they don't have any money anyway. So, why get a judgment against somebody who has no funds?"

"Scott, how much does it cost to process just one of these frivolous lawsuits?"

"About $50,000 for each and every one," McAlister responds.

When asked for an approximate number of cases the prisoners had filed against the State in the past year, McAlister says, "About 1,400 cases this year, which is up 100 percent in just one year. It's job security."

"Do the same rather lenient rules apply to people who are not in jail, if they want to sue?"

"No, that's one of the ironies," McAlister says. "If the person is on the outside, the court decisions have not given them the same kind of benefits that prisoners enjoy. The prisoner is entitled to, in essence, every break. He is not held to any formal rules of pleading, and any mistakes he makes will be forgiven."

In an interview with another convict, Safer is told, "I can write that you slugged me in the mouth and I can run down and file a suit. And you have to prove that you didn't."

The practice of filing prisoner lawsuits falls to an elite prison population that call themselves Legal Clerks. Safer is told that the charge for one of these lawsuits could be cartons of cigarettes, drugs, or cash, based on how complex it is to write up. The cash is handled by relatives on the outside.

After watching the whole segment I was impressed by how well Morley Safer presented the truth about Rod Addicks. For the first time, Addicks' abuse of the legal system and his harassment of me were made perfectly clear. All the legal proceedings my lawyers went through never exposed Addicks and his frivolous lawsuits as well as Safer had. I began to hope that the legal processes in the courts of the United States would eliminate future frivolous lawsuits filed by prisoners. I also had hope that prison policy would be changed to restrict prisoners from writing, contacting, or harassing prosecution witness.

After the show ended, Norm and Dolores Winningstad, Dick and his wife, and I sat down for a wonderful steak dinner. We toasted to the successful *60 Minutes* segment, which they titled "Plague of Justice," with Dick's expensive bottle of wine. It was an honor to share the moment with them.[1]

When I got back to the office, I was overwhelmed by phone calls. Our clients and most of our 80 company employees weren't aware that I'd been deluged with lawsuits over the past few years. Many of them called in to congratulate me. I received calls from Oregon's senators expressing their outrage at what had been going on. When they asked what they could do to help, I suggested that they call the U.S. District Court office in Portland to call a halt to prisoners filing frivolous lawsuits against their victims and anyone else they had a grudge against.

---

[1] The *60 Minutes* episode, "Plague of Justice," is available on YouTube.com (type in "Stan Turel" or "Plague of Justice" in the SEARCH blank), or go to http://www.plagueofjustice.com.

Chapter 31: *Ha, Ha, Ha* by D.B. Cooper

No direct, immediate improvements to the State's judicial system, or changes in the myriad lawsuits occurred after the *60 Minutes* segment was broadcast. A few of the local reporters I had worked with over the years called to say that they were disappointed that I hadn't let them know in advance about the *60 Minutes* segment.

As 1982 drew to a close, Columbia Bookkeeping staff was getting ready for the eighth tax season since Dad died. Our operations were all in place and although we were busy, the office staff had become pros and the work proceeded without any major glitches. My goal for 1983 was to make sure all our operations ran smoothly. We had spent a lot of money on continuing education seminars, mostly organized by Judy Krussow and Sherri Cronin, a former ADP manager who was in charge of the Computer Processing Department. The seminar handouts included over 600 pages of tax updates and computer software instructions for the computer input sheets. I cannot tell you how priceless Sherri was in running the computers, software, and processing department. She worked tirelessly with me even on Sundays to get ready for the upcoming employee seminars. The only problem with Sherri was she smoked three packs of cigarettes per day.

By then, Columbia Bookkeeping was totally computerized with a very efficient processing department. Judy, Bob Rounds from our Beaverton office, and several other employees worked with me to design additional tax forms that focused on specific transactions for individuals. By the time tax season began, we had created 30 different schedules that our tax preparers were required to complete and attach to each client return, depending on the specific complexities of their situation.

By March 25, 1983, the U.S. Court in Portland charged Rod Addicks, Floyd Forsberg, and Dennis Lee Cartwright with nine counts of a 13-count indictment involving schemes to get Addicks out of jail, for perjury, and for filing numerous frivolous lawsuits. Dennis Lee Cartwright was named in one conspiracy and two perjury cases relating to the frivolous lawsuits. Of course, all three men—Addicks, Forsberg, and Cartwright—pleaded innocent to perjury, even though they had already confessed that the lawsuit scam, including their prior testimonies, were based on lies to get Addicks out of jail. Again, court time and taxpayers dollars were spent on these cases.

An article about the indictment published in the Portland *Oregonian* contained a small item that caught my eye. It said that Rod Addicks was scheduled for parole in 1984. "Oh great," I told Judy Krussow, our general manager. "With all that's going on now, how can I launch a fight with the parole board to contest Addicks' release? Damn it, he's been in jail for murder for only nine years of his life sentence. What happened to the promise of no chance for parole?"

Larry Roach, executive assistant to Oregon State Penitentiary Superintendent Hoyt Cupp, said that Rod Addicks had been transferred last June to the Washington State Prison in Walla Walla for "administrative" reasons, but he declined to explain further. An assistant chaplain at the prison said he believed Addicks was sincerely attempting to live a Christian life now. Right, I thought.

In early 1983 a detective brought in a book called *Ha Ha Ha*, by D.B. Cooper and said he believed Rod Addicks wrote it. The Portland *Daily Journal of Commerce* had been contracted by Signum Books of Oregon City to produce the book, a fictional first-hand account of the Boeing 727 hijacking and parachute jump that had taken place on November 24, 1971. The detective's assumption that Addicks wrote the book did not surprise me as we had found his 60-page manuscript about D.B. Cooper in the Columbia Bookkeeping office in 1974. However, this book was mostly a cops and robbers mystery that provided nasty characterizations and bad drawings of people including someone who looked a lot like Blackie Yazzolino. The book claimed to contain seven clues that would lead the reader to Cooper's stolen $200,000. Twenty thousand copies of the book were printed.

I called the *Daily Journal of Commerce* to find out if they had been paid for the printing of the book. They said they'd received a down payment, but had not been paid the balance, and would be taking the publisher to court to collect the money owed. I explained my suspicions about Rod Addicks using the alias "D.B. Cooper," and they were quite distressed to learn that a convicted murderer inside the Oregon State Prison was the author. I suggested that they might check with the publisher. The newspaper subsequently took legal action against Signum Books, Ltd.

Judith Van Cleave was the owner of Signum Books located in Oregon City, the same city where Addicks' new wife lived; the woman he'd married in jail after she befriended Floyd Forsberg. My question was, who is paying for this whole book distribution operation? The answer arrived in my mailbox.

I received a long letter from a retiring, anonymous prison employee, who warned me that Addicks was running various enterprises and making money while inside the prison. Maybe the *60 Minutes* show was right. Addicks could have received cash for assisting other prisoners in lawsuits, and then sent the cash he received to relatives or friends outside the prison to fund this D.B. Cooper book or *The Innocents* publication. The letter also warned me about an upcoming parole hearing for Addicks.

On May 13, 1983, a letter regarding the printing of *Ha Ha Ha* was sent to the *Daily Journal of Commerce* in response to their effort to collect money for printing the book. The letter, signed by "D.B. Cooper," said that because the printer fell far short of ordinary professionalism and should have caught the numerous punctuation errors, he was therefore refusing to pay. Handwriting analysis indicated a close resemblance between the script of the letter and the handwriting of Rod Addicks. The paper pursued their lawsuit.

In June 1983, Addicks pleaded guilty to one conspiracy count in the perjury case. Eight other perjury counts against him were dismissed. He received a one-year sentence for conspiring to commit perjury in a scheme to have his murder conviction reversed. U.S. District Judge Owen Panner said he would permit Addicks to serve the term concurrently with his life sentence for murder, along with the other concurrent sentences imposed by Washington State, plus the three other Oregon felonies. This meant that although he was found guilty and sentenced, he would not spend even one extra day in jail!

Judge Panner said the material submitted by Addicks' defense attorney, Ronald Hoevet, was quite convincing, but he refused to make that material public. Great, I thought.

I asked Jim Auxier, "Why don't victims have the right to address district judges?"

"They just don't have that right," my attorney said.

Years later I learned, through court records, that Addicks had been ratting on his fellow inmates and helping the authorities solve several crimes involving other prisoners ever since Forsberg exposed his get-out-of-jail schemes. Apparently, Rod Addicks was cunning enough to gain the ear and trust of fellow prisoners who would tell him about their crimes or escape plans and Addicks would forward the information to the police. Addicks had transformed himself into the perfect prisoner, impressing the parole board and judge with his willingness to work on the side of good. Personally, I wondered where was the justice for all the money and harm he had already caused? There is none.

I wish I'd had the right to submit a summary to the judge in charge of Addicks' latest conviction, prior to his sentencing. I would have included a list of all the frivolous lawsuits he filed. But the judge was never presented that information by anyone, including the Federal prosecutor. The State government, prisons, and Federal government did not work together; Addicks' latest conviction appeared to be a plea bargain because the judge was led to believe that Addicks would be in jail a long time for his arson, murder, and securities fraud convictions. Boy, were they wrong!

According to court records, Assistant U.S. Attorney Lance Caldwell told Judge Panner in Pendleton, Oregon, that Addicks admitted that he, Addicks, was responsible for the murder of Jim Turel and that he was present when Turel was killed. However he denied strangling Jim Turel to death.

When I checked with a private psychiatrist, a specialist whose focus was the criminal mind, I was told, "It is apparent that due to the brutal way Jim Turel was murdered, Rod Addicks may, in his warped sense of truth, believe he strangled Turel after Turel was already dead. That way Addicks could continue to rationalize to himself that he did not kill Turel. Addicks' admission does prove that Addicks was involved in the murder. By admitting that he was responsible, but not the one who did the killing, it mitigates his sentence according to the parole board's determination of time he should serve for the murder." This was a very clever legal maneuver in Addicks' attempt to reduce metrics of the mandatory sentence guidelines.

However, the law states that if a man set up and arranged a murder, that man is as guilty as the one that actually performed the murder. In

Addicks' November 4, 1980 admission that he was morally responsible for the murder he states, "I don't feel I have the same physical capability as the co-defendant, but my moral capability is much greater."

But in June 1983, he told U.S. Attorney Lance Caldwell that he was responsible for, and present at the murder of James Turel. In addition, Sam Moll testified that Addicks admitted to him that he had murdered Turel, and Cartwright also testified that Addicks strangled Turel. Yet none of these key admissions were ever clearly pointed out to the parole board prior to Addicks' hearings. This was the fourth time Addicks confessed a connection with James Turel's murder. But it was just another attempt to convince the judge that he had turned over a new leaf.

Looking back, in early 1981, Doctor R.J. Mead conducted a psychiatric evaluation of Rod Addicks and his report stated that Addicks should be considered a dangerous offender. However, on May 18, 1981, after Addicks had numerous follow-up meetings with the doctor claiming he'd been framed, Mead changed his mind and issued a third report removing Addicks' dangerous offender designation. At the same time Addicks continued with his frivolous lawsuits, claiming witnesses had been bribed with cash and were guilty of perjury. The subsequent psychiatric reports from Washington State doctors and the Oregon parole board hearings relied entirely on Doctor Mead's third opinion, unaware that Doctor Mead's updated analysis may have been based on incomplete and misleading information provided by Addicks.

One paragraph in the doctor's report includes information taken from Addicks' description of events leading up to my dad's murder, rather than the official trial transcripts. Not even the District Attorney's office was allowed to submit an alternative perspective to the doctor. Nor were they allowed to submit a list of Addicks' other convictions and crimes for which he had never been charged. I'm including an excerpt from Dr. R.J. Mead's May 18, 1981 report here:

> After reviewing the official account of the crime and then speaking with Mr. Addicks as to situations which prevailed at the time of the crime and after discussing with him his feelings about his future, I am lead to the opinion that he is not a habitual criminal who is likely to repeat his crime in the future. In the absence of a personality disorder or any type of lifelong antisocial type of behavior, I would suggest that his crime was situational and not one due to a constitutional defect.

SITUATIONAL MY ASS! I could not believe that this doctor had any idea of what was going on right in front of him. Did Addicks' superior and cunning 120 I.Q. and psychopathic personality overwhelm the doctor's perception what really happened?

In 1981, Addicks had been turning in a number of other criminals, reporting on schemes to get in the good graces of prison officials. Maybe his good-citizen act convinced Dr. Mead that he had really turned over a new leaf. One scheme Addicks reported involved convicts filing false tax returns with the IRS. Addicks had enough details to provide sufficient information to the IRS, so they knew which tax returns to watch for. Did the IRS consider that Addicks could have been the mastermind of this project, set up deliberately in another attempt to make him look like the perfect prisoner?

Other doctors examined Rod Addicks and prepared reports. A few point out that Addicks never had a problem with alcohol. Yet according to the testimonies of Sam Moll, Dennis Cartwright, and assorted tavern waiters, Addicks had a serious drinking problem. Most of the planning regarding all their crimes took place while drinking, during their heaviest drinking days. The prison doctors evaluating Rod Addicks did not research enough of his record. Apparently, they just skimmed his rap sheet and took Addicks' word as a truthful response to their questions.

I had to back myself away from researching Addicks' latest scams. The aggravation of learning of each new manipulation was causing me too much stress. There was nothing I could do to convince the doctors or parole board to uphold Addicks' prison convictions and sentences. I had to get on with my own life.

In the fall of 1983, Columbia Bookkeeping was again gearing up, preparing for the onslaught of the 1984 tax season. I had a rule that we could not spend over five percent of our budget on advertising so I took the time to study all our marketing options. We also bought out a tax practice called Tax Reducers that had 10 locations in Oregon and Washington. In an effort to be distinctively different from other tax businesses, and first in all advertising angles, I came up with what I thought might be an effective, innovative idea.

Remember how, years ago, we would go to theaters and stare patiently at a blank screen while waiting for the movie to start? Well,

Columbia Bookkeeping made a deal with various Act III Theaters throughout Oregon, Washington and Idaho. We bought and installed hundreds of slide projectors in the theaters, then started selling ad space to local companies. The ads were shown before the movie began. We had over 161 theatre screens set up in Eugene, Salem, Corvallis, Medford, Bend, McMinnville, Hillsboro, and on the Oregon Coast. In Washington State we were the first to introduce theater advertising in Seattle, Belleview, Tacoma, Olympia, Bellingham, and Spokane. Columbia Bookkeeping furnished most of the start-up money in exchange for free advertising, plus we gave a man who had commercial slide projector experience a 20 percent interest in the company for serving as the company's president. He had already set up 14 screens in the Eugene area. We named the company Entertainment Media, Inc.

I wanted Columbia Bookkeeping involved because using a slide program for ads would provide year-round advertising for our company at a very low fee per month. We paid just 25 percent of the regular price; the other companies who placed ads made up the difference. Besides, advertising in movie theaters was a fun business that allowed us to start a branch office in Seattle. The slide show advertisements were more effective than TV ads on the networks. However, we found that buying ads on cable TV stations such as CNN and The History Channel also brought in a good return. To balance our advertising budget, we cut back on network advertising.

Then we created our own in-house advertising agency, which gave us a 10 to 20 percent discount on most of our ads. I wrote and directed the production of all our marketing, TV, radio and half-hour infomercials for our combined businesses. To me, marketing is the most creative and enjoyable part of building a business.

An additional advertising idea came about on a bright Sunday morning in 1984. While I was scanning the classifieds of *The Oregonian,* I came across an ad for a used hot air balloon. Hummm, I pondered. That would sure make a large sign for advertising the company. I also thought it would be a good summertime activity for a team of company employees and their kids. So, I arranged to buy the balloon at the bargain price of $4,500, since it had already used up half of its expected lifetime.

The balloon was seven stories high when inflated. It was truly a beautiful sight! We'd take it to the various cities in which we had tax offices and then show up at their local events where thousands of people were expected. I always made sure the balloon team had a good time.

We printed up thousands of flyers and pictures to hand out describing the balloon and what it could do. Each flyer had our company name and logo prominently displayed. Then, rather than take off at the big balloon festivals, we would stay tethered to the ground and give free rides to thousands of kids. The lines of waiting kids would be a block long. I got my exercise lifting the kids in and out of the balloon for hours on end.

The marketing tactic worked better than we expected since TV and radio crews at major community events focused on us because we were the only hot air balloon there. I made sure the 40-by 20-foot tax sign attached to the side of the balloon would be facing directly at the media crews as they filmed. We even ended up on the front page of the Sunday *Oregonian* during Rose Festival weekend. You cannot buy that kind of advertising.

Months later, when I was negotiating with an IRS agent on behalf of a client, the IRS auditor interrupted to say, "Stan, I want to tell you my son still has that picture of your hot air balloon on his wall and it's been three months since he had a 30-second ride from you." I explained to the client with me, "That proves my point. Our hot air balloon is tax deductible as an advertising expense!"

Many times we drifted free flight over the Interstate-5 freeway exposing our sign to rush-hour traffic. We would lift off by 6:30 a.m., drift for a while, then land by 8 o'clock. After packing up the balloon and feeding the volunteer staff, we would be back at the office by 9:30 a.m. From time to time a school would request that we set up the balloon on their school grounds for special events. It was a great marketing scheme and a fun thing to do, but a lot of work for the volunteers and me.

On one occasion I set up the balloon at a park east of Wilsonville, Oregon. We took off drifting south over the Willamette River. I let the balloon descend slowly over the river. Just before we touched down in the river, I hit the burner and waited ten seconds for the heat to start lifting us off of the water. It was really quite a thrill. A few months later the local FAA office announced that we could lose our license if we did not carry life preservers onboard. I never tried that stunt again, but will always remember my passenger's excitement and squealing laughter as our balloon started drifting upward with six inches of water draining out of the bottom of the wicker basket.

Eventually, it wasn't feasible to make myself available for all the balloon-flying requests, so I let other professional balloon pilots fly it for special events. But, my goodness! What a way to start a morning—to drift over farms and cities like a hawk drifting in the breeze, not knowing where we would land.

Throughout 1984, I continued making personal property investments which added about ten hours to my workweek. I spent 40 hours a week at Columbia Bookkeeping between tax seasons, but from December through April of each year I worked at least 70 hours every week. In an effort to become more efficient with my time, I began delegating more duties to my executive secretary, Wanda Fuller, and to my general manager, Judy Krussow. Sherri Cronin, in charge of our Computer Processing Department, was putting in 60-hour workweeks, which allowed me to reduce my hours during tax season to about 50 each week.

Then I got word Rod Addicks had been granted a parole hearing in late December 1984. One of Addicks' attorneys sent a very compelling letter to the Oregon parole board, explaining why Addicks should be paroled. In it, according to Addicks' version, he did not murder James Turel, had nothing to do with planning the murder, but he was present—a bystander. He never touched the victim. He admits he could have stepped in to save Mr. Turel but did not since the fight was between Mr. Cartwright and Mr. Turel regarding a property dispute. His explanation should have been recognized as outrageous since four people testified that Addicks had offered them money to kill James Turel, and because Rod Addicks had gone to extreme lengths to cover up Lee Cartwright's involvement and activities in Portland prior to the murder. In addition, there was Sam Moll's admission that Addicks told him he killed Mr. Turel on December 10, 1974. I have to assume that Addicks gave Doctor Mead and Doctor Maneman his own version.

My opinion is that each time Addicks was in serious trouble while incarcerated he would fess up solely to impress whatever authorities were bothering him. And, in front of Judge Panner on June 21, 1983, prior to the judge's sentencing regarding Addicks' frivolous lawsuits and conspiracy to commit perjury, Addicks said the following in hope of reducing his Federal sentence:

> One of the things that I think should be clarified, and I have never said
> this publicly before, I want to tell you that I was present when Mr.

Turel was killed. There was some things I could have done, had I been acting as a mature and responsible citizen, which may have saved him. I got convicted of that crime. I got convicted of a murder and I did not feel I was guilty of a murder. I didn't personally get involved in it, but I feel that there is some things I should have done and could have done had I been acting like a mature responsible citizen.

I guess Rod Addicks figured that since Dennis Lee Cartwright delivered most of the killing blows to James Turel, Addicks felt justified in claiming he did not cause Turel's death. Thus, we get another glimpse into the world of denial and the self-justification of a diagnosed psychopathic personality.

Chapter 32: Making Things Happen

In the summer of 1985, I sold my interest in my beautiful twin-engine airplane to my brother. I'd been using that plane for Columbia Bookkeeping business for years, but the only compensation I ever requested was reimbursement for the cost of gas, even though gas represents only a third of the cost of flying. Insurance, maintenance, and depreciation takes up the bulk of the expense. I felt it was time for the family business to own its own plane. By then, the Turel Family Trust had an interest in four different businesses located in 15 locations throughout the Northwest.

I had heard that auctions of government-seized airplanes would be taking place in Florida, so I sent Del Hendrickson, my instrument flight instructor and expert mechanic, to check things out. Hendrickson went down to Florida five days before me to inspect four twin-engine Cessnas. I planned to join him before the auctions began and to use his expertise before making my decision as to which aircraft to bid on. If I could buy one for half price, I figured that would be a good deal. Hendrickson and I drove all over the state of Florida, covering 1,000 miles in two days, looking at those four aircraft. I made bids on two aircraft and was the successful bidder on a pressurized twin engine Cessna 340 at the Dade County Sheriff's Department auction. The plane was okay mechanically, just out of license. Someone had removed the main radios, but the wiring was good. The plane had been confiscated by Dade County agents in a case involving a drug dealer.

I was prepared to use either a cashier's check or banker's draft to pay the full $62,000 bid price, but the sheriff's department refused those. They suggested that I go downtown to obtain cash, then drive the cash back across town to hand it over to them. I felt their plan could be the set up for a robbery and that I'd be crazy to do it. So, I insisted they come to the bank with me to get the money. Never before, nor since, have I had to count out that many hundred dollar bills. We used the bank manager's conference room where the piles of money were laid out on a large oak table. The bank manager and I smelled something fishy in the way Dade County officers were handling the money. We requested a notarized receipt from the two officers. Years later the press exposed Dade County Sheriff's Department officers in a scheme to embezzle cash out of these types of deals.

The next day a man approached me and offered to sell me radios for cash that I suspected had been removed from the plane I bought just before its sale. I flew back home on a commercial flight that night to attend business meetings in Portland while Del Hendrickson spent three days in Florida getting the plane in flying condition before ferrying it back to Troutdale, Oregon. I had done what I set out to do—buy a plane for Columbia Bookkeeping at half price. These sideline adventures helped to reinvigorate my positive attitude as an offset to hearing about Addicks' escapades.

In 1985 I became even more involved in legislative efforts that would give victims, and the family members of victims, the right to show up at parole hearings. Crime Victims United and Concerned Oregonians for Justice were at the forefront of this effort. Eventually, Oregon voters had the chance to vote on this statewide measure and I helped fund the effort and the endorsement in the Voter's Pamphlet. I was surprised that Norm and Dolores Winningstad had quietly made a sizable donation to the cause. Again, my brother, sisters and I appeared on a number of TV and radio talk shows to promote the ballot measure. In November 1986, the measure passed by a whopping three-to-one margin. Now we supposedly would have access to the parole board hearings and all information presented.

Around the same time, I contacted Scott McAlister at the Oregon State Justice Department to catch up on the latest regarding Rod Addicks. McAlister said Addicks had been writing harassing letters to him and to Detective Rod Englert. Here is a response letter McAlister sent back to Addicks:

DAVE FROHNMAYER
ATTORNEY GENERAL

DEPARTMENT OF JUSTICE
Justice Building
Salem, Oregon 97310
Telephone: (503) 378-4400

May 30, 1985

Mr. Rod Addicks
Box 520, 276419
Walla Walla, WA 99362

Re: Your letter dated May 19, 1985

Dear Mr. Addicks:

Your letter reinforced my belief in the overall consistency of LIFE, you know, a leopard never changes its spots and all? Here I have not heard a word from you in several years and when I do, what? Back to the same old style -- threats of courts and press. Did not work then, will not work now! I have not changed either.

Actually, personally I do not mind if your "serious and widely read media representatives" go public with what happened. As I recall the last time you went public, we both ended up on <u>60 Minutes</u> and you undoubtedly recall which of us ended up smelling like what. However, onto the meat (less threats) of your letter.

Enclosed is a copy of the Board Action Form (BAF) dated June 30, 1982. It <u>clearly</u> states that an initial parole release date was not set because you are under the discretionary system. The Board position reflected by the BAF is legally correct.

The Board of Parole does not have an option of treating you as a dangerous offender. Either you were sentenced as a dangerous offender or you were not. In the event that you were sentenced as a dangerous offender under ORS 161.725 and 161.735, you are entitled to a psychiatric and physical examination every two years and other specific treatment which I am certain the Board of Parole will make every reasonable effort to provide.

I note that the first appearance of an "adjusted inception date" is on the BAF of December 18, 1984. I find no reference to earlier calculations, however, it appears that the Board actually granted you credit to more time than you should have received. I have enclosed a copy of that order for you to review.

Your letter also claims that your request for administrative review has been ignored by the Board. Enclosed is a copy of a response dated March 14, 1985 which appears to reveal an error in your contention.

Finally, your representation that I would go to the Governor to assist in getting you a commutation to Manslaughter is, at best, slanting the truth. As you should recall, <u>you told me</u> that you were at most guilty of Manslaughter and I told you that <u>if</u> that representation were true I would forward the supporting materials to the Governor.

As it turns out, your representations were totally false! I expended a great deal of time and energy in investigating your case, with the ultimate result that your claims broke down completely. I believe I now know you as well as anyone alive, including yourself. In my opinion you should be released from prison upon your demise and not one second sooner.

First, you beat a crippled man to death using his own crutch, a cue ball in a sock, and various other items. The death had to be slow and brutally painful. Your motive was one of pure profit and you took great pains in both planning the killing and attempting to avoid apprehension after the killing. After conviction you conspired with another inmate to attempt to get the conviction set aside based upon his confession. Although we had broken the charade before it occurred, ultimately your co-conspirator admitted his confession was false. The admission was triggered by your failure to pay him as agreed. For revenge, you then attempted to frame him and several other inmates for an escape attempt.

At the same time as your brutal murder for profit, you were also engaged in burning houses down to defraud insurance companies, and apparently both California and Washington authorities were closing in on you involving fraud of some other kind.

Finally, during your incarceration you have persisted in filing frivolous litigation, not only against the state, but also against the son of the man you premeditatedly executed.

In short, in my personal opinion, you are <u>by</u> <u>personal</u> <u>choice</u> an individual who will stop at nothing including murder, (but short of honest employment) to take from others and avoid the consequences of those acts. I do not believe you will ever change and, therefore, you should never be paroled. Thus innocent citizens need not risk falling prey, perhaps fatally, to your criminal activities.

I trust I have satisfactorily addressed your inquiries.

Sincerely, *(signed)*
Scott McAlister
Attorney-in-Charge

SM:sms
Enclosures
cc: Governor Atiyeh
Honorable Owen Panner
Parole Board Members
Stan Turel

On January 22, 1986, Rod Addicks was evaluated by Doctor R.A. Maneman, Ph.D., at the Washington State Prison at the request of the Oregon State Parole Board. The board wanted an updated psychological review so they could rule on Addicks' request to remove his 10-year Dangerous Offender sentence based on Dr. R.J. Mead's favorable 1981 diagnosis. Due to time limitations, the report dealt only with Addicks' psychological makeup and his adaptation while at the Washington State Prison. The doctor based his report on the limited information forwarded by the Oregon Parole board, a copy of Dr. Mead's report of May 18, 1981, and his personal interview with Rod Addicks.

In his report, Dr. Maneman summarized favorable letters received from Addicks' religious chaplain, his college attendance record, and a letter regarding employment in the prison's Educational Department as a paid clerk. I checked around, but no one from the Oregon District Attorney's office, and no one in my family, was contacted about these latest doctors' interviews. It is my opinion that Dr. Maneman was not aware of all the conclusive evidence involving Addicks' criminal convictions in Oregon, and had never been provided with a detailed summary of Addicks' numerous admissions to the Turel murder. He did not receive the detailed descriptions from the testimonies of Addicks' co-conspirators. Was the doctor aware that Addicks had recently taken courses in psychotherapy?

I have to assume, however, that Addicks provided Dr. Maneman with copies of his voluminous lawsuits regarding Addicks' alleged false testimony of key witnesses who testified against Addicks.

Doctor Maneman wrote:

In my opinion, a man's performance in a penal setting cannot be construed as predictive of his subsequent performance in the free community. By all accounts, Mr. Addicks is a bright and capable man, sophisticated and well-versed in presenting himself in a most favorable light. By history, there is little in the central file to suggest any motivation other than financial gain for Mr. Addicks. All alleged criminal activities are in the past. During his time in this institution, his motive for his exemplary conduct and programming efforts here, as well at the OSP appear to be pro-social in all respects, however, in my experience, many offenders are capable of sustaining such activity over a protracted time period, only to fall back into old habit patterns once they are released in the free community.

I would have to regard him as a non-violent offender who appears to have been enlightened, if not humbled, by his prison experiences. Diagnostically, I would categorize this offender as Axis One, an adult antisocial behavior, by history.

Signed by RA Maneman, Ph.D.

1-22-86

On June 16, 1986, Rod Addicks received another evaluation from Doctor R.A. Maneman, Ph. D. This Addendum Review was requested for another of Addicks' parole hearings. In Maneman's second evaluation, Addicks had another chance to make sure Maneman reviewed Dr. Mead's evaluation from May 18, 1981, in which Mead rescinded his earlier diagnostic conclusions and recommendations, which lead to the removal of Addicks' official designation as a Dangerous Offender.

Every parole hearing was conducted without any prior notice to anyone in my family. I received all this information after the fact. I contacted members in my family asking them to join me in an effort to attend future parole hearings.

I found it disturbing that the doctors may have ignored the fact that four people testified they had been solicited by Rod Addicks to kill my dad, as well as Addicks' own admission to a Federal judge that he had been present during my dad's murder. Rod Addicks was manipulating the judicial system and conning the doctors, just as he had attempted to from the very beginning. But by then, he'd convinced them he'd undergone a religious awakening as well.

Meanwhile, the year-round tax business went on as usual with the constant stress of growth and financial obligations of the Turel Family Trust. In 1986, the State Tax Board required that I visit each of our offices at least twice a week. So, I would hop into the plane two days every week and visit each city. A typical flight during tax season, using Instrument Flight Rules (IFR Rules are regulations and procedures for flying safely through clouds using aircraft instruments) was demanding. I would take off IFR, in the clouds, to Hillsboro, then to McMinnville, Salem, Corvallis, and end the day in Eugene. By the time I was done visiting each office for 15 minutes, the day would be done and I would get back home around 9:30 at night. For most of the flights I was flying by myself, often in treacherous winter weather. The twin-engine aircraft was equipped with de-icing equipment, radar, and dual instrumentation similar to that of commercial airliners. This flight schedule allowed me to keep tabs on each office. I would pop in unannounced. You'd be surprised what a boss can learn with that style of management.

I took a great deal of pride in how well we did when our clients had audits with the IRS. It was like a chess game. Our success rate was based on the excellent records we had in our files. Our accountants were doing a great job.

Just after that tax season ended, I received a panicked call from my friend John Winters, the man who had helped me expand my father's home and had stood by me through tough times.

"Stan, I've been fired from the Rockwood Water District! They fired me because when the two bosses were at a seminar in Las Vegas, my crew ran out of work to do on Friday. This time of year, every year, we load up the Water District truck with all the scrap copper we collected during the past year. Usually the bosses take it down to Schnitzer's scrap yard themselves. Since the bosses were not here, me and another worker took it down to Schnitzer's steel yard. When they weighed it, they asked if we wanted it in cash as usual, or by check. I said, 'Give us a check.' When we turned the check in at the office, the bookkeeper said she didn't know what to do with it since they have never heard of this before. When the bosses got back, they fired me for insubordination because I took the scrap metal down to Schnitzer's without instructions from the boss!"

"John," I said, "this sounds fishy. It seems as though the bosses have been skimming cash and putting it in their pockets and you just ruined their scheme. Let me call the sheriff and a reporter I know from *The Oregonian*, and I will attend the Rockwood Water District board meeting in a few days."

An investigation started after that Water District board meeting revealed that the two bosses had been taking thousands of dollars a year, over several years, from their copper theft. The bosses said they used the money for employee turkeys at Thanksgiving. With only 14 employees, the paper's headline read, "Great Turkey Caper Exposed." The two bosses were forced to resign, but they retained their pension rights and John got his job back. We felt it was unjust that the two men were not convicted of any crime and that they went out on early retirement. The District Attorney said they did not have the time, or staff to handle such a case.

Saturday, July 5, 1986, Gresham, Oregon   4 Sections, 36 Pages - 25 cents

Stan Turel stands next to plane at Troutdale Airport. It took a family tragedy to launch him into his tax business.

Staff photo by Terry Farris

"Saturday Profile" on Stan Turel in the *Gresham Outlook*, July 5, 1986.

Meanwhile, I had plenty on my plate to keep me busy.

In 1986, I received over 500 votes from various businessmen and was elected to be a delegate to the White House Conference on Small Business. During my first trip to the convention in Washington D.C., only 12 proposals made it to President Reagan's desk. My proposal on how to consolidate the myriad business forms required by the Federal government was one of them. At the convention, I met Jim Bernau, head of Oregon's National Federation of Independent Businesses. Under Bernau's guidance, I was soon appointed to Oregon Governor Atiyeh's committee to consolidate the filing requirements of Oregon's governmental agencies. Eventually that friendship with Bernau led to a large family investment in Willamette Valley Vineyards, which Jim had formed and taken public. That company is now one of Oregon's largest and most successful wineries (WVVI on the NASDAQ).

While going over my apartment accounts two weeks before Christmas of 1986, I realized we had too many apartment vacancies, which made me nervous. Plus, some of our tenants had lost their jobs and stopped paying rent. On one day in mid-December, I was in court twice, dealing with four Forcible Eviction and Detainers for two separate apartments. There I was in a courtroom with 60 people, all of them facing evictions from their respective landlords just before Christmas.

When it came time to hear my two cases I stood up in my three-piece suit, looked at the crowd, and said, "Your Honor, in a spirit of Christmas, I would like to stipulate, no matter what your decision is, that I do not want my tenants evicted until after Christmas." Everyone in the room applauded. The judge said, "That's wonderful. Will they agree to move out by January 4?" The tenants agreed. Actually that was the fastest way to get them out, as it would have taken longer if the tenant had requested a trial, which was their right.

Sometimes you must do what you feel is right in your heart. I couldn't help but think, what if I was the person sitting there and being forced to move out just before the holidays?

However, sometimes I get burned by being too softhearted.

One of our tenants at the Tristin Manor Apartments was a 19-year-old who was eight months pregnant and past due on her rent. I told her not to worry; she could stay in the apartment for free until one month after the baby was born. However, I made it clear that I would enforce the eviction process if she wasn't out within 30 days after the baby's birth. The woman was so appreciative that she gave me a big hug. But the manager of the apartments gave me a big lecture. She said I was a sucker and that the pregnant lady and her boyfriend were taking advantage of me. We had a big argument as a result. It was my decision even though the manager didn't like that particular tenant.

But the manager was right. One month after the baby was born we asked the young lady to move. Her unemployed, live-in boyfriend said, "Do you think we're stupid? We'll delay moving as long as possible and there's nothing you can do about it." It was April 1 before they were forcibly moved out by the sheriff. They also did over $3,000 worth of damage, including smearing excrement all over the walls as a departing thank you.

Chapter 33: Co-Conspirator Asks for Forgiveness, and Parole Hearing Nightmares

One day a few weeks later, when I was sitting quietly in my office reviewing the past month's bills, the front desk receptionist buzzed me on the phone and said, "There are a couple of gentlemen in the office who have something private they wanted to talk to you about."

"If it's another salesman, find out what they're selling and have them leave their card." I was used to dozens of sales people stopping by and calling every day and generally tried to limit my time with them.

She buzzed me back a few seconds later and said, "It is a Mr. Sam Moll with his parole officer. They would like to speak to you in private."

"Wow," I said. "Give me a few minutes to consider this. Have them wait in the lobby."

I invited Dorothy, the bookkeeper across the hallway, to come into my office. "You will not believe who's in the lobby," I said. "Sam Moll. I can't imagine why he's here. The man is scum and I want nothing to do with him."

Dorothy went down the hallway, peeked around the corner, and came back into my office. "It's really him," she said. "I can't believe he's here."

I spun around in my swivel chair to look out the bulletproof window, remembering how Sam Moll described how he almost shot my dad through this window. Then, turning to face Dorothy, I said "Okay, I'll talk to him but I want you in the room taking notes. When he comes in the room leave the door open and don't even let him sit down. This won't take long."

Sam Moll entered the room with the man who introduced himself as Sam Moll's parole officer. "Sam wants to ask you something," the man said.

As Moll began speaking, I noticed he was much shorter than I remembered. I'd last seen him when he was with my father during the 1974 tax season, five months before Dad was murdered. He was chubby, but looked healthier. He still had a friendly, but earnest look about him.

Sam Moll looked me right in the eyes. "Mr. Turel," he said. "I have had a hard time living with myself since I could have done something to stop your father from being murdered. I allowed myself to get involved in bad things, but I now I have found Jesus in my heart." Sam Moll looked at me with what could have been a sincere expression. "I am asking for your family's forgiveness for what I have done. That is all I wanted to say."

I asked him if Rod Addicks had admitted to him that he had murdered my dad. He looked down and quietly said, yes. I did not want to get into any long discussions with him. You sure have a lot of nerve coming in here, I thought. You're probably doing this to get early release from jail.

"Sam," I said, standing up. "It's between you and God whether or not you will be forgiven, not me. Don't you ever come around my family or to any of our offices. If I ever see you again, even in a restaurant, I will walk up to you and personally deck you. However, I will consider what you have asked." I was shaking with anger. Sam Moll got the message very clear. He turned and left the room.

"Dorothy," I said, "Type up your notes of that conversation and file them away in the Rod Addicks file." Sam Moll left the building promptly. I sat down slowly, turned to the window, and watched him walk out onto the street. Seeing him at the tax office brought back a flood of bad memories, which led to a very stressful headache.

For years after Sam Moll's visit, I continued to ponder his apology. I came to believe that he had a deep soul somewhere and probably meant what he said. After all, he got within a few feet of murdering my father and backed out. He was one of the accomplices who couldn't follow through on the murder. In my heart, I hoped he turned into a good citizen. Sam Moll was the first in Rod Addicks' crime circle to crack and tell the detectives what happened. God will be his judge, not I. I have never seen or heard from him since.

In January of 1987, I wrote to the Oregon State Parole Board that I, and my extended family, wanted to be advised of all upcoming parole hearings regarding Rod Addicks. I told them I planned to attend all hearings and requested copies of all documents that the parole board would be privy to based on the newly passed Crime Victims Rights initiative. Eventually I amassed over 300 pages, including, for the first time, a copy of all Addicks' prior pleadings with the parole board.

At the first hearing after the passage of the initiative, the Parole Board barred reporters from the hearings. *The Oregonian* learned that I planned to attend the next parole hearing for Rod Addicks and in early March 1987, Rollo Creek, a reporter from *The Oregonian*, called and asked me to contact a reporter named Wallace Turner who worked for the *New York Times*. When I called Turner, he asked if I would be willing to answer a few questions. I said, "Sure." We met at my office and as usual, I had all the parole information and transcriptions ready so there would be no doubt that Addicks should be refused parole under the merit system for inmates who behaved well in prison.

On March 16, 1987, the *New York Times* published Wallace Turner's article about Oregon's new parole process. The article states, "The board's second such hearing is scheduled for April 21, 1987, to hear objections to the parole of Roderick Raymond Addicks, convicted of the 1974 murder of James Turel, his partner in a bookkeeping company. Mr. Turel's son, Stanley Turel, said he has examined the parole board's file on Mr. Addicks and found it to be deficient, which he will point out when he testifies in opposition to the parole."

In early April, the *Oregonian* crime reporter, Jim Hill, asked me if I would assist him in gaining access to the upcoming parole hearing. I said, "Of course," as I felt it would put more pressure on the parole board and hopefully they wouldn't go easy on Addicks. I filed an affidavit with the *Oregonian* in Marion County courts requesting the right of the public, the press, and victim's families to attend parole board hearings. Attorneys from the Portland *Oregonian* armed their reporter with a Temporary Court Order, forcing the parole board to open up the hearing to the reporters.

On April 21, 1987, my brother, sisters, and I appeared at the parole hearing in Salem at the Oregon State Prison. The prison's administrative building is made of stone and marble and as we entered the lobby, the echo of our footsteps was deafening. The Parole Hearing room was small, with one oversized conference table in the middle.

Reporters Jim Hill, from *The Oregonian,* and Wallace Turner, from the *New York Times,* were already there. We thought Rod Addicks would attend in person, but a teleconference was set up between the courtroom and the prison, and Addicks' voice could be heard over the speaker system. Addicks was absolutely charming as he expressed remorse to my family, saying he had no hard feelings, he was just following his rights as prisoner to pursue getting out of jail on parole. He was still the smooth talker he always was.

At the hearing I asked, "Have you folks considered all the millions of dollars worth of frivolous lawsuits Rod Addicks has filed as you deliberated as to whether or not he should be considered for parole?"

The chairman of the parole board answered, "Mr. Turel, we cannot bring that into our evaluations as it has nothing to do with this hearing and we cannot consider his civil lawsuits outside of the prison."

I just about dropped dead upon hearing this.

"Why are you treating his arson and murder sentences concurrently rather than consecutively?" I asked.

Their answer was a vague excuse, even though Multnomah County Assistant District Attorney Norm Frink contested their position. I was horrified to see that the parole board had more power than the authorities that placed Addicks in jail.

My brother, sisters and I walked out of that short parole hearing shaking our heads. It was obvious to us that all the outrageous trouble Rod Addicks had initiated during his stay in jail meant nothing to the parole board. And I could tell they did not appreciate the press or our presence at the hearing. At that time we did not realize that Addicks had become a primary snitch for the prison officials and the IRS. Maybe this was why he was receiving preferential treatment from the board.

On April 26, 1987, reporter Wallace Turner's article was published in the *New York Times*. Here's an excerpt:

Victim's Relatives Opposing Parole
by Wallace Turner

Exercising a new right given to crime victims, Stan Turel appeared before the Oregon Parole Board today to warn, "Rod Addicks is better at crime now than he was when he went into prison." Mr. Turel continued to speak in opposition to paroling the prisoner, who is serving a life sentence. In 1982, only six states allowed victims to appear at parole hearings. Now there are 32 states that allow this.

When asked to respond to the statements opposing his parole, Mr. Addicks said he told the board his story at a previous hearing and would stand on that. No victim's representatives were present at that hearing, which had been held before the new law was voted in. Five years ago, Mr. Addicks was transferred to the Washington State

Penitentiary at Walla Walla, Washington, under an interstate prisoner exchange agreement. Last fall, in what is now described by state officials as an error in judgment that led to an act beyond its authority, the parole board set a March 1987 release date for Addicks. When Stan Turel, his sisters, and brother Gary heard of this, they began a campaign to block the parole.

"I came here to see how the parole board might let the guy who murdered my father go free out on the street," Gary Turel told the board. Stan Turel testified that he was astounded that the board's file did not contain the information that Mr. Addicks had pleaded guilty in Federal District Court in 1983 to the charge of conspiracy to commit perjury. Chalmers Jones, acting board chairman, told him it was not the panel's responsibility to gather such data. Mr. Turel said he would provide it.

While in jail, Mr. Addicks filed suit for millions of dollars against a wide range of defendants, including Turel who was forced to spend $18,000 to defend himself, Stan Turel told the board. After hearing the family testify in closed session, the board decided that Mr. Addicks would stay in jail until a new hearing to be held on April 21, 1989.

In that article Turner also pointed out several other cases where a parole was being contested, including Sirhan Sirhan's murder case regarding Robert F Kennedy, Jr. in 1968, and Charles Manson, the man who murdered actress Sharon Tate and her unborn child.

Sadly, the article didn't mention the parole board's response to my presentation, which read, "The Oregon Parole Board does not have the right to evaluate Addicks' actions without considering his malicious civil proceedings while incarcerated in prison."

On April 27, 1987, an article appeared in *The Oregonian*. That article said the same thing as the *New York Times*, but included a photo of my brother, sisters and me. We all had a very grim looks on our faces.

On July 20, 1987, Rod Addicks requested to be placed on the parole board's docket as a Matrix Case rather than a discretionary case, which meant it would become easier for Addicks to be released on parole, as the merit system was more lenient than the discretionary system. I found it incomprehensible that after the Parole Board set a new hearing date of April 21, 1989, Addicks started right in again, trying to reset the parameters of his parole.

On September 24, 1987, another parole teleconference was held. I attended with my brother and sisters, as well as Norm Frink, the Deputy District Attorney for Multnomah County. He reassured us by saying that the District Attorney's office, with the assistance of Scott McAlister, would do everything in its power to keep Addicks in jail.

On October 19, 1987 my brother and sisters attended Rod Addicks' third parole hearing. Norm Frink, and Sarah Hames a reporter with *The Oregonian*, were also present. Again, we were not allowed to discuss anything other than stating we contested the removal of the Dangerous Offenders Sentencing designation, under which Rod Addicks had been sentenced. The parole board chairman, Mr. Faatz, clarified the board's action from the June 11, 1981 hearing. He said, "Our interpretation of the psychiatric report of May 18, 1981 by R. J. Mead, Ph.D., is that there is an absence of a personality disorder and therefore the inmate is not to be considered as a dangerous offender."

Oh great, I thought. Then I realized, oh my God, Addicks appears to have totally conned the prison doctors. I said, "Remember, this man murdered someone in a preplanned contract killing, and he was involved in numerous cases of arson while he was working as a Certified Public Accountant." I could tell the board was again annoyed by my presence and uncomfortable about engaging in a discussion with me since the press was in the room.

Parole board members Dinsmore and Groener applied one standard variation for Aggravation, set a parole date at 204 months hence, for a release on March 16, 1992. Board Chairman Faatz recommended 240 months, for a release on March 16, 1995. Board member Robinson recommended no parole date due to the particularly violent and otherwise dangerous criminal conduct of Rod Addicks, and the manifestation and extreme indifference he showed to the value of human life. Board Member Samuelson suggested 168 months with a parole date of March 16, 1989. The board noted that no release shall be considered without a current psychological evaluation. Since no quorum could be reached at that hearing, they voted to reschedule another hearing of the full board, by teleconference, as soon as possible.

My brother, sisters and I did not believe that murder was worth just 15 to 20 years behind bars. My sense was the parole board did not want to make a decision with our family and the press in the room. They adjourned that meeting for a final decision at some later time.

Twice during the hearings, Michael Schrunk, the Multnomah District Attorney, and Norm Frink attempted to submit a three-page report from Dr. David Myers, Ph.D., P.C. that presented a determination of Addicks' psychopathic personality. Both attempts at submission were refused by the parole board. Here is District Attorney Schrunk's letter contesting the board's refusal to reconsider the evaluations by Dr. Mead and Dr. Maneman. The parole board refused to consider Dr. David Myer's letter:

MICHAEL D. SCHRUNK
District Attorney for Multnomah County
600 County Courthouse
Portland, Oregon 97204

(503) 248-3162

November 9, 1987

Mr. Vern L. Faatz, Chairman
2575 Center Street N.E.
Salem, OR 97310

Re: State v. Rod Addicks

Dear Mr. Faatz:

Since the Board is to hold a new hearing, I would ask that the report from Dr. David Myers that I offered at the last hearing now be made a part of the official record and provided to Mr. Addicks 10 days prior to the hearing. I have enclosed a copy.

Thank you very much for your cooperation in this matter.

Yours very truly,
MICHAEL D. SCHRUNK
District Attorney
Multnomah County, Oregon

By (signed) Norman W. Frink, Jr.
Chief Deputy, Circuit Court

NWF: je
Enclosure
cc: Michael Swaim
Stan Turel
Parole Board Members

David A. Myers, Ph.D., P.C.
Clinical and Consulting Psychologies

17 10 S.W. Harbor Way #201   Telephone
Portland, Oregon 97201   (503) 223-9238

October 13, 1987

Norm Frink
Deputy District Attorney
Multnomah County Courthouse
1021 SW 4th Ave.
Portland, Oregon 97204

Re: Roderick Raymond Addicks
OSP 37945

Dear Mr. Frink,

At your request I have reviewed the Parole Board packet pertaining to Mr. Addicks. Per your request I have carefully reviewed, as well as other documents, the psychological evaluation of R.A. Maneman, Ph.D., dated January 22, 1986 and the psychiatric evaluation of R.J. Mead, M.D., Ph.D. from May of 1981 and December 29, 1980, and October 8, 1980. I also reviewed the presentence psychological evaluation from an assessment completed on December 24, 1974 by Constantine Columbus, Ph.D. The purpose of this review was to provide an opinion regarding Mr. Addicks' diagnosis and possible dangerousness.

It is noteworthy that the original PSI report in 1974 found Mr. Addicks to be a "psychopathic personality" with a superior intelligence. He was full of anger, denial, and projection of blame. Those of us who have evaluated and attempted to work with psychopathic personalities know that the implications of this designation are far reaching. Essentially, a psychopath is a conscienceless, glib, manipulative individual who can demonstrate enormous persuasive talent. The rule of thumb in dealing with a psychopath is to ignore what they say and observe carefully what they do. I have seen psychopaths who have repeatedly persuaded counselors, probation officers and judges that they have "reformed"; only to reoffend as soon as the opportunity in the community was provided. The psychopath is frequently an extremely likable person because they tend to be masters of telling you what you want to hear.

In view of his certain involvement in a brutal murder and his subsequent total denial regarding responsibility for this crime; and in view of the fact that others were somehow induced to confess to these crimes in a failed effort to exonerate him of responsibility for this murder; and in view of the fact that he was also found guilty of arson and securities fraud, I found it hard to comprehend how Dr. Mead and Dr. Maneman could reach the conclusions that they did regarding Mr. Addicks. It would appear obvious to me that Mr. Addicks worked his persuasiveness on them.

I found some of the language in Dr. Maneman's January 1986 report incredible. On page 2 he writes, "By history, there is little in the central file to suggest any motivation other than financial gain for Mr. Addicks' alleged criminal activities in the past." It seems that Dr. Maneman doubts that the murder of Mr. Turel is Mr. Addicks' crime. And, if you grant for a moment the assumption that there was no other motive than financial gain for his crimes, this is even more chilling.

For years, Mr. Addicks absolutely denied any involvement in the murder. Now he is accepting some moral responsibility for it. At the time of his conviction I don't think anyone had the slightest doubt about his intimate and personal responsibility for the murder. (I must note for the record that I was familiar with the details of this crime because I performed the psychological evaluation on the co-defendant Cartwright.) Accepting peripheral, passive responsibility continues to reflect denial and an unwillingness to be honest.

I was particularly alarmed by the brief report of Dr. Mead that was received by the Parole Board on June 9, 1981 in which Dr. Mead wrote:

"After reviewing the official account of the crime, and then speaking with Mr. Addicks as to situations which prevailed at the time of the crime, and after discussing with him his feelings about his future, I am led to the opinion that he is not a habitual criminal who is likely to repeat his crime in the future. In the absence of a personality disorder or any type of lifelong antisocial type of behavior, I would suggest that his crime was situational and not one due to a constitutional defect."

In truth, the way in which Mr. Addicks participated in the murder as well as other criminal conduct suggested overwhelmingly that he was a psychopath. And according to witnesses who spoke to the Corrections Division Staff who prepared the presentence evaluation, there was a vast body of evidence that suggested Mr. Addicks was a liar and a conscienceless psychopath. There was never any doubt that Mr. Addicks had an antisocial personality disorder.

However, Drs. Mead and Maneman have chosen to conclude that, on the basis of Mr. Addicks' institutional performance and Mr. Addicks' word, he is not a personality disorder predisposed to criminal behavior.

I also think the report of Dr. Maneman dated January 22, 1986 deserves some close inspection. I think line 18 of the second paragraph of this report is very revealing. My reading of the meaning of this sentence is that essentially, "...if Mr. Addicks participated in the crime as indicated by Oregon authorities, then he would be properly diagnosed as antisocial." However, the author immediately then cites the fact that Mr. Addicks doesn't possess the typical history of an antisocial person.

Perhaps Dr. Maneman is not aware of the research that shows that perhaps 70% of the people who seek psychiatric help do not fit neatly into one single diagnostic definition. Having an atypical history only suggests that he would not be classified strictly as an Antisocial Personality according to DSM III. Rather he would, again, strictly speaking, be classified as a Mixed Personality Disorder or Other Personality Disorder (because the disorder is not classified in the DSM III.) The point is that DSM III specifically recognizes that there are personality disorders that are not specifically named in their schema. I believe Mr. Addicks, technically, and appropriately, would be classified as DSM III, Axis I, 301.89 Other Personality Disorder (Psychopathic Personality Disorder).

While Dr. Maneman would point out that Mr. Addicks' early history doesn't suggest a personality disorder, I would point out that his criminal behavior, his denial, his blaming behavior, his manipulativeness while in prison, and his glib, likeable personality that has been manifest since his incarceration are all perfectly consistent with the diagnosis of psychopathic personality.

It is my opinion that Drs. Maneman and Mead are unduly influenced by Mr. Addicks' verbal presentation to them and their opinion fails to adequately note the facts associated with the actual murder. If Mr. Addicks was a psychopath at the time of the murder, he is still a psychopath. Regardless of how glibly he (Mr. Addicks) denies it. In the absence of credible evidence to the contrary, I would view Mr. Addicks as a person who presently has a severe emotional disturbance such as to constitute a danger to the health and safety of the community. This opinion is based upon the fact of Mr. Addicks' continued denial that he was the architect of, and active participant in, Mr. Turel's murder.

In my judgment, if Mr. Addicks is released from prison, the seriousness of his crime will be gravely derogated and the safety of the community will be greatly diminished.

Your request for my consultation on this case is greatly appreciated.

Very truly yours,
David A. Myers, Ph.D., P.C.
Clinical and Consulting Psychologist

By this date, Rod Addicks had taken at least four previous polygraph exams. The first one, which he passed, was in connection with a prison break, not the murder. He refused to answer any questions about the murder. In later testimony, Addicks explained how he managed to fool that polygraph test into giving him a false passing score. His second polygraph test, four years after the murder, was extremely thorough and administered by the independent Court of Last Resorts. After that polygraph test, which Addicks failed, and a comprehensive investigation, their report indicated Rod Addicks was deceptive during the polygraph test and that he was guilty of murder as convicted. Since the report was undertaken independently, neither the State nor the prosecutors were notified until the Court of Last Resorts made the information public. Addicks sued the Court of Last Resorts for violating his privacy. The third polygraph test related to the Boss Convict scheme. Addicks failed that test but explained under oath that he knew why he failed. The fourth polygraph exam concerned his police informant offerings from 1979. There were probably more polygraph tests, but those are the ones I found in the files. Only one of those tests had to do with my Dad's murder, and he flunked badly.

Finally, after more than ten years, Rod Addicks agreed to take a limited lie detector test on an affidavit statement he signed, allowing just two questions about the murder. In my opinion, the affidavit containing the questions was so cleverly worded and limited that it was easy for Addicks to pass, especially since he had spent years practicing how to fool the sensor probes. The parole board accepted the results of this polygraph test and ruled that they remain in his file, yet they refused to allow the results from the extensive test administered by the Court Of Last Resorts in 1978, which he requested and failed miserably.

Addicks admitted in sworn testimony that he knew how to trick a polygraph examiner when questions were not asked correctly. For instance, to the question, Are you a part of an escape plan?, Addicks admitted in prior testimony that he could reply 'No' and have his answer register as true because the escape plan had already been abandoned. Also, Addicks admitted he had read numerous books, including Dr. Stan Abrams book from the prison library on how polygraph machines worked. I decided to ask Dr. Abrams to evaluate Addicks' history and the recent evaluations of Drs. Meade and Maneman.

Below is Dr. Stan Abrams' independent doctor's report completed after reviewing Addicks' parole file, testimony of his conspirators, doctor reports, and the limited information from Addicks' fifth polygraph test:

STAN ABRAMS, PH.D.
Clinical Psychologist

GOOD SAMARITAN MEDICAL BUILDING
2222 N.W. LOVEJOY • SUITE 601
PORTLAND, OREGON 97210
(503) 221-0632

October 8, 1987
Mr. Stan Turel
13909 S.E. Stark   RE: RODERICK ADDICKS
Portland, OR 97344

Dear Mr. Turel,

At your request, I read through the victim notification data that you provided with particular emphasis on the polygraph findings. Obviously, in regard to the latter, I was handicapped by having neither the full set of questions nor the charts. I would have the following concerns about the results:

1. The subject has been diagnosed as a psychopath. By definition, they are charming, manipulative, bright, anti-social, without guilt or loyalty, and they do not change. Research indicates that they can be accurately tested through polygraphy because its pyschophysiologic basis is not guilt but the fear of being detected in a lie. Still the psychopath is quite clever and it would be expected that he would read about his procedure, thereby learning various counter-measures that could be employed. It is reported that polygraph books are some of the most used in the prison library.

2. Mr. Addicks has had the opportunity of taking a polygraph test at least three times prior to the examination in question making him more familiar with its operation and giving him the opportunity to practice any techniques that he has learned.

3. Some examiners would feel that testing on a case almost ten years old reduces the emotional impact of the crime. While there may be some blunting effect, it is not felt that this would have a major impact on the accuracy of the results.

4. My major concern, however, is that the questions are much too narrow to the extent that they could be missing the issue:

1. Prior to the time Turel was killed, I did not plan for the events to occur resulting in his death on August 28, 1974.

   a. Using the phrase "plan for the events to occur resulting in his death" complicates a very simple question. The query really deals with whether he planned for the events not planned for the killing. If, in fact, not all of the events that occurred were planned, then he could pass the test.

   b. This does not appear to be a question that a polygraphist would develop because the question should be formulated so that they are brief, clear, and to the point; "Prior to his death, had you planned Turel's death?" This does not allow any room to evade the issue.

2. I did not strangle James Turel to death.

   a. Because the victim had also been bludgeoned, could the perpetrator have rationalized that he would have died anyway, therefore, the strangling really did not cause the death. In polygraphy, one has to be very wary of question formulation to be certain that the issue involved is quite clear. For example, if three men beat another man to death, one could not ask, "Did you kill John Smith" because the subject really would not know if his punch caused the death. There is considerable concern about the use of intent questions such as "Did you purposely fondle the child while you were washing her?" because of the fear that the individual is capable of rationalizing his act that his intent was only to clean the child.

It is my feeling that the test risks loss of accuracy when more details are not considered. Specifically, what role did Mr. Addicks play. He should be asked if he stood and watched, struck or held the victim, used any of the weapons -- crutch, pool ball, or cord -- against him. This way it would also allow for more opportunity to determine his exact role. The additional testing would also provide more time to evaluate the subject for the use of counter measures. Hopefully, this will answer your questions.

Cordially,

Stan Abrams, Ph.D.

I was surprised at Dr. Abrams response because he was right. According to Addicks' own testimony explaining the scheme he and Floyd Forsberg concocted to make it appear as though Forsberg murdered my dad, Addicks and Dennis Lee Cartwright went over every detail of the murder so that Forsberg could imagine himself there. Addicks said this was an effort to make sure Forsberg's false confession to the murder of Mr. Jim Turel fit the crime scene exactly.

Maybe Rod Addicks, who was by then well-versed in taking polygraph tests, was able to say he did not plan the exact events that led to James Turel's death on August 28, 1974 because the "plan" may have been to knock the victim unconscious, strangle him and haul the body away to another location where others would be implicated. But according to Addicks *Innocents* article, since they could not remove the body due to the amount of blood from the brutal killing, they had to improvise by making the office look as if a robbery had taken place. Addicks could rationalize he had not planned the *exact* events that took place the night of the murder, since the blows with the cue ball did not knock Turel out as planned.

On December 14, 1987, another parole hearing took place in Salem. Once again, I was there with my brother, Gary, my sisters, District Attorney Norm Frink, and Rod Addicks' attorney, Michael Swain. Addicks, who was still incarcerated at the Walla Walla Penitentiary in Washington State, appeared via teleconference. I was proud of my sisters and brother for keeping their cool, as I was having a hard time staying calm as we left the parole hearing. Again, the parole board rejected every attempt by the District Attorney to submit Dr. David Myers' report for their review. The board did review the technical aspects of the seriousness of the crime based on the Matrix System, then deliberated on release date. Board members Dinsmore, Groener, and Samuelson voted for release on March 16, 1989. Board members Faatz and Robinson suggested 240 months, for a release date of March 16, 1995.

Meanwhile, Dennis Lee Cartwright was released on parole on January 18, 1988 and moved to the Portland area. A few months later Aunt Grace Turel, my grandfather's brother's wife, was found dead in her burning house. Grace was the only Turel listed in the Portland phone book and at 73 years of age, lived alone. Her autopsy revealed that she was strangled and the murderer set fire to her home. The investigating detectives said Dennis Cartwright had an ironclad alibi for that night, and it was determined he was not a suspect. The case has never been solved. That same year, three of our offices were broken into on the same weekend.

Addicks' arson conviction incarceration was supposed to be served consecutively with his Oregon murder conviction, meaning the arson sentence clock would start ticking after his life sentence for murder was completed. The parole board was supplied a copy of the original sentencing, and we presented a sworn statement from the judge's clerk asserting that Rod Addicks' sentences were supposed to be consecutive, but somehow the courts failed to clarify this point with the parole board. A mistake was made, they said. Somehow Addicks' lawyer arranged to have the parole board consider the two crimes as running concurrently, meaning he would not serve one extra day in jail for his convictions on arson, murder, and perjury regarding frivolous lawsuits. And, against our pleas, after numerous jailhouse doctors' examinations, the Dangerous Offender designation was eliminated. Our only comfort was that Rod Addicks was still in jail in Washington for securities fraud. What next, I wondered. It seemed as though every decision was going in Addicks' favor.

Ultimately, and without me or my family, or even Norm Frink being present, the parole board selected a release date of March 16, 1989, just fourteen years after the brutal, premeditated murder of Jim Turel and the multiple arsons. They would not consider the many years during which he had harassed us, the victim's family, with threatening letters and frivolous lawsuits. Nor did they consider the years during which Addicks conspired with inmates to con the system and his alleged escape plans. The parole board stipulated that prior to release, another psychological evaluation would need to be performed. I guess that was supposed to be our carrot. What is life worth? I wondered. Surely more than fourteen years.

After a few calls to the Washington State Penitentiary, I found out that I did not have the right to intervene in the Washington parole hearings since his crime in Washington had nothing to do with his Oregon convictions. Justice would not be served and there was nothing more I could do to stop Rod Addicks from being released. Okay, I told myself, it's time to move on. My brother and sisters also wrote the parole board, but they, too, found out there was nothing they could do to prevent Addicks from being freed. I reluctantly decided I was done. I was busy with business and family obligations, and totally exhausted from wasting my time on Rod Addicks. With the parole date for his murder conviction scheduled for March 1989, I just gave up. Addicks would still be in prison for securities fraud, but for how long?

I stopped tracking Addicks' manipulations of the parole board and tried to distance myself from his criminal world, but information sporadically made its way to me.

On March 18, 1989, Addicks was paroled from Oregon on his murder and arson charges, but remained in the custody of the Walla Walla State Prison to serve out his sentence for securities fraud. In September 1989, he was released from the Walla Walla State Prison after serving less than six months for his securities fraud convictions. He was placed on a two-and-a-half- year parole, but I was assured by the Washington Parole Board that he was restricted from traveling to Oregon. Meanwhile, the State of Oregon refused to reconsider his parole release date again because he had received a favorable psychological analysis examination from Dr. Maneman.

A few years after Addicks was paroled, I found out he had set up a tax preparation office north of Seattle. When I contacted the IRS to find out why they allowed a convicted murderer and arsonist to be licensed in Washington and why they had granted him an Electronic Filer account, they said they had no idea of his past. For some strange reason none of their background research identified Rod Addicks as a person with numerous felonies who had spent time in prison.

The following excerpt comes from a recent article titled "The Psychopathic's Parole Trick," published in *The Week Magazine*:

> Psychopathic criminals are more likely to be released from prison than are the garden variety criminals, new research shows. Psychopaths like Ted Bundy, who was handsome and gracious, and Jeffrey Dahmer, who appeared shy and sweet, have an inherent ability to charm and deceive people, and parole board members are no exception. Canadian researchers found that psychopaths were two and a half times as likely to be released than ordinary criminals, even though they were more likely to commit another crime within a year. "Psychopathic offenders are far more likely to re-offend, so they should be far less likely to be released," study author Dr. Stephen Porter told BBCnews.com. "But psychopaths," he said, "know what a parole board wants to hear, and as skilled actors and liars they often

make a convincing case that they've been rehabilitated. Even trained experts, such as psychologist, doctors, criminologists, and lawyers generally are not better than the layperson in detecting deception," Porter said.

I checked with the State of Washington Accounting Board to see if Addicks could renew his expired CPA status and they said yes. All he had to do was complete the application form and attach a list of his continuing education hours. After I forwarded his conviction record to that board, they called back to thank me. They said, "We'll put a warning note in his file not to renew his license to practice in the State of Washington."

Again, it was time for me to let go and move on. Addicks had been set free and there was nothing I could do about it. Despite my efforts and the letters my brother and sisters wrote to the parole board, all our protests and requests fell on deaf ears. It's their system and we had no way to stop them from releasing Addicks or Forsburg. The reality is that all the attempts made by the people closest to the truth and severity of the crime—the detectives, prosecutors, and doctors who originally evaluated him—to keep Addicks in jail made no difference at all with the parole board's final decisions. In Oregon, Floyd Forsberg, Rod Addicks, and Dennis Lee Cartwright served between 14 and 15 years for their crimes of premeditated murder. This seems to be the average sentence for murderers in Oregon under the metric system.

As far as the U.S. justice system goes, I still believe we must work within the system in our own pursuit of justice. This country is one of the fairest in the world when it comes to justice. However, sometimes it takes personal involvement to make sure it functions properly. Yes, there are inequities.

My family was lucky because the men who murdered my dad were caught and did serve some time for their crimes. Of course my family members and I were upset that these killers did not spend more time in jail. It bothers us to this day. Our story reveals how a psychopath, when smart enough, can work the prison's merit system to obtain early parole. Since these murderers were released, the State of Oregon, like other states, have tightened regulations regarding early parole of convicted murderers. My heart goes out to the families and victims of crimes that haven't yet been solved. Perhaps with the use of DNA evidence, the criminal justice system will be able to solve more cold cases.

One of my main goals in writing this book is to alert the reader that you have rights, too. Nationwide Crime Victims Rights legislation has been enacted and if you or a friend are the victim of a crime, I want to stress that there are many state and local organizations now that can help. Your rights may include compensation from the criminal, the right to assist in solving the crime, the right to be heard at sentencing, the right to speak at parole hearings, and financial assistance at no cost. The Appendix at the end of this book contains a list of organizations and agencies that can help. Or better yet, call your local district attorney's office for assistance.

The United States of America is not a perfect country, but the Constitution is a fair one.

God bless America.

Jim Turel built and moved into this large office complex two years before he was murdered.

Chapter 34: Update—Time Changes Everything

Realizing there was nothing I could do about Addicks, I had to move on and focus on business and family. In 1988 and 1989, we expanded Columbia Bookkeeping to even greater heights. By then we had about 22,000 annual clients and 3,000 small business clients. Plus, I had personally purchased several more apartment buildings and investment properties.

Independent of the family business, I formed a cable TV company with one partner, Mr. Smith, the man who came up with the idea. Relying on Smith's experience, we set out to develop a community cable TV service that stretched throughout the unincorporated areas of southeast Portland, Oregon City, Damascus, Happy Valley, and Pleasant Valley. The larger cable companies, TCI and Paragon, didn't want to mess with the unincorporated areas because of the lower house density.

Mr. Smith had an engineering background, but no money. So, I mortgaged every dime I could to expand and build this company from scratch. We formed the company with $1,000; $490 from Mr. Smith and the remaining $510 from me. In 1989, our first year of business, I loaned $250,000 to the company because my bank would not loan any money on a company they deemed too risky, plus, they reminded me, I had already signed a guarantee for the Columbia Bookkeeping credit line, which reduced the amount I could personally borrow for the cable TV company.

During that lean time, John Winters loaned me $20,000 to expand the cable TV company. John wrote me a check in a Safeway parking lot and did not even want a signed note. I insisted, so he handwrote and I signed an interest-bearing note on a brown shopping bag. John was such a trusting and good friend.

We obtained 3,000 pole permits from the local utility company and rapidly expanded our service to the edges of the large cable TV companies in Portland and Gresham. I was really sticking out my neck to the max.

Mr. Smith's job was to operate the business and be in charge of expansion and development. He, his wife, and I would meet at the end of every day to schedule each street's construction, and then go over the budget for our day-to-day operations. I enjoyed marketing the business. Smith and I quickly developed a customer base of 60 percent sign-ups on every street before we even started operation.

However, within a year, competitors to the national cable TV companies bought us out. After Oregon Community Cable TV repaid the money it borrowed from me, Mr. Smith and I split the profits 49/51. Then I bought a majority interest in a small cable TV company in Central Oregon. Soon I was making more profit in my spare time with my personal properties and the sale of the cable companies than I ever made from my salary running the Turel Family Trust or Columbia Bookkeeping.

In 1990, we expanded Columbia Bookkeeping even further. We went from just providing tax services into numerous diversified investments including a 250-acre RV park near San Diego, a large investment in Willamette Valley Vineyards, helicopters, residential and commercial rentals, an insurance agency, plus properties in four states. Also, in my spare time, I oversaw management of my apartment buildings, the central Oregon cable company, and the movie theatre advertising business. I did not join any organizations, nor did I ever learn how to golf. With such a busy schedule, I had no time left for anything else. My life was just business and the time I spent with my family.

By the mid-1990s, Columbia Bookkeeping consolidated and eventually bought out my brother's business, College Crest Tax Service, which included three offices. Gary and I signed an agreement that he would show up with me at all TV and radio appearances and that Gary and I would have equal status. We wanted to make sure the public still saw us as a locally owned family business even though we were a large and diversified company by then.

Each time we expanded the Turel Family Trust business investments, I had to personally guarantee over $1,500,000 (a million and a half) in credit lines and loans, which restricted my personal credit lines for the cable company. So, I talked my older sister, my Uncle Ray and Aunt Lorraine, and Chris Cheney into investing. Within several years, we sold the Central Oregon cable TV company and I was able to return double their investment. After the sale, I used the money to invest in even more apartment buildings, eventually owning over 200 units. Without the backing of kind bankers like Mary Lightfoot and Cal Tobata, the Turel Family Trust would never have been so successful.

We changed the name of the tax business to Columbia Turel. We knew our competitors were claiming we were just simple bookkeepers, even though we were state-tested and licensed tax professionals. By changing the name of the company we removed the bookkeeping stigma.

Then Gary and I decided to set up a helicopter sightseeing business at the Troutdale Airport. It seemed reasonable that during summers and between tax seasons, we could fly people up the Columbia River Gorge or over Mount Saint Helens, all within a 25-mile radius. We even bought two helicopters in partnership with Arden Danielson with the hope of starting operations.

I didn't have the time to take helicopter lessons, but Gary pursued at company expense his private and commercial helicopter license. We were both excited about the helicopter possibilities but we never did start that business. After a helicopter belonging to a friend sank in the Pacific Ocean, I decided the potential liability of a sightseeing helicopter business was too risky for the Turel Family Trust, and sold the two helicopters.

By 2000, when the Columbia Turel tax business had over 27,000 annual clients in our combined 15 offices, we sold out for millions of dollars to Fiducial, one of Europe's largest privately owned accounting firms. Gary received a large sum of money for his sale of College Crest Tax Service to the Columbia Turel family business. This sum was in addition to his share of the Trust fund.

The Turel Family Trust had been able to support Bernie Turel, my stepmother, until she passed away in 2001, which signaled the time to close the Trust. All the Trust's net assets, valued at millions of dollars by then, were distributed to the Turel children as remainder beneficiaries. Distribution followed the directions of the Turel Family Trust agreement stipulated in Jim Turel's will. I felt a great satisfaction that the Turel Trust was able to support Bernie for over 27 years—20 years more than the estimate I was given by the First Interstate Bank Trust Department in 1974. I was proud that Rod Addicks and his co-conspirators had not destroyed my dad's lifelong efforts.

Epilog

Rod (Roderick Raymond) Addicks married his second wife in 1980 while incarcerated in the Oregon State Prison. She divorced him in 1986. Addicks was transferred to the Washington State Penitentiary in June 1982 to serve out the remainder of his Oregon murder and arson convictions. On March 19, 1989, while still incarcerated in Washington, Addicks was paroled from Oregon regarding those convictions, and ended up serving only six months more in Washington for his 10-year securities fraud conviction. He was released on October 18, 1989 and placed on a two-and-half-year probation. The Washington State Parole Board assured me he would be restricted from entering the State of Oregon as a condition of his parole.

According to State of Washington filings, Addicks now owns, or is the registered agent or governing person for at least eight separate businesses, all but one located at the same address. In addition, there are 14 other registered trade names recorded and attached to those state records, including tax preparation businesses in Mt. Vernon and Burlington, Washington although Rod Addicks is not registered as a CPA with the State of Washington Accounting Board. The records also indicate he has had numerous District Court filings, mostly involving Driving Under The Influence, for which he has either been found guilty or received deferred prosecution.

Billy Anglin, who was offered money to kill Jim Turel, turned that information over to Kennewick, Washington, police prior to the actual murder. He appeared as a witness against Rod Addicks in the murder trial. In August 1980, Addicks filed a frivolous lawsuit against Anglin and it appears Anglin did not properly respond to the lawsuit or adequately defend himself. Court records show Addicks filed a foreign judgment of $120,000 rendered against Anglin in 1990 in the State of Washington King County Superior Court. Billy Anglin died on November 15, 2002. He was the only recipient of the reward money offered in the Turel homicide case.

Jim Auxier, my lawyer for over 20 years, died of cancer in 1996.

Sheriff Lee Brown left Portland to become sheriff of Atlanta, Georgia, and then Houston, Texas. Next he served as President Bill Clinton's drug czar, and ultimately was elected mayor of Houston.

Dennis Lee Cartwright was paroled on January 15, 1988, after serving only 13 years for murder.

Chris Cheney retired early as an airline pilot, and now has a large farm in Washington State, where he is a state lobbyist for the farm industry. He and his wife, Pam, spend their leisure time yachting on their 57-foot yacht in the Puget Sound plus relaxing at their condo in Hawaii. We enjoy yachting together.

D.B. Cooper has never been found and the hijacking investigation has never been solved. However, a small portion of the marked money was found washed up alongside the Columbia River.

Sherri Cronin was vice president of Columbia Bookkeeping's computer department for over 20 years. She died of cancer in 2002.

Detective Rod Englert retired in 1995 as Chief Deputy of Multnomah County's Sheriff's office and became a nationally recognized investigator, expert witness, and advisor to prosecutors on several of the country's most famous trials. Englert's current business is Forensic Consultants, Inc. of West Linn, Oregon, which specializes in reconstructing crime scenes, particularly homicides, and officer-involved shootings.

Officer Dennis Fitz, who recovered the murder victim's flight bag from the Columbia River, eventually married the waitress who served Jim Turel his last meal. Fitz joined the Multnomah County Sheriff's River Patrol and as a pilot established the Multnomah County Narcotics Division's Air Surveillance Team. He is now retired.

Floyd Forsberg was released on a two-year parole in 1990.

Norm Frink still works for the Multnomah County District Attorney's office. Over the years he has devoted tireless personal time in pursuit of crime victim's rights.

Wanda Fuller was my loyal executive secretary for over 20 years. She still works part-time for Fiducial Accounting.

Judy Krussow left Columbia Bookkeeping in the late 1980s and now works for a CPA firm in Gresham, Oregon.

Sam Moll, who was a co-conspirator in the murder and arsons, passed a lie detector test during the initial investigation by Detective Rod Englert. He was granted immunity, but years later was convicted on a separate crime. Sam Moll is not his real name.

Forrest "Joe" Rieke retired as Multnomah County Senior Deputy

District Attorney in 1976, but maintains a private law practice.

Morley Safer is still a commentator on the CBS show *60 Minutes*.

Ernesto Santos and his family still live in Mexico City, operating their perfume shops. He married his college sweetheart from Washington State and may retire in the USA someday.

Michael D. Schrunk has been the elected District Attorney in Multnomah County, Oregon, since 1981.

Julie Syler eventually left Columbia Bookkeeping, and then retired.

Maddock Tollocko passed a lie detector test regarding his testimony during the initial investigation by Rod Englert. Maddock Tollocko is not his real name.

Dr. Ronald Turco is a consulting psychiatrist, author, wilderness enthusiast, Diplomate of the American Board of Psychiatry and Neurology, and has served as an Associate Clinical Professor of Psychiatry at Oregon Health Sciences University for more than 30 years. He assists homicide departments by developing psychoanalytic profiles of murderers.

Bernie Turel died in 2001, at the age of 84, of natural causes. She never remarried after her divorce from Mr. Cosmo.

Gary Turel now owns and operates Seaside Helicopters Sightseeing and Fun Park on the Oregon Coast Highway. His still loves flying and remains a commercial pilot. He has two lovely children.

John Winters left his job at the Rockwood Water District and started his own excavation company. He became a multi-millionaire dealing in real-estate investments and is now semi-retired. He is the hardest working man I have ever known.

Norm and Dolores Winningstad retired and still live in Oregon. Over the years, Norm founded Floating Point Systems, Lattice Semi-Conductors and several other Oregon companies. Norm was still flying his Augusta jet helicopter from his private helipad at 80 years of age.

Louise Whitfield, the murder victim's ex-wife, retired from *The Oregonian* in 1998 and passed away two years later of natural causes.

Detective Joe Woods retired after a career in the Homicide Department of Multnomah County. He became involved in real estate investments and developments.

Detective Orlando "Blackie" Yazzolino ran his own bar and grill in downtown Portland following his retirement from police work. He died on March 23, 1999.

Summary of Lawsuits Filed by Three Oregon State Penitentiary Inmates

Inmate Rod Addicks: Convicted of Murder, Arson, Fraud, and Theft
Inmate Floyd Forsberg: Convicted of Murder, Bank Robbery, Escape
Inmate Dennis Lee Cartwright: Convicted of Murder

	People Sued	Inmate's Name	Damages Sought	Alleged	Who paid to defend lawsuits?	Case #	Date Filed	County of Filing
1	Court of Last Resorts	Addicks	2,000,000	Defamatory statements	Court of Last Resorts	115,618	11/1/79	Marion
2	Stan Turel (murder victim's son)	Addicks	5,000,000	Violated Addicks' 4th & 5th Amendment Rights. Claims Turel was police agent.	Stan Turel	10,522	6/6/78	Mult.
3	Stan Turel	Addicks	5,000,000		Stan Turel	79,701	6/27/79	Mult.
4	Oregonian	Addicks	2,000,000	Libel	Oregonian	115,618	10/25/79	Marion
5	Oregon Journal	Forsberg & Addicks	2,000,000	Libel	Oregon Journal	115,619	11/1/79	Marion
6	Andy Stack (writer)	Cartwright	2,000,000	Libel	Official Det. Stories	98,891	1/7/77	Marion
7	FBI	Addicks	3,000,000	Claiming illegal conduct	US Gov't.	N/A	8/3/79	N/A
8	Official Detect. Stories	Cartwright	2,000,000	Libel	Official Detective Stories	98,891	1/7/77	Marion
9	Rod Englert (Mult. Cty. Detective)	Addicks	5,000,000	Rights violated	Multnomah County	78-522	6/6/78	Mult.
10	Rod Englert	Addicks	5,000,000	Civil Suit	Multnomah County	79-701	6/27/79	Marion
11	Rod Englert	Cartwright	2,000,000	Libel	Multnomah County	98,891	1/7/77	
12	Rod Englert	Addicks	1,000,000	Illegal wiretap	Multnomah County	78-521	N/A	
13	Rod Englert	Addicks	10,000,000	Illegal wiretap	Multnomah County	N/A	N/A	
14	Orlando Yazzolino (Mult. Cty Detective)	Addicks	$5,000,000	Rights violated	Multnomah County	78-522	6/6/07	Mult.
15	Orlando Yazzolino	Addicks	5,000,000	Rights violated	Multnomah County	79-701	6/27/79	Mult.
16	Orland Yazzolino	Cartwright	2,000,000	Libel	Multnomah County	98,891	1/7/77	Marion
17	Joe Woods (Detective)	Addicks	5,000,000	Rights violated	Multnomah County	78-522	6/6/78	Mult.
18	Joe Woods	Cartwright	2,000,000	Libel	Multnomah County	98,891	1/7/77	Marion
19	Joe Woods	Addicks	5,000,000	Civil	Multnomah County	79-701	6/27/79	Mult.
20	Joe Woods	Addicks	1,000,000	Civil	Multnomah County	78-521	6/6/78	Mult.
21	Joe Woods	Addicks	10,000,000	Civil	Multnomah County	N/A	7/1/79	Nevada
22	Stewart Wells (Detective)	Addicks	5,000,000	Rights violated	Multnomah County	78-522	6/6/78	Mult.